BusinessAge

# The Rich 500

## The Richest 500 people in Great Britain

Edited by
**TOM RUBYTHON**

The *Rich 500* is published by:
**HARRIMAN HOUSE PUBLISHING**
in association with ***BusinessAge Books***

The *Rich 500* edited by Tom Rubython

7 The Spain, Petersfield, Hampshire, GU32 3JZ
Tel: 01730 233870    Fax: 01730 233880

**British Library Cataloging-in-Publication Data**
A CIP record for this book is available from the British Library.
ISBN 1 897597 11 8  *Hb*   ISBN 1 897597 10 X  *Pb*

First Edition

The text of this book is set in Plantin
Printed and bound in Hong Kong by Midas Printing Ltd
Reproduction by Triffik Technology & Colour Connection, London
Research by Anil Bhoyrul, Peter Kirwan and Richard Halstead
Book design by Jo Wardle
Cover design by Richard Sprinks
Photographs by Desmond O'Neill

Portions of this book appeared in a previous form in *BusinessAge* magazine.

# The Rich 500

# The Prologue

Individual wealth has always fascinated the British public. When someone succeeds in business, entertainment or sport, what we really want to know – but are never told – is how much money they have made. How much is pocketed by the king of the British supermarket scene David Sainsbury every time you buy groceries in his shop? How much did George Michael earn from his two albums? Why is Paul Raymond so rich?

For every publicised financial success story, there are twice as many people who have, unknown to anyone but themselves, accumulated substantial wealth. These are the people we are even more hungry to find out more about.

Yes, many others have tried to publish lists of Britain's wealthy individuals. But most have failed miserably on two counts. Quite commonly, they fail in their basic calculations. Otherwise, such lists will include family wealth, which obviously gives no indication of what really counts – an individual's wealth.

Many members of the *Rich 500* have

**We have fully researched the backgrounds of every member of the *Rich 500*. We publish not just their source of wealth, but also details of their personal style and extravagances.**

acquired their wealth in business. In looking at either public or private companies, we didn't merely content ourselves with a direct calculation of an individual's shareholding. Instead, we have gone on to carefully analyse corporate performance and judge the company's real value. This often gives a completely different value from that quoted in the accounts – and also leads to a far more accurate assessment of an individual's wealth.

Where our subjects are not in business, we have left no stone unturned in the effort to pin down every possible source of wealth, right down to how much Mick Jagger is being paid by the marketing company which is designing silk ties featuring his lips.

But wealth is only part of the story. We also tried to find out as much as possible about the personal style of our subjects. What type of home does Sir James Goldsmith live in, and what football team does Simon Keswick support?

The result is the definitive guide to individual wealth in Britain.

# Part One

## *The Rules of the Game*

**B**ritain's 500 richest individuals have had done well recently – largely courtesy of the early 1990s bull market in equities and the general rise in property values as the economy once more climbs out of recession.

This was the conclusion reached by *BusinessAge* magazine in its most recent annual review of the nation's wealthiest individuals. Known as the *BusinessAge Rich 500*, and published every summer, this listing is the most detailed and authoritative guide to British wealth available. For the first time, the 1994 edition of the *Rich 500* appears in book form.

Overall, as measured in July 1994, the wealth of individuals on the *BusinessAge* list has risen by some 13 per cent from 1993. Last year, their combined wealth added up to £44.03 billion. In 1994, the total wealth of *Rich 500* members stands at £49.78 billion. Looking toward the bottom of our list, the threshold for membership of the *Rich 500* club is now £27.7 million. In 1993 it was £23.75 million.

**On average, members of the *BusinessAge Rich 500* are 13 per cent wealthier than they were in 1993.**

That's an increase of 13.6 per cent – similar to *BusinessAge*'s figure for the overall rise in wealth on the list.

At first sight, the task of compiling a list of the 500 richest individuals in Britain looks like a serious case of tilting at windmills.

Naturally, questions arise. For instance: can a passing journalist tell you how much loose change you are carrying in your pocket? (Unless he or she is clairvoyant, the answer's no.) Or: can a journalist tell you how much cash is in your bank account? (The answer here is yes, up to a point – but finding out such things is a shady business, and anyway, it's costly, and in the case of Britain's 500 high net worth individuals, far too costly.)

So how do we did we produce the *BusinessAge Rich 500*? The main thing to notice is that this is a listing of individuals' wealth – not wealth owned by families or attributable to dynasties.

Clearly, current accounts are not usually too important, given the sums we're talking about. And at this level, if loose change enters the picture at all, it tends to do so packed into neat piles in attaché cases. Assets are the deciding factor. In the case of individuals listed here, wealth tends to be held in paper form (ie shares), or physically (ie, property or land). Assets in these forms are usually fairly well identifiable – through wills, company accounts, press reports, and so on.

But there are a large number of variations on these themes. Aristocrats tend to boast large land holdings, for example. But land varies in quality and value according to its location or use – and so we have tried to allow for broad regional trends in our valuations.

The main source for our figures, of course, are the accounts of both public and privately-held companies. In many cases, that's just the start. Compiling a list of this kind is a big job. One researcher at *BusinessAge* works year round, spotting information on our entries and maintaining our stock of accounts and returns for relevant private and public companies.

Lists of rich individuals generate intriguing responses. People frequently call the magazine to enquire after our researchers' opinions on a *Rich 500* member's wealth. In the case of people from the same family, they often say that *BusinessAge* appears to know more than them.

One classic case comes to mind. Last year the magazine estimated the wealth of former Page 3 girl Sam Fox at around £4 million. This sum astounded Sam herself, and led to her embarking on legal proceedings against her father who had also acted as her manager. In the end, Fox's father settled out of court. It's fair to say that *BusinessAge* made the topless model Sam Fox at least a million pounds richer.

Putting together the *BusinessAge Rich 500* becomes a marathon task that occupies an average of 10 people working over several months. The result, however, is an indispensable guide to high net worth

Sir Terence Conran is the biggest winner in the 1994 *BusinessAge Rich 500*. **His wealth showed a 304% increase during the year**

individuals in the British Isles – and to the inner sanctums of power and influence in the 1990s. What follows are the rules and resources that *BusinessAge* used in compiling the *Rich 500*.

1. The *BusinessAge Rich 500* is based on individual personal wealth including holdings in shares in public and private companies, real estate, land, art, antiques, cars, bonds, value of pensions and controlling interests in trusts. Each individual's wealth has been calculated with a non-identical formula depending on the source of wealth.

2. When liquid assets are referred to, this does not necessarily mean cash. Instead, "liquid" assets are those that seem not to be held long term. Such assets are easily realiseable – convertible to cash – to meet immediate demands.

3. Public company shares are for the most part calculated at the face value when the particular subject was researched in July 1994. In the vast majority of cases, shares have been valued according to values ascribed to them in the *Stock Exchange Daily Official List*. However, in some cases, where the stock market is valuing a company at more or less than its net assets, adjustments have been made up or downwards as appropriate. In less than a dozen cases we found examples where the stock market – for reasons best known to itself – was severely undervaluing or overvaluing the assets of particular companies.

4. Private companies: As a very general rule, by no means liberally applied, where a price/earnings valuation has been used, it has been set at 14 times after tax profits or 10 times pre-tax profits. This ratio has been used in less than a third of the private company valuations. Often, we found a price/earnings ratio valuation entirely inappropriate. In such cases, we valued a company on its assets at today's prices. In such cases,

more often than not, a company's balance sheet did not reflect the current market value of those assets and further adjustments were made. Private companies often sell for very low price/earnings ratios – as low as six and not much higher than 12. Private companies have been valued between these parameters. There were odd occasions when it was appropriate to judge private companies on a price/earnings ratio as low as two. Companies have been sold on that basis in the past.

5. Domicile: Only British and Irish nationals are included. This included anyone who has become widely known as British. There were one or two people whose nationality was uncertain. But the nationality rule was adjusted on no more than five occasions to include someone who does not technically qualify, but whose omission would have rendered the list a farce.

6. Taxation: Many fortunes are not subject to tax considerations because they are domiciled in tax havens where no tax on capital is paid. Or else such fortunes are stowed away in tax efficient trusts. Tax has been taken into account on assets sold: the date of sale and the prevailing tax rate at the time has been taken into account. Some aging assets are free from capital gains although most newer fortunes are not. On the whole, members of the *BusinessAge Rich 500* paid a capital transfer tax of less than 10 per cent on transfer of assets, but tax bands have been calculated at between 10 and 40 per cent.

7. Real Estate: Rough valuations have been calculated for personal-use real estate holdings for all members of the *Rich 500*. A conservative figure has been used, especially for valuing overseas estates. In some locations, a realistic sale price is unlikely to he achieved.

8. Land: There can be no set criteria for

In the wealth game, some have missed the rising economic tide predicted for so long by John Major's government. **For whatever reason, many see their boats either holed below the waterline or becalmed.**

valuing the land holdings of the members of the *Rich 500*. Setting criteria is almost impossible, as land values vary greatly. For instance, many great land tracts in Greater London are subject to vagaries of long and complicated leases. Others are not. Land in different parts of the country varies greatly in quality and value. Each individual's land holding have been separately assessed according to circumstances.

9. The sources for material within the *Rich 500* include *Who's Who, Debretts, Jordans, Dunn and Bradstreet, Extel, Datastream, MAID, Daily Express, Sunday Express, International Who's Who, Women's Who's Who, Key British Enterprises, Press Association, Companies House, Daily Mail, Mail on Sunday, Dunns Europa, Arthur Andersen Corporate Register, Hambro Companies Guide, Nigel Dempster's Address Book* (Weidenfeld and Nicholson), *Sunday Times, The Times, The Sun, News of the World, Business and Finance (Ireland), Wall Street Journal, Autosport, Autocourse, Sunday Telegraph, Daily Telegraph, The Observer, The Stage, Variety, Music Week, Tatler, Vanity Fair, Harpers and Queen, Esquire, Hello, Reuters, Forbes, Fortune, BusinessWeek, Barrons, Financial Times, The Independent, the Independent on Sunday, Sunday Mirror, Daily Mirror, The Guardian, Amusement Business, OK, Investors Chronicle, Insurance Age, Time, Life, U.S. News and World Report, Times 1000, European Business Who's Who, Henderson Top 1000 Charities, Estates Times, Estates Gazette, Register of Shipping, List of Shipowners, Guardian Guide to Top Companies, The Performance Ranking Guide.* Authors, City analysts and company secretaries of most of Britain's quoted companies provided information that was greatfully received by the *BusinessAge* research team.

# Part Two : The People
## *Paul Raymond*

Someday someone will produce "Paul Raymond – The Movie." It will be a cross between Dynasty, Only Fools and Horses and Mona Lisa – the story of an abandoned five year old who skips school, skips conscription, trains as a mind reader and eventually creates Britain's biggest sex, property and publishing empire.

Then the story gets interesting. His rivals whisper that the mob is pulling his strings; his only son and heir apparent, Howard, turns to cocaine; his daughter, Debbie, gives up her cocaine habit and comes to his rescue. The empire is safe again. But it all ends in tragedy – Debbie dies of a heroine overdose and Howard remains estranged. As for Paul Raymond, well, he becomes Britain's richest man with £1.65 billion, but he can't spend 20 pence on a newspaper without being accompanied by two burly minders.

That movie may be a while coming yet, as 68-year-old Raymond is alive, kicking

*The past few years have been tough on Paul Raymond emotionally if not financially.* **After the death of his heir daughter Debbie, his son Howard remained estranged. Although the relationship is said to be on the mend.**

and adding to his loot. On top of the 20 property deals a year he still does, Raymond controls 30 acres of Soho, where the smallest sex-shop on the corner of Beak Street, often selling the magazines he publishes, pays him £60,000 a year in rent. Officially, the companies he runs are part of the Paul Raymond Organisation Ltd, valued at £250 million. Add to that his other interests, and the figure rises seven fold. (See page 32)

So what is Paul Raymond actually like? In the past two years, he hasn't given a single media interview and has made only the occasional public appearance. But those close to him – and his friends are still mostly the same as they were 40 years ago – know the two sides of his complex character – so complex, in fact, that Charlton Heston would have trouble as the star of *Raymond The Movie*.

First there's the royalist, the Catholic and the Thatcherite. The man trying to clean up sleaze on the streets of Soho, the business guru who snaps up the best property at the bottom price. He wears the best suits, never gets into a fight and holidays alone in Antigua.

Then there's the other Raymond, the one we all know: publisher of *Escort, Men Only* and *Club International*, owner of legendary Soho sex haunt the Raymond Revuebar. He is usually pictured with 20 topless leather-clad blondes, has a slight stammer and he once offered Esther Rantzen £500,000 to pose nude.

Can these two versions of Paul Raymond really be contained in one person? Raymond has proved beyond reasonable doubt that while sex can generate money, money can't buy happiness. After 40 years in the sex business, the only thing that's really changed is his bank balance. When he opened the Raymond Revuebar in 1952, he paid husband and wife team, Ted and Renee Haskell, £5 a week to perform what was seen as an outrageous sex act – Ted wore a gold lame jockstrap and Renee a G-string. They appeared on stage as statues, covered in gold dust, slowly coming to life. The audience of 30 working class men loved it, splashing out £10 each.

Forty two years later, Ted and Renee have been replaced by Carmel and Lola. The show is pretty much the same, except the duo skirt £300 each for a night's work. The audience is mostly German tourists, and the cash tills take several thousand pounds a night. Raymond, who played the role of bouncer, waiter, manager, owner that night in 1952, is most probably sitting on a beach alone in Antigua, pondering what to do next with his billion.

The past few years have been particularly tough on him, after the death of his daughter Debbie. Raymond's natural heir, his son Howard, was kicked out of the home several years ago after one drugs binge too many – the highly "moral" Raymond, who disapproves of unmarried mothers, would have none of

In October 1992, in her last interview before dying of a drugs overdose, Debbie Raymond said: **"When he dies we'll be putting him twelve feet under, not six feet under! By the time he does kick the bucket, Christ knows what we could have done. We could have bought London or we could have bought the moon."**

it. In Debbie, herself a reformed wild child, he had found the perfect heir to allow him a graceful retirement. She joined his £50 million magazine empire as a trainee, rising to editor-in-chief on merit. In October 1992, in her last interview before dying of a drugs overdose, she spoke to *BusinessAge*: "When he dies we'll be putting him twelve feet under, not six feet under! By the time he does kick the bucket, Christ knows what we could have done. We could have bought London or we could have bought the moon."

He hasn't bought the moon yet, but he's taken just about all the best parts of London, owning more than 400 properties in Soho. If the wealth hasn't always brought happiness, it has done even less for his reputation. His former wife, after taking £250,000 from him in a divorce settlement, claimed he refused to donate £1 for a cancer research charity "because you have to draw the line somewhere". When he tried to buy Watford Football Club from Elton John, the homosexual pop star said Raymond "wouldn't be a suitable chairman". Instead, he did a deal with pension thief Robert Maxwell. Ironically, this year, Elton John asked Raymond if he could borrow one of his Soho properties as a base for his AIDS Foundation charity. Raymond said "no" – politely.

But he has never let the knockers get him down, saying once: "What I give is sex plus a laugh. That's the trick. If you want education, try the Royal Shakespeare Company." He doesn't mind being labelled as a pornographer, but prefers to describe stripping as an "art" and his clubs as a "business". As for himself, he says: "My staff say I am one of the few gentleman left. It's automatic for me to open a door for a female and to walk by the kerb."

The bouffant hair and Clark Gable moustache, coupled with his untouchable position as the Duke of Soho, constantly leads to gossip that Raymond has connections with the mob. This, too, he has always humbly rejected, saying: "People who don't know me think I'm like Al Capone with a bald head and gangster's molls on each arm – a wide boy with a massive cigar. Maybe they even think I'm a crook, but I'm not any of those things. I wouldn't knowingly do anyone any harm. I have very few emotions".

Few emotions maybe, but what's there is emotionally complex. Raymond was one of three sons of a haulage contractor in Liverpool. By age of five, his parents separated and the young Raymond, or Geoffrey Anthony Quinn as he was christened, was ordered to tell classmates his father was "working abroad." Daddy never re-appeared. Brought up by his mother, grandmother and aunt, he quit school at 15 to work as an office boy in Manchester. The boredom of the job led him to play drums in his spare time. Unwittingly, Raymond had begun his journey on the road to Soho.

His career as a musician was interrupted by the Second World War, and for two years Raymond was on the run from conscription. After eventually getting caught, he served two years with the RAF before hitting the drums again.

The transition from drummer boy to sex club owner, if he is to be believed, was almost accidental. His somewhat humble version is that after the war, he went to Clacton-on-Sea where he purchased a clairvoyant act for £25. He chose the stage name Gene Raymond, which then became Geoff Raymond before he settled for Paul Raymond. His mind-reading act was supported by two female dancers, and the trio toured the halls and venues of northern England. Success was limited. One night he took the show to Manchester's Queen's Park Hippo-

**On Boxing Day 1951, Raymond came to London to start his first club, the Raymond Revuebar. Few would have guessed that Britain's richest man had arrived.**

drome. "The manager wouldn't let us in. He said: 'Sorry son, not here unless you have nudes.' Two of the dancers said: 'All right, we'll show our boobs for an extra ten bob.'"

Within a week, Raymond realised his audience had quadrupled. The punters wanted a sex show, not a mind-reading drummer boy.

On Boxing Day 1951, he came to London to start his first club, the Raymond Revuebar. Few would have guessed that Britain's richest man had arrived. Reflecting on the move, he said recently: "I thank God I wasn't a good drummer because if I had been, I'd probably still have been playing the damn things today."

Instead, his days are mostly spent playing the property market or sitting on a beach. The dream of retirement was squashed by Debbie's death. Her young daughters appear to be his only inspiration for carrying on working.

But it can only be a matter of time before he calls it a wrap and the moviemakers get to work.

# *James Goldsmith*

Jean Paul Getty once said that if you can count your money, you're not seriously rich. By that measure, Sir James Goldsmith can't count; nor, for that matter, can he read or write. All the more reason why the world's most famous gambler should now be openly canvassed as a future president of France.

Over 8,000 flag-waving French citizens attended Goldsmith's final rally in Paris when he stood for the Euro-elections. "The billionaire with the sexy eyes" was how the women (and some of the men) described him. Princess Diana, Lord Rothschild and Michael Caine were among the guests at his victory party. Meanwhile, customs officials at New York's Kennedy airport still greet him with the words: "Hey, you're that dude who made half a billion on the stock market crash. Way to go, Jimmy."

Somehow, Jimmy has found respectability again.

The turnaround is quite remarkable. Only a decade ago he attained dollar billionaire status in the US, by selling every-

Goldsmith sat in a New York hotel room on Black Monday laughing his head off. **He had sold a billion worth of assets beforehand according to his biographer.**

thing, including his house, on the eve of the 1987 stock market crash. Having correctly called the boom of 1971-72 and the bust of 1974, Goldsmith's legendary 1987 call sent him once again to the top of the financial genius class.

But life for Jimmy Goldsmith has always been a roller-coaster ride. Once, famously, he erred badly by selling his 1.5 million acres of timber forests to Lord Hanson in return for shares in the gold company, Newmont Mining, whose shares then went through the floor, while the price of timber went through the roof. This piece of bad luck was followed by a gaffe at Rank Hovis McDougall, where he took a bath for several millions after a failed take-over bid. The genius once again tarnished, Goldsmith publicly retired to his 40,000 acre Mexican ranch with £730 million in the bank, three concurrent relationships and eight children.

Suddenly, he's back with a new career. His right wing French political party, L'Autre Europe (the Other Europe) won 13 of France's 87 Euro seats in this year's

European elections, taking just two per cent fewer votes than President Mitterand and almost as many seats as the Conservative Party managed in Britain. He cleverly mined a rich vault of French frustration with unemployment, declining living standards and EC bureaucracy to pull off this surprising coup.

With dual nationality, there was never any doubt that Goldsmith would choose France, not Britain, in his bid for political respectability. Sir Bernard Ledwidge, biographer of Charles De Gaulle, summed perfectly what was on offer when he noted that in France, "personal behaviour does not come into the political scene... The only French king not to have a string of mistresses had his head cut off."

Goldsmith knows he would have been crucified for his past if he ever stood as a candidate in Britain. Never mind the fortune he amassed by cherry-picking his way through the food, pharmaceutical, banking and financial and retail sectors. The fact is that in Britain, we'd primarily be concerned with his behaviour in bed.

Here, Goldsmith's career as an international playboy has been as notable as his financial successes. More than anything, he is famous in Britain for having said that when a man marries his mistress, he creates "a job vacancy". Goldsmith's liaisons – with his wife, former wife and mistress – always made the headlines, and still do. "I was not willing to tailor my personal life to my career," he admitted recently.

Goldsmith was a tabloid editor's dream in the Fifties. He eloped with Bolivian heiress Isabel Patino, whose father had warned him they couldn't marry because Goldsmith was Jewish. Goldsmith replied that, for his part, he "didn't usually marry Red Indians" and promptly fled with his lover to Scotland, pursued Benny Hill-style by her father and most of Fleet Street.

Nothing much has changed, except that

Some of the women in Sir James's life have enabled him to lead an extraordinary existence.
**Eldest daughter Isabel was from his first marriage.**

today Goldsmith stands on the threshold of the ultimate power. With France due to elect a new president next year, Goldsmith is seen as kingmaker. Whoever he backs can pack his backs for a spell at the Elysee Palace. Five years from now, most French political analysts believe, Goldsmith will want the favour returned.

Even if he doesn't, Goldsmith is set to cause political waves in Strasbourg. One sure indication of this is the many compliments he receives from maverick Tory MP, Bill Cash. The big question is whether, as a politician, Goldsmith will change his style.

The early indications are that he won't. His primary agenda, he believes, is to throw a spanner into the EC's bureaucratic machine. Apparently, his MEPs will disobey every instruction the Eurocrats give them, right down to where they should park their cars at the parliament building in Strasbourg. Inside parliament, he will campaign for the Community to return to its original aims, as set out in the Treaty of Rome: preference for European goods and services and regard for member nations' welfare as against the rest of the world. Protectionism, in other words.

His critics claim Goldsmith would be singing a different tune if he was still a businessman and not a politician. But that's Jimmy's trick: he takes positions as a gambler, opting for whatever gives him the best return at that moment. As a six year old in 1939, he played the fruit machines at the Hotel de Paris in Monte Carlo, with one franc coins borrowed from an American lady. Young Jimmy would wait for hours until a punter moved off a slot machine, sensing his moment had come. Ten years on, he had changed little, winning £8,000 on a £10 accumulator bet at the Lewes races.

Nearly fifty years later, his biggest gamble paid off – selling off all his investments before the big crash of 1987. Among the assets to go was the London casino in which he had invested £800,000 with John Aspinall. This was sold to Peter de Savary for £90 million. Goldsmith personally trousered £34 million. The clear-out continued across the board. Goldsmith set about liquidating his investments with a vengeance.

By October 19th 1987, he had transferred around $1 billion into his Lichtenstein-based family trust, the Brunneria Foundation. His friends, Rupert Murdoch, Donald Trump and the legendary investor Carl Icahn lost over £1 billion between them that day, while Goldsmith sat in a New York hotel room laughing at them on the phone. When asked why he wasn't at his office, he said: "I sold it just before the crash." The next day he flew to Mexico to begin work on his dream home, a 40,000 acre estate with a 40-room mansion.

Retirement, it seemed, was a foregone conclusion, but Goldsmith couldn't resist playing the markets one more time – and in doing so, he managed to squander some of the fortune he made on Black Wednesday. Why he's made another comeback, this time as a politician, is hard to judge.

Whatever his reasons, Brussels and Strasbourg are filled with a mixture of trepidation and excitement. MEPs are aware that Goldsmith's pet hate is bureaucracy. He is renowned for tearing up files once he's finished with them, and boasts that he hasn't sat behind a desk for 25 years. The chances are he views the Brussels bureaucracy machine with the eye of a corporate raider, preparing to end the bandwagon of Eurocrat free-loading. As his friend Charles Hambro recently remarked: "MEPs should beware. Jimmy is going to take away their lollipops."

Goldsmith's critics – and there are many – take heart from the fact that he has few academic credentials. He dropped out of

He is famous in Britain for having said that when a man marries his mistress, he creates "a job vacancy".

**Goldsmith's liaisons – with his wife, former wife and mistress – always made the headlines.**

Eton and only went into business because his brother, Teddy, was conscripted, leaving him with a skin cream business to run. When his second wife, Ginette, had a baby in a Paris hospital, he kept her there for two weeks as he tried to raise the cash to pay the hospital bill. Goldsmith only managed it by winning backgammon at the Traveller's club.

While other financial gurus bury themselves in the financial press to spot market trends, Goldsmith has always read closely all the raw economic data he can get his hands on. He admits he has never invested in the stock market without first ringing half-a-dozen analysts for their advice – and then doing the opposite. He says: "When 90 per cent of people are thinking exactly the same thing, you can be certain that if you do exactly the opposite, you'll make a fortune."

The chances are whatever the lobbyists and advisers tell him to do, he'll follow the same rule now. At 62, Goldsmith's cocktail of wit, infectious laughter and serious thought can still captivate an audience. It is a testament to his charisma that he has been able to persuade moderate-thinking people to consider a manifesto that owes more to Hoover's disastrous reaction to the crash of 1929 than sensible modern economic thinking.

Any lingering doubts that Goldsmith isn't being taken seriously on the political stage were quashed in July when a group of Tory MPs invited him to Westminster to deliver a political address. He didn't disappoint. Among his judgements was the idea that President Clinton's lack of wisdom was paralleled only by his ignorance of history. Meanwhile, the Americans are likening Goldsmith to Ross Perot, another tycoon turned politician. But the similarities are few and far between. Perot is history. He's busy writing his memoirs. Goldsmith has only just begun – again.

# The Golden Couple

The banner headlines in Dublin proclaimed the marriage of "two mature romantics". For all that, the wedding of 55-year-old Tony O'Reilly and 45-year-old Christine Goulandris in September 1991 seemed straight out of a blockbuster novel.

Here was a new golden couple, a kind of alternative Charles-and-Di thrown up by two of the poorest nations in the Europe – Greece and the Irish Republic.

The ceremony took place at the bride's family home in Lyford Cay, the exclusive Bahamas resort. Tony O'Reilly, chairman and chief executive of HJ Heinz, and at the time the world's best-paid businessman, turned up with a £50 million pay packet in his pocket. The bride brought along much more serious money; namely, her share of a £850 million Greek shipping fortune.

It had been a short, secret courtship. First, O'Reilly got the bride's brother, Peter Goulandris, to bring her along to a Heinz-sponsored race meeting. But from then on, the couple's meetings were only known to close friends. By this time, O'Reilly watchers were commenting that the bride seemed more Irish than Mediterranean. Though in her forties, she was said never to have had a serious boyfriend. But when the *Tatler* magazine went along to see O'Reilly at rest in Ireland after a full year of marital bliss, it found a man whose "voice softened" when he talked about his new wife.

The marriage contract was no doubt drawn up by a Wall Street rocket scientist. Between them, the couple possessed three stud farms, eight residences and a restored medieval chapel – properties spread around five different countries.

But who was richer, the bride or the groom? When the Irish newspaper, the *Sunday Tribune*, suggested to O'Reilly that his wife was wealthier, he shrugged his shoulders. "I hope not," he answered. Remarkably, he added that he hadn't looked into the matter, and could only hazard a guess that his new wife was a "wealthy woman".

> Tony O'Reilly, chairman and chief executive of HJ Heinz, and at the time the world's best-paid businessman, turned up with a £50 million pay packet in his pocket.

Quite so. According to our latest estimates, Goulandris personally is worth some £300 million. O'Reilly's worth tops out at some £230 million – hardly poverty-stricken, but certainly poorer than his wife.

But if Tony O'Reilly is an Irishman who works in Pittsburgh, and if Christine Goulandris is a Greek shipping heiress, what are they doing on a list of the 500 richest individuals in the British Isles?

The simple answer is that both of their families have substantial assets in London and Dublin – and in the case of the Goulandris family, that means Capeside Shipping, the London-based company that controls 25 ships worth around $1 billion, according to the Lloyd's List. For good measure, the couple also spend much of their free time in Ireland – at Castlemartin, O'Reilly's large estate in Co Kildare.

Castlemartin is the most evident badge of Tony O'Reilly's successful career as a salesman of baked beans and newspapers. His estimated fortune of £230 million has been the product of very hard work. As boss of HJ Heinz in Pittsburgh, O'Reilly works in a tough business, in the toughest market in the world. His personality matches the task: according to one fellow Irishman he has a "neck like a jockey's bollocks," meaning he is tough.

In addition to Heinz, he chairs two other Irish-based quoted companies: Independent Newspapers, with a market capitalisation of £340 million; and Fitzwilton, which is valued at £95 million. His investments in these companies are currently worth about half of his total fortune. The rest is made up from accumulated profits and dividends – and £75 million-worth of Heinz stock at current prices.

For O'Reilly, the road to riches started 30 years ago. At the age of 26, O'Reilly was a qualified solicitor and had already

**The bride, Chryss Goulandris brought along much more serious money; namely, her share of a £850 million Greek shipping fortune.**

carved out a successful career as an Irish rugby international player. A year later, he created his first wildly successful brand – Kerrygold, for the Irish Milk Marketing Board. At the age of 32, he turned down the offer of a job as Minister of Agriculture.

Instead, O'Reilly went to work for HJ Heinz in London. He rose rapidly at Heinz, but kept a close eye on developments in Dublin. When one of the nation's largest quoted companies, Gouldings, fell on bad times, O'Reilly was there to bail it out. With subsequent additions, the company became Fitzwilton. In 1971, he moved to Pittsburgh as a senior executive for Heinz.

Then, ironically, there followed the deal that set him up as a press baron – the skilfull purchase of Ireland's largest news group, Independent Newspapers. Then aged 37, O'Reilly was selling tomato ketchup round the world, publishing newspapers in Dublin and running the largest conglomerate on the Dublin Stock Exchange. In the same year, he became president of HJ Heinz. The first individual outside the Heinz family to occupy the post, he's been there ever since. Since then, fortunes have fluctuated, but nothing has changed very much overall. Only his companies' turnover is larger.

By the time he tied the knot with Goulandris at Lyford Cay, O'Reilly had been round the block a few times. He was born out of wedlock in Dublin in 1936, to Eileen O'Connor and John O'Reilly, a senior Irish civil servant who already had an existing family in the rural county of Wexford. Today, this would be unexceptional. In Ireland in the Thirties, it was remarkable. Perhaps because of his government job, O'Reilly's father apparently concealed the fact that he was living with a woman who was not his wife. Whatever the reason, his son's birth certificate listed the father's occupation as "traveller".

The memory is presumably painful. In the grounds of his mansion, Castlemartin, in Co Kildare, O'Reilly later reburied his father. Alongside, there are plots for O'Reilly's six children – the offspring of his long marriage to Australian mining heiress Susan Cameron, which ended in divorce in the late Eighties. Friends and family insist the break-up was "amicable". But doubts remain, visible in O'Reilly's frequent confession that his career as a newspaper proprietor and American corporate executive exerted intolerable strains on his family in the early years.

O'Reilly and Goulandris have been together for three years now. At O'Reilly's frequent dinner parties, she is a shy presence – short on words, long on girlish charm. She is his junior by a decade, but has been richer for a longer stretch of time – ever since she inherited her father's share of a Greek shipping fortune at the age of three.

In terms of temperament, she is O'Reilly's opposite. Her upbringing and education only deepened a natural reserve – most of her youth was spent with an uncle, living on a stud farm in Normandy.

Horse racing remains her primary interest. In France, she now owns the Haras De La Louviere farm and the Skymarc stud farm. There, she cultivated a talent with horses – today, she owns the prize-winning colt Priolo, one of the most successful flat racers in France. Just before their marriage, she sold off a few million pounds-worth of yearling bloodstock at Deauville and lashed out around £300,000 on four new horses – a wedding present for her husband, we think. Besides the Normandy property, she has developed a smaller farm in Kentucky.

The family's pedigree is substantial.

**Tony O'Reilly travels with six different brief cases each stuffed with details of different projects**

This is evident from the old story of how Christine's brother, Peter Goulandris, was able to turn down Christina Onassis as a marriage partner – despite a promise to Ari Onassis, who at the time was on his deathbed, that he would go through with the wedding. He didn't. To refuse took some clout. But the Goulandris family have rarely been short of that particular commodity. The Goulandris family is one of the richest and most influential in Greek shipping circles. On her mother's side, O'Reilly's bride is related to Costa Lemos, possibly the wealthiest of all the Greek shipping owners.

From an early age, Christine Goulandris has grown accustomed to a jet set existence. And that's just as well, for at any one time, her husband's whereabouts on the planet is a matter for debate. Heinz has interests on most continents – from processing plants in Australia to factories in Zimbabwe. Independent Newspapers, meanwhile, has operations in the UK, Mexico, France, Australia and Germany.

There's also the occasional takeover battle to take care of – like the unsuccessful bid against Conrad Black for a chain of Australian newspapers, or last year's bid for *The Independent* in London. Meanwhile, there are his non-executive posts – including a seat on the board of the Washington Post, for which he receives a cheque for $25,000 annually.

Highly organised, O'Reilly crisscrosses time zones in a a Gulfstream jet. With him travel half-a-dozen briefcases, each stuffed with details of separate ventures. So does Chryss Goulandris.

Thankfully, his exterior charm is matched by remarkable stamina. "I've only really got two speeds: stop and full speed ahead," he once said. Married for a second time, he's now hoping to stop more often – at home, as one-half of Ireland's golden couple.

# Part Three

# The Rich 500

STEVE FINN

### 1 (1) Paul Raymond 68
### £1.65 billion
(£1.5 billion)
### ◆ Property

## Source of wealth

Paul Raymond doesn't like his label of Britain's richest man. When interviewed he will admit to a worth of between £50 and £200 million depending on the mood he is in. As he approaches his 70th year, he has decided to stop giving media interviews.

He never announces his property deals – some 20-plus each year – and will only make a statement when he feels it is necessary. For the most part he owns a string of companies where he is not listed as the director, or the owner. It is all hidden away. The only companies he is formally identified with are: Paul Raymond Organisation Ltd, Paul Raymond Publications Ltd, Soho Estates Ltd and Victor Green Properties. These all come under the auspices of the Paul Raymond Organisation where profits have been rising for years. His publishing company is the star performer with sales at £23.5 million and profits of £12.2 million, pre-tax.

The PRO as a whole has sales of £28 million and profits of £14.2 million. However, this is clearly only part of the story. Raymond owns some valuable leisure concerns including Madame Jo Jo's and Raymond's Revuebar in Soho. Neither of the activities of these companies appear to be included in the PRO accounts indicating they are in separate companies.

The visible Paul Raymond trading companies are therefore conservatively valued at some £250 million and would easily be worth that on break up.

It is clear from the publishing companies' growth of the last few years that his late daughter, Debbie, had become a very successful businesswoman. Before her death, she took over the PRP business which profited mightily, meaning she was a worthy heir for his whole empire. His son, Howard, was never in the running to take over the business.

But it is the property side of Paul Raymond's empire which is the key to his fortune. Most of his holdings are concentrated within the 87 acres of Soho. He has grudgingly admitted that he owns a third of these acres. His daughter revealed, in her last interview before she died, that he owned 65 per cent of the area.

When *BusinessAge* reviewed Raymond's wealth two years ago, reporters walked the streets identifying Raymond-owned properties. Out of the 2,000 odd freeholds in Soho, it was estimated Raymond owned 374 properties. That figure is well over 400 – now some 20 per cent of the real estate total.

He started buying those properties 40 years ago at prices then between £5,000 and £15,000. In 1974, at the very bottom of the property cycle, he added about 50 properties. In 1977 just as property was about to recover dramatically, he added no less than 100 properties to his portfolio.

And he has not just stuck to Soho. In 1993 he bought an old cinema site in Chelsea. This year he has added another big chunk to his Soho holdings when, in a rare admission, he revealed that he was the buyer of the old Rialto cinema, the Cafe de Paris and most of the rest of Rupert Street that he didn't already own. It was bought from a bankrupt subsidiary of Brent Walker plc for £15 million. Typically, the payment came from Raymond's own resources. He had no need for any borrowings. This is just one of the deals he has done this year as he senses the turn of the property market and thus the end of the window buying opportunity. We estimate Soho property values have increased by at

least five per cent this year. And that does not take into account the incredible yields Raymond obtains from renting his properties to sex-retailing concerns. The tiniest shopfront can command £60,000 a year rent.

Raymond's wealth has come after 40 years of property buying, in which he has ploughed every penny of his cashflow from the sex, publishing and leisure business where net margins were often in excess of 50 per cent.

In 1994, whatever Raymond might say for public consumption, and despite the idea that the British Establishment hates the fact that a pornographer is the richest man in Britain, he is worth a minimum of £1.65 billion.

## Personal style

Raymond is true rags-to-riches. He started off his career as a washer-upper for £1 a day in Soho, at the Rialto site he has just bought, fifty years ago. Later, he debuted in the sex business as the owner of Raymond's Revuebar and the hugely successful *Men Only* magazine.

His personal life has been marred by tragedy. Married in 1951, he divorced in 1971. He is semi-estranged from his son. His daughter, Debbie, whom he was grooming to take over his empire, died of a drug and alcohol overdose two years ago. Apart from his son, his only heirs are his two granddaughters from Debbie's two marriages. Fawn, who is now nine, and India Jane, will one day both be very rich and Raymond is likely to endow them directly with his fortune. The loss of Debbie, a very capable businesswoman, who had inherited his best business traits, robbed him of a next generation heir. He seems to have little regard for the abilities of his son Howard.

## Extravagances

Now nearing the age of 70, Paul Raymond does not live like a billionaire and has little use for public shows of wealth. He neither desires nor has any need of the kudos of Britain's wealthiest individual. He owns a grand London, and country, home and a holiday beachside villa at the St James's Club in Antigua. He now prefers his own company, and that of his granddaughters, and often holidays alone in Antigua. His heirs are looked after by Debbie's last husband, John James, at Debbie's country house in Surrey.

Surprisingly among very rich people, Raymond has no pretensions. He does not mind being described as a pornographer and has not the slightest shame about his activities. He is not a great charity giver and lives a very quiet life.

**2**
**(2)**

## David Sainsbury 53
## £1.38 billion
(£1.425 billion)
## Retailing

### Source of wealth

Ever wondered why your £20 dividend cheques have a "£millions" column? Meet the reason: David Sainsbury owns 317 million shares – 18 per cent – of J Sainsbury plc, worth an astonishing £1.28 billion. The family firm wrote him a dividend cheque for £33,616,292.40 last year. He got £32 million the year before, and indeed has raked in similar income for the last ten years. The shares have suffered in the last year, reducing his wealth to below £1.4 billion

David Sainsbury finally took over the top slot at Britain's biggest food retailers in 1992. In succeeding his cousin Lord John Sainsbury, he also looks likely to be the last of the Sainsburys to head the company founded by his great-great-grandfather in 1869, in London's Drury Lane. He is the natural heir-apparent, being the largest shareholder and by far the richest family member.

### Personal style

Text-book Machiavellian. According to David, 1993 was a tough year for the company. It lost a legal battle to keep discount rival Costco out of the British market, started a price war, and had to swallow a £350 million hit on its balance sheet through property value writedowns. Curiously enough, all three events are connected. The threat of warehouse discount clubs caused Sainsbury's to embark on a property buying spree that at one stage bid up retail sites to £10 million an acre, far in excess of their true value. Costco was threatening to undermine the whole plan by opening massive warehouses on sites zoned for industrial use. It won the right to open in Thurrock, Essex, but shortly thereafter David Sainsbury's friends in government slammed the door on any further "quasi-retail" developments on non-retail land. Just for a good measure, Sainsbury cut 200 own-label item prices the day that Costco opened. Battle has been worthwhile: Warehouse clubs are neutered, and Sainsbury's position has never been stronger.

### Extravagances

Although David Sainsbury may not be a self-made millionaire, he has a valid claim to the title of self-made billionaire. One weakness is that he'll buy prime retail sites seemingly at any price. He put millions into the ill-fated SDP led by David Owen, a rare failure in his life. But, come what may, that £1.3 billion nest egg will be around for David's three daughters to enjoy. By then it may be worth treble that and Britain may be sporting its first women billionaires.

**3**
**(4)**

## Sir Evelyn Rothschild 64
## £1.35 billion
(£1.1 billion)
## Banking

### Source of wealth

Unlike other noble dynasties, the Rothschilds seem never to leave the family fortune in the hands of a profligate or incompetent heir. The cash keeps on rolling in. The Rothschild family has remained largely cohesive for 200 years. Sir Evelyn is chairman of the London 'branch' of the bank. NM Rothschild, which is privately controlled through a trust, the aptly named Rothschild Continuity. He is able to vote for about 40 per cent of the trust.

Little is really known of how the family operates. Given two centuries of consistent banking success in London and worldwide, the real value of the ultimate holding trust, which may not be Rothschild Continuity itself, could be as much as £10 billion. Whatever its size, this fortune has been passed down the generations, relatively tax free, through the hands of several astute inheritors.

As for the trading arm, the family bank, NM Rothschild, 1993 was for most City institutions a bumper year. Sir Evelyn's gross worth has increased significantly as a result.

In Britain, the Rothschild story began in Manchester in 1804, when a wealthy German Jew, Nathan Rothschild, arrived with the modern equivalent of £2 million to start a textile business. By 1815 he had moved to London and set up a bank; he also staged the coup that is still a banking legend. That year, Wellington defeated Napoleon at Waterloo. The first man in London with the news was Nathan Rothschild, and he used it in order virtually to corner the nascent stock market. He learned of the victory a full 24 hours before either the Palace or the prime minister.

Sir Evelyn is the great-great-grandson of Nathan Rothschild. Apart from being the chairman of the bank, he is also a former chairman of *The Economist*, and has led the key banking organisation, the British Merchant Banking and Securities Housing Association.

NM Rothschild has always specialised in advising governments, and the London arm has been the foremost western bank to the People's Republic of China, soon to become the pre-eminent economic power in Asia.

### Personal style

Sir Evelyn is as obsessive about his personal affairs as the bank is about its affairs. He is married with two sons and one daughter. During the Eighties, under the chairmanship of his cousin, Baron Edmond de Rothschild, the bank was the leading adviser to the British government on its privatisation programme. The government, which boasted two ex-Rothschild employees in the Treasury (Norman Lamont as Chancellor and Anthony Nelson MP as economic secretary), recently refused to tell MPs how much the bank had been paid in fees. In the 19th Century, when the Rothschilds bailed out even the Bank of England, the family were seen as parvenus – a perspective abetted by the deep historical anti-Semitism of the City. These days, however, blue blood doesn't come much thicker than it does at the House of Rothschild.

### Extravagances

Sir Evelyn is a notoriously conservative figure – in business and in life. Hence his split with the more commercially flamboyant Lord (Jacob) Rothschild, who left the family banking business to pursue his own interests in the late Seventies. At the time, it was widely whispered that while Sir Evelyn loved doing business with the state of Israel, Jacob would do business in virtually any situation that offered the chance of a highly leveraged return. Shy of publicity, Sir Evelyn keeps out of the limelight, leading a personal life that is much less swanky than that of his cousin, Baron Edmond, whose continental parties were the talk of European gossip columnists for much of the Seventies. Wine and vineyards remain an abiding passion.

Astoundingly, *Forbes* magazine, in its 1994 survey of the world's billionaires, left the whole Rothschild family off the list. By our reckoning, there are maybe six family members who would qualify in addition to Sir Evelyn and Lord Jacob.

**4**
**(3)**

## Viscount Rothermere 68
## £1.22 billion
(£1.2 billion)
## Media

### Source of wealth
Viscount Rothermere, through various trusts, has a controlling 74 per cent interest in the *Daily Mail* and General Trust. A canny 9-for-1 share split, in February of this year, saw the stock market wake up to the inherent values of the group and the price has virtually doubled this year.

Previously the market grossly undervalued the company, which is stuffed with assets and has few debts.

A queue of buyers would form if the three newspapers were ever offered for sale, and bidding would start at £1.5 billion. Add in the £800 million of other assets, less the debt, and even the stock market values the business at nearly £1.8 billion. It is difficult to decipher Rothermere's exact holdings in both class of shares, as most are tied up in obscure Jersey trusts, but we estimate he controls an overall 74 per cent of the company. Last year we valued him on a brand and asset value and, as the market has merely caught up with valuation, we have revised it slightly upwards to take into account dividends.

### Personal style
A press man all his life, the present Viscount was educated at Eton and became chairman of the *Daily Mail* and General Trust in 1978. Ten years ago, Rothermere had three second-rate papers, and made all three world-beaters.

The family assets are held in tax haven Jersey and Rothermere has long been a tax exile. Assessments of the Viscount's wealth have suffered from other people's confusion between his personal wealth and the Jersey-based family trusts.

Although he is a member of the House of Lords, where he has taken the oath, he appears to have voted only once in the 15 years he has been a peer.

He married a film starlet and actress, Patricia Beverley Brooks, in 1957. She became famous as the socialite "Bubbles" Rothermere but died of a heart attack last year in Paris. He has one son and two daughters, and a step-daughter. He married his long-time companion, Maiko Lee, in 1993. His heir is Jonathan Harmsworth.

### Extravagances
For tax reasons, he cannot spend more than 90 nights a year in the UK and has residences he can use in London, New York, Kyoto, Japan, Paris and Jamaica. Nothing much personal is held in his own name and the houses are registered in the names of his children and wife.

**5**
**(5)**

### Duke of Westminster 42
### £900m (£750m)
### Property

### Source of wealth
On paper, the Westminster fortune remains in decline, despite the cost-cutting efforts of the 6th Duke, and legislation to allow leaseholders to buy freeholds will erode it still further. But we think things are recovering strongly and, despite a deteriorating balance sheet, the Westminster property empire has appreciated considerably over the last year.

For over a century the successive Dukes of Westminster have been regarded as the richest men in Britain. The core of the Grosvenor fortune is based on 300 acres of land in central London, around the Mayfair area, the most expensive and prestigious area in the capital. Westminster was never Britain's richest man as propagated by the *Sunday Times* for years. *BusinessAge* discovered that many of his properties were in fact 999 year leases with Westminster receiving hardly any income. A substantial proportion however did retain value.

The Grosvenors acquired most of their land in 1677 when Sir Thomas Grosvenor married Mary Davies, heiress to the medieval manor and lands of Ebury, which included Mayfair and what is now Pimlico. By the late 1800s London was a boom town and the not inconsiderable Grosvenor fortune, originally based on a 13,000-acre estate in Chester, multiplied in value by perhaps a hundred-fold between 1800 and 1874. When the sec-

ond Duke (known as Ben Dor) died, taxes on his estate came to £19 million, the equivalent of £600 million today. This was despite the fact that he had tied all the family wealth and lands up in 20 trusts, most of them overseas.

The estate, to all practical purposes, by-passed the 3rd, 4th and 5th Dukes, and the present incumbent of the title, His Grace, Lieutenant Colonel Gerald Grosvenor, is the first to enjoy full control and benefit of the fortune. From a peak value of over £2 billion in 1989, the net value of the estate has fallen to £504 million. While Grosvenor Estates has returned to after-tax profits of £2.4 million after a disastrous 1991 which saw losses after exceptional items of over £20 million, the Duke isn't out of the woods yet. The master company has an overdraft of some £200 million – not the mark of a very rich man.

On the other hand the £504 million net asset valuation is very cautious – even at the bottom of the property market the Duke's holdings were worth at least 30 per cent more. But how the leasehold legislation affects these assets is still open to question. We believe there has been an underlying recovery in the Duke's wealth that the balance sheet doesn't reflect. This is tempered by that worrying overdraft.

With works of art and his personal property combined with a recovery in the value of both types of assets, we think Grosvenor is worth some £150 million more than last year.

### Personal style
The Duke chairs Grosvenor Estates Ltd, and takes an active part in its management. In defence of his estate, he recently resigned as the Conservative whip in the House of Lords in protest at government plans to give leaseholders a right to buy the freehold of their properties. Such "retroactive" legislation would, it is argued, have a severe detrimental impact on the assets of the man once hailed as Britain's wealthiest.

### Extravagances
Gerald Grosvenor has focused his family life on the original Chester estate. He is married to Natalia Phillips, a descendent of the Tsar Nicholas I of Russia; they have four children. He drives an Aston Martin, and takes an active role in the Territorial Army, where he serves as a colonel.

He can have any lifestyle he likes but realises he is merely the caretaker of a family empire that will go on forever.

## Lord Rothschild 58
## £775m (£725m)
## Finance

### Source of wealth
Lord Jacob Rothschild's wealth has been seriously underestimated in other publications, which have ignored his continuing interest in the main Rothschild family business. But he was said to be far from miffed that American *Forbes* magazine completely missed him and his family from its 1994 billionaires list. Everyone knows the Rothschilds are dollar billionaires even if *Forbes* doesn't.

In 1994 Lord Rothschild's wealth has been boosted still further by his remarkably successful spate of speculation in world gold markets last year. His life assurance partnership with Sir Mark Weinberg has also turned in good results this year adding to his wealth for the first time.

He is the eldest son of Lord Victor Rothschild, the former top government adviser, chairman of NM Rothschild in London, and ex-M15 officer, who died in 1990. As one would expect, he cuts a flamboyant figure, having inherited the Rothschild family entrepreneurial edge that occasionally seems lacking in the safe, blue-blooded, precincts of NM Rothschild, which remains under the control of his cousin, Sir Evelyn Rothschild. Jacob Rothschild is also the holder of the family's UK peerage, a fact that would normally entitle him automatically to a position as chairman of the bank. A split with Sir Evelyn in the late Seventies ensured this would not happen.

At the end of the Seventies, Baron Edmond de Rothschild, the chairman, was expected to nominate his cousin Sir Evelyn de Rothschild to succeed him. Instead, he chose Jacob's father, Lord Victor, who in turn ignored his son and nominated Sir Evelyn to the chairmanship he had expected in the first place. In practice, by a process that is not understood outside the Rothschild family, Lord Jacob ended up able to vote only 10 per cent of Rothschild Continuity, the trust which controls the bank and the source of his main wealth.

### Personal style
Occasionally buccaneering, very much entrepreneurial. Still very friendly with the increasingly likeable Sir James Goldsmith, whom he partnered in raids on the gold market with George Soros in 1993.

### Extravagances
Total. He is cashed up and can afford any lifestyle he chooses with the time to enjoy it as well. In business, a lack of caution may be his biggest extravagance. He is a big buyer of art adding, maybe, £50 million-worth a year to his collection.

## Sir James Goldsmith 62
## £730m (£700m)
## Finance

### Source of wealth
By scything through the British food industry, French pharmaceuticals and banking, and then American and British supermarkets, Sir James Goldsmith built a moderate fortune – less than £100 million. He became immensely rich - certainly dollar-billionaire class - in America in the mid-Eighties with a variety of deals in timber, tyres and natural resources. He was a feared corporate raider and made a billion dollars exceptionally quickly during the Eighties. The Nineties, however, were not so kind to him financially.

### Personal style
Maybe Jimmy Goldsmith chose the wrong career. After retiring from business and experiencing a few lacklustre years he has enjoyed instant success as a French politician. He created a new organisation called L'Authre Europe and won 13 of France's 87 seats in the European elections of 1994. Emulating Silvio Berlusconi in Italy, he may become a full-time politician and – perhaps –even turn his hand to the problems of Britain.

## Viscount Cowdray 84
## £700m (£475m)
## Aristocracy

### Source of wealth
Octogenarian Viscount Cowdray is one of the fastest movers in this year's *Rich500*. The best known public face of the Cowdray fortune is the *Financial Times*, owned by the Pearson group, in which the family has a 20 per cent stake. The company itself is very much the personal creation of Viscount Cowdray, who took over the running of the firm after World War II.

Before turning to politics, however, he took a few baths – in financial terms. There followed a very distinguished career as the ultimate international financier. After shrewdly buying up acres of timber forests, he then failed to gain when he sold the lot to Lord Hanson in exchange for shares in the gold company Newmont Mining. This was the worst deal that Goldsmith ever did. It was followed by remarkable losses stemming from the failed bid to take over British food group, Ranks Hovis McDougall, where he took a bath for more than a few million pounds. Goldsmith lost money on Newmont (after taking the holding costs into account). Gallingly, he then had to watch as the value of the timber interests, which he swapped with Hanson, trebled in value.

Thus, he lost out three ways. In addition, Goldsmith was a constant bear in the stock markets during that period (which was the reason why he'd swapped into gold). As he watched the markets go through the roof, his reputation as a shrewd reader of markets took a hammering. Now, his dwindling fortune is in liquid assets, earning building society rates of return.

### Extravagances
Goldsmith has a breathtaking 40,000-acre Mexican estate which contains all the usual billionaire trinkets: A 40-room mansion, a smaller mansion for his daughter, lakes, tropical forests, a profusion of wildlife and an extensive private coastline. But his back garden also contains something unique: An active volcano. But Goldsmith's main extravagance is women. As a womaniser, he has been likened to Orson Welles.

Not surprisingly, he has been married three times, and maintains a relationship with his current wife, his former wife, and a French mistress. His various liaisons have produced seven children.

His motto is: "When you marry your mistress you create a job vacancy."

Currently, Pearson is chaired by Viscount Blakenham, Viscount Cowdray's nephew, and he remains as president of the company. Like many of the fortunes in the list, the Pearson fortune is almost entirely held in trust and Lord Cowdray remains the key trustee and representative beneficiary. It's been a good year for Pearson and accordingly, we have boosted the Viscount's fortune to match. The Pearson group as a whole is currently valued at £3.2 billion, up on the back of large profits, from last year's £2.5 billion. Consequently Cowdray's worth has risen significantly. Via trusts, Cowdray's share in that capitali- →

sation runs to around £650 million, with the rest of our figure comprising property interests.

In Scotland, Cowdray owns the 60,000 acre Dunecht estate near Aberdeen. He has been married twice, on both occasions to daughters of the aristocracy. His first wife was a daughter of the fifth Earl of Bradford and his second wife was a daughter of Sir Anthony Mather-Jackson. His own mother was a member of the Churchill family.

## Personal style

One of the nation's great post-war corporate adventurers. His management style, however, was smooth and steady.

## Extravagances

Despite being seriously injured in World War II during the retreat from Dunkirk, the Viscount is an expert shot and was once a keen polo player. That's why he had his own pitch constructed at his 17,000 acre Cowdray Park estate in Sussex.

## 9 (12) Richard Branson 43 £650m (£410m) Leisure

## Source of wealth

The finances of Richard Branson are becoming increasingly more difficult to fathom as time goes on. As well as being a master businessman, Branson is a master financier who thinks for the long term.

Last year we assessed his wealth based on the Virgin Atlantic profits, plus the amount that he had trousered after the sell-off of the record division to Thorn-EMI. It now appears that the airline had made a thumping loss in 1991, rather than the £6 million profits it first seemed to have made. Voyager Group Investments shows a loss in its latest accounts, to the end of 1991, of £32 million on a £424 million turnover. There are no later accounts and the airline is thought to have lost money in 1992. It may have broken even in 1993 – but maybe not. Debts are also impossible to quantify but looked to be in excess of £100 million in the accounts. This explains why Branson was worried about his finances during the battle with British Airways and why, in the end, he was impelled to sell the record business. Quite simply, he needed the cash.

Since selling, he has purchased four new planes and bought out his Japanese partner's 10 per cent stake in the business for £45 million, ostensibly valuing the whole business at £450 million. It is uncertain, however, whether that £45 million included buying out any loans his partner had made.

The rest of the Virgin companies, some 200 registered around the globe, turnover about £250 million and make profits. The

video game business, Virgin Interactive, is thought to be on the verge of being sold and will net Branson some £80 million overall.

Supposing that he still has £200 million cash stashed away after the airline investments and losses and that the rump of Virgin is worth £50 million to him. Finally, take the airline at a face value of £450 million, then Branson's net worth is probably some £650 million.

In times of recession we would have scaled that down considerably, but taking into account that boom times are on the way, combined with the fact that Richard Branson is a brilliant manager, then we are happy with the £650 million valuation – up some £240 million in 1994.

This makes Branson one of the big winners of the year. The crystallisation of the value of his companies, the end of the recession and investment in new planes means a profitable, if somewhat cashless, medium-term future for the airline.

And Virgin Atlantic is exceptionally well managed. Last year business guru Professor John Kay, using his concept of added-value said: "For every £1 of input by way of costs, Virgin is getting £1.07 pence in output, compared with £1.03 pence for British Airways. 'Added value' is one of the most important long-term indicators of company viability, and it says much for Branson's skills as a financier and manager."

## Personal Style

Branson comes from a middle-class background and went to a top private school, Stowe. He left at the age of 16 with just three 'O' levels making him classic tycoon material. This year has been as active as any other. He defied death when his Range Rover overturned on the M4 late on a Friday night.

He lost out in the battle to run Britain's national lottery and got annoyed about it. And most significant of all, he spent, or rather leased, at bargain basement rates (and we mean real bargain basement), $400 million worth of brand new aircraft.

## Extravagances

He lives the life of a tycoon in an unrestrained way. Whilst he is not the type to surround himself with servants and chauffeurs, he has a luxurious London home, a country manor and his own Caribbean island. He is married with three children.

## 10 (8) Garry Weston 67 £650m (£600m) Food

## Source of wealth

Tax is Garry Weston's big headache at the moment. His proposed reorganisation of

family firm AB Food's convoluted ownership structure – to fold it into George Weston Holdings, a Weston holding company, and reward shareholders with a 10 pence special dividend – is designed to thwart the taxman and retain family control of the Sunblest-to-Silver Spoon Sugar conglomerate. The Weston family will realise £130 million tax-free as a result of the deal. The £16 million "for your trouble" dividend to minority shareholders will come from family, not company, funds.

But problems loom: 36 per cent of AB Food's share capital is tied up in the Garfield Weston Foundation, Britain's third-largest charity whose £860 million assets come almost exclusively from this holding. Garry is chairman, and only family members can be trustees.

Other rich lists have lumped in the charity's wealth with that of the Weston family. This isn't strictly correct: no one knows this better than the Charity Commission, who nearly upset Garry's reorganisation plans by arguing that the new AB Food ownership structure may not be "expedient in the interests of the Foundation". While the objection was resolved in the High Court, it demonstrates that charities – even family-controlled ones – are not such unaccountable fiefdoms.

Garry Weston, second son of the late Garfield Weston, has been chairman of AB Foods since 1967. The company is Britain's largest baker (Kingsmill, Allinson, Sunblest) and also owns British Sugar (Silver Spoon) and Twinings tea interests. Last year the company reported pre-tax profits of £338 million (up 27 per cent) on turnover of £4.4 billion. Weston says he has no plans to retire.

The accounts of the various family-dominated companies suggest that Garry Weston's personal investment in AB Foods is now a lowly £8 million-worth. The Foundation owns a hundred times that amount, but there is also a £650 million gap which, again, it is evident from the accounts, is in trusts which he controls. All the documents spell out that he has a "controlling interest" in AB Foods, although the exact nature of that interest is not detailed. Taking all the family fortunes and the Foundation together, the Weston family controls 63 per cent of AB Foods.

Weston also has an entirely separate 90 per cent interest in Fortnum & Mason, grocers and retailers to the gentry and royalty, worth £15 million.

## Personal style

Garry Weston runs a conservative, cash-rich company: "When we were sitting with more than £1 billion in the bank, that was money we earned ourselves, by being very good at what we do," he told Canada's

*Financial Post*. He prefers commodity items (bread, sugar) to brands, and is particularly scathing about 'brand value accounting': "It's another form of leverage," he says.

His curmudgeonly style has not endeared him to teenage City scribblers. He has no time for them, he says, nor for the Cadbury Code of corporate governance. He keeps his six children on a tight rein (four of them work full-time in the business), and barely conceals his disapproval for flamboyant younger brother Galen, who runs the large and entirely separate Loblaws supermarkets business in Canada.

## Extravagances

He was born in Britain and has lived here

### Galen Weston 53
## £630m
(New entry)
## Food

## Source of wealth

Galen Weston has been excluded from previous *BusinessAge* lists, and everybody else's for that matter, because it was believed he was Canadian born. However, it was recently disclosed he was born in Britain although he works and lives mainly in North America. Galen Weston was born in 1940, while his father was sitting as a Tory MP and his wealth derives primarily from his 57 per cent interest in Canadian firm George Weston Ltd., the company established by cockney emigré George Weston in the late 19th century. George's son Garfield turned the company from a wheat trading operation into a dynamic baking and retailing conglomerate in the Twenties and Thirties and then went on to establish what is now AB Foods in Britain.

Profits recovered last year at George

for about 60 years, but still travels on a Canadian passport. He was one of the few who publicly supported Margaret Thatcher when everyone else thought she should go. His family holding company, Wittington Investments, gave £100,000 to the Conservatives last year.

He owns a house in Kensington and a 400 acre farm in Hampshire. Garry Weston earned a £165,000 salary from AB Foods last year, and his dividends from all the family companies totalled £99,000. Other than Galen, Garry Weston has no non-executive directors on the board at AB Foods. As he said two years ago, "Why do we need outside directors? The first thing they would tell me to do is double my salary."

Weston to C$70 million (1992: C$48 million). At current exchange rates that holding is worth about £560 million. He also owns £70 million worth of AB Foods – ironically, substantially more than brother Garry's "personal" holdings, though he doesn't attend board meetings – and co-owns a Florida residential complex.

## Personal style

Galen Weston is a curious character. While abstemious elder brother Garry runs Britain's AB Foods, British-born Galen controls the entirely separate Canadian supermarkets and chocolate company George Weston Ltd.

The brothers could not be more different. Galen acts the socialite tycoon, playing polo with Prince Charles regularly and shooting his mouth off in the press, while Garry keeps a low profile and concentrates on squeezing penny margins from his massive baking operations. Galen's company has suffered relatively as a result: last year's C$150 million operating profits on C$12 billion sales would have been satisfactory, but the company's substantial borrowings mean an C$80 million interest bill every year. In contrast, Garry can expect to add that much to his bottom line every year from interest on AB Foods' £1 billion cash mountain.

Says Garry of his brother: "Our personalities are different. He's done his thing, I've done mine. Galen's more of an owner than a manager."

## Extravagances

He has many. He married Irish model Hilary Frayne in 1967, and is the father of two children. He owns the Maple Leafs, a polo team, and, in addition to several homes in Canada and the US, he leases Fort Belvedere, a "castellated folly" in Windsor Great Park, from the Queen. He spent a reputed £250,000 on his daughter Alana's 21st birthday party there last year. But what's the point of being a *Rich 500* member otherwise?

### Bruno Schroder
## £503m (£380m)
## Banking

## Source of wealth

The elusive Bruno Schroder, head of merchant banker Schroders, has almost doubled his already staggering wealth in the past year, thanks to an increase in pre-tax profits to £196 million in 1993 – a rise of 85 per cent. Schroders is now capitalised at £1.17 billion, making it Britain's richest quoted merchant bank. Its shares are the third best performing in the world over the last 13 years.

Bruno Schroder himself has, through various trusts, a 43 per cent stake in the group, putting his current wealth at £503 million.

## Personal style

Although he is head of one of Britain's most important banks and goes by the title "Count", Schroder makes no appearance in *Who's Who*, reflecting the City's, and his, traditional secretiveness. Curiously, his brother-in-law George Mallinckrodt, who chairs the bank, does appear.

The bank was first set up in the UK in 1804 as the British arm of a German bank, but one branch of the family, now headed by Bruno, settled in England. Although an Eton scholar and Oxford graduate, Schroder is anything but the front man – chairman George Mallinckrodt takes most of the credit and chief executive Win Bischoff does most of the work. When Bischoff took over in 1983, Schroder's shares were worth just £48 million.

## Extravagances

The title "Count" was conferred by the last German Kaiser on Schroder's grandfather, but Bruno will do if you're close to him – which few people are. With Win Bischoff running the show in London, Schroder prefers the country life on his Scottish estate, fishing and shooting.

### Paul McCartney 52
## £482m (£420m)
## Music

## Source of wealth

Some say that Paul McCartney's earning power is in decline, but not us. We estimate that, after taxes, McCartney's worldwide companies and activities brought him in a staggering £42 million last year. This means that, before tax, he is earning well over £1 million a week. In addition, his other business interests, and the income on his assets, amount to another £20 million.

The reason McCartney is so wealthy is because he works hard at earning it. It is how he keeps the score and his own sanity.

His wealth is the most invisible of all. He hides it through a myriad of companies and it is no one else's business but his own. His master company, MPL, is small by comparison with those of other stars, such as Phil Collins and Elton John, and he pays himself a comparatively moderate salary of just over £500,000 a year as chairman of MPL Communications. But that is just the start. There is an equivalent MPL Communications Inc in the United States.

MPL was set up in the early Seventies and grossed £5 million every year for McCartney, in its first 11 years. He gets a three per cent composer's royalty every time a song he has written is played or used. The performance copyrights for the first 159 songs which he wrote for the Beatles were owned by Michael Jackson, who bought them for $47 million in 1985 and has since sold them on again for a rumoured $75 million.

McCartney's wealth is estimated by adding up his royalties, touring fees and income from the Beatles days. Whilst that faded away, the advent of the CD has meant that income recovered to £20 million last year and McCartney's share of that is £5 million or thereabouts. He probably netted £10 million from touring last year, and the balance of this year's earnings is made up of royalties and profits from money invested. Add in the value of his rights and titles and his performing income, and it comes to a new total of £482 million. But this can only be roughly calculated, because it is impossible to ensure that all the companies in the McCartney empire have been traced. It is the most speculative figure in the *Rich 500*. Nothing about Paul McCartney's wealth is transparent.

## Personal style

McCartney runs his empire from an old five-storey Georgian house converted to offices in trendy Soho Square, London, where he often travels by train from his 160 acre Sussex farm.

McCartney has a general reputation for being mean with his money although whether this is fair or not is impossible to say.

The only question mark is his health. Despite healthy living under the auspices of his wife Linda, an American, he has been a long time user of recreational drugs.

## Extravagances

With £400 million in the bank it is difficult lead the ordinary existence that McCartney craves. The McCartney family live the tycoon's lifestyle all over the world, with houses on many continents and a private jet to shuttle them between homes. And no ordinary Lear either – his is a converted gas-guzzling BAC1-11.

**14** (14) **Lord Cayzer** 84
**£400m**
(£375m)
**Finance**

### Source of wealth

Lord Cayzer was one of the shrewdest financiers in the City of London in his day. It all started in 1938, when he took the helm of the original family company, the Clan Line shipping empire, founded by his grandfather in Scotland in 1878. Later, he diversified the company into finance and insurance, grafting on the quoted investment company, Caledonia Investments. Later, Clan Line Steamers Ltd changed its name to British & Commonwealth Shipping, while Caledonia Investments was kept separate. The Cayzers repeatedly made profitable investments in banking and aerospace.

In 1987, Lord Cayzer recruited high flying former Exco boss, John Gunn, to be chief executive of his sprawling conglomerate. The canny Cayzer quickly saw he had made a mistake and sold his stake back

to the company for the irresistible price of £427 million. He retained a small 4.9 per cent holding.

The money was paid out in stages but was fortunately guaranteed in full by Barclays Bank, amongst others. This was a shrewd move: B&C was bust within three years and the remaining stake was rendered virtually worthless. B&C collapsed after Gunn acquired the Atlantic Computer leasing company.

Many of the original B&C businesses were strong, but were sold off. Ironically, Lord Cayzer bought a minority share in the money broking company Exco, Gunn's original company. He made a £20 million investment which values Exco at about one-third of its price in the Eighties.

On the back of satisfactory profits, Caledonia Investments is currently capitalised at £560 million, of which the Cayzers own 48 per cent. Lord Cayzer recently retired from the company – in a year of record profits.

### Personal style

An old Etonian, he has a magnificent flat in Eaton Square and a country estate at Walsham-le-Willows in Suffolk. In 1982, Margaret Thatcher raised him to the ranks of the peerage.

### Extravagances

For such a traditionalist, the absence of a male heir seems contrary. Cayzer has two daughters.

His peerage is of the lifetime variety. But the inherited baronetcy he holds will become extinct on his death – unlike his wealth. He is a staunch supporter of the Conservative party and a leading donor to its central funds.

**15** (15) **Sir Adrian Swire** 62
**£390m** (£373m)
**Business**

### Source of wealth

Sir Adrian is the younger of the two brothers who now head the family firm of John Swire & Sons. But he is not as rich as legend, due to a complex financial structure which confuses the position. He was most confused two years ago when *Sunday Times* columnist, Ivan Fallon, described him as head of Britain's richest family.

For sure Sir Adrian is rich – but not that rich. The company has its headquarters in London and was first set up in Hong Kong in 1867 by John Swire, a successful Yorkshire businessman operating out of Liverpool. The parent company in the Swire Group is the London-registered John Swire & Sons Ltd. In 1992, it increased its turnover by £1 billion to £3.6 billion. After-tax profits were almost 40 per cent

higher at £488 million.

But most of the parent company's profits come from subsidiaries which are not wholly-owned, such as the Hong Kong-registered Swire Pacific. Therefore, there is a very large deduction in the profit and loss account to take account of the minority profits (the profits which are really attributable to the other shareholders in the partly-owned subsidiaries). In 1992, this charge was £398 million, leaving John Swire & Sons Ltd with just £90 million attributable to its own shareholders.

John Swire & Sons Ltd's assets amount to £5.3 billion. But most of those assets effectively belong to the other shareholders in Swire Pacific and the other subsidiaries which are not wholly-owned by the parent. Stripping these out, the parent's net assets are around £1.6 billion. Because the parent is, to a large extent, an investment vehicle for these assets, it would be appropriate to value the company on the stock market at a discount to its net asset value. Therefore,

John Swire & Sons might be worth £1.4 billion.

And what of Sir Adrian Swire's holding? He is listed as being personally interested in 23,124,970 shares in John Swire & Sons. He also owns 10 million shares in the quoted subsidiary Swire Pacific. His personal wealth, as determined by these two shareholdings, adds up to £360 million. Sir Adrian Swire also received a £202,157 salary in 1992 for his work as chairman of the parent company. He also trousered £2.6 million in dividends. Sir Adrian Swire has considerable personal assets in Hong Kong and England worth a further £25 million which can be added to his identifiable holding.

## Personal style

Sir Adrian was knighted in 1982. Like his brother, he went to Eton. Next came University College, Oxford, and finally the Coldstream Guards. He is married to a daughter of the 6th Marquis of Northampton and they have two sons and a daughter. Despite the Hong Kong business base, the family home is a manor house in an Oxfordshire village, where Sir Adrian is a popular local figure.

## Extravagances

A keen flier with a private plane, Sir Adrian was a long-term member of the Royal Hong Kong Air Force, and is involved with various RAF charities.

## 16 (38) Ronald Hobson 73
## £350m (£197m)
## Property

### Source of wealth

Talk of takeover has placed under the spotlight the value of National Parking Corporation, the parent company of National Car Parks and the vehicle recovery business founded by Ron Hobson and Sir Donald Gosling. As a result of these takeover offers, Hobson's wealth has virtually doubled to £350 million. He has also aged by six years in the space of 12 months courtesy of a misprint in last year's *Rich500*.

Ronald Hobson is credited with conceiving the idea of National Car Parks, currently the largest parking operator in Britain. An ex-services man, like his partner Sir Donald, Hobson was convinced there would be a post-war motoring boom as war-time restrictions and rationing came to an end in the Fifties. He went to see a young surveyor at Westminster City Council to get planning permission for the bomb sites which he proposed to use as his first car parks near London's West End. The surveyor was Donald, now Sir Donald, Gosling, who almost immediately left the Council to work with Hobson.

The company made pre-tax profits of £53.3 million on turnover of £233.5 million in the year to March 1993. NCP has little by way of borrowings and controls valuable inner city land sites. After a flotation was ruled out earlier this year, the company's bankers began seeking buyers for the 64 per cent of the shares that remain in the hands of Hobson and Gosling.

Heading the queue of interested parties are the Prudential, Electra and CinVen, the venture capital arm of the British Coal pension fund.

The limited over-the-counter trading in the group's shares currently values the company at around the £700 million mark – a figure pushed upwards by steady demand in recent months. That makes Hobson himself worth some £250 million from this source alone, way above last year's estimate, which was made before buyers started circling the business. Accrued dividends take his worth upward to some £350 million.

## Personal style

Modest and publicity-shy, Hobson has never appeared in the gossip columns, unlike his flamboyant partner Sir Don Gosling.

## Extravagances

There is no doubting that as well as his shares Hobson boasts some £100 million of liquid funds. Wining and dining with remaining military contacts is high on his list of priorities.

## 17 (41) Sir Donald Gosling 65
## £335m (£191m)
## Property

### Source of wealth

Due to his far greater extravagance, Sir Don Gosling is a few million poorer than his partner Ron Hobson. Together they founded National Car Parks. There can be few towns in Britain, however small, which do not sport, somewhere or other, the yellow hoarding of NCP. It is one of the largest and most profitable private companies in the country. In fact, the original idea was Hobson's and the two men only met when Hobson asked Gosling how he could get planning consent to use an old bomb site in London's Holborn district as a car park. Gosling was working as a trainee surveyor with the Westminster City Council in London, and left to join Hobson. That was 43 years ago.

Sir Donald was knighted by the Labour Prime Minister Harold Wilson in 1976, mostly for his services to the Royal Navy charity, the White Ensign Organisation. He had originally planned a career in the Royal Navy himself, but was made redundant in

1949 in a round of post-World War II cuts. He married a daughter of the key shareholder in the Huntley & Palmer confectionery business, and is credited with turning round that company, which he heads as chairman, when it ran into a sticky patch. Remarkable levels of interest in purchasing NCP from institutions – and the company's own undervaluation of its assets – mean that we have significantly upgraded Gosling's wealth this year. It is likely that the company will be taken over in 1995, further crystallising the wealth of two of Britain's richest pensioners.

## Personal style

Far more used to the limelight than his partner. He has offered to partly finance the building of a replacement for the Royal yacht Britannia. He can well afford it.

## Extravagances

He lives the hedonistic life of a tycoon with a large yacht and all the other accompaniments of tycoonery. Leander, the current vessel, is one of the grandest private yachts in the world. Sir Don enjoys entertaining Elizabeth Taylor on board.

## 18 (16) Jack Walker 64
## £325m (£345m)
## Business

### Source of wealth

British Steel bought Jack Walker's family company, C Walker and Sons, the steel stockholder better known as Walkersteel, in 1990 at the start of the Nineties recession. Even though the company – owned by Jack Walker and his elder brother Fred – was making £50 million a year, that was the peak. British Steel paid £330 million cash but the Walkers cannily kept all of the property assets of the 50-odd steel stockholding depots spread throughout the UK. The total sell-off was therefore worth £400 million, most of which was taken tax-free in Jersey. The actual sale price set a record for the most money ever paid for a private company in Britain. British Steel had wanted to buy Walkersteel because of its strategic position, being responsible for selling nearly 10 per cent of British Steel's production. British Steel overpaid and is suffering now, while Walker enjoys a relatively quiet retirement in St Helier, Jersey.

If you add in the enormous dividends taken over the years, Jack Walker is worth a staggering £325 million and his brother Fred £95 million. But we believe that Walker in tax exile minds the money for Fred and theirs is an equal financial partnership. Unlike many other multi-millionaires, the Walkers are spending the money quicker than it is coming in, meaning a slight decline in Walker's worth this year.

## Personal style

Jack Walker would be a much richer man if he had left his money in the building society. He has instead invested £100 million in two of the biggest financial black holes that are known – that of an airline and a football club.

True to form, both have swallowed large amounts of cash maybe £100 million between them.

In addition he invested £100 million in property at the base of the recession and has lost money on that as well. He spent £100 million buying up commercial property in London. The only consolation is the yield, thought to be at least 10 per cent. The airline, Jersey European, is highly speculative

but at least the football club, Blackburn Rovers, is proving successful and Walker showed that money was no object when he signed Chris Sutton for the British record fee of £5 million plus a rumoured retainer of £500,000 a year.

Walker made his name and fortune as a salesman extraordinaire. He went out and did the business where others couldn't. He is still doing it but this time a profit is a bit lower down the scale of things in priority. However, the Walkers are long-term players. Don't count out them doubling the family fortune before they sign off.

## Extravagances

Very, very few and they are all called football.

### 19
### (77)
## Simon
## Keswick 53
## £320m (£129m)
## Business

### Source of wealth

The younger brother of Henry Keswick was Tai-pan of Jardine Matheson for six years, from 1983 to 1989. Previously, the close-knit, blue-blooded colonial company had hired an outsider as its head – an experiment which didn't work. Simon Keswick is generally credited with turning Jardines around in the late Eighties and jettisoning troublesome investments in South Africa and Hawaii.

Now he is running Trafalgar House in London – courtesy of his leading role over the past few years in Jardine subsidiary Hong Kong Land, which now effectively controls Trafalgar.

Simon Keswick has never given any signal that he has political ambitions. Unlike his elder brother, who left Hong Kong in

the mid-Seventies embarking on a vain quest for acceptance by Edward Heath's Tory Party. Again, unlike his brother, Simon Keswick appears to have left the vast majority of his fortune invested in the family firm.

Recently, Jardines has performed superbly. In the year to December 1993, the holding company turned over £5.6 billion, up 20 per cent from 1992. Pre-tax profits were also up by 20 per cent – to £550 million. After tax and minority interests, that figure was reduced to £259.2 million.

Keswick owns 8.7 per cent of the company. At the very least, that makes him worth nearly £310 million. This figure is significantly up from our valuation last year, chiefly because of the remarkable boom – now somewhat cooled – that pushed Hong Kong asset values through the roof earlier this year. Add in accumulated dividend payments and minimal outside assets, and we currently value Simon Keswick around the £320 million mark.

### Personal style

Smooth-talking corporate raider. Relished his own inexorable march to victory over Sir Nigel Broackes at Trafalgar; followed up with a ruthless purge.

### Extravagances

The younger Keswick's pastimes include watching Tottenham Hotspur play football.

### 20
### (22)
## Edmund
## Vestey 62
## £320m (£260m)
## Food

### Source of wealth

In 1991 Edmund Vestey stepped down as managing director of Union International, the Vestey's colossal ranch-to-freezer meat empire which was then in the grip of serious financial problems stemming from the Gulf War. Along with his cousin, Lord Sam Vestey, he still performs a chairmanship role. His retirement saw his wealth crumble but the changes since have meant a sharp recovery in his net worth this year.

Edmund's grandfather, Sir Edmund Vestey, set up Union Cold Storage in Liverpool in 1897 with his elder brother, William, who became the very first Lord Vestey. Their idea was brilliant and simple: meat for the working classes. They saw that the newly invented cold storage techniques would enable them to import cheap meat from all over the world.

Just before the Second World War, Sir Edmund's son Ronald – Edmund Vestey's father – took up the reins and, by a series of shrewd deals, he built the Vestey group into a truly global empire. The businesses fell neatly into two halves: Frederick Leyland (refrigerated ships and shipping insurance) and Union International (meat producing and processing). The two halves are controlled by the Vesteys through a holding company, Western United Investments, which also acts as the family's private bank.

Edmund's 50 per cent share in United International is worth £300 million based on the latest results and its potential break-up value. He also owns the vast 100,000 acre Sutherland estate in Scotland and is part-owner of the 11,000-acre Vestey compound in Essex.

### Personal style

Unlike his brother Sam, Edmund Vestey likes to live it up a bit. He owns a string of polo ponies, hobnobs with royalty, and generally enjoys his privileged position. Vestey observers blame Edmund's laid-back approach to business for the family firm's recent difficulties.

### Extravagances

Polo and parties.

### 21
### (17)
## Sir John
## Templeton 81
## £315m (£285m)
## Finance

### Source of wealth

Sir John Templeton is an English knight of American origins, who made his name as one of the great financial managers and investors of the 20th century. He was one of the first investors to spot the potential of Japan in the early postwar years.

He is able to sport the knighthood because he became a naturalised British subject. The honour was conferred on him in 1987, largely in belated recognition of his enormous charitable donations. In 1992, he sold his stake in his master company, Templeton, Galbraith & Hansberger, for £300 million.

## Personal style

A lot of people would have been satisfied with retirement at 79 on £300 million. Not Templeton: he oversees the Templeton Emerging Markets Investment Trust, whose net asset value increased by nearly 40 per cent in the six months to last October. He has a high opinion of his own investment tips – but with a record like his, why shouldn't he? Latest pearls of wisdom: go long on gold and oil; don't invest in Germany.

## Extravagances

He has been married twice: He was widowed in 1950 and remarried in 1958. He has two sons and one daughter. He lives quietly at Lyford Cay in the Bahamas.

## Earl of Iveagh 24
## £310m
(£270m)
## Inheritance

## Source of wealth

The current young Earl inherited the title and his share of the Guinness fortune in the middle of 1992. The family fortune was founded in 1752 by two brothers. Arthur Guinness became a brewer and Samuel Guinness a goldsmith; his descendants diversified naturally into banking.

By 1920, the 1st Earl of Iveagh had £200 million to leave to the family funnelled into a web of trust funds. The English branch of the trust funds, the Guinness Trust, today operates "outside London" – a possible reference to British Pacific, the Canadian family interest set up by the 1st Lord Iveagh. The Guinness Trust, meanwhile, was the first of the family trusts: it operated to provide housing for workers in Dublin and London. The Dublin-based branch of the trusts, the Iveagh Trust, is most commonly associated with the personal fortunes of the Guinness heirs and heiresses. Another Guinness family trust, Burhill Estates, controls large swathes of land, from which it aggressively extracts income.

The Canadian-based interests of the Guinness family, set up by the 1st Earl, were partly consolidated in British Pacific, a property investment company. Until being put up for sale in 1984 for C$100 million, British Pacific had 35 shareholders –

## Chryss Goulandris 47
## £300m
(£280m)
## Inheritance

## Source of wealth

Half Greek, half British, Chryss Goulandris is the richest woman in Britain. As the wife of Tony O'Reilly, she is worth a good deal more than her husband's own, not inconsiderable, fortune. Although of a Greek-originated family, London-born Chryss Goulandris is thought of as British, and she and her family have lived here all their lives, controlling their empire from London. She is one of two children of John Goulandris, who died in 1950, leaving her a half-share of his shipping fortune when she was barely five years old.

Under the control of her brother Peter, once destined to marry Christine Onassis, the fortune has expanded considerably. Chryss and her brother are the British element of an interlocking family fortune which spans the globe. One part of the family wealth is controlled by the descendants of Basil Goulandris from Switzerland. That wealth was put at $1.5 billion by *Fortune* magazine in 1993, which also estimated the wealth of her maternal uncle, Constantinos Lemos, at $2 billion. The Goulandris family has a major ship-

ping operation in New York, and her New York cousins are married to the $2 billion Livanos family.

## Personal style

At the age of 44, Chryss was, like her brother, unmarried, and the family had almost resigned themselves to the situation. Then, after a modest and unnoticed courtship, she announced that she was marrying Tony O'Reilly, the divorced head of the Heinz food empire.

Quiet, shy and charming, she can sometimes seem gauche and is not afraid to interrupt her husband in a business meeting. She often hosts important events for him extremely capably.

## Extravagances

Apart from the family company, Chryss Goulandris's main interest is horse racing – and her prize-winning colt, Priolo. She owns a stud farm in Normandy. Likewise, O'Reilly owns a stud farm on his Irish estate. In England, the Goulandrises have owned a number of stately homes, including Glympton Park, bought from bakery billionaire Garfield Weston, and Ashdown Park, near Reading, once the home of the Earls of Craven. She now divides her time between Ireland, Australia and New York, or wherever her husband travels in his Gulfstream jet in an increasingly global business.

presumably mostly Guinness heirs and heiresses. The sale went through because of the "differing interests" of shareholders.

The 3rd Earl's recent death ended the family connection with the huge Guinness drinks combine. What remains is a shareholding of a few per cent only – worth under £200 million. Accordingly, the problems experienced by the brewing group last year have had minimal effect on the overall family fortune, which has been managed, since last year, by Julian Robarts, formerly the

managing director of Coutts & Co.

## Personal style

The young earl has yet to choose a career – although learning to help manage the family's dispersed holdings should prove challenging enough. Seems dedicated to a life outside the City and one of anonymity, for he has yet to be seen in London.

## Extravagances

Much the same as most young men in their early 20s: girls, motor cars and music (not necessarily in that order).

## 24 (30)
## Lord Vestey 53
## £300m (£230m)
## Food

### Source of wealth
Along with his cousin, Edmund Vestey, Lord Sam Vestey still controls the Vesteys' shrinking worldwide meat empire.

The Vestey family is the oldest of the nouveau riche. Lord Vestey's great-grandfather, William, started the business with his younger brother Sir Edmund Vestey in 1897. Their revolutionary use of cold storage technology brought meat from around the world within the reach of millions of ordinary Britons and in the process they became millionaires. In 1922, William bought himself a peerage for £22,000 .

Because the brothers wanted to live in Britain and still enjoy their enormous income tax-free, they set up an ingenious tax-avoidance scheme which has kept several generations of Inland Revenue inspectors entertained ever since. This enabled them to pay just £10 tax on an annual income of £2.5 million. Despite serious attempts by the Revenue to divest them of some of their tax-free fortune, the Vesteys have held on to it and avoided paying the government £88 million in tax.

Due to the dramatic improvement in Union International, 50 per cent owned by Sam, to after-tax profits of £30 million in 1992 (1991: £100 million loss), Vestey's fortune has recovered to a fair valuation of £300 million though the Vesteys still owe the banks £330 million.

### Personal style
The combination of Eton, a spell in the Guards, and a lifetime of privilege has made Sam Vestey an unrepentant boor. He is renowned almost as much for his fearsome temper as for traditional Vestey characteristics of secrecy and thrift.

### Extravagances
Compared to his high-living brother Edmund, Sam Vestey lives quietly but still in the grand style.

## 25 (28)
## Andrew Lloyd Webber 46
## £290m (£240m)
## Entertainment

### Source of wealth
At the age of 20, Andrew Lloyd Webber, composed *Joseph and the Amazing Technicolour Dreamcoat*. A quarter of a century later, Lloyd Webber is still raking it in. In 1992, he sold a one-third stake in his Really Useful Company to Polygram for around £70 million. This is the same price that the stock market valued the whole company at barely two years earlier when he took it private. Two years later, his 70 per cent interest in the Really Useful Group is probably worth around £250 million on its own. In the US, Lloyd Webber's productions continue to take the theatrical world by storm. In part, the useful boost to Lloyd Webber's wealth from US developments of his productions – in Las Vegas and in Hollywood – has lead us this year to uprate his wealth substantially to around £290 million.

Other assets include a few thousand acres surrounding his country estate Symington Hall, and a substantial property at Cap Ferrat in France.

This is a few millions less than the *Sunday Times* value him at. But its valuation includes many millions from the worldwide success of *Les Miserables*, with which he has no involvement and from which he hasn't earned a penny.

### Personal style
Despite being pilloried in the press he is a remarkably pleasant and fair man, adored by his staff at Really Useful. They know that when Lloyd Webber throws a rage and fires them, the next morning he will have forgotten all about it. When a staffer did take him literally and believed she had been fired, he rang next morning to enquire if she was ill. Despite ill-informed comment in the past his third marriage currently looks strong and is set to last the distance.

### Extravagances
The purchase of wildly expensive works of art by Canaletto, private helicopter, jet, and yacht. You name it – Andrew Lloyd Webber has it. And why not? He is one of the greatest creative talents Britain has ever produced.

## 26 (19)
## Cameron Mackintosh 47
## £286m (£278m)
## Entertainment

### Source of wealth
It is not only curtains that have been rising for Cameron Mackintosh this year. Profits from his personal production company Cameron Mackintosh Ltd zoomed ahead in 1993, meaning Mackintosh has even less need to worry about money. Turnover was up more than 20 per cent, rising from £29.6 million to £36.5 million. Profits, before tax, doubled to 14 million. After a chunk was chopped away in tax, the company was left with £8.4 million. Mackintosh rewarded himself with a salary increase of £500,000, taking his pay up to a huge £10.2 million a year. He makes sales of £23 million in the United States and total overseas sales of £34 million. In fact, turnover in the UK counts for only £7.7 million, and Australia for £3.4 million. His profitable sideline is in theatrical costumes, which represents £1.2 million in sales. Staff costs remove £16 million from his company's profits.

Cameron Mackintosh's organisation has over 50 musicals running all around the world and more than 30 are under his direct control. Mackintosh is currently producing *Oliver*, which opens in December 1994, at the London Palladium. Rumour has it that he is also planning a new musical about French legend Martin Guerre for next year, teaming up with the writers of *Les Miserables* and *Miss Saigon*. Cameron Mackintosh's organisation would be a tasty nugget for anyone to buy and he is said to get offers all the time. On the net present value of the copyrights, an appropriate sale price, should he ever desire it, of not less than £250 million can be placed on his empire. Add to this past salaries and dividends, and Cameron Mackintosh is easily worth £286 million.

### Personal style
Cameron Mackintosh is not only Britain's most successful impresario of all time, he is also probably one of the UK's top exporters. The government has not yet seen fit to award this prodigy with either a knighthood or a Queen's Award for Export. He has a joint venture, owning theatres with First Leisure Corporation and has eyes on the Stoll Moss empire owned by the widow of Robert Homes á Court, Janet.

### Extravagances
He has homes in Scotland and the English home counties, and most of the accompaniments of a tycoon.

## Stephen Rubin 57
## £275m (£450m)
## Business

### Source of wealth
What a bad year for Stephen Rubin who is one of the biggest fallers in this year's *Rich 500*. The market capitalisation of the main vehicle of his wealth, the Pentland Group, has halved to £192 million. But that is seriously undervaluing the company. The stock market still values Pentland at only slightly more than the £185 million cash in the bank. Pentland is now a £460 million turnover company. But it has more potential than that, and when the business is fully sorted out it will probably be showing a 10 per cent pre-tax margin. We still think Pentland is worth £500 million despite the problems.

Rubin holds over 50 per cent of the company's shares personally, and is therefore probably not particularly protected against punitive taxation in the event of a sale of those shares. But he has received substantial dividends over the years, and would certainly be able to raise a net worth of £275 million on the liquidation of his assets. Despite his big fall in the *Rich 500* he still has one of the more tangible fortunes on paper in Britain.

### Personal Style
Stephen Rubin is the most successful businessman of his generation never to have been given a knighthood. Whilst other, less able, less rich and less philanthropic men have been given gongs, Rubin, more deserving than most, has been passed by.

### Extravagances
He lives for the business and dreams of recreating the Pentland of old.

---

## Harry Hyams 66
## £270m (£215m)
## Property

### Source of wealth
Harry Hyams had built up his Oldham Estates property company into a £500 million conglomerate by 1987. Forced to sell to the MEPC group in a contested takeover in 1988, he personally netted £140 million out of the deal – but kept what is now a 5.5 per cent shareholding in MEPC itself. That shareholding is currently worth some £100 million. Within the lumbering giant that is MEPC, Hyams's old businesses now account for the lion's share of profits.

Harry Hyams was the quintessential property man of the Sixties. Best remembered for having built – and then holding empty – the huge Centre Point building on the corner of Tottenham Court Road and Oxford Street, he had started Oldham with less than £50,000 and, even at the time of the Centre Point controversy, his company was worth several hundred times his original stake.

### Personal style
Born the son of a bookmaker in London's East End, he is a noted racegoer. For many years Hyams was featured in the gossip columns. He was a regular litigant against those whom he felt unjustly criticised him.

### Extravagances
He owns the Ramsbury Estate in Wiltshire, which he bought from Lord Rootes, and which is reputed to have some of the best shooting in the country.

---

## Duke of Devonshire 74
## £268m (£255m)
## Aristocracy

### Source of wealth
Chatsworth, the Devonshires' family seat and one of Britain's foremost stately homes, was constructed on the creation of the dukedom in the late 1600s. Around 70,000 acres of land, part in Eastbourne and the rest evenly divided between Derbyshire and Yorkshire, remain in family hands. Art works by Rembrandt and Rubens, among others, push the value of the Devonshire estate into the hundreds of millions. Good taste doesn't stop there: the Duke's power as a landowner in Eastbourne means that he dictates the colour of shopfronts – and their content. (On the seafront at Eastbourne, chip shops are confined to side streets, hidden away from the naked eye).

The aging Duke's family connections branch out toward the Mitfords (he married the sister of Unity Mitford, an acquaintance of Adolf Hitler) and John F Kennedy (the Duke's brother married the great man's daughter).

The Duke has passed Bolton Abbey and 30,000 Yorkshire acres plus Lismore Castle and 8,000 acres in Waterford, Ireland, on to the Marquess of Hartington, his heir, whom we value at £35 million. All the same, the Duke of Devonshire remains one of Britain's seriously rich aristocrats. Conservatively, we have valued his art collection, land and physical property at £268 million, up from last year's £255 million.

### Personal style
Continues a great family tradition of paternalism, with conservationist tinges. After a tentative career as a junior Conservative minister in the Sixties, the Duke revoked his Tory loyalties in the 1980s to become an early supporter of Dr David Owen's SDP.

### Extravagances
Horse racing remains a prized pastime. The Duke's colours are among the best known at Britain's racecourses. His son, the Marquess of Hartington, is senior steward of the Jockey Club.

---

## Tom Jones 54
## £265m (£252m)
## Music

### Source of wealth
As far back as 1973, Tom Jones earned £800,000 in one year – a sum of money equivalent to approximately £12 million today. This is the equivalent minimum sum that we estimate Jones has earned over the last 25 years. Looking back at his live performances in America reveals an incredible work rate during this period. Jones established himself in the Frank Sinatra class of earnings in America. In the early Eighties, as Atlantic City grew to challenge Las Vegas, Jones was earning $50,000 for every performance. The trick was to have the presence of the big singing stars, which increased the casino drop (or earnings) out of all proportion to the fee paid to the entertainer. Therefore, Jones could name his own price. By 1980 he was the biggest regular crowd-puller on the US casino/cabaret circuit - and that included Sinatra.

By the mid-Eighties he was earning £2 million a week in Vegas. But that was not all: he was also working incredibly hard and could be seen all over America - albeit not always at those rates. For 20 years Jones took £20 million a year out of America. In today's money, Tom Jones has earned the equivalent of £700 million from his performing, singles, albums and business interests. From deductions of tax, manager's commission and his not inconsider-   ➜

able living expenses, his net worth is around £265 million.

## Personal style

Tom Jones's eternal luck was to be managed by the most remarkable music industry manager of all time: Gordon Mills. Mills took Jones and made him into an international singing star. The foundations which he'd laid made Jones richer than his wildest dreams. He started a public company, MAM, on the back of his success.

When Gordon Mills died suddenly of cancer in the summer of 1986, Jones was devastated and his fortunes went into temporary reverse. Jones took a few years off, but then made a comeback, managed by his son, Mark. He badly missed Mills, however. His secret had been to spread Jones around America for low fees to build his reputation and establish fan clubs, thereby increasing his appeal to the casinos. In eight months, at the height of his powers, he made 150 performances in 1980, right across America. Jones realised only too well that if it hadn't been for Mills, he would have been a simple Welsh labourer.

## Extravagances

He lives as quietly as he can in California. This means that his great wealth has never been recorded, whether by *Forbes* magazine or the *Sunday Times*.

### 31
### (25)

## Lady Brigid Ness *73*
## £265m (£250m)
## Inheritance

## Source of wealth

Lady Brigid Ness stood helpless as the family gradually lost control of the great drinks empire. Not that it mattered – for years she has been one of the world's richest women. She watched her brother lead an unhappy existence and finally die worn out, two years ago. She is the youngest daughter of the 2nd Earl of Iveagh, and part of the Guinness brewing dynasty.

In 1945 she married Queen Victoria's great-great-grandson, HRH Prince

### 32
### (31)

## Viscountess Boyd *76*
## £235m (£225m)
## Inheritance

## Source of wealth

Wealthy in her own right in 1938, Lady Patricia Guinness, daughter of the 2nd Earl of Iveagh, married Alan Lennox-Boyd MP, thereby creating a second line of Conservative parliamentary influence within the famed Anglo-Irish clan. (The other stemmed from Henry "Chips" Channon, father of Paul Channon MP, who married into the family in 1933).

Lennox-Boyd was given the title Viscount Boyd in 1960; his wife became the Viscountess. He came from a modestly wealthy background in Scotland. In 1959, he resigned his post as Colonial Secretary under Churchill's government and moved on to the board of Arthur Guinness & Co, next to his wife, Lady Patricia. Through his time with the company, he amassed shares which, with his wife's endowment, made their partnership the second-wealthiest in terms of Guinness family fortunes. Only the 3rd Earl of Iveagh was richer.

The accounts of the Iveagh Trustees demonstrate the wealth which has flowed in their direction. Lady Patricia holds

Friedrich Georg Wilhelm Christoph of Prussia. The marriage caused a sensation, for Prince Friedrich was the grandson of the last German Kaiser. He had also, for a brief period, been a Nazi stormtrooper. In 1947, Prince Friedrich became a naturalised British subject, but in 1951 he resumed German nationality and the use of his title. They had five children: three boys and two girls. In 1966 Lady Brigid sued for divorce: later that year the Prince was found drowned in the River Rhine.

In 1967, Lady Brigid married Major Patrick Ness. She was given away by her eldest son, Prince Nicholas, an officer in a British cavalry regiment.

Neither of her marriages brought much cash into her life: even before the war and her marriage to Prince Friedrich in 1945, the Hohenzollern family estates in Germany were much reduced.

Yet Lady Brigid continues to hold around 10 per cent of the shares in the Iveagh Trust, which has a total estimated value of £2.2 billion.

## Personal style

A great society beauty in her day, Lady Brigid belongs to a rapidly dwindling band of Anglo-Irish aristocrats.

## Extravagances

Art and charitable activities befitting the 2nd richest woman in England.

55,000 shares in the trust – the same amount as was held by her late nephew, the 3rd Earl of Iveagh. Viscount Boyd retired from the Guinness board in 1979. He died in 1983.

Among their children was Simon Lennox-Boyd, who succeeded his father, becoming the 2nd Viscount Boyd. He was cross-examined during the Guinness trial in 1990. The couple's third son, Mark Lennox-Boyd, has carved out a career in Westminster, most recently as parliamentary private secretary to Margaret Thatcher (1988-1990). As a junior foreign office minister, he has been given the uncomfortable task of explaining the government's policy on war-torn Rwanda and Bosnia to an incredulous parliament.

## Personal style

The marriage of Lady Patricia and Viscount Boyd was commonly described as one of the most stable of the Guinness girls' many matrimonial partnerships.

## Extravagances

A remarkable wardrobe of clothes.

### 33
### (34)

## Tony O'Reilly *58*
## £230m (£219m)
## Food

## Source of wealth

The bulk of Tony O'Reilly's wealth comes from his shares in the Pittsburgh-based Heinz Corporation, currently struggling to shore up its large margins and big brand names in a sluggish North American market.

In 1992, Heinz paid O'Reilly £50 million in salary, bonus and options. With the addition of subsequent, more modest, wage packets, that remarkable deal took his paper value, in terms of Heinz shares alone, to around £75 million over the past five years. More recently Heinz has been less generous. In 1993, O'Reilly took a 15 per cent pay cut – to £600,000 – as his company struggled to preserve its remarkable earnings record.

But HJ Heinz is only one strand in O'Reilly's multi-faceted business career.

In Dublin, he owns 10.5 per cent of Fitzwilton, an underperforming mini-conglomerate that he set up with colleagues in the early Seventies. That stake is now worth about £10 million. In addition, O'Reilly holds shares in Waterford-Wedgewood, the Irish glass maker, where he is chairman.

Perhaps his greatest non-Heinz money spinner, however, is Independent Newspapers plc, the Dublin-based group that recently failed in its bid to buy the similarly named *Independent* broadsheet in London. Independent Newspapers controls the vast majority of newspaper circulation in the

Republic – plus diversified media holdings in Australia, France, Mexico, South Africa and the UK. Its market capitalisation is around £340 million. Of this, O'Reilly himself owns 28 per cent, valued at £95 million.

Meanwhile, a range of property investments, including commercial investments in Ashford and Dromoland Castles in the Irish Republic, are worth up to £2 million.

Beyond identifiable shareholdings and assets lie the accumulated profits of a lifetime's wheeling and dealing – in investments ranging from fertilisers to natural gas exploration. Counting these, and with accumulated dividends included, we rate O'Reilly at £230 million overall. This makes Tony O'Reilly easily the richest man in Ireland.

Small dents have occurred in his wealth after his divorce from first wife Susan. This was easily made up when he married Britain's richest woman Chryss Goulandris. Together they have become Britain's golden couple with a combined net worth in excess of £500 million.

BUSINESSAGE LIBRARY

### 34 (20) Robert Edmiston 48
## £225m (£275m)
## Business

## Source of wealth
The uncertainty surrounding almost all of his vehicle franchises has caused us to downgrade the personal wealth of Robert Edmiston substantially.

It has certainly been a bittersweet year. His £50 million wrangle with Vauxhall over the Isuzu franchise has finally been settled, but the agreement reached means that Edmiston's IM Group will be selling a decreasing number of Isuzu Troopers over the next three years. After this time, Vauxhall will take over the franchise and sell their Vauxhall Monterey instead.

Last summer, Edmiston sold IM Group's control of the Hyundai car import business to Lex for an initial £9 million. He effectively sold the Hyundai franchise to Lex Group for £30 million,

## Personal style
An unparalleled charmer. In the City of London, they used to say you could never trust a man whose ties were of a brighter hue than his shirts. Tony O'Reilly – who typically wears yellow ties and blue shirts – has conclusively proved how much things have changed.

## Extravagances
Food, wine, after-dinner speaking – all part of an extravagant entertaining style. At Castlemartin, his mansion in Co Kildare, guests rarely get to sit down for dinner before 10.30pm. O'Reilly bought the place from the Earl of Gowrie in the 1970s: previous tenants had included the Rolling Stones in their wild heyday. Now a photograph of O'Reilly playing tennis with George Bush sits on the mantelpiece. In the grounds stands a medieval chapel, renovated by O'Reilly himself. O'Reilly's other residential property interests are his residence in Pittsburgh, a holiday home in Glandore in West Cork and a second vacation property in Barbados. These have a combined value of several millions.

spread over three years, and half of IM Finance for £8 million. However, Edmiston is not in the poorhouse, yet, and the dividend pay-out last year for this car and property group director, totalled £4.13 million.

IM, which originally stood for International Motors, made nearly £32 million, before tax, for the year to December 1992 from a £308.5 million turnover. Most of the profit came from the Japanese import franchises and increasingly from the property side, which last year absorbed another private company, BHH, with the spare cash thrown off by the import and finance operations. For the year to December 1992, property sales counted for £17.8 million of the company's entire turnover.

Edmiston owns all of the shares in IM outright, making him a very wealthy man indeed but because of the nature of the business it is totally inappropriate to calculate his worth on a profits multiple. Assuming that his compensation for eventually losing the franchises will be modest, that there are five years of profits left and including the value of the property portfolio, we have downgraded him to £225 million. We also believe that he has made several multi-million donations to charity in the past 12 months.

## Personal style
He was brought up as a Roman Catholic and became a Pentecostalist at 17.

## Extravagances
As a god-fearing man he exists only to give and to work.

### 35 (36) Patrick Murphy 83
## £221m (£208m)
## Property

## Source of wealth
Patrick Murphy is one of Britain's oldest chairmen, having turned 83. Part of his motivation for still turning up to work every morning is the continued growth of Charles Street Buildings (Leicester) Ltd which he owns.

The latest accounts, for the year ending November 1992, show a £19.8 milion profit with £102 million of assets on the books. The company is worth close to £300 million, given that it owns 6 million square feet of industrial property on 350 acres of land. It also has a large bank of industrial land, which will be developed once the economic climate improves.

Murphy, himself, is registered as owning 30 per cent of the shares, largely because he is transferring as many as possible to other family members to save inheritance tax – a large number going to his daughter, Winifred. Any reduction in his wealth through inheritance tax will be compensated by the upturn in the property market.

Most of the holdings are in the Midlands, producing another £15 million a year through rental income. The property market has failed to take-off in the last year but, more significantly, the slump is over. We have upgraded our valuation to include his share of the 1993 income, less tax.

As an example of the sheer wealth that pervades the family, his brother Hugh Murphy died in 1991, leaving £27 million in his will. The majority of Hugh's shares are being held in trust by other members of the family.

## Personal style
Like most family-run property/construction outfits, Patrick Murphy's style is not to let anyone know what it is. He has not given an interview, or for that matter made a public appearance, in the past two years, but we are assured he is alive and kicking at the helm of the company.

The company started as Murphy Brothers Ltd in the aggregates business, operating over 250 heavy earthmoving vehicles and 400 delivery lorries in the Thirties. In 1968 this side of the business was bought by BET for £8 million – the cash was used to move into property.

A new site was purchased in Charles Street, Leicester, which was turned into Murphy's HQ – hence the new company name.

## Extravagances
Keeping a low profile, and staying up till the early hours discovering new ways to transfer his shares to his family.

BUSINESSAGE LIBRARY

**36** (29) **Donatella Moores** 32
**£218m** (£235m)
**Inheritance**
▼

## Source of wealth

The delightful and unassuming Donatella Moores is one of the brightest business brains in the Moores family and semi-active in making the important decisions.

She is the only daughter of Peter Moores CBE, former chairman of the Littlewoods store and pools group. Peter Moores has transferred most of his 12.5 per cent stake to her, making her the richest female in the family. Last year *Business-Age* estimated that the Littlewoods empire would be worth £2 billion, if quoted on the stock market. We have downgraded her wealth this year, as in our view, the

advent of the national lottery has devalued the Littlewoods business substantially, and we now rate the private empire at around £1.7 billion.

Peter Moores married Luciana Pinto in 1960, and Donatella was born in 1962. She has one brother, Alexander, born the following year. Her parents divorced in 1984. The death of her grandfather, Sir John Moores, who founded the Little-woods organisation in 1924, made no difference as he had already long passed on his shares in the company to his descendants just as Donatella's father has chosen to do.

In theory, each of the children of Sir John Moores, and his brother Cecil, who founded the company, should have one-seventh of the shares, which would give Donatella only one fourteenth of the company. In practice, the shares have not been split that way: about 12 per cent of the company is registered in the name of Donatella, or jointly with her father at his Lancashire mansion home.

## Personal style

She is more active in the family than most and sits on the Littlewoods Organisation plc group board, as a non executive director.

## Extravagances

She lives quietly with homes in London and Brighton. Neighbours can't believe that the unassuming girl is worth so much money.

**37** (39) **Jack Dellal** 71
**£218m** (£195m)
**Property**
▲

## Source of wealth

If insider trading in property was a crime then Jack Dellal might have problems. Too often Dellal has been on the inside of cosy property deals and people have questioned the relationships between buyer and seller. Nothing wrong in this, of course, just as there were no insider trading laws on the stock exchange when Dellal created his first fortune.

He made this via the sale of his financial group Dalton Barton to City merchant bank Keyser Ullman. The price Keyser paid, £58 million – about £580 million in current money – is the foundation stone of the Dellal fortune. Originally from Manchester, he did a stint at Keyser's as deputy chairman, resigning just as the secondary banking crisis hit the City in 1974. Since then he has operated as an investor through his master company Allied Commercial Holdings. In 1987, he bought the freehold on Bush House, home of the BBC World

Service, for £55 million, and legend has it that he later sold it on to Japanese Group Kato Kagaku for £130 million. In 1990, a 650 per cent increase in profits prompted him to award himself a pay packet of some £6.2 million.

Not all his investments have been so successful. A backer of William Stern in the Seventies, he is thought to have lost heavily when Stern's Wilstar properties went under. He was a heavy investor in property and was still in a number of situations when the recession began.

## Personal style

Sharp eye for yields. The old secondary banker in him has never lost the taste for elbows-first tactics. Formerly married to an Israeli air hostess, with whom he had one son and six daughters. One daughter died of a drug overdose 12 years ago, and there was more tragedy when his son Guy became involved in drugs and narrowly escaped prison in the early Eighties.

He is substantially wealthy and has made many gains, but also losses.

In the mid-Sixties he was heavily involved in activities in South Africa, he is virulently anti-Communist and his politics

are right-of-centre. He is reportedly close to the Conservative Party, although there is no record of any political donations. Dellal and his family are close friends of Elliot Bernerd, another very successful property trader, and they have apparently done deals together in the past.

Bernerd advised Dellal's sister, Violet Seulberger-Simon on the purchase of Guinness shares during the Guinness/Distillers scandal. A commission was paid to an offshore company, Rudani Corporation, for which no public explanation has ever been given.

Currently edging back into the property market, via the £10 million freehold purchase of a giant West London leisure site from developers THI. In summer 1993, he underwrote just under half of a £2.2 million capital raising exercise for Tony Berry's Business Technology Group.

## Extravagances

A yacht in the Mediterranean and an estate in Hampshire. His son is said to have harboured Michael Jackson, while the pop star fled law enforcement officials on suspicion of child abuse.

**38** (72)  **Steve Morgan** 41
**£216m** (£132m)
**Construction**
▲

## Source of wealth

This has been a trying year for Steve Morgan. A lot of people would be happy to see an already large fortune double and £62 million materialise in their bank account overnight, but not Morgan. The flotation of the housebuilder Redrow, which he founded 20 years ago, stalled in a jittery market earlier this year. From an opening price of 135 pence the shares now stand at 113 pence, capitalising the company that builds "heritage" homes at £250 million. Predictions in March of a £350 million capitalisation have gone out the window, and Morgan is said to be less than pleased with advisers BZW as a result of effectively losing £100 million in a day. Morgan still owns 60 per cent of the shares.

At least, however, Morgan now has the cash to endow trusts for his children and the company's borrowings are no more. In 1993 Redrow made £13 million pre-tax profits on £130 million turnover.

## Personal style

Morgan comes across as an extravagantly self-made Liverpudlian. He claims to make decisions based on instinct. Entering the private housebuilding market in 1982, just on the cusp of the housing boom, for example; or getting out of building in the south-east of England in 1988, the graveyard for so many construction firms in the subsequent recession. "I turned up on a building site [in 1988]," he recalls, "and no work was being done. They were all off fishing, I was told. I knew then I had to get out."

Last year Steve Morgan bought Costain Homes for a paltry £17 million to re-establish the Redrow Group in the South East, confirming himself as the UK's largest homebuilder with a capacity of 2,000 houses a year. Factories, offices, pubs, as well as a luxury hotel and country park owned and managed by him, complete the portfolio – at least temporarily.

### Extravagances
He is a fanatical Liverpool supporter, and so far cannot quash rumours that he will invest some of his flotation lucre in the Premier League side. On the eve of the flotation, he transferred a £6 million hotel and golf course complex from Redrow to one of his private holding companies. The purchase price? Just £100.

### Paul Hamlyn 68
### £215m (£245m)
### Publishing

### Source of wealth
The source of Paul Hamlyn's wealth has always been Reed International, the all-embracing publishing giant. Twice he has sold his company to them, and twice made millions - the second time hundreds of millions. His first company, the Paul Hamlyn imprint, was sold for £2.5 million in 1964; his second, called Octopus, went for over £500 million in 1987. In between, he bought his original company back from Reed, and merged it into Octopus. Therefore, he effectively sold the Paul Hamlyn imprint to Reed twice.

With dividends, salaries and the rise in his Reed shares, plus some shrewd investments, Hamlyn has easily netted £450 million.

He has, however, given over £100 million to charity since he became super-rich, pegging his personal fortune at £350 million. Then the taxman took a chunk. So we valued him last year at £245 million. We believe that he has given a further large chunk of money to charity this year and the uncertain position at Reed, with the resignation of Chairman Peter Davis, and the half-hearted merger with Dutch publisher, Elsevier has made the real value of his share stake more uncertain. It is not something that he could sell easily, without severely devaluing the worth of the whole of Reed. The conclusion that he came to as a result of the forcing out of his friend, Peter Davis is anyone's guess.

Taking into account his donations, the fact that there is now no possibility of Reed

Elsevier being taken over, and his stake in the company being worth a premium, we have marked him down £30 million. For now, he is stuck with the shares.

### Personal style
He is German by birth, but now more British than most, as he chose to escape the

BUSINESSAGE LIBRARY

### David Wilson 52
### £212m (£206m)
### Construction

### Source of wealth
At the start of the year Wilson Bowden chairman, David Wilson, was worth nearly £300 million after the housebuilder's share price rose to 571 pence. The price slump, to just over 400 pence, values Wilson's stake in the company at £185 million – similar to last year. However, he netted £7 million in a share sale last year, pushing his worth, with dividends, to £212 million.

### Francis Chamberlain 62
### £210m (New entry)
### Drink

### Source of wealth
Francis Chamberlain controls 33 per cent of William Grant & Sons, producer of Glenfiddich, the pricey single malt whisky that dominates the world market for this type of Scotch. And yet he has escaped the attention of all rich lists before. Our mistake.

Based on expected profits of some £25 million for 1993, and a theoretical price/earnings ratio of 20, the company would be worth just over £400 million. Chamberlain's stake comes to £130 million. However that is not the end of the story. We estimate that the Glenfiddich brand alone would be worth £400 million, if ever put up for sale. We have therefore val-

regime of Adolf Hitler in the mid-Thirties. Surely a knighthood cannot be far away after his gigantic donations to charitable causes.

### Extravagances
He loves flying the world in his private jet and floating around on his big yacht.

The City continues to admire Wilson Bowden which, in spite of being in a depressed sector, more than doubled pretax profits last year to £31.2 million. This is largely thanks to the strategy of concentrating on building four-bedroom houses in the Midlands and, more significantly, none in the South East. The five year land bank also gives it a useful cushion against changes in government policies on planning applications.

It's all a long way from the company's origins in the gritty Leicestershire mining town of Ibstock. David Wilson joined what was his father's business as an 18 year old, floating the company in 1987. At the start of this decade, his stake, after his father's death, was already worth £148 million.

### Personal style
Much of his working life was in partnership with his father, whose death has only further inspired him to succeed. Not a man to be deflected from his work, he is devoted to the housebuilding industry where he concentrates all his efforts.

### Extravagances
Not that keen himself on four-bedroom Wilson Bowden homes, having splashed out £1 million on Lowesby Hall in Leicestershire where he lives with his second wife. Farming and fox-hunting are heavily pursued while waiting for the housing recovery.

ued William Grant on a brand basis at some £600 million including other assets, making Chamberlain one of the highest new entrants in the *Rich 500* at a valuation of £210 million.

### Personal style
Over production of Glenfiddich may have undermined its "exclusive" label, and more discerning customers are turning to less well-known single malts. Also, William Grant's structure is a bit voluminous: the paper trail extends to at least a dozen registered companies, with William Grant and Sons Ltd as the prime trading entity.

### Extravagances
For one so wealthy – and producing such a well-known product – Chamberlain keeps his head down: no playboy lifestyle, no ostentatious sampling of his product (or the competitions for that matter). Not even a *Who's Who* entry.

BUSINESSAGE LIBRARY

**42**
(27)

## Tiny Rowland 76
## £208m (£242m)
## Business
▼

### Source of wealth

Rowland's own personal wealth was relatively easy to assess, until Tom Bower published his unauthorised biography in 1993. In that, he virtually accused Rowland of not always telling the whole truth.

Paul Spicer, Lonrho's former deputy chairman, stated, for the record, that Tiny Rowland had £120 million cash in his bank account two years ago. That seems unlikely. But Rowland does boast that he is, in his own words, "a fully paid-up member of the Inland Revenue". There is no question that much of his fortune is now liquid. Rowland likes to have his money where he can see it, and he has been earning very substantial dividends from Lonrho for some time. For some years his dividend, after tax, has been as much as £7 million. Most of his expenses are paid for by Lonrho and, with his million-plus salary, it is likely that he has accumulated that much cash in the last 30

**43**
(32)

## David Thompson 58
## £206m (£220m)
## Business
▼

### Source of wealth

David Thompson made over £300 million when he sold his shares in the company. He founded Hillsdown Holdings plc and he got out at the right time, as the company went into sharper decline after his exit. Since then, Thompson has chaired the family company, Union Square plc, and Thompson Investments, run by his son Richard. He also owns Queens Park Rangers Football Club. He owns two large

years. We put it after taxes at some £60 million. He also has the £50 million which he received from new Lonrho boss, Dieter Bock, when he sold half his shareholding two years ago. He can expect another £80 million before he retires in an agreement he has, with Bock, to buy the other half in a few years' time. After tax, we have downgraded his wealth to £208 million simply because, after Bower's extensive research, we have a much better feel for his true financial position.

### Personal style

These are the Autumn years of Tiny Rowland's life. He would give up all his wealth if he could turn the clock back 10 years. He was the ultimate tycoon who recovered from so many financial scrapes that he was at one time nicknamed Houdini. He lives with his talented wife Josie and children in his Buckinghamshire home, famed for its beautiful garden.

### Extravagances

Since Robert Maxwell died, Tiny Rowland has been Britain's finest example of a true tycoon. The yacht, the private Gulfstream jet and the country house are all his to savour.

studs in the south of England, countless horses and a controlling stake in Windsor racecourse. The *Sunday Times* values his horse-racing empire at £30 million. This is probably an underestimate.

He invested in a troubled estate agency called Glentree and bought some property at the wrong time. He had well publicised troubles at Queens Park Rangers, the passion of his son. But the new company he is building, Thompson Investments, is doing well with sales of around £50 million and profits of over £1 million. Even after his mistakes, he is still worth nearly £250 million.

After a relatively good year when the

value of his properties increased, we still rate Thompson slightly lower at £206 million because of other problems.

### Personal style

David Thompson is one of the most private men in British business. He was virtually unheard of until Hillsdown Holdings was floated on the stock exchange in 1985. He is most famous for his passion for the turf: his horse *Party Politics* won the 1992 Grand National, only days after he bought it for his wife. He lists running the family businesses and horse-racing as his recreations in *Who's Who*.

Thompson has one son and two daughters. He is an extraordinarily private man without being a recluse and, despite what would seem to be a relatively high profile career in business and horse-racing, there has never, ever been a photograph published of him anywhere. In fact he goes to extraordinary lengths to avoid being photographed. Friends speak highly of him and he is an extremely charming man – especially when turning down photo requests.

### Extravagances

Football – the weakness of so many members of the *Rich 500* - and horses, although he appears not to lose too much money from this activity.

**44**
(74)

## Graham Kirkham 50
## £204m (£131m)
## Retailing
▲

### Source of wealth

When a private company is floated on the stock market, value is crystallised up or down. There were two extremes to this rule for the members of last year's *Rich 500* in 1993. For Graham Kirkham, it meant a virtual doubling of his wealth; for John Hayes, the motor dealer, it meant that he was wiped out, he lost his company and all but a few millions of his net worth.

Graham Kirkham and his family owned all the shares in the Doncaster-based furniture retailing company, Northern Upholstery Group. His annual salary last year was the fourth highest in Britain, at £5.72 million. We thought flotation would value it at £100 million. But he renamed the company DFS plc and got his timing right. A £275 million valuation was made possible by a huge burst of profit.

Kirkham cleared some £130 million from dividends and share sales on flotation. He will eventually have to yield £30 or so million of that to the tax man. He already had liquid assets of £31 million before the sale and the remaining shares held, are worth £140 million.

But not all the shares belonged to him and after deducting the ones he does not hold personally plus the tax he will have to pay after the flotation, we value him at £204 million.

## Personal style

The bluff miner's son is a genius retailer. He keeps it simple and he keeps it sweet. Simple – by only offering three piece suites for sale in his shops and sweet – because 0% finance and no deposit credit, comes as part of the deal. You can pay cash if you like, but what is the point? Kirkham marks his sofas up 100 per cent and out of that he deducts the credit costs which he pays for typically now some 20 per cent over three years, leaving him with 30 per cent. He doesn't keep any stock and the customer pays a deposit on order, taking delivery later. It is a superbly simple business and they simply don't come any better.

## Extravagances

He has few. Running the DFS money machine is exhausting.

**45** (40)
### Lord Wolfson 66
### £200m (£194m)
### Retailing

## Source of wealth

Leonard Wolfson joined Great Universal Stores after his father, furniture salesman Isaac Wolfson, made it part of the family business. Since 1966, the current Lord Wolfson has been chairman of GUS.

His father was one of the greats of British commerce, with the giant GUS racking up huge profits towards the end of his life. His start in business, though, was by all accounts a rough and tumble affair. Leonard has not had the same problem and, although he inherited only a fraction of his father's great wealth, he has still been made a very rich man indeed.

The largest stockholder in Great Universal Stores, the home shopping-to-finance group, is the Wolfson Foundation, a charitable trust. The Wolfson fortune held in non-charitable trusts – referred to in GUS's accounts as 'other trusts etc' – appears to amount to roughly £185 million. To that must be added Lord Wolfson's direct personal holdings in the company, which are valued at around £9 million.

Add to this existing personal wealth and dividends and Wolfson's wealth comes to around £225 million. However, some £25 million appears to have been passed onto his heirs, tax efficiently.

In the UK, GUS owns the CCN credit-checking business, Burberry and Scotch House. Net turnover for the year to March 1993 totalled £2.8 billion, up from £2.5 billion in 1992. Pre-tax profits were £475 million.

## Personal style

Wolfson's links with the Conservative Party are evident from his loyalties in the House of Lords, where he has taken the Tory whip since 1986. Not to be confused with his more politically active cousin, Lord Wolf-

**46** (42)
### Albert Gubay 64
### £198m (£185m)
### Retailing

## Source of wealth

Albert Gubay's first fortune came from the Kwik Save supermarket chain. He took it public, and then sold his stake for £14 million. He moved to New Zealand and did the same thing with a chain called 3 Guys, for £46 million. Then he set up another 3 Guys chain in Ireland and, 17 months later, Tesco paid him £17 million for the lot.

Then he went to America, that graveyard of retailing for the unaware, and caught his first cold. Gubay says he picked the wrong area (South Carolina), and the wrong time, to do it. He claims he made £40 million. In truth, he got his money back and made a bit, because the exchange rate moved with him.

His supermarket days left him with a net £80 million after tax, and he moved to the Isle of Man and developed property sites to house supermarkets in Britain. He also set up the Celtic Bank there, financed by

**47** (83)
### Martyn Arbib 55
### £195m (£121m)
### Finance

## Source of wealth

It's been a great year for Martyn Arbib, as the value of his Perpetual shares raced ahead. Arbib has made himself rich by making other people rich too. Even his hobbies make money.

Twenty years ago, he founded the Perpetual unit trust group. Today, chairman

son of Sunningdale, who also chairs a clothing retailer – Next plc.

## Extravagances

Wolfson has endowed colleges at Oxford and Cambridge, and he is a trustee of the Imperial War Museum.

his cash.

He made another cool hundred million during those years so that, by the start of the Nineties, he had amassed a personal fortune of £180 million. Since then, he has been treading water, like many entrepreneurs, preserving the status quo with his bank accounts. Nowadays his money is tied up in a massive property portfolio - which would probably be worth £185 million in a sensible liquidation – as well as his private bank.

## Personal Style

Gubay's original formula for supermarket success was very simple. He bought supplies for his supermarkets by the week, sold out and then ordered another week's supplies. He took four weeks' credit and, by the time he came to pay, he had earned interest from four weeks' takings. He sold the goods at next to cost, and the investment income was his profit. Clever stuff because his low prices brought in huge business.

He is currently in the middle of building a luxury complex on the Isle of Man for an American group, which will include a 100-bed hotel and 18-hole golf course. And he really is building it: he apparently takes on all the jobs alongside everyone else – even shovelling concrete – and works 12 hours a day, seven days a week, fitting in other business in between. His drive is quite phenomenal, and must explain much of his success.

## Extravagances

Gubay is a non-drinking, non-smoking, non-waste tycoon, although he does have the luxury of a Gulfstream jet for his trips to Europe. However, all is not entirely rosy: he has had serious run-ins in the past with local tax bureaucracy, and has threatened to pack up his tent and move to Switzerland.

Arbib and his team of fund managers look after a few billions of other people's money – and they do the task superbly well. Perpetual's two dozen unit trusts have won many awards. The consequent inflow of cash from investors reflects this and has helped push up profits – particularly in the past year, when the company's share price has been on a constant upward trend. Market capitalisation currently stands at around £260 million. Arbib's 70 per cent share is worth some £180 million.

Arbib floated Perpetual on the stock

market in 1987, and trousered more than £10 million when he sold almost a quarter of his shares. Accrued dividends and outside investments make up the total of £200 million.

## Personal style

One of the secrets that makes Arbib's company such a successful City player could be that it isn't based in the City at all. The headquarters are at Henley-on-Thames, "far from the maddening crowd," as one of his colleagues put it.

This base is said to give a more relaxed atmosphere for investment decision-making, increasing the chances that Perpetual

will lead the stock market pack, not just follow it.

Arbib's style is laid back and he runs the company lean, and mean, on overheads so low that it frightens his competitors to death.

## Extravagances

Arbib's racehorse, Snurge, has won over £1.2 million – a world record. As if the real thing wasn't sufficient, Arbib is the proud owner of a life-sized bronze statue of the beast.

He has a lovely country home, where his wife frequently entertains. Fast becoming a part of the establishment.

BUSINESSAGE LIBRARY

### Alexander Grant Gordon 63
### £195m (£124m)
### Drink

## Source of wealth

Every second bottle of single malt whisky sold in Britain is a bottle of Glenfiddich. The distinctive, triangular green bottle comes from the Speyside distillery owned by the family firm, William Grant & Sons, and is also the leading malt brand in overseas markets. Over the last thirty years, William Grant has turned the whisky market on its head: blended products used to dominate, while malts were, for generations, regarded as a local preference, rarely found outside Scotland.

In 1993 the company will probably have made £25 million pre-tax on a turnover of £250 million. Highland Distilleries, which is of broadly similar size and profitability compared with William Grant, and which also has one particularly strong brand (the Famous Grouse blended whisky), trades in the stock market on a price/earnings ratio of 20. A similar figure would give

William Grant a market value of more than £400 million, of which the interests allocated to Alexander Grant Gordon (personal holdings as well as a Jersey nominee account that controls 43 per cent of the equity) amount to just over £170 million. However, we believe a price/earnings ratio value of Grants now highly inappropriate. On a brand value basis we value the company at £600 million in 1994 and believe it would fetch more were it ever to be for sale, meaning a large increase in the net worth for Alexander.

## Personal style

Ever since the first drop of malt flowed from the Dufftown stills on Christmas Day, 1887, the company has been owned and run by the Grant family, with some Gordons marrying in along the way.

Alexander 'Sandy' Grant Gordon is the chairman of the company; he recently handed over his role as managing director to 35-year-old Glen Gordon.

The company has recently spent millions of pounds buying in shareholdings from some family members who have no involvement with the running of the company. Many shareholdings have also wound up offshore, like that 43 per cent of William Grant & Sons' ordinary shares parked in Jersey. Sandy Grant Gordon discloses no beneficial interest in the shares held by this nominee but, as he is the effective patriarch of the family of distillers, we have included a portion of this offshore holding in his wealth calculation. Furthermore, it is understood that shareholders are restricted from selling their stock without first offering them to other members of the family.

## Extravagances

Few, as the family has never cashed in on the undoubted bonanza that would come if they were ever to sell. There would be a stampede. No wonder the family is keen to buy in as many shares as it can.

### Paul Channon 63
### £190m (£180m)
### Inheritance

## Source of wealth

Britain's richest MP has held the seat of Southend (West) for the Conservatives since 1959. The seat has been held for so long by a member of the Guinness family that it is affectionately known as Guinness-on-Sea in the House of Commons.

Paul Channon's mother was the eldest daughter of the 2nd Earl of Iveagh, who ruled over the Guinness brewing fortune until his death in 1967. She married Chips Channon, the anglicised US politician. On his death in 1959, Chips Channon left an estate valued at £73,646 after death duties, which was passed entirely to Paul Channon. In 1969, Paul Channon inherited around £2 million-worth of Guinness shares previously held by his mother – an inheritance which apparently had accumulated outside the assets of the family's Iveagh Trust.

Paul Channon's marriage to his cousin's former wife, Ingrid Guinness, may well have bolstered his standing within the family. In the past year he has become a director of the Iveagh Trustees. Perhaps the ritual handing over of the income to the younger beneficiaries is taking place.

Paul Channon's relationship to the Iveagh Trust is shrouded in mystery. Despite his status as grandson of the 2nd Earl of Iveagh, and cousin to the 3rd Earl, he does not appear as a shareholder in the Iveagh Trust. Possibly, given his insistence in 1990 that "my people" have always dealt with his inheritance, his legacy is concealed within the nominee company, Scotia, which holds 35,000 shares – around 6.25 per cent – in the Iveagh Trust. In terms of the Guinness family hierarchy, Channon may be as wealthy as his aunt, Lady Patricia, Viscountess Boyd, as his mother's assets would have passed to him on her death.

## Personal Style

Paul Channon has one son and one daughter. A second daughter, Olivia, died after a drugs overdose at Oxford University in the mid-Eighties.

During the Thatcher era, Channon held a number of Cabinet posts, including portfolios at Trade and Industry and Transport. Oddly, perhaps because of his suspicious status as a 'wet', he made no lasting mark on the politics of the period. Sadly, there is no sign that he will emulate either his father or his friend, Alan Clark, in publishing a scurrilous autobiographical memoir.

## Extravagances

Few, as he has to remember that he is a Member of Parliament subject to public scrutiny.

## Andrew Brownsword 46
**£189m** (£170m)
### Business

### Source of wealth
The phenomenally high margins in the greetings card sector have led to Andrew Brownsword's multi-millionaire status. On sales of £44.9 million in the latest accounts, a profit of £19.6 million was achieved. The turning point was the company, Gordon Fraser Gallery Ltd,

acquired in 1989, the best known brand in the greetings card business. Profits soared from £3 million in 1989 to the astounding 1991 results. In a private deal he merged the company with the relatively unsuccessful UK subsidiary of Hallmark cards and took management control.

Valuations in the order of £300 million are wildly excessive but Brownsword is worth an easy £189 million.

### Personal style
The Andrew Brownsword Collection, established in 1975, didn't come into its own until the 1980s, with its famous Forever Friends, Dino and Country Companion cards. His direct management style ensures very high margins. He is also an expert financier, as well as a brilliant manager. He has expanded into gifts and his never-ending ideas mean designs are popping up everywhere.

### Extravagances
He has more money than he ever dreamed of, but still loves the greetings card business. Billionaire status is almost inevitable by the time he retires.

---

## Eddie Healey 56
**£188m** (£69m)
### Property

### Source of wealth
Eddie Healey's father, together with his three sons, began as suppliers of decorating materials after the Second World War. Eddie built the business up to profit from the 1970s DIY boom, trading as Status Discount in Hull's former Dance de Luxe ballroom. More branches were added, and Eddie Healey floated Status in 1972. He sold it to MFI for £30 million in 1980 and left when his contract ran out three years later. In 1983 he formed Stadium Developments, specialising in the construction of retail warehouses. Then came his biggest coup. He bought into the Meadowhall shopping centre project with Paul Sykes. The timing was perfect and Stadium Developments owns 60 per cent of a site that is said to be worth some £500 million.

Be that as it may, Healey has a net worth that has spiralled in 1994 and we estimate it at £188 million, well over double that of a year ago and overtaking his up until now richer brother Malcolm.

### Personal style
His was a classic road to riches, climbing the ladder to the source of the wealth, with complete family commitment. When Eddie Healey was born in 1938, his father was a painter and decorator in Hull, pushing a handcart from door-to-door to generate business. During the war, with her hus-

band away fighting, his wife Sarah kept the business going. Healey's wife, Carol, provides that same support today.

### Extravagances
A member of the young, northern ratpack who all made fortunes in the Eighties and survived to enjoy them in the Nineties. He is now enjoying his success. He has just bought his first jet with the proceeds of his Meadowhall success but otherwise Healey lives quietly near Hull and is regularly seen in the village pub. A rare extravagance, five years ago, was his 50th birthday party (combined with his daughter's 21st). The band of the Royal Artillery played and the party set him back £250,000.

---

## William Brown 57
**£187m** (£175m)
### Finance

### Source of wealth
William Brown controls Walsham Brothers, a 73-year-old business. Insurance brokers cannot be valued on a price/earnings basis. The only effective valuation is its net asset value, which is around £90 million, giving Brown a small increase for 1994 in net worth combined with salary and investment earnings.

The company has gone awry in the last few years and Brown has only drawn a £3 million a year salary. Operating profit has dropped to virtually nothing, and investment income of around £10 million saved the company.

Three Brown brothers direct and control Walsham, but William Brown, the eldest, has control of the company through non-beneficial deferred shares, and we estimate that his influence means he controls around 70 per cent of the company, giving him a capital worth of £60 million. But to that must be added the salary and dividends he has been receiving for the past years.

We estimate that Brown has drawn around £155 million in salary and dividends in his business career. He also received a private inheritance when his mother and father died.

After tax and with his shares in the company, Brown is now worth £187 million.

### Personal style
William Brown has had more publicity than he cares for, as a result of being dubbed the man with the biggest salary in the UK for some years. This was never actually the case, it was just that he was the most visible. Walsham Brothers made ridiculously high profits because of Brown and his brothers' skills.

### Extravagances
For all his cash, Brown lives quietly in Hove, Sussex whilst his brothers Jim and Henry are Essex boys.

---

## Malcolm Healey
**£186m** (£165m)
### Business

### Source of wealth
Malcolm Healey, younger brother of Eddie, created Humber Kitchens and renamed it Hygena in 1981. By 1987, it was making pre-tax profits of £20 million. At this point, he sold out to MFI for £200 million in cash and shares.

### Personal style
The Healey brothers, Eddie and Malcolm, are a unique phenomena in British industry. Both are independently self-made, both are very, very rich and both made their first fortunes by selling different businesses to MFI. Their father was a painter and decorator in Hull, pushing a handcart from door-to-door to generate business. During the war with her husband away fighting, his wife Sarah kept the business going.

Malcolm left the family firm of Status Discount in 1976, frustrated by the inability of suppliers to deliver on time and to the required quality.

After the lucrative sale to MFI, he went to America to seek fresh opportunities.

### Extravagances
He lives to work and is said to be all cashed up and ready to go on to a new project. Non-complete contracts prevent him from entering the furniture business for a long time.

### Simon Sainsbury 64
### £185m (£220m)
### Retailing

## Source of wealth

In the J Sainsbury accounts for the year to March 1993, Simon Sainsbury is shown as holding five per cent of the company's shares, beneficially and as trustee. Assuming a rough 50/50 split between trust and personal holdings, as in the case of his brother, Tim Sainsbury MP, Simon Sainsbury's personal paper fortune amounts to around £180 million at current prices. That 2.5 per cent gives him an income of £5 million a year.

## Personal style

The late Lord Sainsbury attempted to steer his sons in different directions during their early careers – and thus into different niches within the family firm – Simon Sainsbury became an accountant.

He left the board in 1979 to devote more of his time to the arts and thoroughbred racing. The *Daily Express* has described him as a "quiet, tweedy bachelor." He is a junior minister at the DTI and filled in for Michael Heseltine while he was ill last year.

## Extravagances

In 1991, Simon Sainsbury endowed the Judge Institute at Cambridge University with £5 million. A knighthood must surely beckon soon.

### Lady Grantchester 71
### £185m (£168m)
### Inheritance

## Source of wealth

Lady Grantchester is the elder daughter of Sir John Moores, the co-founder of Littlewoods. She is both a shareholder and a director of the main company, as she has been all her adult life. In recent times she is rumoured to have played a decisive role in bringing in the first non-family chairman of the operation, Leonard Van Geest, of the Lincolnshire fruit company. It was a particularly difficult task for her as one of her brothers, Peter, had already been chairman and knowledgeable observers of the Moores empire thought that he and his brother John were once more contending for the key post in the most valuable private company in Britain.

Lady Grantchester and her children still have a total of 14 per cent of the equity. She has already transferred a number of the shares to her offspring but about £170 million-worth are still in her name. Her title comes from her marriage to the second Lord Grantchester, an eminent barrister and son of Alfred Jesse Suenson Taylor, a Liberal peer and one-time treasurer of the party.

## Personal style

One of the great matriarchs of the Littlewoods family. Has operated alongside influential and powerful men all her life.

## Extravagances

Membership of the great and the good.

### Frederick Barclay 60
### £184m (£144m)
### Business

## Source of wealth

The second of the two Barclay twins, Frederick is as publicity shy as his brother, David. Both live and operate out of Monaco.

Two years ago, the brothers rescued London Club's casinos where, after a Gaming Board raid, they managed to save the licences - a feat never achieved before in the history of UK gaming. The Barclay brothers turned a disaster into success after the company's flotation.

This year, like many others, they have plunged into property, adding to the hotels they own in the US and Monte Carlo. But the bulk of their wealth came from the Ellerman Line they acquired at bargain basement rates, plus the associated drinks interest sold at inflated prices to a gullible George Walker of Brent Walker.

Because of the complicated structure of their companies, it is difficult to fix a value on the wealth of the two brothers: £144m is a conservative figure. They are exact equal partners in everything . Their wealth is ultimately controlled from Bermuda.

The only loser is *The European* newspaper bought in 1992. After a few management upheavals, it is still losing money, but remains as a flagship for the brothers and gives them great prestige in Monte Carlo where they ensure it has a very high visibility – out of all proportion to its importance.

Their wealth has risen significantly in the last year as property has recovered and gaming has come good after near disaster.

## Personal style

Raised on Glasgow's mean streets, the Barclays have little time for fools. Rarely have two brothers been blessed with so much business acumen. They have close political connections with the Conservatives via fundraiser Lord McAlpine.

## Extravagances

Yachts and fine food. Recently, the brothers purchased their own personal tax haven – the isle of Brechou, near Sark in the Channel Islands. The price tag was said to be £3.5 million. But they love Monte Carlo and its hedonistic lifestyle – plus the low taxes. For them tax exile is no inconvenience.

### Sir David Alliance 62
### £181m (£165m)
### Textiles

## Source of wealth

Sir David Alliance has two sources of wealth, the Coats Viyella textiles and clothing business, and a small family-owned home shopping firm, N Brown, of which he became chairman in 1968.

At Coats Viyella, the larger business, which Alliance founded 40 years ago, he has one per cent of shares, worth around £13.5 million. The company operates in 60 countries, produces more thread than anyone else in the world and owns the brand names Jaeger and Van Heusen in the UK. Alliance has been busy slashing its workforce and reducing gearing after the takeover of Tootal three years ago. At Coats, profits have been promisingly healthy this year – up 50 per cent to £150 million on increased turnover of £2.4 bn.

Meanwhile, N Brown, one of Britain's largest home shopping catalogue outfits, has reported only slightly less impressive percentage gains. There, pre-tax profits were £22.5 million, up 18 per cent, on turnover of £186.8 million.

Sir David beneficially owns shares valued at nearly £140 million in the company. A separate large slice of shares is held in trust for his children.

## Personal style

Spent three years looking for a compatible chief executive at Coats Viyella. When he found one, Alliance spent much time haggling over whether the word "openness" should be agreed as an organisational aim of the company. The poker-playing mentality comes naturally. Sir David is one of a small community of Iraqi-Jewish businessmen who came to Britain after the Second World War.

## Extravagances

Happiness is a warm balance sheet.

## Robert Madge 42
## £180m (New entry)
## Computers

### Source of wealth
Robert Madge comes charging into the *Rich 500* this year, on the back of his computer networking company's flotation on the New York NASDAQ stock exchange. At the moment it's a "hot" stock: networks are sexy according to the analysts, a £1.3 billion industry, and Madge is making some serious money (£11 million net off a £100 million turnover during 1993).

The limited offering in August 1993 raised $30 million. Madge NV, Robert's Dutch-registered flotation vehicle, now trades at $12 a share, valuing the company as a whole at around £250 million.

### Personal style
Madge has built his fortune on Token Ring technology. It may sound like witchcraft, but in layman's terms Madge sells the hardware and software that computers use to talk to one another efficiently across a network.

This is the second entrepreneurial venture for the former architecture journalist. "I was an impossible employee," he told journalist Patience Wheatcroft earlier this year. "I always believed I was right." However, his first computer venture – which designed the first personal organiser – went bust for lack of customers and British venture capital houses were highly sceptical about the prospects for Madge Networks. But America welcomed Madge, and now British venture capitalists are kicking themselves as the company continues its stratospheric growth.

The volatility of the shares is almost farcical however: in 12 months they've been as high as $17, and as low as $9. Madge's 70 per cent stake currently makes him worth £180 million – tomorrow it could be over £200 million, or even under £100 million. Fortunately Madge doesn't worry about his wealth too much.

### Extravagances
Chocolate biscuits, and a love of things American. He remains single at 42, which, when combined with his wealth, inevitably attracts a sackful of scented letters.

## Patricia Martin 61
## £179m (£184m)
## Inheritance

### Source of wealth
Patricia Martin is the youngest daughter of Doris Moores and the late Cecil Moores who, with his brother, Sir John, founded the Littlewoods pools and stores group.

Last year *BusinessAge* estimated that the Littlewoods empire would be worth £2 billion, if quoted on the stock market. We have downgraded her wealth this year as, in our view, the advent of the national lottery has devalued the Littlewoods business substantially, and we now rate the private empire at around £1.7 billion.

Just under 10 per cent of the shares are registered in Patricia Martin's name meaning her wealth is slightly down this year at £179 million.

### Personal style
In 1955 Patricia married Francis Xavier Velarde at St Patrick's Church, Soho. She had three children but the marriage ended in divorce. She married again in 1986 and lives in the Isle of Man.

### Extravagances
It is impossible to live an extravagant life on the Isle of Man.

## Duke of Buccleuch 71
## £175m (£169m)
## Aristocracy

### Source of wealth
The rise and fall of land values means little to the Buccleuch family, who have held their massive acreage in Scotland since the time of Robert the Bruce. With a total of 277,000 acres, the Duke is the largest private landowner in the UK, with slightly more land than the Queen if the Crown estates are excluded. He has often protested that he actually owns nothing, a claim partly substantiated by the accounts of the Buccleuch Estate which show that the bulk of the land is owned by the company, which in turn is almost wholly owned by shareholders who hide their identity behind a nominee account with an Edinburgh firm of solicitors. There are a few shares, in the Duke's name, of course.

### Personal style
It isn't just land that makes the Duke rich. There is an estate in Northampton centred on Boughton House, which contains no less than 37 oil sketches by the Dutch master Van Dyck, as well as almost priceless works by El Greco and Gainsborough.

The principal family seat is Drumlanrig Castle, and that contains a Rembrandt, *Old Woman Reading*, which could fetch up to £20 million if it ever came on the market. Prior to succeeding to the title, the Duke was a Conservative MP for an Edinburgh constituency, and he takes the Tory whip in the Lords, where he has been active from time to time.

### Extravagances
Crowning the family's art collection, a painting by Leonardo da Vinci which is too valuable to insure and which the Duke takes with him as he travels between his four homes. A great supporter of the nearly extinct red squirrel. In the Lords, he has made speeches suggesting that "some form of birth control substance" be distributed in areas where more aggressive grey squirrels are in the ascendant.

## John Asprey 56
## £171million
(£155million)
## Retailing

### Source of wealth
John Asprey owns just under 50 per cent of the shares of the 200-year-old family jewellers and antiques dealing group, of which he is chairman. He has a shade over 39 million shares, worth around £118 million. He has collected substantial dividends over the years, and has £50 million of personal assets besides his shareholding.

### Personal style
Asprey now acts as a gentleman chairman, with non-family member, Naim Attallah, as Group Chief Executive. Asprey's profits are now nearly £25 million annually.

Family feuding has twice resulted in family members being bought out, or in a pruning of the board. Recession-proof confidence is indicated by the acquisitions over the year: an Edinburgh silversmiths and several Swiss watchmaking businesses and distributorships, the latter being part of a desire to expand into Europe – particularly into the Swiss watch industry. Most are already justifying the bank loans used to finance them. Other parts of the group include Garrards and Mappin & Webb.

### Extravagances
Naim Attallah to run Aspreys, but it hasn't worked out well.

## Henry Keswick 55
## £170m (£105m)
## Business

### Source of wealth
In June, with Henry Keswick in the chair, Jardine Matheson held its final AGM in Hong Kong. The trading conglomerate, built on the back of 19th century opium trade profits, has now moved its registration to Bermuda. The jewel in its crown is the 34 per cent owned Hong Kong Land, which is chaired by Henry Keswick's brother, Simon.

The move to Bermuda has been received bitterly in Asia, where the *Business Times* in Singapore ran the headline: "Wake up, Jardine, this is the 20th century". The subtext was acidic: in Hong Kong, Jardine Matheson was being outclassed by Chinese mainland money. Now in Bermuda, when Henry Keswick speaks, "the government listens".

Henry Keswick has been chairman of Jardine Matheson since 1989, when he succeeded his brother. It was his second spell as chairman. In 1975, he resigned the post for the first time and returned to Britain after pocketing the fruits – reput-

edly £15 million – of several well-timed interventions on the colony's stock market.

Back in Britain in the late Seventies, Keswick embarked on a long search for a wife – and a safe Tory seat. The Tory Party, it seems, just couldn't organise a parliamentary seat for him. But in 1985, Keswick wed Tessa Reay, daughter of Lord Lovat, the multi-millionaire Scottish laird. Jardine Matheson's business interests span pizza, limousines, elevators, financial services and Britain's late night shopping chain, 7-Eleven. Despite his return to the helm, Henry Keswick appears to have withdrawn much of his wealth from Jardine Matheson Holdings, the parent company. He currently owns shares valued at around

## Bernie Ecclestone 58
## £167m (£41.75m)
## Sports

### Source of wealth
Grand Prix motor racing is a sport that generates £200 million a year in total revenues world-wide and another £200 million in sponsorship. The drivers take 10 per cent of that, and it costs another 20 per cent to keep the teams running. The rest disappears to the team owners, circuit owners and the motor racing authorities, and some sticks to Bernie Ecclestone and his organisation. He has negotiated an unknown percentage, thought to be around 5 per cent, for his services. Known activities are the profits of his two registered UK companies which total over £16 million. But there is much more in Geneva where the television-rights money is stashed away. Now at the height of his powers we think Ecclestone is making some £22 million a year for himself even after taxes.

He has never revealed much about his own commercial interests, nor where

£10 million but sold off around £500,000-worth earlier this year. His paypacket is supplemented by bonuses paid from shares held in trust for the company's directors. We have upgraded him this year.

### Personal style
Conservative in the extreme. Keswick once bore the nickname 'Scotch egg' – a self-evident reference to his complexion and girth. His style at AGMs is to read straight from a script without pausing, without expression, and without glancing at shareholders.

### Extravagances
In the late 1970s, he bought loss-making magazine the *Spectator* from oil man Algy Cluff. Over six years, Keswick's sickly investment lost him around £300,000.

much of the £400 million that motor racing earns every year goes. But then again, he doesn't need to. It is rumoured he is paying much of the fee needed to lure Nigel Mansell back to Europe.

### Personal style
Bernie Ecclestone is the owner of Grand Prix racing in everything but name. He rose through the ranks to the position as head of FOCA, the commercial arm of Formula One motor racing. Before that he was team manager to the late 1970 world champion Jochen Rindt, and was a driver of some talent himself. After Rindt died, Ecclestone bought the Brabham Grand Prix team from Jack Brabham and his partner Ron Tauranac, for a sum thought to be less than £100,000. After a decade of success he lost interest, when ace driver Nelson Piquet and ace designer Gordon Murray, both his protégés, left the team. He got more than £5 million for the brand name and the assets.

Ecclestone's outside commercial interests include motor dealing and property.

Rumour has it that he actually owns some of the Grand Prix circuits where the races are held. If he does, he ain't tellin'. He is a close friend of Paddy McNally, the former boyfriend of the Duchess of York, who runs Allsport.

But it is the finances of FOCA – effectively the commercial side of Grand Prix racing – which intrigue everybody. They are kept secret, and if Bernie has his way, they'll stay that way.

### Extravagances
A diminutive, married man with a beautiful Yugoslavian wife. He has a tycoon lifestyle and lives in a house once owned by Adnan Khashoggi. There is a Lear jet for his personal use, and a luxurious motorhome which he takes when travelling in Europe. The Lear jet is somewhat essential as he spends 800 hours in the air very year.

**64**
**(46)**

## David Sullivan 45
## £166m (£173m)
## Media

### Source of wealth

Porn merchant David Sullivan may not quite be in the Paul Raymond pay league, but he proves again that porn pays – big time. By the age of 23 he was already a millionaire. Today, through his holding companies Roldvale, Conegate and Sport Newspapers, he owns half the *Sunday* and *Daily Sport,* Birmingham City Football Club and produces money-spinning adult magazines (as he would call them).

Titles such as *Adult Fantasy* and *Parade* helped build Sullivan his cash mountain, of which he ploughed £700,000 into Birmingham City Football Club, with the promise of £6 million more to come. Despite poor results on pitch, last year BCFC returned its first trading profit in a decade. The *Sport* papers have seen circulation dwindle and been affected by curbs on 0898 sex line advertising, (worth about £2.5 million revenue) but are still profitable. Sullivan also owns 12 racehorses, and made an unsuccessful £20 million bid to take-over Epsom, Sandown and Kempton Park racecourses.

Sullivan has tried to move into respectable publishing but his attempt to buy the *Bristol & Evening Post* was thwarted. In May 1994 he tried to sell off his interests in *The Sunday News & Echo* for £150,000. Six days after agreeing terms with Michael Savage, Savage pulled out, claiming Sullivan hadn't told him about the paper's true financial position. The paper was a true dog and a surprise mistake for Sullivan, who has backed more winners than losers. Publication has been inevitably suspended; the paper was never viable and will have cost him maybe £3 million since it was launched.

The last accounts Sullivan filed for 1992 show he collected a £1.9 million salary at Roldvale, making him one of Britain's 20 best paid chairman. He will have taken at least the same amount in 1993. Even with the selling of some of his horses, a £10 million pension fund and the improved performance of his football club, we have nudged Sullivan's net worth down £6 million to £167 million.

### Personal style

Sullivan is the bad boy of British publishing, although he always rejects this. A former student at the London School of Economics, Sullivan's business acumen should not be underestimated. He managed to make the *Sport* papers profitable from day one, by getting United Newspapers to do most of the production work – and take much of the risk for little of the reward. Asked how he would describe himself, he said "I hope you will appreciate I am a businessman."

Apart from producing porn magazines, Sullivan tends to say what he thinks. This tends to land him in hot water, and he has a libel writ to contend from Midland Independent Newspapers over comments he made about the group just before it was floated.

Sullivan is also noted for his outspoken criticism of the Jockey Club, who generally want nothing to do with him. He says this is because "they are all posh snobs."

### Extravagances

He lives in a £6 million Essex mansion. The extravagances have been curtailed by ill-health, and he underwent major heart by-pass surgery in early 1994.

**65**
**(54)**

## Trevor Hemmings 57
## £165m (£156m)
## Business

### Source of wealth

Trevor Hemmings controls numerous companies, including a massive share in Scottish & Newcastle, the northern brewery firm, as a result of its takeover of a business in which he had a large stake.

Hemmings' career took off when he met Sir Fred Pontin in 1967, and built two holiday camps for him in record time. Sir Fred was so impressed that he bought the company, and Hemmings became his right-hand man.

Later, when Pontins itself was taken over by Coral, and then by giant brewers Bass, Hemmings decided that it would not flourish as part of such a large group, and so organised a management buy-out in 1987.

By 1989, this business had been sold to Scottish & Newcastle for £100 million.

He now runs S&N's leisure division, which is one of their most successful elements, and which has made him some tidy profits. A sale of some of his S&N shares in March 1992 realised £16 million cash. He has around £80 million worth left.

In addition he owns stakes worth £30 million in private companies he is associated with. We value him at a minimum of £165 million.

### Personal style

Trevor Hemmings is a real self-made man. He started out as a builder's apprentice in Leyland, Lancs, after the Second World War, then set up with his first independent venture: building two semi-detached houses.

### Extravagances

Horses.

**66**
**(109)**

## Martin Bromley 79
## £165m (£98m)
## Leisure

### Source of wealth

Martin Bromley was born in the United States, but is now an Anglo-Japanese citizen who is the epitome of the words 'financial colossus'.

We have almost certainly understated Martin Bromley's wealth in the past. We have good reason to believe it could be in excess of £1 billion and that he is one of the world's secret billionaires.

His visible interest in the UK is Family Leisure Ltd, which runs half a dozen amusement arcades in London, including the Trocadero, Piccadilly Circus. But this is small fry to Bromley, who only keeps it because it was one of his first businesses in London.

He began his career in the Sixties during the Vietnam War, shipping out slot machines for use by American GIs. The legality of this operation was always in doubt but Bromley had a monopoly, because he was the only one who thought of doing it and he had secured an exclusive supply of the one-armed bandits.

Naturally, he made up his own rules, and there were no limits on the prizes or stakes. It was like running Las Vegas for the whole American army: they had nothing else to spend their money on. He made a fortune – and in cash – which was put away for the future. In today's money, Bromley cleared £250 million in those years on that operation. It has financed everything else he has done. But except for Family Leisure, run in London by his faithful lieutenants, Alan Rawlinson and Michael Green, no one actually knows what he really does.

We have increased his known wealth substantially this year as our knowledge about him increased.

### Personal style

He is one of the most successful businessmen ever to walk the streets of London, and has lived in a penthouse in Victoria, where it is said that 100 people can sit down to dinner in comfort. But we have included only the known, public face of his wealth.

He only surfaces in the press in times of controversy. His business is video games and gaming machines – but that is just about as definite as you can get. That he is the biggest mover and shaker in the international gaming and coin-operated business, is in little doubt.

He once wrote out a cheque in court for evasion of customs and excise duty on fruit machine takings. The cheque was in excess of £1 million, and that was 12 years ago – worth an equivalent £8 million today. The

London listings magazine *Time Out* wrote a long piece 10 years ago which tried to unravel his fortune but got nowhere.

**Extravagances**

Cashmere coats. But for all his wealth and power, he is an approachable man who can be found at all the amusement machine exhibitions around the world.

### John Madejski 52
### £164 m (£142m)
### Publishing

**Source of wealth**

John Madejski had a very simple idea which he got from America to publish advertising only cars-for-sale magazines.

As a result, he has a lock on the market and is one of the few big independent publishers that dominate a market. He owns nearly 70 percent of the Hurst Publishing Group, which publishes unglamorous but highly profitable publications. *Autotrader*, which is now published all over the country, is a weekly magazine the size of a phone book full of small ads – plus pictures – advertising cars for sale. He now also has joint ventures with the *Manchester Evening News*.

On a £33 million turnover in 1992, Hurst made £2.65 million profit. But this is not the whole story, as Madejski paid himself a whopping salary of £3.7 million, slightly down from the previous year of nearly £4 million. Add that back onto the profits, and the company would be valued on a very high price/earnings ratio, simply because of the type of business it is.

He also owns nearly 60 per cent of quoted printing and newspaper publisher Goodhead Press and 90 per cent of Reading Football Club. If sold, the magazine business on its own would fetch £120 million. But we think that, with the joint ventures, the business would probably be worth nearer £160 million. John Madejski's empire is worth an easy £160 million today. But because of his dalliances with Reading Football Club we have rated his wealth only slightly higher this year as we do not believe football, in the current environment, is particularly lucrative.

He gets constant offers to buy the company and may take it public one day.

**Personal style**

Madejski was an advertising sales executive when he started Hurst 18 years ago and has remained a sales oriented person since. He was undoubtedly lucky that he was on his own in the market for the first ten years.

**Extravagances**

He wears a monocle and has a fleet of very expensive cars in his vast garage at his Reading country home. He is unmarried.

### David Crossland 47
### £160m (£137m)
### Leisure

**Source of wealth**

For 18 years, David Crossland was running a nice little travel business. It started off as a chain of travel agents (the first one cost £8,000), but soon expanded into package holidays. Then two things happened: in 1990, Crossland decided that it was time for Airtours to start its own charter airline, rather than feed passengers into other fleets; the next year, Intasun went bust.

The effect on Airtours' share price was nothing short of fantastic: it was the star stock of 1991, soaring from 42 pence to 225 pence, taking the market value of the company from £27 million to £193 million. It currently trades at 457 pence, valuing the company at over £500 million. Turnover rose almost 50 per cent to £615 million in 1993 – four times its 1990 turnover.

Crossland's 33 per cent stake in Airtours is now worth £138 million, and generates nearly £3 million a year in dividends. He sold £12 million worth of shares last year. In all he has realised nearly £30 million since the company floated in 1987.

**Personal style**

Crossland puts the success of Airtours down to excellent management – the best in the industry, he claims, as a result of his top-level hirings – and technology, which helps keep tabs on every corner of the business. He also claims that his airline is not as vulnerable as Air Europe or Dan-Air were: Their mistake, he insists, was to try to expand into the scheduled airline business, and to do so out of Gatwick, not Heathrow. "In this business you do not get a second chance," he says.

He keeps wanting to get bigger – whatever the cost. In the last 12 months the company has spent £25 million acquiring Hogg Robinson's 210 retail travel agents which, when added to the existing Pickford's chain, make Airtours the second largest high street travel agent after Thomas Cook.

It also bought Eastern Med travel specialist Aspro for £20 million – about twice what it turned out to be worth. It has just acquired SAS Holidays, the package tour arm of Scandinavian Airways, for £74 million. Next year Boeing will deliver two brand new 767s to Airtours.

It's some consolation for Crossland's failure to acquire Owners Abroad last year in a £290 million battle that cost him £9m in advisers' fees and other costs. The charge has been taken against 1993 pretax profits of £45 million.

**Extravagances**

Crossland lives to work and the years since Harry Goodman went bust have been frenetic. The possibilities gnaw at him that he may one day slip and follow the Clarksons and Intasun down the slippery slope.

### David Barclay 60
### £160m (£144m)
### Business

**Source of wealth**

David and his twin brother, Frederick, are the ultimate financial entrepreneurs, taking stakes in undervalued companies and selling off parts which don't fit in with their core interests: hotels, brewing and leisure. In 1992, they added Robert Maxwell's *The European* to their empire.

The brothers started in London in the Sixties, first in the real estate business and later moving into property development, specialising in hotel conversions. Their various companies are controlled through a series of holding companies, mostly based in Monaco, with the holding company based in Bermuda.

**Personal style**

David is the older of the twins by a matter of ten minutes, and is the chairman of the operation. His son has joined him in the business.

The operation is highly tax efficient, based in Monaco, and the Barclays recently issued strongly-worded denials that they had donated a free loan of over £1 million to the Conservative Party. Only Lord McAlpine, the party's former fund raiser, really knows and he isn't telling. The brothers' City-style attire hides razor-sharp financial minds.

**Extravagances**

Same as his younger twin Frederick, the two are indistinguishable. Sometimes a huge asset in the middle of a complicated deal.

### Kenneth Morrison 62
### £160m (£171m)
### Food

**Source of wealth**

Even a supermarket giant such as Wm Morrison, valued at nearly £900 million, has been affected by strong competition in 1994. As a result, chairman Kenneth Morrison's 15 per cent stake in the company is now worth £129 million, down £12 million on 1993. He probably now regrets the 14 million shares he gave his son on his eighteenth birthday last year. Nevertheless, with dividend payments, he is still worth £160 million.

He deserves the cash too. Wm Morrison was once a small family grocery and market stall in Bradford, which grew into a self-service store and eventually a series of supermarkets in the North and the Midlands. By 1987, he had opened Britain's largest supermarket complex, in Idle.

But the group's share price hovers around 120 pence following the half year results for the six months up to September 1993 which showed profits up only 5.5 per cent to £38.2 million.

## Personal style

Morrison is renowned for keeping a very low profile – rarely spotted in his own stores. When he does, he usually poses as a customer to see how the staff are performing.

## Extravagances

A very private man, awarded the CBE in 1990, a year after buying the Grade One listed Myton Hall near Boroughbridge. Noted for his charity work.

### Sir John Swire 67
### £160m (£131m)
### Business

## Source of wealth

Sir John Swire joined the family firm in 1948 and played a major role in rebuilding the company, which had been devastated during the Second World War. The elder of the two Swire knights, he received his knighthood in 1990, eight years after his younger brother, Sir Adrian.

The family company of John Swire & Sons has always been profitable, but has shown exceptional growth since the mid-Eighties. Because of the structure of the group, net income is much smaller than one would expect on turnover reported at £3.5 billion.

This is because of the string of subsidiaries (particularly Swire Pacific and airline group Cathay Pacific) which are only partly-owned by the parent, John Swire & Sons. We have assigned to the two senior members of the family a valuation approximating to those shares which they personally control directly or through their own trusts.

There is no disclosure of Sir John having any shares personally in Swire Pacific or Cathay Pacific, nor is he is a director at either company. Within John Swire & Sons Ltd, the London-registered parent company, he is named owning shares that are probably worth around £110 million – significantly up on last year's valuation, on the back of Hong Kong's asset boom. The major portion of Swire shares associated with his name is held non-beneficially. Therefore we have not counted these in assessing his wealth.

It is his considerable controlling share in the family holding which gives him the wealth, plus personal assets acquired over his lifetime: These add up to almost £50 million.

## Personal style

Sir John has held a number of key posts outside the main company, including directorships in Royal Insurance and at Hong Kong

### HM Queen Elizabeth II 68
### £158m (£150m)
### Royalty

## Source of wealth

There are various ways to calculate the true wealth of the Queen. The most ludicrous would be to value her investment portfolio, as is often done, rather then her earnings from it. Our valuation this year is based, primarily, on her accumulated income and massive art collection – in other words, what she would walk away with if Britain became a republic tomorrow. The same basis is used to calculate the wealth of any company chairman, that is the value of their shareholding if they quit. In fact, that is the best parallel – the Queen is in many ways the chairman of the Crown Estate, which turned in a profit of £79 million for the year to March 1994. Under the provisions of the Crown Estate Act 1961, the Crown Estate manages the hereditary possessions of the Sovereign. Its portfolio in 1993 was £1.95 billion. Any surplus, after paying for the running of Buckingham Palace and 100 other Royal buildings, is handed to the Exchequer in exchange for the Civil List, from which the Queen receives her direct income.

& Shanghai Bank, and has been active in the educational life of both Hong Kong and the UK. Sir John Swire was educated at Eton, followed by Oxford University and a spell in the Irish Guards. He is married and has two sons and one daughter.

## Extravagances

Keen flyfisher. Lives the life of a country squire.

This amounted to £7.9 million last year, on which she faces a substantial tax bill. At 40 per cent, this would be over £3 million but her accountants are no doubt piling up the invoices to claim tax allowances. Her accumulated income from the Estate is around £55 million.

If anything, the bulk of her wealth stems from a huge art collection. Rumours have long circulated on the value of these, but we feel comfortable with no more than £100 million. Although she has more, many belong to the state. The Queen does, of course, have the burden of the Windsor Castle fire bill to settle, but to date the £5.6 million Government donation and the £8 a head she's charging to visit Buckingham Palace more than covers the costs she has incurred. Our present assessment of the Queen's wealth is therefore up £8 million, from the Civil List payment, to £158 million.

## Personal style

Inside the Palace, the Queen has had her mind on cost-cutting. Although the Palace points out that the costs of maintaining 400 staff on the Royal Household is covered by the Civil List (about £24 million), the decision to pay tax seems to have made her more cash conscious. Some of the perks of working for her have been replaced by cash bonuses: instead of receiving half a bottle of champagne for working at Royal functions, staff receive £30 a year. Staff who serve more than 50 guests at a function received an extra miniature spirit bottle – now they get £30 a year extra. Days off to watch Wimbledon and Ascot are taken as annual leave, and free Palace soap is being replaced by a £6 annual cash bonus. And all bonuses are now taxed. Some consolation is if you've worked over a year, you still get free Christmas pudding.

## Extravagances

Private use, though thankfully for her not ownership, of a fleet of private jets, the Royal yacht Britannia and a large London home plus various country houses. As yet, no holiday home abroad. In between not abdicating she enjoys free world travel, looking after the Corgis, playing with grandchildren and collecting expensive paintings.

### Felix Dennis 46
### £155m (£154m)
### Publishing

## Source of wealth

Felix Dennis was made famous by *Oz* magazine in the Sixties and the obscenity trial which followed, at a time when Britain's courts had nothing better to do. Dennis was the business brains of *Oz* and had little to do with the content. After that, he wrote a biography of Bruce Lee, which sold two million copies, and launched *Kung Fu Monthly*. It was published for nine years and printed in 11 languages.

He bought a fledgling magazine called *Personal Computer World* from a Yugoslavian newsagent, Angelo Zgorelec, for a pittance. Dennis soon sold it and retired, but got bored and went off to America to start *MacUser* for the developing Apple Macintosh market. He sold that for $16 million and started Micro Warehouse Inc which markets computers and peripherals by phone. MW now employs over 1,000 people and has a $400 million turnover. Dennis and his partners have just floated it. His shares are worth £50 million. He caught a trend again by launching *Windows User* magazine in the USA. Simultaneously, he developed Dennis Publishing in the UK which is now worth some £20 million.

We estimate he has taken £60 million in profits and dividends from his activities, but he has to support a significant lifestyle. Consequently we rate him at £155 million, slightly higher than last year. He disagrees with this valuation but he is one of the most astute businessman/ publishers in the world and he is merely being modest.

## Personal style

He leads a colourful private life, has never married and enjoys the company of his many girlfriends. He has never ever learned to drive a car and merely says: "I was born to be driven." In typical tycoon style, he left school with no O-levels – the perfect qualification to make money.

## Extravagances

He has set up his personal life to function almost exactly the same, whether he is in England or America. In England, he has a huge country estate in Warwickshire and a flat in Soho. In America, a flat in New York and a country estate Bridgeport, Connecticut.

### Lord Ashburton 65
### £152m (£146m)
### Banking

## Source of wealth

Formerly plain old Sir John Baring, Ashburton finished a fifteen year spell as chairman of family bank Baring Brothers in 1989. One of the most prestigious – and intensely secretive – merchant banks in the City of London, Barings has used its strong Far East connections to become one of the most profitable Western banks in Asia/Pacific.

The Baring family arrived in Britain from Germany in 1717 to set up in the cloth industry in the West Country, but soon expanded into finance. At the end of the eighteenth century, one of the family, Francis, became chairman of the East India Company, just as the great imperial expansion into India was really getting under way. Working from London, which is still the headquarters of the bank, Francis set up Baring Brothers, which later led the Duc de Richelieu to remark that, "There are six great powers in Europe: England , France, Russia, Austria, Prussia and Baring Bros."

Baring Bros remains in family control, despite disappointing after tax profits of £12.3 million in 1992 (down from £26.4 million in 1991), its net assets of £255 million and its commanding position in Asia – which made fifteen times more money than its British operations last year – the bank would fetch £300 million on the auction block.

## Personal style

The latest offspring of that powerful family would not have disappointed Richelieu. He currently pays his club drinks bills by working as chairman of British Petroleum.

Ashburton muscled his way back into the ranks of power by deposing unpopular and over-empowered BP chairman Bob Horton in 1992 and taking the job himself. Since then he has restored BP's battered credibility and improved profits.

## Extravagances

He has all the advantages of old money and therefore doesn't have to do the day job for money. However, he makes sure his executives do. As chairman of the remuneration committee he has authorised a highly lucrative share options scheme that will ensure BP's top 500 managers get options on 80 million BP shares at deep discount to market price. But he doesn't think that an extravagance. More like public service.

### Duke of Atholl 63
### £150m (£145m)
### Aristocracy

## Source of wealth

George Murray, the 10th Duke of Atholl, lost his war hero father in 1945 at the age of 12. Later he inherited the dukedom. There's other industrial nous in the family: the duke's uncle is Viscount Cowdray, the inspiration behind the Pearson conglomerate.

Blair Castle may work as a going concern. According to the Duke, his home is the most frequently visited stately home north of the border – despite its lack of theme parks, safari animals or fun fairs. His land and property assets are worth a minimum of £100 million. Add in the artifacts and art works he lovingly maintains and his fortune has shown a modest rise this year of £5 million.

## Personal style

Atholl is a typical assets rich, cash poor aristocrat. But he sees it as his duty in life to maintain the family tradition and keep the heritage intact. He divides his time between the family's 135,000 acres, including Blair Castle in Perthshire (the setting for BBC TV's Strathblair series) and London. In 1993 he resigned as chairman of Westminster Press. His mother was a member of the owning Cowdray family. As yet unmarried and likely to stay that way in his mid-60s. The heir is therefore his older cousin, 64-year-old John Murray.

## Extravagances

The Duke of Atholl has the distinction of maintaining Britain's only private standing army, known as the Athollmen. Permission for the Duke's force was given by Queen Victoria in 1845, in recognition of the 6th Duke's prowess at jousting. But, generally, he lives frugally.

He has to. He hasn't any cash. When he needs money he simply sells something small from the house. The duke compensates by eating, drinking and making merry in his Scottish seat. In other words, conspicuous consumption in kilts.

### 76 (65) Lady Elizabeth Nugent 55
### £148m (£141m)
### Inheritance

## Source of wealth

Lady Elizabeth's wealth stems from her stake in the Guinness dynasty's holding trust, the Iveagh Trust. Her share is worth

### 77 (76) Duke of Northumberland 41
### £146m (£130m)
### Aristocracy

## Source of wealth

In 1991, the Duke of Northumberland sold a 13th century encyclopedia and invested the proceeds in a grouse moor. If this was evidence of cash flow problems, the Duke must have been well pleased the following year when art experts reclassified an 11"x 8" item in his art collection, long thought to be a fake, as the genuine work of master Renaissance portraitist, Raphael.

Overnight, the Duke of Northumberland's fortune expanded by around £25 million – the price tag attached to the canvas. According to a Sotheby's expert, the precious painting was housed "in a horrible 19th century frame and was under dirty glass" at the ancestral home, Alnwick, in Northumberland. (The Duke also lays claim to 100,000 acres up north, as well as Syon House, the only non-royal stately home in Greater London.) We have upgraded his wealth to include a rise in value of his property and art in the last year.

## Personal style

Languid – though this is said to reflect a bout of "yuppie flu". Much involved in charitable work. He is famous because of a relationship of several years - which is now rumoured to be over – with Nicaraguan-born actress, Barbara Carrera, 51, who once removed her clothes for *Playboy* magazine. He has made films with Carrera who is one of the most beautiful 50 plus year old women in the world.

£150 million, held offshore.

## Personal style

Lady Elizabeth is quiet, understated, stylish and very, very wealthy. She is a member of the Guinness family and is the sole surviving child of Viscount Elveden, the heir to the 2nd Earl of Iveagh. Viscount Elveden never succeeded to the title: he was killed in the last year of the Second World War during the battle of Arnhem, immortalised in the film *A Bridge Too Far*.

Lady Nugent's brother, who eventually succeeded to the title and the chairmanship of Guinness in 1967, died only last year. Meanwhile, Lady Elizabeth's sister, Henrietta, committed suicide at Spoleto in Italy in 1978, apparently while suffering severe depression. She married David Nugent, a prominent horserace trainer; the marriage has been stormy.

## Extravagances

Usual Guinness interests, and bloodstock.

## Extravagances

Who needs extravagances when you own Syon House but Northumberland's burgeoning film career, which is reported to have sprouted wings with the completion of *Wildlands*, a £2.5 million epic in which the Duke appears. The film has yet to be publicly screened.

Meanwhile, the Duke is said to have moved on to other projects of a similar budget to the money already spent. Girls have been his biggest extravagance now he is finding his feet in Hollywood.

### 78 (69) Matthew Harding 40
### £145m (£135m)
### Finance

## Source of wealth

Matthew Harding is a 40-year-old financial genius and the chairman of the Benfield Group, an insurance broker operating in the international reinsurance market. He also owns one-third of the company's 48 million shares. Benfield had a remarkable 1992, making £30.6 million profit on turnover of £39.7 million. It followed up in 1983 in a more difficult year with a £41.2 million turnover and profits of £31.2 million. Harding has just launched a re-insurance company that will take on insurance risks itself. The venture is jointly funded by Benfield and venture capitalists to the tune of £50 million. The performance of Benfield is typical of the high margins of the very best Lloyd's registered brokers, of which Benfield is one. Same again sales and profits mean only a marginal increase

in Hardings overall wealth.

## Personal style

The big event of 1993 was his decision to invest £8 million into Chelsea Football Club after a session with the silver-tongued chairman, Ken Bates. Whatever Bates said, Harding took the bait, in what is regarded as being not a particularly astute deal. Harding is unlikely to see all his money back, if any. But that doesn't matter, as football and Chelsea, in particular, is his one extravagance and he travels to most games.

Football aside, Harding likes to speak his mind and has strong views on the whole insurance industry. He describes today's attitude in the market with a topical metaphor: "Gone are the days when the answer to our difficulties was akin to the cricket captain who, when fielding, always placed a fieldsman where the batsman has just hit the previous ball." Who could disagree about Lloyd's? It appears that Harding has taken cash out every year, recently to the tune of some £6 million a year. Everything included, we calculate he is worth £145 million.

## Extravagances

Football and Chelsea are his weaknesses. Now he is a major shareholder and director he has left the terraces for the directors' box. He hires Jackie Stewart's private jet to fly to away matches, and has his own chauffeured London taxi for transport around the capital. Warren Buffet, the richest man in America, and a legendary investor, is his hero. Perhaps a portent of things to come for Harding's ambitions. Don't bet against it.

### 79 (67) Mark Lennox-Boyd 51
### (£145m) £138m
### Inheritance

## Source of wealth

In 1990, Charles Sherwood, managing director of the Iveagh Trust, told *The Sunday Times* that Lennox-Boyd had "no interests" in Guinness-related trusts. Since then, the position must have changed. Returns for the Iveagh Trustees Ltd for the year to March 1991 show that Lennox-Boyd holds 35,000 shares. He also owns shares in Guinness itself. Not surprising as his grandfather was the recently departed 2nd Earl of Iveagh.

## Personal style

At least in the sense of surnames, Mark Lennox-Boyd, currently parliamentary under-secretary at the Foreign Office, qualifies as one of the Guinness family's concealed heirs. Like his cousin, the Rt Hon Paul Channon MP, Mark Lennox-Boyd also followed in his father's footsteps. In Lennox-Boyd's case, the path to Parliament was first taken by his father, Alan Lennox-Boyd, who married into the Guinness clan in the Thirties and subsequently ran the Colonial Office for Churchill, before assuming a seat on the board of Arthur Guinness & Co in the Sixties.

He is one of those junior Foreign Office ministers that get to fend off tough questions in the House when Douglas Hurd is away globe-trotting. Lennox-Boyd was the third son in the family. Yet, given his background, he reached Parliament rather late in life – in 1983 at the age of 40. He is married with one daughter.

### Extravagances
Membership of the Pratt's and the Beefsteak. Said never to tire of travelling – whether for his employers or on his own account, plus the usual accoutrements of great wealth.

## 80 Paul Sykes 51
## (134) £145m (£83m)
## Property

### Source of wealth
Paul Sykes owns 40 per cent of Meadowhall shopping centre in Sheffield which has a likely value of £250 million. That alone makes him worth £100 million.

Sykes is only known of because of the £6 million salary he paid himself in 1989. He leant that lesson, and last year his salary was under £200,000 – he didn't like the publicity. His business interests are all funnelled through Paul Sykes Group Ltd which had a profit of £4 million and assets of £36.5 million in the last published accounts. We estimate his net worth at some £145 million, a big leap from last year entirely on the back of Meadowhall's obvious success.

### Personal style
He teamed up with former DIY retailer Eddie Healey to develop Meadowhall.

Healey and Sykes were planning to develop rival centres but they came together to pool their different skills to make Meadowhall a success. And a success it has been, almost at the John Hall scale at Gateshead.

Meadowhall is probably the best-sited shopping centre in the country, lying just beside the M1 motorway at Sheffield, on vacated British Steel land.

Doubtless the land was bought for a song and probably there was some British Steel aid to develop the site, as the package was put together before the Eighties boom and completed before the recession struck. Virtually perfect timing. It probably wouldn't have mattered, because this project would have worked whatever the timing.

### Extravagances
He has none of the trappings of tycoonery.

He once bought an aeroplane and a yacht and found no use for them. He prefers cycling but you see a different view of life from a bicycle – especially if you are worth £145 million.

## 81 Sir Humphrey Cripps 79
## (99) £145m (£105m)
## Business

### Source of wealth
Sir Humphrey Cripps is furious when his name appears on a wealth list of any description. His angry letters bludgeoned the *Sunday Times* to remove him from theirs some years ago.

But the point is that Sir Humphrey, whether he likes it or not, is very rich. Why deny it and why be ashamed? After all he is one of Britain's great self-made inventor millionaires.

The source of his great wealth is the fiendishly simple but unlikely Velcro strip – and this device made much of his fortune. But he is an inventor-entrepreneur of rare distinction, founding companies in the UK, USA, Canada and Australia.

He still controls companies which manufacture and license Velcro and has made an enormous amount of money from his simple idea. The patents have now long run

## 82 HRH Prince of Wales 45
## (66) £142m (£140m)
## Royalty

### Source of wealth
Prince Charles's primary income source is from the Duchy of Cornwall. This portfolio includes the traditional West Country land holdings, the Oval Cricket Ground and several adjoining properties in the Kennington area of South London.

The land estate was created in 1337 and covers 130,000 acres in 13 counties. During the Eighties, under new legislation, it has been able to build up a substantial portfolio in stocks and shares.

His revenue from the Duchy of Cornwall in 1993 was just over £4 million. Since

out but to his surprise he found the Velcro name was worth far more than the original patents and it still provides a vast income.

His holding companies are registered in the Netherlands Antilles and his American operation alone is worth well over £100 million. We must confess we have little idea as to the final worth of Sir Humphrey Cripps as it is concealed that well, but we have added £40 million to last year's assessment as being the very least this remarkable man is worth.

### Personal style
He is a Northamptonshire man, born and bred, and had the good fortune to be educated at Northampton Grammar School – one of the finest in the country and regarded as an equal by the top public schools – before the degradations of recent governments. He has given millions to charity and lives in simple style in Stoke Goldington, Buckinghamshire. He was knighted in 1989. Nurses and staff at Northampton General Hospital owe him a great debt for the hours of fun they spend at the Cripps Centre, built with his money. He is a member of the council of management of the Cripps Foundation.

### Extravagances
Giving his vast wealth away as quick as he can. But it is impossible as he is worth so much.

1981, the Prince has voluntarily submitted 25 per cent of his earnings to the Treasury, (£853,000 in 1992). This September he will submit a tax bill instead. After deducting allowances, his disposable income is £3.2 million. It's worth noting that the separation from the Princess of Wales means his accountants cannot claim tax allowances on her spending. From the £3.2 million, his 62 staff have to be paid, leaving the Prince with around £2 million extra in 1993. His accumulated wealth – and he was one of the only Royals not to be paid from the Civil List – stands at £142 million.

### Personal style
Despite not getting a penny from the Civil List, unlike his mother, the Prince is a more shrewd investor than the Queen. The value of his portfolio has increased threefold in the past ten years. Of some help is the fact that Lord Cairns, vicechairman of SG Warburg, and Lord Ashburton, director of Barings, are on the Duchy's council. He also pays no capital gains tax from share dealings or land sales.

### Extravagances
Large country estate in the Cotswolds and a penchant for old Aston Martins. Walking, polo, conservation, architecture, and confessing all on national television.

### John Moores II 66
### £140m (£160m)
### Inheritance

## Source of wealth
John Moores II holds 8 per cent of the Littlewoods company's shares, worth some £136 million. Last year *BusinessAge* estimated that the Littlewoods empire would be worth £2 billion, if quoted on the stock market. We have downgraded his wealth this year, as in our view, the advent of the national lottery has devalued the Littlewoods business substantially. We now rate the private empire at around £1.7 billion.

## Personal style
John Moores II is the eldest son of Sir John Moores, the founder of Littlewoods. He was groomed to take over from his father at the top of the company but in 1971, he had a public row with his late father about selling off a German mail order subsidiary. Sir John decided that the firm was losing too much money. Sir John had his way, and John II angrily resigned from the executive. He is still on the board. He has filled the gap by becoming involved with charities of his own although he is said to miss the business greatly. He has been married twice, and has four children from each marriage.

## Extravagances
Breeding prize cattle.

### Nicholas von Preussen
### £140m (£85 m)
### Inheritance

## Source of wealth
"Instead of George Mansfield, I wish to be known as Mr von Preussen." Those were the words of Friedrich Georg Wilhelm Christoph, Prince of Prussia, spoken to a *Daily Telegraph* reporter in 1951. This was fully six years after the Prince's secret marriage to Lady Brigid, the Guinness heiress, at which the Prince had posed under the assumed name of George Mansfield. The ruse was intended to not evoke anti-German sentiment, for Prince Friedrich was directly related to Kaiser Bill, of First World War fame. The Prince and his wife produced five children. Nicholas von Preussen lays claim to around £140 million-worth of shares in the Iveagh Trust, the ultimate resting place of the Guinness family billions. Similar amounts are recorded in the names of his brothers, Prince Rupert, 38, and Prince Andrew, 46.

## Personal style
Pan-European member of the international jet set.

## Extravagances
Vintage cars.

### Marquess of Northampton 48
### £136m (£80m)
### Aristocracy

## Source of wealth
The Marquess of Northampton's fortune is an inherited one, based on 25,000 acres of land, mostly in Northamptonshire. He has two superb stately homes at Castle Ashby and Compton Wynates, in the Cotsworlds.

He owns the ultimate freehold of large areas of Islington in London. But it is perhaps his great art collection which gives him his fabulous wealth. The extent of it is unknown to anyone but the family – and perhaps his insurers. The paintings he holds are worth a minimum £30 million. And the houses are stuffed with treasures. As an example, in 1985 he sold the Renaissance masterpiece, Mantegna's Adoration of the Magi, to the Getty Museum in California, for £7.5 million.

Legal wrangles as to who exactly owned a collection of Roman silver were settled in Northampton's favour, and the Marquess stands to gain some £40 million from a sale. We have revalued him to include this windfall in 1994.

## Personal style
The present Marquess's father was married three times, and now his son, known as 'Spenny', is on his fifth marriage. This has cost him an average million pounds a time. A hunting accident a few years ago left him with facial scars and forced him to grow a beard, but he is now, perhaps, even more popular with women.

The Marquess has abandoned the home of his childhood, Castle Ashby, to live at Compton Wynates, a picturesque house that is the world's finest example of Tudor architecture. The magnificent family pile at Castle Ashby now hosts conferences and was recently used as the venue for Will Carling's celebrity wedding.

## Extravagances
Women and his two marvellous houses.

### Phil Collins 43
### £135m (£118m)
### Entertainment

## Source of wealth
Philip Collins Ltd continues to flout Cadbury Report guidelines: last year it paid its only director, singer-songwriter Phil Collins, some £10 million. Yet the 99 per cent shareholder, one P Collins, isn't exactly complaining. Over the last seven years he's realised £50 million from the company, which channels the royalties from his numerous bestselling albums,

including *Face Value, No Jacket Required*, and most recently *Both Sides*, which was the seventh-biggest selling British album of 1993. He's also contributed £10 million into a pension fund.

The company's been around since 1977, but Collins's millions really began to flood in when his solo career took off with his first personal album, *Face Value*, in 1981. As well as his solo records and performances, he continues to net money from his lucrative career with the band Genesis, still releasing the occasional record and royalties continuing to come in.

Collins's own album, *But Seriously*, released in 1990, is the third-biggest selling record ever in the UK, and reached number one in 22 countries, establishing Collins as an international star. It has also generated fabulous wealth for Collins in the last three years, and taken his solo record sales past 57 million.

The last few years have seen that income soar. He earned a cumulative £23 million income up to 1984. But he earned nearly £12.7 million in 1991 alone. He has been involved in a series of companies, and owns 20 per cent of Genesis Music Ltd, the remainder of which is owned by the original band members, Peter Gabriel, Mike Rutherford and Tony Banks.

Rutherford, Banks and Collins are equal shareholders in Fisher Lane Farm Ltd, based in Surrey, which includes a recording studio. With their manager, John Smith, they have long-term investments in Scotland, with the Isle of Mull Salmon Farm Ltd and Pennyghael Estates Ltd.

## Personal style
Collins has cashed in on burgeoning music sales (almost exclusively on CD) to the over-30 age group. But he's also had plenty of success in the singles charts, which indicates that he still has a youngish following. In March Warner Brothers confirmed that Collins has signed a worldwide solo record deal with them, snatching him from the grasp of Virgin-EMI. The terms were undisclosed, but are reputed to be in the region of £10 million advance per album.

## Extravagances
Collins has admitted that the last few years have seen his wealth multiply and agrees he has more money every year than he can possibly begin to spend. He has been trying hard however with a lavish home in Beverly hills. But a very British sense of irony keeps his feet on the ground, which is why he is still around and lucid enough to really enjoy his money. He works for the Prince's Trust, and received the Lieutenant of the Victorian Order award in the Queen's 1994 Birthday Honours for this. He recently announced the break-up of his second marriage, to American-born Jilly.

## 87 (112) Viscount Portman 60
## £135m (£97m)
## Aristocrat

### Source of wealth
The total land still held by Viscount Portman's trust in London is around 100-acres in varying states of freehold and leasehold and, like the Grosvenor Estate, its value has fallen considerably from a peak of about £200 million in the mid-Eighties. Recent resurgence of activity in the West End property market has led us to boost Portman's valuation this year. The Portman Estate, first created in 1533 by a gift from Henry VIII to Lord Chief Justice Portman, is the fourth of London's great aristocratic estates. Centred around the north of Oxford Street and Baker Street, it is now tied up in trusts, following severe death duty problems at the end of the Forties. Part of the London Estate, about 25 acres, was sold off, as well as a 3,800-acre estate in Dorset.

### Personal style
The present Viscount, the 9th, is a former racing driver, who now officially describes himself as a farmer. He has an agricultural qualification; shoots and fishes as often as possible.

### Extravagances
Former racing driver, still keen on the business and has homes in the Caribbean and London.

## 88 (58) Ken Scowcroft 65
## £132m (£148m)
## Insurance

### Source of wealth
Ken Scowcroft was all set for a happy retirement in 1993 after spending the previous five years selling off his vehicle insurance group, Swinton, to Sun Alliance, trousering well over £100 million along the way. Scowcroft no longer has any role in Swinton, which he founded in 1957. But the holiday plans and cash counting have been badly disrupted by a £28 million lawsuit he faces from five separate shareholders at Swinton.

The dispute, due to come to court by the end of 1994, stems from the 30 per cent stake Scowcroft sold to Sun Alliance in 1988 – the same day the five shareholders claim they sold their shares to Scowcroft, unaware of the Sun Alliance deal. If their claims of "fraudulent deception" stand up in the High Court, Scowcroft's massive fortune will begin to evaporate.

The action has sparked off a separate lawsuit between Sun Alliance and Scowcroft. With interest, Scowcroft's for-

tune should top £150 million, but we have discounted for the mounting legal costs and the strong possibility he will have to pay out some sort of settlement.

### Personal style
Since he began building up Swinton from scratch in 1957, Ken Scowcroft's main aim was to keep it in the family. He did just that, with son Brian becoming chief executive and daughter, Janice, as deputy chief exec-

## 89 (84) Ian McGlinn 55
## £131m (£120m)
## Finance

### Source of wealth
Ian McGlinn is one of Britain's most unlikely richest men in the UK on paper, and one of the most mysterious. He invested £4,000 in the Body Shop in 1976 and now has a stake that is worth – on paper – around £125 million. He has 52 million shares worth 240 pence each.

But Body Shop manages a yield of barely 2 per cent and McGlinn collects a dividend of around £1 million a year and lives relatively frugally for a man of his worth. It is thought he sold some shares at the flotation and raised around £2 million. Since then he has received about £6 mil-

## 90 (92) Viscount Petersham 49
## £130 m (£110 m)
## Aristocrat

### Source of wealth
Viscount Petersham's daughter, Serena Stanhope, 24, recently married Viscount Linley, son of Princess Margaret. The son of Earl Harrington and heir to the Stanhope family fortune, Viscount Petersham has at various points declared himself a tax

utive. He is obviously a shrewd man with a good sense of timing– since selling off his stake in Swinton, the company has seen profits drop because of tough competition from Direct Line.

### Extravagances
Playing the stock market and buying and selling shares on the same day for a turn. He can afford the gamble and the diversion from hedonistic pursuits.

lion in dividends and has conserved most of it.

### Personal style
McGlinn is a permanent tax-exile, flitting between five-star hotels across the world with a small flat in Majorca as his base, and a yacht. He is divorced with a school-age daughter who reputedly will inherit all 52 million shares her father owns in Body Shop.

McGlinn has a reputation as something of a hell raiser, chasing girls and indulging in drinking binges across the world. He gets far more publicity in the tabloid newspapers than he does in the serious newspapers.

### Extravagances
Ian McGlinn was thinking about settling in Jersey last year, seeking a permanent home at last.

exile. In the Seventies, he followed his father to Ireland, in anticipation of a Labour government's soak-the-rich policies.

Irish tax rates proved less than comfortable. More recently, Petersham parked much of his loot in Monte Carlo, maintaining a home in Wiltshire.

Petersham's company, the Bingham Land Company, owns large chunks of the imposing mid-Victorian terraced buildings in west London – most notably around

Stanhope Gardens. The area has been run down in recent years.

Last year, we reckoned that the Stanhope possessions merited a price tag of as much as £90 million. If anything, that estimate now appears cautious. Petersham has been negotiating the sale of one-half of the squares of terraced buildings he owns. The price tag is said to be in the region of £20 million. And there's plenty more where that came from. A substantial art collection further boosts the value of the Stanhope estate. The family assets were transferred to Petersham over a decade ago by his father, who opted to remain in Ireland.

### Personal style
The lack of a university education – Eton was as far as he got – appears not to have held him back.

### Extravagances
Sailing, and lots of it.

## Peter Johnson 54
## £129m (£90m)
## Food

### Source of wealth
Peter Johnson has seen a spectacular rise in his wealth thanks to the even more spectacular growth of his quoted mail-order food hamper business, Park Food Group.

Profits moved up to £6.9 million after tax in 1993 on a £116 million turnover, with the group now capitalised at £184 million. The group's 70,000 UK sales agents sold one million hampers last Christmas, and Park Food's share price has soared to 116 pence after the purchase of the rival group Heritage Hampers. As a result, Johnson's customer base has expanded by 15 per cent. Notably, the group's shares are outperforming the market sector by 800 per cent and the price has increased tenfold since 1990.

Johnson owns around 65 per cent of the company, making his stake worth £118 million. With dividend payments we value him at nearly £129 million.

However, Johnson is about to go on a spending spree, with aspirations to become chairman of Everton Football Club. The former Tranmere Rovers' chairman is underwriting Everton's £9.75 million rights issue and is set to gain control of the club, with the backing of the Moores family who currently hold a majority stake.

Assuming Johnson takes over, we have adjusted his new wealth down to £130 million, but is still a huge £40 million up on 1993. Included in this is his share of a parcels delivery company he backed which is now starting to flower.

### Personal style
Johnson's management style is to let the money roll in without interfering too much. All the hard work was done at the beginning, starting the business from scratch in his father's Liverpool butcher's shop. Now he effectively has 70,000 employees who bring money to him for 45 weeks every year, making the group extremely cash generative.

### Extravagances
Football and more football. Will do – and is doing – anything to become chairman of a big club. Everything went right for this very astute businessman in 1994 and he has found the knack of enjoying life as well.

## Marquis of Tavistock 54
## £128 m (£122 m)
## Aristocrat

### Source of wealth
Henry Russell, the Marquess of Tavistock, is heir to the 76-year-old Duke of Bedford. His father – brought up in South Africa and never apparently groomed for aristocratic life in the shires – opted for tax exile status in Monte Carlo in 1974 after 20 years of running the family estate. That estate still contains some prime chunks of London property – up to 20 acres – around Bloomsbury. Unfortunately, the Bedford family fortune was diminished somewhat with the sale of most of the family freeholds around Covent Garden in the early Fifties. The sales were designed to meet death duties on the estate of the 12th Duke of Bedford.

### Personal style
Transatlantic – and European. Educated in Switzerland and then at Harvard, he served a five-year stint as a trustee of the Kennedy Memorial Trust – set up to commemorate America's youngest president. He seems to have recovered from an illness that restricted his mental capacity for some years. He was nursed back to health by his elegant wife, the mistress of Woburn.

### Extravagances
Horseracing: he is a long-time director of United Racecourses.

## Martin Naughton 55
## £127m (£119m)
## Business

### Source of wealth
Earlier this year, Martin Naughton's privately-held Ulster-based company, Glen Dimplex, failed in its attempt to purchase the French electric goods producer Moulinex. For Naughton, who sells £300 million-worth of electric kettles and hairdryers annually, the Moulinex bid was a rare failure.

Glen Dimplex ranks among Ireland's most successful companies. From its headquarters in County Louth, in Ulster, its operations span Ireland, Northern Ireland, Canada, Holland, the USA, Germany and the UK. Among the brand names owned by the business are: Morphy Richards and Belling (both well-known in the UK), as well as Hamilton Beach (US) and Chromalox (Canada).

The company was founded in 1973, and has been held entirely privately since Naughton bought back an equity stake held by Northern Ireland's development agencies. Naughton himself owns 75 per cent of the company, with the rest split among partners. The company has little, or no, debt burden. On that basis, his fortune amounts to pretty near £130 million. Because of the opacity of the Irish company disclosure regime, it is impossible to be more precise.

But Naughton isn't immune to losses. In 1991, he took up a 13 per cent shareholding in the Dublin-based *Sunday Tribune*, the Irish newspaper group. The company – in which Irish media mogul Tony O'Reilly recently took an opportunistic stake – is now in a shambles. Latest estimates point to a negative net worth of around £2.5 million. A few months ago, Naughton combined with O'Reilly to fire the paper's editor.

### Personal style
A man with a head for figures, Naughton has so far managed to keep clear of the limelight that so often neuters talent in big city Dublin. Up in Ulster, he's just another businessman.

### Extravagances
In business terms, property investments seem to be a weakness. Naughton has dabbled extensively in property in the Irish Republic. Among his investments was UPH, the ill-starred property company which came to prominence after making a £12 million profit on the sale of premises to Irish Telecom. The deal became one of the major business scandals that marked the end of Charles Haughey's rule as premier. A government inquiry cleared UPH investors' of wrongdoing in 1993.

## Alan Lewis 56
## £126m (£120m)
## Textiles

### Source of wealth
In the last ten years, the main source of Alan Lewis's wealth, Illingworth Morris, has been twice rationalised, floated once and then taken private. In 1988, Lewis's personal holding in the then-quoted Illingworth Morris business was valued at £42 million. The following year, Lewis took it

private, in an offer which valued the entire company at around £74 million. Lewis, reportedly, financed the buy-back chiefly "from his own resources". Illingworth Morris is currently 100 per cent owned by the Hartley Investment Trust, Lewis's controlling vehicle.

Among the company's most successful products are tennis ball and snooker table coverings, which account for a large slice of profits. In mainland Britain, as part of the Illingworth Morris empire, Lewis owns the Crombie brand name.

An associated textile processing business, Woolcombers (Holdings), was pulled back from flotation in the late Eighties. Taken together, Woolcombers and Illingworth Morris – dividends included – push Lewis's wealth well beyond the £100 million mark. The companies made profits of over £5 million on turnover of £85 million in 1993.

Lewis's other interests include the Anglo-Manx Bank on the Isle of Man. He also controls banking interests in Baton Rouge, Louisiana, originally purchased from the Slater Walker empire.

In 1988, Lewis moved the bulk of his personal fortune to the Netherlands Antilles. In 1991, he received a CBE – a signal that he had progressed some distance beyond his humble origins as a car dealer.

## Personal style

Unusual. Lewis is unmarried, but romantically connected to a Spanish flamenco dancer. An evangelical Christian, he is also a vegetarian, a karate black belt and a prominent donor to the Conservative Party.

Alan Lewis says that he owes his control over his clothing and textile empire to a chance meeting in 1982 with John Dean, former aide to President Richard Nixon and a leading figure in the Watergate scandal. (At the time, Dean was acting as attorney to the firm's American owner).

## Extravagances

Few and far between. Lives an austere life. Outwardly, at least, maintains the image of a northern textiles boss.

## 95 Maurice Hatter 63
### (86) £125m (£120m)
### Electronics

## Source of wealth

Maurice Hatter probably has as much as £80 million readily at hand in liquid assets. Add in the value of his shares in private IMO Controls Ltd, and it seems ludicrous that the *Sunday Times* chose to halve his net worth in its last rich list. Agreed, it is difficult to value Hatter's company, as

## Lord Sainsbury 65
## (59) £124m (£147m)
## Retailing

## Source of wealth

Lord John Sainsbury stood down last year as chairman of J Sainsbury, Britain's biggest and most profitable high street food retailer. He remains on the board as president.

obviously he is vital to the operation, and profits are very up and down. A realistic sustainable profit seems to be around £5 million and there are net assets of £7.5 million ratio. Put that on a moderate price/earnings and you get £57 million. But then add the huge dividends and salary that Hatter has taken in the last 30 years, and you can see that he is worth at least £130 million – and much of it is liquid wealth, even after the taxman has plundered it.

In the last available accounts, profits dipped from £11.7 million to £5.8 million, with turnover surprisingly taking a dip from £27 million in 1992 to £14.3 million in 1993. And Hatter has a good excuse. He was just in the middle of launching a new range of products when the IRA bombed Staples Corner and put his HQ out of action. The disruption affected the company for 18 months, so expect profits to bounce back in 1994.

The company has actually recorded a retained loss for the last two years of £11 million because Hatter has paid himself a

He handed over the reins to his cousin David, who has long been the largest shareholder. The stockmarket has gone off the shares of late, reducing Lord Sainsbury's paper wealth, but like the Walton family in America, the company makes the Sainsburys the richest family in Britain by a wide margin.

## Personal style

After 14 years of Lord Sainsbury at the helm, the company is reaping the rewards of one of the most carefully devised and executed strategic business plans ever seen in the UK. But cousin David runs the show now: Lord Sainsbury apparently hasn't interfered.

## Extravagances

Private passions include the Royal Opera House, where he is chairman of the Trust, and the Royal Ballet, where he is a governor. He is married to Anya Linden, the former ballerina; they have two sons and a daughter.

staggering £24 million in dividends which, on top of his salary, makes him one of the top three highest earning people in the country. Only in the latest accounts did Hatter think it prudent to pass on the dividend.

But the company can well afford it, as it always keeps plenty of cash in the bank in case of any rainy days. Like the day the dividend is paid.

## Personal Style

Maurice Hatter set up IMO Precision Controls Ltd in 1958, with £100 capital. He had left the army with no idea what to do and just dabbled and out came IMO. Hatter needs just 105 employees to makes sales of £27 million.

## Extravagances

Constant desire for vast amounts of cash. He lives in Queens Grove, near Regents Park, and drives every day to his North Circular Road premises before he was rudely interrupted by the IRA. He is believed to be one of Britain's highest individual taxpayers.

### Michael Smurfit 58
### £123m (£108m)
### Business

## Source of wealth

At Jefferson Smurfit's recent AGM in Dublin, chairman and chief executive Michael Smurfit admitted the company had weathered "four terrible years". Now, he added, demand for its staple products – paper and board – was "tremendous". There was a little exaggeration involved, but not much. Jefferson Smurfit hit a brick wall in 1990. Ever since, Michael Smurfit has been leading a delicate rescue operation and it seems to have started working. Perhaps his ebullience at the AGM can be attributed to the thought of receiving a £1.4 million personal bonus on the long-awaited flotation of JS Corp, the debt-laden US subsidiary in which Jefferson Smurfit held a 50 per cent share.

Currently, Michael Smurfit beneficially holds shares worth £82.5 million in the company, which the market values at £1.72 billion. That's significantly up from last year's valuation of £60 million. To be added to this amount are various finance and leasing businesses, unconsolidated within the accounts of the Jefferson Smurfit Group.

## Personal style

Doesn't give a damn about the Cadbury Report. Despite the company's difficulties, he has stubbornly kept the posts of chairman and chief executive united. Meanwhile, the Jefferson Smurfit board contains three other members of the family: Tony, his son, and Alan and Dermot, his brothers. Remarkable considering that this is a public company that avoided bankruptcy by the skin of its teeth.

## Extravagances

Wine and racehorses – including a mount named Fortune and Fame. The joke in Dublin is that Smurfit competes with Tony O'Reilly to endow the maximum possible number of institutes and professorships. Notably, both men acquired doctorates after becoming success stories.

### Sir Anthony Bamford 49
### £122m (£80m)
### Business

## Source of wealth

Destiny beckoned Sir Anthony Bamford in 1962 at the age of 17, when he joined JCB on the factory floor.

In 1989 profits were £38 million on a turnover of £422 million, and JCB was valued at over £450 million. The Bamfords lived accordingly. Profits dropped to as low as £8 million in the recession, and for a while it looked as though JCB could be in trouble. However, Sir Anthony pulled the company round last year and turned in a magnificent £26.5 million on a £399 million turnover. Not as good as 1989 but it meant that JCB was probably worth around £300 million. This meant that Sir Anthony's personal net worth is up considerably.

The JCB Group is owned by Transmission and Engineering Services Netherlands BV, and the true ownership is hidden, but control of the family fortune has now passed to Sir Anthony from his father and mother (who remains wealthy in her own right).

The empire is already being passed to Sir Anthony's 16-year-old son, Joseph Cyril Bamford II, or JCB Mk 2 as he is affectionately known. The end of this recession will see what sort of inheritance he is handed. We estimate that the value of the JCB empire to be around £300 million at present, down from the undoubted half billion pounds it was worth at the end of the Eighties.

## Personal style

A fierce supporter of Margaret Thatcher, Sir Anthony was knighted in 1990 for services to exports. Ironically, his father never received an honour higher than the CBE which he was awarded in 1969.

JCB is one of the great standard bearer companies of the United Kingdom. No one can begrudge the Bamfords their great wealth: they have created many jobs and done the country huge service. If only the rest of British industry had followed suit.

## Extravagances

Sir Anthony knows how to spend it. In 1990, out of the dividends from the record 1989 profits, he paid £12 million for a stately home in Gloucestershire to add to a holiday property bought in Barbados in 1979 for £1 million.

He also runs a large estate in the Midlands.

### John Murphy 70
### £121m (£118m)
### Construction

## Source of wealth

The aging John Murphy, now in his seventieth year, may not be calling all the shots but still takes the cash at one of Britain's best known builders John Murphy & Sons. John has the biggest stake in the family firm which, despite the depressed nature of the construction industry, delivered £8.3 million profits after tax on a £140 million turnover in the year ending December 1992 (the last time accounts were filed).

We value the company at around £80 million, but John Murphy is noted for taking hefty dividends – £16 million was paid out to shareholders in 1991 and 1992, leaving just £370,000 bottom line profits. As a result, we estimate John Murphy's private wealth has nudged up to £120 million.

Murphy's success in the industry is largely on the back of its reputation as an aggressive and reliable sub-contractor that takes no prisoners when working for main contractors.

In 1991 the company's share structure was changed with a new holding company set up to account for interests in construction, property and motoring. Shares are now held in an Isle of Man registered company.

## Personal style

Most sub-contractors suffer heavily from late payments from main contractors. The name Murphy is a good way to get round that, and few big companies would dare cross John Murphy. One of his most trusted executives is nicknamed "Elephant John", after allegedly surviving a beating from the Sunshine Gang. Murphy himself is no stranger to controversy, with questions asked in the House of Commons regarding the number of contracts he has won from British Rail.

## Extravagances

Little is seen of John Murphy, leading to speculation that he has retired in all but name. He lives in North London with his nurse wife, some 40 years his junior. That explains why he hasn't been around much.

### Jacques Murray 74
### £120m (£97m)
### Business

## Source of wealth

Jacques Murray seems to enjoy controversy. True, he turned fire protection group Nu-Swift into a profitable company, after he bought his way in 1982. His best deal at Nu-Swift was the 1986 purchase and 1990 sale of French group Sicli, yielding a £115 million extraordinary gain. But profits have taken a mild roller-coaster ride over the last six years, dividends have been suspended (despite the company's cash pile from the Sicli sale), and the company's decision to buy in its shares rather than spend its cash on an acquisition or two has led some to conclude that Murray has run out of ideas.

At the start of the year Murray made Nu-Swift private, making it a wholly-owned subsidiary of his Dutch-registered European Fire Protection BV; major shareholder ADT got property, cash and loan notes for its 23 per cent. The remaining 11

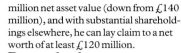

per cent of shareholders got cash and loan notes. The buyback was financed – Amstrad-style – by the company's cash pile.

On the buyback price of £3.98, his 66 per cent stake was worth £97 million. Now 100 per cent owner of a company with £110 million net asset value (down from £140 million), and with substantial shareholdings elsewhere, he can lay claim to a net worth of at least £120 million.

### Personal style

But Murray has raised eyebrows in other ways. Last May he finally succeeded in gaining a seat on the board at industrial services group Andrew Sykes, using his 29.7 per cent stake (worth about £4 million) for leverage. The battle was dirty: the Sykes board pointed out that Nu-Swift forgot to reveal in its accounts that it had bought a corporate jet, forcing a correction in the 1991 accounts. They also turned the tables by pointing to Nu-Swift's recent lack-lustre record. But the "backdoor takeover" appears for now to have succeeded. In between times, Murray has made a little profit for himself by taking a sizeable stake in the tiny Downiebrae Holdings. It is hard to see what, if anything, Jacques Murray intends to do for an encore. Observers wonder when he is going to settle down to retirement and to enjoy his near-£100 million fortune – or at least help his son look after it for him.

### Extravagances

That company jet. Murray also owns homes in Acapulco and Geneva. Then there's his son and heir, now director of Nu-Swift, who at 27 is the youngest director of a major British company.

In 1991 he cashed in £33 million of Amstrad shares three months before the share price crashed. Amstrad's flotation brought in a £2 million cheque, he has a £7 million stake in Tottenham Hotspur, and his Jersey offshoot, Amshold, is worth close to £25 million. In the past year, his value at Amstrad has slid £11 million, with the share price continuing to fall, putting his overall wealth at £122 million. He holds a number of properties through a company called Amsprop Ltd.

But the future looks brighter with the recent £60 million purchase of Viglen, the direct-selling computer group, widely applauded by the City. It is unlikely his fortune will dwindle any further.

### Personal style

As the City, shareholders and retailers have found over the years, Sugar is a one-man-band who takes no prisoners. The City are treated with disdain, "assholes" being the kindest description he can offer. Retailers, who have cut Amstrad margins in the past five years and, as a result, cut profits, are "prostitutes". Shareholders are no better. They were offered 30 pence to sell back Amstrad to Sugar two years ago. They rebelled, and the wounds are still to heal.

But, in the past year, Sugar appears to have calmed down. In March he admitted, "If it all went down the pan tomorrow, it wouldn't bother me personally." He finally appointed a chief executive in May, suggesting he no longer thrives on total control.

### Extravagances

Though his appearance doesn't suggest it, Sugar enjoys the high life. He drives a Rolls Royce, number-plate AMS 1, lives in a luxury mansion in Essex and takes, whenever possible, the family on exotic holidays. Since taking over Spurs, he has actually become a passionate football fan – and quite a knowledgeable one. If it does all go down the pan tomorrow, a job as team coach would be less of a shock than some previous appointments at Spurs.

### Sir Peter Michael 55
### £118m (£82 m)
### Electronics

### Source of wealth

One fortune might be enough for most. Maybe two? Well, for Sir Peter Michael it's three and counting: UEI, Cray, and now Classic FM.

Trained as an engineer, he has some 40 patents to his name. His first company United Engineering Industries was bought in 1988 by Carlton Communications, run by Michael Green, in a lavish £526 million deal, netting Sir Michael a tidy £76million or so.

He then took on the problems of Cray Electronics, bringing them back into profit after hard times. 1992 saw profits of £4.8 million before tax, at which point Sir Michael left, unloading his entire shareholding for a £10 million profit.

Now as chairman and 35 per cent shareholder in Classic FM, he is presiding over perhaps the most exciting (in financial terms at least) radio station in Britain. Ad sales targets have been smashed, and the startup cost – £6 million for the licence and another £12 million in capital expenditure – is all but paid off after only two years. The company will float before the end of the year, and talk is of a £100 million price tag.

He also picked another couple of winners: in the 1970s he bought land in California for viticulture: today, with California wines acknowledged to be among the best in the world, the Peter Michael Winery pro-

### Alan Sugar 47
### £119m (£133m)
### Electronics

### Source of wealth

Alan Sugar's first job was in 1963 as a clerk at the Statistics Department of the Ministry of Education and Science. Not surprisingly, he found it "boring as hell", and two years later was selling second-hand radios from the back of van. Four years later AMS Trading was formed (Alan Michael Sugar Trading), which grew into Britain's biggest electronics company. On flotation in 1980, £8 million was raised and, by the mid-Eighties, Amstrad was worth £1.3 billion. Cut-price stereos, satellite dishes, personal computers and videos were lapped up by a grateful public, and Sugar was worth £580 million.

Not now. The share price, hovering just below 30 pence, is down a staggering 900 per cent on the good days, with the stock market valuing the company at £170 million. Sugar himself told *BusinessAge* earlier this year that a more realistic share price for Amstrad would be 9 pence.

Nevertheless, he is still a wealthy man.

duces some of America's most exclusive vintages.

Adding up Sir Peter's numerous interests, he is worth at least £118 million.

## Personal style
He is one of the few businessmen who have survived being awarded the 'Young Businessman of the Year" by *The Guardian* newspaper. He is generally regarded as being a very gifted businessman.

## Extravagances
Squash and tennis, and is also an opera fan. He owns a large farm in Wiltshire.

### Chris Blackwell 56
### £116m (£112m)
### Entertainment

## Source of wealth
The basis of this Old Harrovian's fortune is the music business. The man who promoted Bob Marley, Bryan Ferry, Steve Winwood and U2 under the Island Records banner, experienced a difficult patch in the mid-1980s, but recovered and sold out to Polygram in 1989 for an estimated £300 million. Of this amount, a portion went to Blackwell's partners in adversity, the members of U2. Debts subtracted another chunk of capital. Reports indicate that Blackwell received around £100 million. He still keeps his hand in, though. In 1993, he sealed a deal to distribute the recordings of legendary Jamaican producers, Sly Dunbar and Robbie Shakespeare, through his recording company, Mango Records.

Blackwell has now started a second career as a Caribbean property investor, specialising in small luxury resorts for the international jet set.

In December 1993, his Island Trading Co announced plans to build three resorts in Jamaica. One of these, Strawberry Hill, a collection of 10 luxury villas on land once used as a British naval officers' club, opened in March. Last year, Blackwell completed the purchase of a long lease on Noel Coward's old home on the same island. These properties are part of a small but intriguing luxury property empire that stretches to the Bahamas and Miami, where he also has a share in three expensive, trendy Art Deco hotels on the sea front. Blackwell's trademark combination of showbiz and sharp deal-making is still in evidence. At his Marlin Hotel on Miami Beach, the model agency Elite has taken an office. Blackwell's partners reckon that merely keeping the lobby full of attractive women results in occupancy rates of 85 per cent and above.

Overall, Blackwell's adventures in the property business have probably cost him

in the region of £20 million. We reckon Blackwell's hotels are now generating some cash returns. Among other things, he seems to have profited mightily from the boom in property prices on Miami Beach, where he was an early entrant. Counterbalancing this have been a few speculative ventures, including investments in feature film production – rarely a crock of gold for investors. Accordingly, we have upped our valuation of Blackwell this year by a tiny amount to £116 million. Next year could provide much greater returns.

## Personal style
Rock 'n' roll legend has it that before recording sessions at his Compass Point studios in Bermuda, Blackwell liked to sprinkle chicken blood around the room. This old voodoo ritual seems to have been discontinued at Blackwell's Miami hotels. Apparently, it puts the supermodels off their food.

## Extravagances
Blackwell has four homes – including Goldeneye, the Jamaican bolt hole once owned by James Bond author Ian Fleming.

### Tim Sainsbury 62
### £115m (£134m)
### Retailing

## Source of wealth
Tim Sainsbury, the highly religious former DTI junior minister, qualifies as the richest government minister around.

Sainsbury's wealth springs, in part, from a £5.2 million trust fund set up by Lord Sainsbury in 1953 on behalf of his two sons, Simon and Tim.

In the March 1993 accounts for food retailers J Sainsbury, Tim Sainsbury is recorded as holding – beneficially and as a trustee – 3 per cent of shares. Sainsbury's shares are split virtually in half between family trust and personal holdings. Currently, Tim Sainsbury's personal holdings apparently amount to 27,936,000 shares. At the current share price (some 13 per cent off its 1993 levels), his fortune totals around £115 million.

In this assessment, *BusinessAge* has taken account of cash resources and investments held outside the Sainsbury trusts. Much of this amount is the fruit of 40 years' worth of dividends on the shares originally allotted to him by his father in 1953. Those shares yield around £3 million a year. He is the MP for Hove.

## Personal style
With one eye on the family's typically irascible temperament, Lord Sainsbury encouraged his sons to take up different specialisations. Tim Sainsbury was steered

toward managing the Sainsbury's property interests – a discipline which ran side-by-side with his early political adventures within the Conservative Party, where he made town planning his personal area of expertise.

Early in life, Tim Sainsbury gravitated toward the Tories, particularly the "wet" wing of the party gathered within the Bow Group.

Accordingly, Tim Sainsbury followed in Michael Heseltine's footsteps for much of his parliamentary career. Sainsbury first shadowed Heseltine at the Department of Environment and then at the Ministry of Defence. He returned for a second spell at the MoD between 1987 and 1989, dealing with defence procurement. "Nobody could ever accuse me of being a Thatcherite,'" Sainsbury has commented.

Regardless, Sainsbury's spells in the DTI (where he was responsible for export licensing, among other things) and the MoD landed him hot water over arms-to-Iraq.

## Extravagances
His children. Sainsbury's son Jamie, a twenty-something graduate, has picked up a reputation as a bad boy, not least via his old habit of offering Nazi salutes at meet-

### Noel Lister 66
### £112m (£107m)
### Retailing

## Source of wealth
Noel Lister founded MFI in 1964 to sell mail-order camping gear and low-cost self-assembly furniture.

In 1973 he abandoned mail order and opened the first of the now famous MFI stores instead. In 1980 the company went public. Lister took the opportunity to sell £11 million-worth of shares but kept hold of a huge stake, then worth some £30 million. By 1984, MFI controlled 40 per cent of the UK self-assembly market, and was approaching £40 million. Lister's dividends came to nearly £1 million a year.

In 1985, with 130 stores operating, MFI was bought for £615 million by the Associated Dairies Group, to form Asda-MFI. Noel Lister got around £60 million and retired from the position of chief executive. He invested the cash in shares and other paper assets.

Recently, he sold most of his shares and bought three properties through his charitable trust. In June 1993 he paid £2.9 million for a Do-It-All warehouse (sub-let to MFI) in Blackpool. Lister is one of Britain's immensely rich, liquid millionaires. Even after his major contribution to the Inland Revenue, we rate him at £112 million in 1994.

## Personal Style

Lister's secret was hiring good managers to run the business for him. His protégé, Derek Hunt, whom he plucked from the ranks of the Police Force, still heads the company today and probably does a better job of running it. Now in its 30th year, MFI has been a consistent success. It has been floated, sold off to ASDA, sold again in a management buy-out and has finally gone public again with Hunt running the show.

In between, Lister led the trend to mega-stores on edge-of-town sites. Lister recognised that town centre rents were too high and the business depended on lots of space bulk selling at low prices. Lister bought Edwin Healey's Status Discount chain of 60 stores in 1980.

A rare failure was an attempt to sell bathrooms but a big success was filling the stores with mostly British-made goods and winning the price war.

## Extravagances

Noel Lister's life has been dominated by sailing, and when he sold out he set off for a long trip on his yacht, Whirlwind XII. The Lister Charitable Trust is actively involved in teaching young people how to sail.

DAVID SHEPHERD

### Sir Terence Conran 63
### £111m (£27.25m)
### Retailing

## Source of wealth

When Butlers Wharf went bust it was generally thought that Sir Terence Conran had lost much of the £70 million fortune that he had built up over the years with investments in Habitat and the Storehouse Group. But Conran only lost his seed money, thought to be around £10 million. Midland Bank took over the site and have now made it into a success with Conran's continuing support. And he lost little from the Storehouse fiasco. He sold his shares when he left and is thought to have netted £70 million.

Some of his fortune has dwindled away after a generous separation settlement with his ex-wife, Caroline, and investments in restaurants and other areas of his business empire. Conran's family is also large and expensive to support.

But his catering and retail empire is now starting to shine making maybe £5 million a year on sales of £50 million. The catering empire now includes Pont de la Tour at Butlers Wharf, Bibendum at the Michelin Building in Fulham Road and Quaglino's in London's West End. He also has two Conran shops in Paris and London and one opening soon in Tokyo. The shops are immensely profitable.

Conran also owns substantial property, which we value at £5 million-plus. He also retains a stake in the book publishers Conran-Octopus, which was founded with his friend, the well-known publisher Paul Hamlyn. Overall, on a conservative basis, we value Conran's assets and liquid investments at £111 million, making him one of the big winners of the last 12 months. This shows how daft other rich lists are, having failed to include one of Britain's most famous businessmen.

## Personal style

Conran was knighted in 1983 at the height of his powers. He was recently subjected to a kiss 'n' tell assault by a former girlfriend, many years his junior. He had known her for barely three months. The story turned on the misconception that she had left him for a younger man. In fact, Conran had dumped her. We are told he was simply bored.

Terence Conran has been twice married to famous women. His first wife was the author Shirley Conran, to whom he got hitched in 1955. From that marriage, he is father to two famous sons, one of which is Jasper, the fashion designer. He is now happily ensconced with Vikki who travels everywhere with him. The two seem blissfully happy.

## Extravagances

He has a summer home in Provence, a manor house in Oxford and a London dwelling at Eaton Terrace. Added to that, there's his endearing weakness for cars. Perhaps his biggest extravagance, however, is cigars. He gets through a lot and they are the hideously expensive variety.

### Sir Jack Hayward 71
### £110m (£123m)
### Finance

## Source of wealth

Starting with both a lead and an inheritance provided by his father, Sir Charles Hayward, boss of the Firth Cleveland Group, Sir Jack made his own fortune by developing Freeport in the Bahamas. The capital of Grand Bahama, Freeport is famed for its status as an offshore centre.

Hayward is chairman of the Grand Bahama Development Company and of Freeport Commercial & Industrial Ltd. He is equity partner with his great friend, Sir Freddie Laker, in Laker Airways (Bahamas) Ltd: Laker's new airline now flies Boeing 727s between many American cities and Grand Bahama Island.

This year Hayward has footed a £20 million bill for new facilities and players at Wolves. It's arguable whether this investment will produce a return that couldn't be bettered elsewhere. Accordingly, we have reduced our estimate of Hayward's wealth.

## Personal style

Known as "Union Jack" on account of his generous support for worthy causes back home in Blighty. Saw active service in the RAF in the Second World War. He is married with two sons and one daughter. He was knighted in 1986 for his services to the Bahamas, and conceivably for his support for the Liberal Party (which is occasionally allowed to nominate someone for a 'gong'). Despite his entrepreneurial spirit, Sir Jack was never a born-again Thatcherite, but it was her government which sanctioned his knighthood.

## Extravagances

Lists his hobbies in Who's Who as "... preserving the British landscape, keeping all things bright, beautiful and British." Typically, his extravagances benefit others. Leads a lively lifestyle as the uncrowned king of Grand Bahama.

### Bernard Schreier 76
### £110m (£104m)
### Business

## Source of wealth

The curious thing about Bernard Schreier is that he makes no attempt to disguise his success or wealth, yet he remains unknown as a major player in business.

Schreier's company CP Holdings, according to its accounts, dabbles in everything – open-cast coal mining, civil engineering, investment management, farming and leisure, and trading agricultural products. These literally span the globe, including ore mining in Africa and petrol stations in Hungary. In 1989, CP Holdings was British Coal's biggest single contractor, producing 22 per cent of its opencast output.

Pre-tax profits in 1992, the last time accounts were filed, show a healthy £27.4 million pre-tax profit on £220 million turnover. The group is worth well over £100 million, which is lower than expected, but the accounts are complicated with substantial minority interest in various subsidiaries.

Schreier himself directly owns 60 per cent of the shares, his family another 17 per cent. His wealth is boosted by heavy dividends – £6 million in 1991 and 1992. In May 1993, the group sold its take in a foreign company, Shell es Ineterag, for a cool £12 million, which means this year's profits are likely to be in line with the past year's. More importantly, so will Schreier's dividends.

### Personal style
Born in Austria, his family fled to Palestine just before the Second World War and came to Britain in the Fifties. He began working in the road-building industry, before setting up his own sub-contracting firm for open-cast mining, which eventually grew to CP Holdings.

### Extravagances
A workaholic, who keeps a low profile and lives in North London.

## Simon Weinstock 42
## £109m (£121m)
## Electronics

### Source of wealth
A double blow in 1994 for the Hon Simon Weinstock: his father and managing director at GEC, Lord Weinstock, announced he wasn't retiring for another two years from the group, and the relative slump in the share price means he's lost over £20 million.

The group returned £866 million profits in 1993, up £3 million – not enough to impress the City which promptly knocked the share price down.

As commercial director, Simon Weinstock still holds a 1.2 per cent stake in the group, which is quite staggering considering the stock exchange capitalises GEC at £7.8 billion. This translates to £94 million, on top of which he picks up around £3 million in dividends each year. We estimate his new wealth at £109 million.

### Personal style
The wealth is as extraordinary as the rise from management trainee to boardroom director in three years, after he joined the group in 1986. Simon would argue this was

down to his expertise and experience as a merchant banker at SG Warburg. Others continue to whisper about what help Daddy gave him. The announcement that Lord Weinstock wants to stay on for two years has led some to speculate that his father wants more time to groom him for the job.

### Extravagances
He may not have inherited his father's job yet, but has inherited Lord Weinstock's love of the turf.

## Terry Curry 55
## £109m (£104m)
## Retailing

### Source of wealth
Terry Curry and his family controlled 35 per cent of the publicly quoted, high street electrical retailer called Currys. It was never highly regarded in the City but was undeniably well-run and profitable. In 1984, however, after a fierce £250 million take-over battle, Stanley Kalms's Dixons won control of the company and Terry Curry received £85 million for his share. Kalms ejected him from the company. Curry paid a substantial amount of tax on this but invested it wisely, and the family fortune has now grown to nearly £110 million.

### Personal style
Terry Curry was forcibly retired at 45 and has had 10 years of bliss spending his money. He is the great-grandson of the founder of the Currys electrical chain. Currys dominate electrical retailing, and have done so almost since electricity came into wide use in Britain at the beginning of the century. The brand name is one of the best known and enduring on the High Street.

### Extravagances
Curry invests in the stock-market, but he has no other known interests and keeps a low profile near his Maidenhead home.

## Leon Tamman 67
## £109m (£115m)
## Business

### Source of wealth
Leon Tamman's Brighton-based pharmaceuticals, media and hotels holding company, Inter Generics, has assets of £35 million – down from £50 million last year – and boasts Leon Brittan as an adviser. It is controlled through a Panamanian company. Inter Generics's main business is selling cheap, unbranded medicines to the third world. But it also manages telecommunications projects in Nigeria, Central America and the Caribbean. Tamman also

owns a £7 million television production facility in Jerusalem, used by CNN, ITN and the BBC.

One of Inter Generics's subsidiaries is the Patio Hotel Group. In 1993, Patio announced plans to spend £100 million developing a chain of 21 hotels in the UK. It already has several hotels in France and plans a further 13 hotels over the next three years. Tamman also owns Sonotel International, which manages hotels in Nigeria and Kenya. Because of the lower assets values of his interest in Britain we have slightly lowered our estimate of Tamman's net worth.

### Personal style
Leon Tamman started out hunting crocodiles on the Nile in the Sudan and selling their skins to traders in Khartoum. In 1953, the rest of his family moved to Switzerland – his brothers now count among the wealthiest people there – but Leon stayed behind and started a pharmaceuticals business. In 1961, he moved to Britain.

An extremely well connected man, he counts among his friends the Zairean President, Mbuto Sese Seko, and the foreign minister of Israel, Shimon Peres. He frequently has acted as an inter-governmental go-between around the world. In 1985 he helped negotiate various technical co-operation and defence agreements between Israel and Zaire, at a time when most African nations had cut off diplomatic relations with Israel. In 1986, he helped set up a £7 million pharmaceutical factory in Zaire producing 107 million tablets a year. Three years ago he set up a company in Geneva to finance Israeli agricultural exports to the former Soviet Union.

An exotic power broker, Tamman is as much at home in Geneva as in Kenya. Tamman's mixing of business ventures with personal contacts is about as serious as these things come. In the 1980s, he pledged $400 million to help Zaire's troubled state airline, Air Zaire, its shipping company, Compagnie Maritime Zairoise and pharmaceutical importer Central Medical Pharmaceutical Depot.

### Extravagances
Tamman has an exquisitely marbled residence in London, and houses in Hove and Monte Carlo.

## Lady Virginia Stanhope 54
## £108m (£105m)
## Inheritance

### Source of wealth
Lady Virginia Stanhope currently lives on her own stud farm, close to her former father-in-law, the Earl of Harrington, in

Limerick, Ireland. But she is an independent heiress in her own right. Her mother, known as Dorro, who died last year, was a wealthy American heiress. Her marriage to Viscount Petersham, himself the son of the owner of one of the most important horse racing studs in Ireland, was the social event of 1966. Prior to her death, Lady Virginia's mother had been bedridden with severe arthritis for many years. She left all her American trusts, said to be worth well over $100 million, to her daughter.

## Personal style
The last time the media spotlight shone on "Ginny" Stanhope was when she was a prizewinning national horse jumping champion in Ireland in the Fifties and Sixties. She is back in the limelight again, now that her daughter Serena has married Viscount Linley, the son of Princess Margaret and Lord Snowdon.

## Extravagances
On her wedding to Viscount Petersham in 1966, there were rumours that the Viscount's father gave the couple, as a wedding gift, a cheque for £1 million. Her mother duly matched the sum in dollars. She also owns a splendid home in Monaco. She received the villa as part of her divorce settlement with Serena's father. She is a horsewoman par excellence, even at 54 years old.

## Michael Heseltine 61
## £108m (£47.75m)
## Publishing

## Source of wealth
The publishing company that Michael Heseltine founded, Haymarket, boasts a tortuous corporate structure – all the better for hiding the true extent of the President of the Board of Trade's fortune. The holding company, Haymarket Publishing Group Ltd, is non-trading, with one share owned by Heseltine's partner, Lindsay Masters, and the rest by a nominee company run by lawyers. Other Haymarket trails lead to either Jersey, or once again to Lindsay Masters. Michael Heseltine's name does not appear anywhere on any share register connected with Haymarket.

Heseltine is generally assumed to own – beneficially or otherwise – 50 per cent of Haymarket which, if it came on the open market, would be worth maybe £200 million. Values have recovered rapidly in the last 12 months. With the company's long-awaited emergence from recession. Aside from trade and business publishing the group has interests in property, local radio and farming.

Heseltine took a substantial cash chunk out of the company when he sold a clutch of prestige trade magazines, including *Accountancy Age* and *Computing*, to the Dutch VNU publishing company in 1980. He is thought to have received £8 million himself from this transaction. It enabled him to pay off his mortgage on his substantial country estate near Banbury in Oxfordshire. With past dividends and his share of the capital value, plus his personal assets, we rate Heseltine at £108 million. The increase is entirely due to the fact that Haymarket has suddenly emerged again as a very valuable commodity after some terribly lean years when it looked as though the company was directionless.

## Personal style
Eschewed the life of a tycoon for politics. Good vote winner; greatly attractive to Tory ladies. Still has an outside chance of achieving his dream of being prime minister. If only he hadn't walked out of Thatcher's cabinet meeting that day, he would be in No 10 now.

## Extravagances
A Palladian-style 18th century estate, Thenford, situated in 800 acres of lush farmland. It was purchased in 1977.

## Peter Dawson 55
## £107m (£75m)
## Business

## Source of wealth
Within a year of truck rental company Dawson Group's 1988 stock market debut, the share price jack-knifed. From a launch price of 155 pence, the company's share lost more than 90 per cent of their value, bottoming out at just 14 pence as the company headed for a 1990 loss. Founder, chairman and chief executive, Peter Dawson, must have thought that being a paper millionaire wasn't all it was cracked up to be.

But the Milton Keynes-based company recovered, and so did the shares. In fact, in the last year they've positively surged. They now stand at their 1994 low of 338 pence, valuing Dawson's 75 per cent stake at £93 million. His family also sold around £11 million of shares at the time of the flotation. Last year saw profits surge - yet again - from £4.7 million to £8 million on sales of £53 million.

## Personal style
The recession wasn't kind to most small businessmen, but ironically in the early Nineties Peter Dawson's company has cashed in like never before. As fleet managers become increasingly reluctant to spend lots of money on their own lorries, they turn to short-term truck and articulated lorry hire – which is where Dawson Group steps in. Dawson has been prepared to renew his own fleet and this has helped improve rental rates.

Now Peter Dawson is looking abroad for new challenges. He now heads up the Dutch-based international arm of Dawson Group, formed in March of this year, while two hand-picked experienced managers look after the British end. "The company is almost running itself," says one analyst.

## Extravagances
Dawson received a £50,000 performance bonus on top of his £100,000 salary and £1.23 million in dividends last year.

## Ben Dunne 45
## £106.5m
(£105m)
## Retailing

## Source of wealth
Journalists in the Irish Republic have spent years trying to assess the value of the family trust that runs Dunnes Stores, the privately-held family retail group that operates 100 supermarkets in Ulster, the Republic of Ireland and the north of England. Irish company law meant that turnover and profit figures never had to be disclosed. But the general consensus last year, held that the company was making £80 million on turnover of around £1 billion. On that basis, we valued what we thought was Dunne's 25 per cent holding in the company at around £100 million. Earlier this year, Ben Dunne himself corrected us. Having been ousted as company chairman in April 1993, after a bitter feud with his two sisters and other brother, he launched a bid to buy, from his siblings, their shares in the family business. Applied to his own stake, the purchase terms valued Dunne's 20 per cent holding at £80 million. The offer was the latest instalment in an Irish corporate soap opera that began in February 1992, when police discovered a £100-an-hour call girl and a bag containing a large amount of cocaine in Dunne's

Florida hotel room. Dunne, it was said, had been snorting the drug for hours, and at one point threatened to jump from his 17th floor balcony. A year later, he was ejected from the boardroom at Dunnes Stores. Nemesis came in the form of his sister, Margaret Heffernan, who disagreed sharply with Dunne's policy of deep discounting. Whatever credit Ben Dunne deserved for building up the group from virtually nothing went out of the window. Ever since, Dunne has been fighting a pitched battle in the courts. His primary aim has been to lay hands on his cash – or else regain control of the company. The case will finally come to court in November. The likelihood is that Dunne will extract his cash, leaving the remaining family the unwelcome prospect of floating part of the group, or inviting outside investors to participate. The company, however, remains tightly controlled. Because of its traditional, harsh methods with suppliers, Dunnes Stores usually owns a cash stockpile, typically invested to good effect on the short-term money markets.

Dunne is still relatively youthful. Last year, he purchased 75 per cent of Dunloe House Group, a small quoted property and investment group. Dunne has pledged to turn its operations around, amid much speculation that he would use Dunloe to threaten his siblings' retail operations. But with gearing at 125 per cent, and pre-tax losses stated at £396,000 for the six months to June 1993, there's still no sign of light at the end of the tunnel.

## Personal style
Once alleged to have burst into the boardroom, started shouting, and then extinguished his cigarette in a glass of mineral water belonging to his sister, who happened to be conducting a difficult meeting with suppliers at the time. She is said to have been unimpressed.

## Extravagances
Contrary to popular perception, which sees him as a boorish and aggressive figure, Dunne undoubtedly boasts hidden reserves of charm. The call-girl whom Florida policemen found in his hotel room clearly experienced the warmth of its glow. On Dunne's arrest, Denise Wojcik, 22, told the *Daily Mail*: "I want him to know that I will be by his side. I had no idea he was so rich."

### Baroness Willoughby de Eresby 60
### £106m (£97m)
### Inheritance

## Source of wealth
Baroness (Jane) Willoughby de Eresby has substantial residences at Grimsthorpe in Lincolnshire, and Castle Drummond in Perthshire. Neither is open to the public. These houses contain some of the loveliest tapestries, porcelain and works of art in the UK. Her wealth arises from the antiques in the castles, and from the vast estates, which were associated with the Dukedom of Ancaster and the Barony of Aveland. The dukedom and the barony are now extinct but the assets, all of them in trust and amounting to 65,000 acres in Scotland and at least 40,000 acres in England, passed to the Baroness.

She is the 27th holder of the title Willoughby de Eresby, one of the oldest baronies in the peerage, dating back to 1313. Hers is one of only 20 hereditary female titles in the House of Lords. The title passed to her when her brother disappeared at sea in 1963. The current heiresses to her title are her two aunts, aged 86 and 81.

## Personal style
A one-time Sixties raver, Baroness Jane has now retreated into spinsterhood, enjoying the quiet life in her castles. They simply do not come any more blue-blooded and she is known as Nancy to her friends.

## Extravagances
Private ownership – no visitors allowed – of works by Holbein and Canaletto. She is the Joint Hereditary Great Chamberlain of England. The job description is vague and the salary unknown, but the holder is required to organise certain State ceremonials and to be present at coronations to carry the Staff of St Andrew. At the coronation of the present Queen, the baroness was a train bearer.

### Lady Anne Cavendish Bentinck 78
### £105.5m (£90m)
### Inheritance

## Source of wealth
Lady Anne Cavendish Bentinck is the sole heiress of the Portland estate, held in trusts. The value of her property assets, we estimate, has risen in line with other property prices in London.

In the last century, when the British aristocracy were the virtual lords of creation, the Dukedom of Portland was the second-richest estate in the country. Lady Anne Cavendish Bentinck's great-grandfather owned a total of 162,235 acres, with an income of £124,925 – in modern money, about £6 million a year. In those days, the Portland estate almost rivalled that of the Westminster's.

## Personal style
The unmarried Lady Anne eschews the Cavendish name, as well she might: many of the holders of the name and title were eccentric. Even the fifth duke had his little foible: he communicated with the world only through a letterbox in his bedroom door. Lady Anne is a noted horsewoman. For many years, she owned her own pack of foxhounds. She still has four horses in race training with Jeremy Clover in Nottinghamshire.

## Extravagances
Lady Anne states, in her *Debrett's* entry, that she has homes in Nottingham (35,000 acres), Caithness (81,000 acres), Northumberland (10,000 acres), and Easter Ross (25,369 acres).

### Marquess of Cholmondeley 34
### £105m (£98m)
### Aristocracy

## Source of Wealth
Mick Jagger and Jerry Hall have been house guests at the home of the Marquess of Cholmondeley, at what is thought to be Britain's finest Palladian mansion. Houghton Hall was originally constructed for Sir Robert Walpole, the 18th century prime minister, whose tenacious grip on office was rivalled only by Margaret Thatcher's. For much of the 19th century,

Houghton was unused and boarded up: as a result, its contents have survived intact and mostly preserved. The other family home is at Cholmondeley, in Cheshire, which is surrounded by a 9,000-acre estate. After his father's death, Cholmondeley decided to sell off one of the family's greatest treasures, a Holbein canvas, to establish a maintenance fund for Houghton Hall. The sale brought in £10 million and opened the floodgates on another of the nation's periodic rows concerning the dispersal of treasured works of art from landed estates. The Holbein was saved for the nation by a private treaty sale. In 1990,

Cholmondeley paid off death duties on his estate with the grant of a Gainsborough to the National Gallery.

## Personal style

Member of the rock 'n' roll jet set. Among the skills demanded of the Marquess of Cholmondeley is an ability to walk backwards.

This is the primary task of the Lord Great Chamberlain of England, a title which was passed down to the youthful Marquess when his father died in 1990, leaving behind an estate valued at around £100 million.

The Marquess is probably accustomed to fancy footwork, having worked as an assistant to Robert Stigwood, the impresario behind Saturday Night Fever. He is related to the Rothschilds, via his grandmother.

## Extravagances

Mostly showered, according to rumour, upon Lisa B, the shapely pop chanteuse in whose company Cholmondeley constantly crops up in the gossip columns.

## John James Fenwick 61
### £105m (£132m)
### Retailing

## Source of wealth

The Fenwick shop chain was set up at the end of the last century by the great-grandfather of its present chairman, John James (JJ) Fenwick. It has finally caught some effects of the recession, with after-tax profits falling to £9.2 million for 1992-93, against £13.7 million previously. Yet with substantial cash reserves of £40 million (interest adds £3 million to this year's profits) and other undervalued assets of £60 million on the balance sheet, this privately held family business is rock solid.

The first Fenwick store was set up in Newcastle in 1882, with the best known shop, Fenwick's in Bond Street, following in 1891. There are now stores dotted all around the country. On the basis of the valuation of the House of Fraser chain Fenwick's would be worth around £155 million, but the cash pile and the prospects for recovery inflate this figure to around £180 million. The only exit route, if the family desired it, would be a flotation, as department stores are still seen as a dying institution everywhere but the stock market.

Judging by a very confused share register – six tiers of shares and littered with tax-saving family trusts – Fenwick personally controls well over half of the company. Including dividend income of £600,000 a year as well as a £500,000 salary, his personal worth is £105 million, down somewhat on last year due to the vagaries of retailing.

## Personal style

John Fenwick, though living in London, retains the family connection with Newcastle as a governor of the Royal Grammar School there, and a director of the Northern Rock Building Society. He is married with three sons.

## Margaret Heffernan
### £104m (£98m)
### Retailing

## Source of wealth

Last Christmas, most large Dublin retailers were saying prayers of thanks to the Great Retailer In The Sky for his permissive attitude toward Margaret Heffernan's management coup at Dunnes Stores, the Republic's biggest retail chain.

Starting last April, Heffernan discarded the price-cutting strategy pioneered by her brother, Ben Dunne, who lost his seat as chairman in a bitter family feud that is still wending its way through the High Court in Dublin. In particular, the change-over seemed to be good news for Dunnes Stores' major competitors in the Republic, Associated British Foods, which reported that its Irish profits doubled in the six months to March 1994.

Dunne's Stores is to Ireland, what Marks & Spencer is to Britain. For the past year, Heffernan has controlled nearly a quarter of the Irish retail trade. Estimates of the family company's annual profits – a subject which Ben Dunne always refused to discuss – run to around £80 million on sales of £1 billion. Until recently, the company was routinely valued in Ireland at £550 million to £750 million – a figure that came with no borrowings.

## Extravagances

Owning a department store might be seen as an extravagance, but as the Al-Fayed brothers have shown, it can also be profitable.

If Fenwick has any personal foibles, he keeps them to himself.

Because of weak disclosure rules under Irish company law, those estimates were the closest anyone had ever come to estimating the family's wealth, which is held in trust on behalf of five brothers and sisters. Now all that has changed – not least because of Ben Dunne's frontal assault on his sister in the courts.

Earlier this year, Dunne offered to buy out his siblings for £320 million – in a proposal that valued Margaret Heffernan's share of the business at £80 million. Given Dunne's hostile position, that figure may represent a very conservative valuation. In reality, the figure may be nearer £100 million.

Notably, Heffernan's sister, Elizabeth McMahon, left behind her an estate valued at £106 million when she died last year.

## Personal style

Heffernan, a noted supporter of charity, appears every bit as hard-headed as her brother, whose negotiating tactics and strong-arm approach to unions and regulation are legendary.

## Extravagances

Not on the menu. Under Ben Dunne, the company's ill-advised attempt to crack English retail markets cost £10 million. Another £20 million was lavished on store development within five years. The company's results this year appear to have suffered from the ruckus taking place in the boardroom.

## Abe Jaffe
**£103m** (£102m)
**Business**

### Source of wealth
Abe Jaffe is the boss of Curfin Investments Ltd, which is the holding company for Currie Motors. Currie has 13 retail motor outlets in the London area, and is the distributor for Nissan, Honda, Toyota, Vauxhall and Peugeot.

Curfin owns the freehold of 12 of the 13 sites. In America, the company has eight branches which hold the franchises for GM, Ford, Chrysler, Subaru and Hyundai, and owns the freehold on five of these branches.

Abe Jaffe and his immediate family possess 95 per cent of the shares of this company through a Netherlands Antilles based holding company called Curfin Holdings BV. The balance of shares are held by an executive director.

Currie Motors has annual sales in Britain and America of £133 million and minuscule profits of £937,000 in the year to end of 1992. Profits have halved from the previous year. The balance sheet severely undervalues the company's freehold properties that have recently undergone extensive refurbishment. We rate the freehold values of the sites from which the group operates at £110 million alone. Add in other assets and the real value is probably £130 million. The group shows some debt of £16 million.

On the basis of that, we rate the wealth of Abe Jaffe at £116 million. Because profits are lower we have assessed the net worth of Abe Jaffe at £103 million slightly up on last year.

### Personal style
A staunch socialist in a list of the super rich. Management of the company has passed to his son who is managing director.

### Extravagances
Remaining as anonymous as possible. Hated it when *BusinessAge* revealed his identity last year

## John Whittaker 53
**£102m** (£76m)
**Property**

### Source of wealth
After gaining control of the Manchester Ship Canal Company in 1993, John Whittaker has even more reason to celebrate: his property group Peel Holdings is now valued at £246 million by the City. Whittaker's 50 per cent stake makes him worth £122 million – on paper at least. However, we have downgraded this, given that several of Peel's properties are empty and

rents are falling. In May 1994, the group's share price took a hit after Whittaker saw his plans to build a one million square foot shopping centre in Greater Manchester, squashed by the Court of Appeal. He plans to go to the House of Lords, but the City is not holding its breath, or the share price.

### Personal style
Whittaker began building his property empire in the Seventies with a business partner, and friend - Leslie Smith. Together they bought three cotton mills and a stake in a fourth. Whittaker gained control of Peel by selling his family's 68 per cent stake in the MSCC to Peel for £79 million of cash and shares in 1991. He is a hardened corporate fighter, having stalked the MSCC for six years before taking over.

Now busy creating a family dynasty, Whittaker nearly trained as a priest, and entered the property business via quarrying and demolition. Surrounds himself with younger men, and is renowned for being hard, abrasive and confrontational.

### Extravagances
Whittaker likes to stress the "Britishness" in everything he does, except when it comes to paying tax – he lives in the Isle of Man. Prefers a pint down the local rather than cocktail parties.

## Engelbert Humperdinck 58
**£102m** (£95m)
**Entertainment**

### Source of wealth
Nearly 22 years ago, Engelbert Humperdinck decamped to Las Vegas. It was the best financial decision that he ever made. At his peak he earnt £1million a week performing in the casinos. It was the idea of his legendary manager Gordon Mills. He tired of Gordon Mills' management in the early Eighties and struck out on his own, which damaged his earnings.

We estimate that Humperdinck has earned around £210 million in his career and that, after management fees and tax, around £95 million has stuck to him, plus investment earnings. He is approaching 60 years of age and his voice is not what it was.

### Personal style
Engelbert Humperdinck was one of the stable of three megastars who were groomed and handled by Gordon Mills even though he was never as successful on the Tom Jones scale. His real name is Arnold George Dorsey and he performed as Gerry Dorsey until Gordon Mills made him change it in 1960.

### Extravagances
He has houses in California and Leicester - which has a real pub in the garden. Plus a fleet of exotic cars

## Charles Saatchi 51
**£98m** (£98m)
**Media**

### Source of wealth
It was Charles Saatchi's good fortune to have invested heavily and wisely – reportedly on the advice of his former wife, Doris – in some of the brightest names in more modern-type art. Mystery surrounds the extent of Charles Saatchi's art sales. In November 1992, he put two Warhol canvases and other works up for sale at Sotheby's in New York. The expected price was £13 million.

His current shareholding in Saatchi & Saatchi is worth a few million. Over the years, they have made share sales and simply seen themselves diluted down. Charles Saatchi's art collection – or that part of it exhibited over the years in his London gallery – has been valued at below £200 million. Of this, 50 per cent was cornered by Doris in divorce proceedings. Assuming recent sales similar to last year's event at Sotheby's, and taking that as a valuation guide, and assuming that the split with his American wife was equally divided, then Charles Saatchi's art-based fortune adds up to £80 million.

We think that Saatchi's fortune has remained virtually static in the last 12 months with the value of his paintings moving lower if anything against the trend.

### Personal style
His collection of paintings led the *Financial Times*, somewhat over-generously, perhaps, to describe Saatchi as a modern Medici. History will judge that. Recently, he resigned from the board of Saatchi and Saatchi after he was turfed out of his Berkeley Square fiefdom with his brother. He still goes to work most days, however, in his original haunt in Charlotte Street. He is regarded as something of a god in the advertising industry.

### Extravagances
Lives well with his new wife in London and is a member of the London brat pack which includes Michael Green and Gerald Ratner.

## Colin Shepherd 66
**£96m** (£92m)
**Construction**

### Source of wealth
The Shepherd family run one of Europe's biggest private construction companies which, for the year ending June 1992, reported £14.9 million post-tax profits on a £279.6 million turnover. On today's ratings, Shepherd Building is worth

£300 million.

Colin Shepherd took over as chairman in 1986 from his elder brother, Sir Peter, and has kept the business very much in the family. Apart from employing his brother, Donald, as deputy chairman, three other Shepherds work directly in the company and, in total, 19 family members own nearly all the company's one million shares.

Colin Shepherd has the largest stake at 13 per cent, currently worth £39 million. But several family members hold his shares, pushing his real worth closer to £100 million. The hefty increase on last year's valuation is based on a price/earnings ratio of 20, which the City would currently give Shepherd. In the past year, the company has successfully pursued "design and build" contracts, involving a single point of responsibility during construction projects. This makes the company less likely to suffer from lengthy claims procedures that often affect the profitability of construction companies.

## Personal style
Carrying on the family traditions as much as possible. The company dates back to 1890 when a joiner/undertaker Frederick Shepherd first began trading. His son Frederick Welton rapidly developed the group through the Thirties, and Colin Shepherd is now the fourth generation of the family running the show.

## Extravagances
Claim to fame is developing the Portaloo. Probably one to avoid at parties.

### Pamela Harriman 74
### £95.5m (£85m)
### Inheritance

## Source of wealth
Pamela Churchill Harriman married for the third time in the early Seventies to an old flame from wartime days, US diplomat Averil Harriman, who had just been widowed after 40 years of marriage. When he died in 1986, he left her £75 million. She was already well off, with a well-furnished flat in Paris. Most of the furniture was Louis XV.

## Personal style
Pamela Harriman is American ambassador to France. She was the daughter of Lord Digby, a Dorset landowner. In the first months of World War II, she married Randolph Churchill, the son of Sir Winston Churchill. Randolph was both an MP (for Preston) and a 2nd Lieutenant in the Queen's Royal Hussars at the time. Her son is Winston Churchill MP, but their political careers are divided by a continent. The marriage did not last and divorce followed. In 1960, she married the Broadway

producer Leyland Hayward, who died in 1971. Then she met Harriman.

He was a legend in US politics but Pamela stepped into the role, providing the Democratic Party with their own version of British royalty: the Harriman name is equivalent to Churchill's in the States and the fact that she carries both has put her on a par with the late Jackie Onassis. She shows no sign of ever returning to Britain.

## Extravagances
Anything her heart desires.

### Felix Grovit 51
### £95.3m (£83m)
### Finance

## Source of wealth
Felix Grovit is the king of London's money changers. But the secretive boss of the Chequepoint bureaux de change chain started out by dealing in property. Cannily, just before the 1973 crash, he cashed in his chips, but was left with a shop in South Kensington. With the help of financial wizard Alistair Holberton, this became the first ever Chequepoint branch.

Today Chequepoint has more than 90 outlets worldwide and is moving rapidly into Eastern Europe. The strong cashflow generated by the company has been used by Grovit to fund other ventures, including the purchase of mining stocks in Canada, Australia and New Zealand, several safe-deposit houses in London and publishing interests in London and Marbella.

Grovit's highly tax-efficient empire has gone from strength to strength. The corporate structure behind his money changing interests meander its way around the world, via Hong Kong and several obscure Caribbean islands, to the Invertrust Corporation registered in the Netherlands Antilles.

In 1987 Chequepoint paid taxes of just 3.5 per cent. The Invertrust Corporation is reputedly owned by Grovit's family trusts, which are based in the British Virgin Islands. The last accounts available list assets of £335 million. This excludes assets in eastern Europe and the former Soviet Union. The organisation is virtually free of debt. The big question still to be answered concerns his ability to ride out the gyrations in exchange rates over the past 12 months. Reports indicate that Chequepoint has done well this year. There is no doubt that this unusual man is one of Britain's hidden super-rich. We rate him at £95 million.

## Personal style
Grovit is a highly autocratic manager. He uses the law in attempts to thwart commercial adversaries and probing journalists alike.

## Extravagances
Attempts to become a media mogul. Grovit's efforts in this area have not been terribly successful. In 1986 he abandoned plans for an alternative to the *London Evening Standard*. He was also a prospective purchaser for Robert Maxwell's newspaper, *The European*. In 1992, frustrated in his attempts to break into the big leagues, he set about producing his own newspaper, *The Europa Times*, which claims half a million readers.

### Fred Walker 68
### £95m (£100m)
### Business

## Source of wealth
Fred and Jack Walker were always equal partners in their steel stockholding business, commonly known across the UK as Walkersteel.

Jack has always been the front man because it was decided many years ago that he should go into tax exile and keep hold of the family money. We have, therefore, taken a very conservative view of Fred's wealth and apportioned the major part to his brother, although we are certain that they share equally.

The Walkers picked up nearly £330 million and kept £100 million worth of properties when they sold their family business to British Steel in the late Eighties. Since then they have been going through the money, investing maybe £50 million in Blackburn Rovers Football Club, and as much as £30 million in the airline – Jersey European Airways. They are also backing other small entrepreneurial ventures that have future potential. We have marked down Walker's wealth slightly as a result of all this spending, which is not reflected in a contrasting capital value appreciation.

## Personal style
Fred Walker is the older brother of Jack Walker. Today he lives in quiet retirement in Lancashire and helps run the family airline, Jersey European Airways. The airline has expanded quickly and there have been changes of management. It is not yet washing its face; unusual for a Walker business.

Despite being the eldest, Fred has always been overshadowed by the go-getting Jack. But it was Fred who was left to successfully run the steel stockholding business after Jack went into tax exile in Jersey. Jack did the selling, chose the executives and had the vision, whilst Fred ran things. He liked it that way.

## Extravagances
Football, football and more football. Fred supports his brother's passion, and witnessed the £5 million splashed out for Nor-

wich player Chris Sutton; a record breaking deal. Blackburn didn't really need Sutton and he was only really worth £3 million. But what the hell. The brothers are determined to dominate the Premier League and Blackburn will surely be champions next season.

## Michael Cornish *41*
## £94.5m (£125m)
## Business

### Source of wealth
Michael Cornish finally took over his father's company, Linpac, which manufactures and markets plastic products, after 28 years.

The transition has not been smooth. The last time accounts were filed, for 1992, profits after tax fell £10 million to £18.8

million. Valued on the market today, Linpac would be worth £300 million, compared to well over £400 million in 1993.

Michael Cornish owns 37 per cent of the ordinary shares in the group. With options, he is worth £110 million. However, as a private company and reflecting worse conditions we believe that a £200 million valuation is more appropriate, but previous dividends and personal assets cushion the fall a little.

### Personal style
Michael worked very closely with his father in making Linpac one of Britain's largest private companies. He is probably finding it hard running the show alone.

### Extravagances
Extremely quiet, appearing only in annual reports and rich lists. He has pioneered a series of racehorse sponsorships carrying the Linpac name.

DAVID SHEPHERD

## Kevin Leech *51*
## £94m (£105m)
## Business

### Source of wealth
Jersey-based Kevin Leech is being widely tipped to reach billionaire status and, on paper at least, is currently worth over £200 million. However, his pharmaceutical company ML Laboratories is highly valued purely on the back of one drug, Icodextrin, which was commercially launched in June 1994, causing no great shakes in the stock market.

Leech founded the company in 1983, and has spent years developing Icodextrin – a cheaper and safer kidney dialysis solution. The potential market is astronomical, with 120,000 new UK patients each year, worth £3 billion.

The Department of Health gave ML the go-ahead to market its product in January, and the stock market is convinced the company will eventually be worth well over £1 billion.

But that's all in the future. The current share price is hovering around 200 pence, well down on the 274 pence at the start of the year. Leech owns 68 per cent of ML, making him worth over £200 million on paper. Last year, we halved this valuation given the uncertain nature of the business and the poor performance so far. We see no reason to change this cautious policy in valuing Leech's wealth.

### Personal style
Leech retired 10 years ago after selling his funeral parlour business. He met an inventor called Jeremiah Milner, who persuaded him to invest £50,000 in the development of Icodextrin, promising him it would soon be worth a fortune. It's taken 11 years and Milner has since died, so Leech is clearly a patient man if nothing else.

### Extravagances
He quit the business because he was "fed up with the quiet life." Not technically minded, admitting "ignorance is bliss." Spends his life as a recluse drinking with friends in Jersey public houses.

## Laxmi Shivdasani *69*
## £94m (£94m)
## Food

### Source of wealth
Laxmi Shivdasani took up the reins of her husband's company after he died. Although they have lived in Britain since the Fifties the family business, a mixture of food, hotels, canning, tea and banking, is still scattered around the world. The banking arm is in Geneva, the vineyards are in France and the hotels are in Thailand and the exotic Maldive Islands.

Her husband began the business by capitalising on a small family inheritance and an unrivalled set of contacts within the various communities, which had emigrated from the Sind province of India, mostly to the old ex-colonies of the British empire. The business is now being taken over by her son Azad and daughter Bina.

### Personal style
Hard-nosed matriarch. Dines with John Major.

### Extravagances
Occasionally gives parties for the wealthy Indian exile community in London.

## James Sherwood *61*
## 92m (£88m)
## Business

### Source of wealth
James Sherwood took Sea Containers public on the New York stock exchange in 1968, raising $8 million. He proved his financial engineering skills when he created a dual structure: Sea Containers Inc in America and Sea Containers Atlantic Ltd in Bermuda. The shares were printed back-to-back on the same stock certificate, meaning that if you held one you also held the other. The paired shares were traded as a unit on the NYSE and were highly tax effective, providing an extra income stream for investors.

He grew a huge business with nearly 200,000 containers and 35 ships. Then he added Sealink, the British Rail cross-Channel ferry company. But net assets were a lowly $300 million as the company had a billion dollars' worth of debt.

In 1990 he sold the container operations to Robert Montague's Tiphook and the Sealink ferry division to Stena, for a total of $1.5 billion. Five hundred million dollars were then used to buy in the company's shares, $700 million to pay off debt and $300 million cash was left, plus a string of exotic hotels in Rio, Cape Town and Venice, as well as the Orient Express leisure company.

Sherwood's stake in Sea Containers is worth £50 million. But he has other liquid assets from past dividends and salary and is worth £92 million personally. His companies are managed from England, but domiciled in Bermuda.

## Personal style

At the age of 31, Sherwood and two partners put in £20,000 each and formed Sea Containers Inc in New York. They bought as many containers as they could, and leased them to shippers and companies. They guessed that container shipping would take over from the break-bulk method. They were right, as the big shipping lines switched over.

Maybe his biggest coup was foiling a hostile takeover from Tiphook and Stena in 1990 and then selling of most of the companies assets, at inflated prices, to both the bidders. It ruined Tiphook which probably overpaid by fifty per cent for the container business. It's rare that anyone comes out of a deal ahead of Sherwood.

## Extravagances

His whole company seems like an extravagance at times.

## Countess of Sutherland 73
### £92m (£87m)
### Aristocracy

## Source of wealth

Elizabeth Millicent Sutherland, the 24th holder of her title and the chief of the Clan Sutherland, inherited 158,000 acres of the Sutherland lands in the county of that name. A little over 100 years ago, the Sutherland estates ran to 1.3 million acres: like most acres of the United Kingdom, there were long ago placed into trusts, some not even domiciled in the UK. This makes them difficult to trace.

## Personal style

She sits in the House of Lords as a countess in her own right, one of only twenty women holders of hereditary titles in that place. The title was originally an earldom but, as with most of the other hereditary female titles, the majority of them Scottish, it automatically became that of countess on being inherited by a woman. Member of the women's Land Army during the Second World War.

An irregular attender at the House of Lords, but with a house in west London, Lady Sutherland is married to the journalist Charles Janson and has two sons, one of whom, Lord Strathnaver, was a member of the Metropolitan Police from 1969 to 1974. Her daughter is married and also lives in London.

## Extravagances

All of those hidden acres.

## David Moores 49
### £91m (£92m)
### Inheritance

## Source of wealth

David Moores owns five per cent of Littlewoods, one of Britain's largest public companies. Last year *BusinessAge* estimated that the Littlewoods empire would be worth £2 billion, if quoted on the stock

## Sir Philip Harris 51
### £91m (£84m)
### Retailing

## Source of wealth

Sir Philip Harris's carpet retailer Carpetright had a spectacular year, with pretax profits rising 79 per cent to £14 million, to August 1994. Since flotation in 1993, the company has taken nine per cent market share and has 149 UK stores.

With 30 more store openings planned and the cash to finance it, Harris's stake as chairman is worth a good £7 million more than last year.

## Personal style

Sir Philip Harris quit school at 15 to take over the running of his father's three carpet shops in London.

They grew into the successful Harris Queensway chain, and he trousered £2 million from the 1978 flotation. Ten years later success dried up so he sold it to James Gulliver for £447 million, trousering another £69 million. James Gulliver renamed the company Lowndes Queensway and retirement seemed an obvious choice for Harris. Not so. He re-started in the carpet retail business in partnership with MFI. The irony is Carpetright has been such a success, the company he sold to Gulliver collapsed.

## Extravagances

Lost £500,000 after guaranteeing an over-

market. We have downgraded Moores's wealth this year, as in our view, the advent of the national lottery has devalued the Littlewoods business substantially, and we now rate the private empire at around £1.7 billion giving him a value of £85 million. He also owns 21 per cent of the 15,000 shares in issue in Liverpool Football club worth some £4 million.

## Personal style

David Moores is the nephew of Sir John Moores, the Liverpool genius who set up Littlewoods Pools after the First World War, with his brother Cecil, David's father. His eldest brother, Nigel, seemed poised to take over the chairmanship of the company when in 1977 disaster struck – he was killed in a car accident.

That same year, David, too, was involved in a car crash with his wife. He was injured but survived. His wife, Kathy Anders – a former Miss England – was less lucky. They had no children.

The Moores family owns 40 per cent of Liverpool Football Club and David took the chairmanship two years ago.

## Extravagances

Football.

draft to former Tory chairman Lord Beaverbrook. Knighted in 1985, he has three sons and one daughter. Was voted Hambros Businessman of the Year 1983, and enjoys cricket, show jumping and tennis.

## Marchioness of Douro 39
### £90m (£82m)
### Inheritance

## Source of wealth

The incredibly beautiful Princess Antonia von Preussen swapped a really grand title for one slightly less grand in 1977 when she married Arthur Wellesley, Marquess of Douro and heir to the Duke of Wellington. She is the youngest daughter of the late Prince Friedrich von Preussen and Lady Brigid Ness, née Guinness. Her twin brother is Prince Rupert who holds their joint stake in the Iveagh Trust.

Princess Antonia and the Marquess have five children from their happy marriage, the eldest of whom is the Earl of Mornington. She is a member of the Royal family and, as such, is entitled to style herself Her Royal Highness.

## Personal style

Beguiling socialite.

## Extravagances

Travel – in the wake of her husband, who probably picks up more air miles than most British executives in pursuit of profit.

## Andrew von Preussen 47
### £90m (£82m)
### Inheritance

### Source of wealth
Andrew von Preussen owes his fortune to the Guinness family. In the 1991 accounts of the Iveagh Trust, he is recorded as holding around 6 per cent. After allowances for inheritances cornered by his two sisters, Antonia and Victoria, Prince Andrew is currently worth around £90 million.

### Personal style
Much photographed celebrity scion of the Guinness family.

### Extravagances
Yachting parties in the Mediterranean.

## Victoria von Preussen 42
### £90 m (£80m)
### Inheritance

### Source of wealth
Victoria, the eldest of the von Preussen princesses, is married to Philip Achache, a director at merchant bankers NM Rothschild. They have two children. Her wealth derives from the master trust of the Guinness fortune, the Iveagh Trustees Ltd, in London.

### Personal style
Very prominent in high society charity work.

### Extravagances
Parties, mostly.

## Duke of Argyll 56
### £90m (£92m)
### Aristocracy

### Source of wealth
The family holdings of the 12th Duke of Argyll have been halved to 80,000 acres since the late 19th century.

Among the losses along the way has been the island of Iona, sold to meet death duties. But remaining assets still mean that he is worth some £90 million – slightly down on last year.

### Personal style
Educated in Switzerland and Montreal. Very history conscious – lists multiple titles in Who's Who. The Duke's temperament is perhaps best illustrated by his lengthy feud with his stepmother, the late Duchess of Argyll, who died last summer. Some years ago, the current Duke was asked what he thought of the proposal that his step-mother's ashes be scattered across the estate. "Under no circumstances," came the reply. "Of course," the Duke added, "if somebody came past in a car and threw

them out of the window there would be nothing I could do."

### Extravagances
Old school attitude. Has been known to refer to the historic dwelling places of his feudal subjects as "mud huts".

He favours country pursuits over City life, and disdains holidaying "Chelsea Highlanders".

## George Moore 65
### £90m (£88m)
### Business

### Source of wealth
George Moore made his fortune in 1987 when he sold his company Moore's Furniture to its management for £80 million. The sale was forced upon him by a heart attack. With interest – and Moore is a canny investor – we have increased his wealth to £88 million.

### Personal style
The retirement is well deserved – Moore started his working life at the age of fourteen working as a joiner repairing toys in Knaresborough, Yorkshire. Four years later he ran a team of skilled tradesman, and by the 1960s was running a huge factory just outside Wetherby.

### Extravagances
All the trappings of wealth, such as a Rolls Royce. And pretty good with DIY round the house.

## Lord Laing 81
### £90m (£80m)
### Food

### Source of wealth
Hector Laing built one of Britain's leading corporations; United Biscuits, the foods group, with a 1991-92 turnover in the region of £3 billion.

At United Biscuits, Laing now enjoys the title of life president. The company he controlled through the past two decades supplies the bulk of Britain's biscuits and controls such brands as KP, Keebler and Ross Young's.

Laing has hardly any shares in United Biscuits now but controls the family wealth believed to be just under £100 million.

### Personal style
A century ago, Hector Laing's grandfather invented the McVitie's Digestive biscuit. A school report once described him as "casual and inclined to be restive under discipline". "My wife says I have dyslexic ears," notes Lord Laing.

In his heyday, Laing was an uncompromising Scots manager with a definitive line in World War Two-style rhetoric – not surprising, given his wartime record as a captain in the Scots Guards, a record which includes the unusual award of a US military medal, the Bronze Star.

After the war, Hector Laing, as he then was, revolutionised McVitie's. Automation upped productivity; sales were helped in part by Laing's tendency to throw packets of biscuits at poorly performing reps.

One of Britain's great postwar industrialists.

### Extravagances
Apart from the Conservative Party, these days, it's mostly gardening. "I find dead-heading azaleas therapeutic," he told The Times. Britain's biscuit baron has little time for highbrow pursuits.

## Earl of Stockton 50
### £88m (£60m)
### Aristocracy

### Source of wealth
Harold Macmillan, the 1st Earl of Stockton, died in December 1986. In his will, the ex-prime minister left a mere £42,000. "If you live to 92, you tend to run down your resources quite effectively," said his grandson, Alexander, who succeeded to the earldom.

Accordingly, three years later, Macmillan's old country mansion was sold off by the family for £5 million. Last year, it was purchased for £5 million by Larry Yung, the son of Rong Yiren, boss of the Chinese government's foreign investment arm, Citic.

But does this mean that the 2nd Earl of Stockton is relatively poor? We think not. He remains head of the family and the family still owns 60 per cent of Macmillan Ltd, the publishing company. Macmillan Ltd made pre-tax profits of £13 million on a turnover of £198 million last year – a highly creditable performance given the economic climate.

The company is private but would be worth a maximum of around £150 million to an outside buyer.

Accordingly, we have valued Stockton at a shade below £90 million. Our increased valuation reflects Macmillan Ltd's higher pre-tax profit figure in 1993 and the fact that it has just paid cash for a fancy new building.

### Personal style
Currently non-executive president of Macmillan Ltd, the earl spends much of his time in the Lords which he enjoys immensely.

### Extravagances
The Earl of Stockton has seen extravagance up close. His wild days of drinking to excess are over.

### Elton John 47
### £87m (£80m)
### Music

#### Source of wealth

The contrast between Elton John and his best pal, George Michael, could not be sharper. While Michael sees his fortune dwindle further and barely scrapes into the *Rich 500*, John continues to increase his wealth at an average rate of £5 million a year. Ironically, John has had just one chart topping single, compared to Michael's seven. Even more ironically, John signed a similarly naive record deal when he was first signed by Dick James Music in 1967. He sued the company and was awarded £5 million in 1986.

In fact, suing people is a profitable business for John, issuing 17 writs for libel against *The Sun*. He has taken £1 million off the newspaper, and last year trousered another £350,000 from the *Sunday Mirror*.

But music remains his main income source. His company, Happenstance, handles his work overseas, paying him £8 million for his services the last time accounts were filed for the year ending 1992. In the five previous years Happenstance paid him at least £5 million. Two years ago he signed the biggest ever music deal in the UK, along with songwriting partner, Bernie Taupin, for £26 million with Time Warner.

He gave up his stake in Watford Football Club in 1989, just about breaking even after 12 years. Elton John uses several offshore holdings to reduce his tax bill, and has invested in publishing, film production and his own record label Rocket Records. We have increased his wealth by £7 million on the back of a new world tour with Billy Joel, royalties from the soundtrack to the new Disney movie, *Lion King*, and his expected 1993 salary at Happenstance. He also sold some of his jewellery in an auction at Sotheby's.

#### Personal style

Were it not for his style of spend, and spend more, Elton John would probably be worth twice as much. Since he found overnight stardom after performing *"Your Song"* in America in 1970, John has kept a loose grip of his affairs, touring and recording "whenever he feels like it." Once married, now homosexual, Elton John was close to a nervous breakdown in the mid-Eighties, following a lengthy drink and drugs binge. The Nineties have virtually been a second birth – apart from financial success, he is an avid charity worker and has set up the Elton John AIDS foundation.

#### Extravagances

The only recreational activity that appears in *Who's Who* is Tennis. Some chance. Just about anything under the sun goes, including dressing up as Donald Duck on stage and having several hair transplants. He has palatial houses and cars that mean little to him anymore as he craves happiness.

### Rupert von Preussen 39
### £86.5m (£82m)
### Inheritance

#### Source of wealth

In the accounts of the Iveagh Trust, which safeguards the Guinness family fortune, Rupert von Preussen is cited as having a six per cent shareholding. However, this is unlikely to give a true picture of Prince Rupert's wealth. Only the three von Preussen brothers are mentioned in the accounts. It is likely, therefore, that their shareholdings must be balanced out to take account of the inheritances enjoyed by their two sisters, Antonia and Victoria.

#### Personal style

As the twin brother of Princess Antonia von Preussen (the Marchioness of Douro), Rupert von Preussen qualifies as the youngest offspring from the 1945 marriage between Lady Brigid, the Guinness heiress, to Prince Friedrich of Prussia, a direct descendant of both Queen Victoria and Kaiser Wilhelm of Germany.

#### Extravagances

Once upon a time a fixture of society nightlife in London. Has now calmed down somewhat.

### John Moores III 42
### £86m (£100m)
### Inheritance

#### Source of wealth

John III owns over 6.5 million shares in Littlewoods, one of Britain's largest private companies. Last year *BusinessAge* estimated that the Littlewoods empire would be worth £2 billion, if quoted on the stock market.

We have downgraded his wealth this year at £86 million with past dividends, as in our view, the advent of the national lottery has devalued the Littlewoods business substantially, and we now rate the private empire at around £1.7 billion.

#### Personal style

John Moores III is the grandson of Sir John Moores, and therefore heir to one of the largest fortunes in Britain. His father, John Moores II, fell out years ago with Sir John, and never became chairman of the company.

Littlewoods now has a non-family chairman, but the shares still rest largely with the family. Looks a likely future chairman if the family ever gets back into the driving seat.

#### Extravagances

Lives the life of Reilly.

### Earl Spencer 30
### £85m (£88m)
### Aristocracy

#### Source of wealth

The brother of the Princess of Wales owns 8,000 acres in Northamptonshire and 5,000 in Norfolk and Warwickshire, an art collection worth more than £10 million and Althorp, one of the finest houses in England.

The value of his late father's estate in 1992 was £88 million, mainly in discretionary trusts. Having criticised the selling of Althorp's treasures and the commercialising of the family name in the last years of his father's life – the influence of his stepmother, "Acid" Raine – he soon found, like an incoming government, that things were worse than he could have imagined in an estate which cost £500,000 a year to run. He could not easily sell family land, and has to keep the house and contents open to the public in order to escape death duties.

Perhaps his most lucrative business initiative has been the use of the estate for corporate hospitality. These measures are not expected to provide for the restoration of Althorp to its traditional glory, and further moves may be necessary. He had few personal assets at his father's death but the best and most accurate valuation of anyone's wealth is a probated estate.

## Personal style

Well-meaning, hard-working and less frivolous sibling of the sometimes daft Diana. Angered residents of his Althorp estate by some high-handed changes and garish yellow signs erected around the estate. Had a well publicised affair with a mistress which, for a short period, threatened his marriage. That is all behind him now.

## Extravagances

A well-publicised trip to Bosnia as a reporter for the US NBC TV network provided a change from being lord of the manor.

## John Menzies 67
## £84.5m (£75m)
## Retailing

## Source of wealth

John Maxwell Menzies is the son of the late John Francis Menzies. John Menzies is as famous and respected a brand name as they come. Founded in 1843 by his grandfather of the same name, John Menzies is Scotland's leading newsagent and the second force to WH Smith in the rest of the UK.

Results to April 1994 show continuing profits growth – up 12 per cent to £34.4 million off £1.23 billion sales – but the City thinks less rosy days lie ahead. The 15 million shares John controls were worth £84.5 million at the beginning of July.

## Personal style

Old Etonian ex-Grenadiers officer John Menzies has been chairman of the firm his great-grandfather founded since 1951. He is also a director of the Bank of Scotland, of the Guardian Royal Exchange group, and a member of the Royal Company of Archers which guards the Queen.

## Extravagances

He farms 2,000 acres in Berwickshire. One of his four daughters, Kate, is famous in the gossip columns as a close friend of the Princess of Wales.

## Thomas Mackie 71
## £84m (New entry)
## Retailing

## Source of wealth

Though Tom Mackie's name appears nowhere in the City Electrical Factors accounts, and the company secretary denies knowing a person by that name, Mackie controls the entire electrical wholesaling and retailing firm through a series of Bermuda shell companies.

Taking that as read, the *Sunday Times* values him at an impressive £186 million. But if he does indeed own 100 per cent of CEF's equity, his net worth is nowhere near that. A quick look at CEF's latest accounts show a company heading for the rocks. It made £9 million after tax on £407 million turnover in the year to April 1992, and paid nearly all of that out in dividends. Yet the accounts also show interest payments of £12 million, on debts of about £120 million, some of which is very expensive junk bond debt. More worrying still, accounts receivable have ballooned to £73 million and stocks to £47 million. The other major asset, a £46 million intangible brand valuation, is curious considering how little-known trading names like Centaur and Proteus are, even within the electrical business.

It is conceivable, therefore, that Mackie might not get net asset value for the company (£52 million) since £46 million of that is the brand valuation. He has however drained an estimated £80 million from the company in dividends over the last ten years. Assuming tax bites and the cost of maintaining his lavish lifestyle, we value Mackie at £84 million.

## Personal style

Mackie was a radio operator for Bomber Command in World War Two, and afterwards became a salesman for GEC. He bought into CEF in 1951, when sales were £28,000, and has grown it aggressively ever since. It now employs 3,800, in 370 nondescript and run-down shops across the country. "He's aiming to make the company twice as big by the year 2000," an "insider" told the *Mail on Sunday* last year. The accounts tell a slightly different story.

## Extravagances

Where do we begin? Mackie resides in Switzerland for tax purposes, in a house on the shores of Lake Geneva, from where he operates nine Swiss and ten Bermudan registered companies.

He owns a £10 million yacht, Klementine, which he bought from the Barclay brothers, a £7 million Gulfstream jet, and two homes in Florida. He has three daughters and a son.

## Earl of Cadogan 80
## £83.5m (£77 m)
## Aristocracy

## Source of wealth

The current accounts of the Cadogan Estate show properties and fixed assets worth a mere £60 million, with income of around £4 million after tax. This would give a maximum valuation of around £65 million on the estate itself, and would not account for other assets of the Cadogan family, which goes back in the aristocracy to 1716. This is a much lower estimate than previous ones, but there is no trace of a vast pile of hidden assets offshore, as there are with some similar estates.

## Personal style

Old soldier, educated Eton and Sandhurst, who served in Second World War. Sufficiently annoyed by the government's reform of leasehold law to withdraw financial support from the Conservative Party.

The estate and the wealth remain in the hands of the current Earl – a much decorated soldier in the Second World War – through family trusts, although the Earl's son, Viscount Chelsea, now runs the company on a day-to-day basis.

Twice married, firstly to a daughter of Lord Churston, a great country grandee and landowner, he has one son and three daughters. The estate itself, which is London-based, was built up through a series of dynastic marriages between the Cadogans, the Sloanes and Cheynes in the 18th century. All three families are commemorated by having their names on streets and squares in the area.

## Extravagances

The family home in Chelsea's Cadogan Square.

## Peter Kindersley 53
## £83m (£80m)
## Publishing

## Source of wealth

A lot can happen in 12 months and it has all happened to Peter Kindersley. The comeback kid is a better description of Kindersley, rather than chairman of book publisher Dorling Kindersley. In the summer of 1993 Kindersley's quoted publisher of illustrated reference books, such as the *Joy of Sex*, was valued at £180 million, along with a host of successful titles in education and health. Microsoft's 26 per cent stake in the company gave him a credible backbone and his 44 per cent stake put him in the *Rich 500*.

By December 1993 he was heading straight out of the list after a series of disasters: managing director Richard Harman →

was fired for losing interest in the job, key distributor Tiptree botched its computer programme, sending the wrong books to the wrong addresses and two profits warnings were issued.

The shares collapsed 89 pence to 221 pence by Christmas. But Kindersley has achieved a remarkable comeback. In May, Dorling Kindersley produced its first five books on CD-ROM, and Kindersley predicts all titles will be produced in a multimedia form within three years. The City is certainly impressed, pushing the share price back up to 300 pence. With his increased share stake and £1 million of dividends, Kindersley is now worth £83 million.

### Personal style
Kindersley is a natural fighter, whatever the cost. After issuing a second profits warning in December 1993, he bought 50,000 shares himself to restore confidence in the business.

### Extravagances
Art school graduate who spends much of his spare time double-clicking the mouse to show off his new CD-ROM book collection.

## Jarvis Astaire 70
## £83m (£78m)
## Sports

### Source of wealth
Varying estimates have put Jarvis Astaire's fortune at between £10 million and £80 million. We believe the actual amount lies at the top end. Simply as a boxing promoter he has earned £45 million over the last 30 years. As a businessman his income has at least matched that, and he holds a monopoly position in certain areas of sports. His famous partnership with Harry Levene and Mickey Duff operated a cartel which dominated boxing for 20 years from 1963 to 1983.

The golden run only ended with the retirement of Levene when ballsy newcomer Frank Warren saw a chink in the armour and set up as a rival promoter. It indicated the sums of money that Levene, Duff and Astaire had been making in the previous 20 years. Astaire fought hard to keep Warren out, and this is one of the few business battles from which Astaire has ever emerged bruised. From his vast cashflow in boxing he expanded into property in the Fifties, where he has been a substantial player. His main vehicle is called Associated City Properties.

### Personal style
Jarvis Astaire has always believed it is possible to make money simply by arranging to make things happen. There was such a shortage of boxing promoters when he first

started out that he flourished and learned the rules of the game cheaply.

His most conspicuous company over the years has been Viewsport which, as its name suggests, broadcasts live sports events but Astaire has had a wide general business career with share stakes in such diverse operations as jewellers Mappin & Webb, James Goldsmith's Anglo-Continental Group, bookmakers William Hill and Technicolor, the American film processors.

Both of his wives, Phyllis and Nadine, died of cancer. He has a son and daughter from his first marriage. He is now involved with the former wife of Lord Leonard Wolfson of Great Universal Stores, Lady Ruth, who was divorced from her husband in 1991. Lord Wolfson named Astaire in the divorce action.

### Extravagances
None – he is married to the buck.

## Charles Hambro 64
## £82m (£80m)
## Banking

### Source of wealth
As chairman of Hambros plc since 1983, Charles Hambro still holds a small stake in the bank. However, much of his wealth existed in 1986 when the family-controlled Hambros Trust, which owned 49 per cent of the bank, was dissolved, releasing some £50 million.

Hambros plc now has assets of over £5 billion, owning three offshore banks, a

## Marquess of Salisbury 77
## £82m (£74m)
## Aristocracy

### Source of wealth
The 6th Earl of Salisbury's family seat is Hatfield House. In Hertfordshire and Dorset, the Salisbury dynasty own a shade under 20,000 acres. The family's local property holdings are supplemented by

bureau de change, several insurance companies and venture capital companies. Latest results show a 44 per cent jump in group profits to £90.5 million.

Charles Hambro himself has stacked up an impressive array of directorships, including the chairmanship of Guardian Royal Exchange, and a board seat at P&O and Taylor Woodrow. He is also senior honorary treasurer to the Conservative Party.

Hambro's wealth nudges up slightly on the basis of earnings from his hectic lifestyle, but he would probably admit it hasn't been worth the trouble. Several MPs are calling for an investigation into allegations that Guardian Royal Exchange dipped into its £7 billion life fund to invest into a subsidiary sales company. Worse still, one of the five City high-fliers he appointed to help write off the £19 million Tory overdraft was forced to resign after admitting he had a US court conviction.

### Personal style
Very well connected with the Major establishment, but noted for his lack of interest in politics. Also close to James Goldsmith and Jim Slater. Similar in personality to his father Sir Charles Hambro, who was head of MI6's Special Operations Executive during the Second World War: gruff voiced, establishment and unmoved in a crisis. As a close friend says, "I wouldn't mind crossing Charlie but I'd rather not play poker against him."

### Extravagances
In between waiting for that peerage, spends much time playing golf and shooting.

freeholds in Central London around Leicester Square – including the building which houses the Hippodrome nightclub – and a treasure trove of art works at Hatfield House. This year's valuation reflects the upward move in London property prices.

### Personal style
Sadly, the family gift for diplomacy seems to have waned over the years. In 1956, as a member of a special ministerial committee, the current Marquess of Salisbury told the government of the "growing and imminent potential danger from the uncontrolled immigration of coloured people". Twenty years later, Salisbury became chief of the far-right Monday Club.

### Extravagances
Certainly not interior design. In the past, Salisbury has had trouble with an architect who exceeded his commission and attempted to transform Hatfield House – the words of a High Court judge – from "a rather severe Jacobean house into an Italianate palace". Salisbury refused to pay the excess charges.

### Christina Foyle 83
### £82m (£102m)
### Retailing

## Source of wealth

Christina Foyle's Charing Cross bookshop has sales of around £16 million a year and Foyle owns the property around the shop which is the source of her real wealth.

But she also owns much art and rare books that could be worth up to £6 million. Inside the shop itself there is the Foyles Art Gallery, which has fostered an enormous number of artists since she founded it in the Thirties. Over the years she has bought works by many of her budding artists.

When Miss Foyle's father died in 1963 he left only £118,000 and she has parlayed that into a £100 million fortune. We over-valued her personal wealth last year as we thought she controlled more of the family trusts than she actually does. It turns out she is the beneficiary of only 60 per cent rather than the 100 per cent we assumed. Therefore, we have reclassified her at £82 million.

## Personal style

Christina Foyle's bookshop on the Charing Cross Road is a metropolitan landmark, and remains one of the very few bookshops which can still get a customer almost any book ever printed.

Despite the uncatalogued chaos which even the 83-year-old proprietress once described as "feudal", the shop is prof-itable, and seems to have been so for most of the 60 years since she started working in it. The shop was started by her father and uncle in 1904.

She and her husband have no children and an attempt to train a nephew, Christo-pher, to take over the bookshop failed, though not totally. He was more interested in aircraft than books and is now running Air Foyle, a large air freighting business. It has always been assumed that he would eventually inherit much of the fortune but there are many other family members who will benefit.

## Extravagances

Books, art and her country house at Beeleigh Abbey in Essex.

### Sir Christopher Wates 54
### £80.5m (£80m)
### Construction

## Source of wealth

Sir Christopher Wates saw no significant change to his wealth in the past year, despite mixed fortunes in the Wates Group which consists of a public property arm and private building outfit. In 1993, Wates

building managed to get back into the red with £2.2 million profits before tax. A simi-lar story at Wates City of London, which came back to marginal profit after a £75 million loss in 1992.

Sir Christopher chairs, and owns, Wates Holdings, which accounts for various other interests, and he will be grateful that he owns less than five per cent of Wates City.

A £31 million rights issue in June com-pletely flopped, and the share price hovers around 70 pence. Valued at £145 million, the group could be ripe for a take-over. If anything, Sir Christopher did relatively well, selling £176,000 worth of shares in December.

His wealth is largely an accumulation of salaries and dividends from his 20 years at the Wates Group, which was founded by his grandfather Sir Ronald Wates at the start of the century.

## Personal style

Publicity shy, very much a family man who has done his best to keep the business in the family. Eternal optimist, never downbeat about the huge variations between profit and loss each year.

Knighted in 1989. He is a Church Com-missioner and a trustee of Chatham His-toric Dockyard, the Science Museum and Lambeth Palace Library.

## Extravagances

Lives in some style in Sussex.

### Evan Cornish 74
### £78m (£95m)
### Business

## Source of wealth

Evan Cornish has handed over the Louth-based packaging company he founded 28 years ago, Linpac, to his son Michael. Evan had built Linpac into a £500 million a year turnover group. Unfortunately, Michael delivered a profits slump and Evan's stake in the group has fallen in value as a result.

However, his wealth remains substan-tial, with interests in a number of car deal-erships in the Louth area.

## Personal style

In building up Linpac to a company employing 4,500 people, Evan Cornish either forgot, or decided not tell anyone about himself.

His name was deliberately dropped from all product launches. But, somebody noticed his work, awarding Cornish the CBE.

## Extravagances

Unlike most men with £78 million to spare, Cornish reputedly drives around in a battered family Peugeot.

### Michael Hollingbery 61
### £76.5m (£73m)
### Retailing

## Source of wealth

Michael Hollingbery sold his 30 per cent stake in electrical goods retailer Comet to Woolworths for £54 million. The Comet name still lives on, and Hollingbery still overlooks the business as a non-executive member on the board of Kingfisher plc (the corporate parent of Woolworth).

On the road he is easily identifiable, as he owns the number plate MH1 – an asset worth a cool £40,000. He is also a non-executive director of Wilson (Connolly), the Northamptonshire builders, and of building materials group Hewetson. He has invested his money wisely if not spectacu-larly, and is now worth nearly £80 million.

## Personal style

In 1958, Michael Hollingbery took over the family business – an electrical retailing business in Hull – and became chairman. In the Seventies he took it public. Comet was one of the go-go companies of the era, but hit harder times in the early Eighties recession. His main claim to fame was 'Currys bashing' and he took the mantle of Britain's top electrical retailer away from them. Hollingbery is renowned for his courtesy and quiet charm. He lives in Humberside. He is interested in local Tory Party activities, but keeps a low profile oth-erwise, both politically and socially. He names his hobbies as hunting and shooting: useful when you have your own extensive estate in Scotland to practice on.

## Extravagances

That number plate and an extensive estate in Scotland where he goes hunting and shooting.

### Sir Tom Cowie 71
### £76m (£72m)
### Motor Industry

## Source of wealth

Sir Tom Cowie spent his entire working life building up T Cowie into one of Britain's biggest motor dealerships. Now retired but still life president, his share stake is worth over £60 million in the group, which is cap-italised at just under £400 million. Cowie has other interests, in a bus and coach busi-ness and a hire purchase firm. Add to that a £5 million share sale, and Cowie's wealth goes up to £76 million.

## Personal style

Cowie's father's hobby was repairing and selling second-hand motorcycles. It grew into a full-time business in Sunderland, and the young Cowie, just sixteen, joined as →

company secretary. He has strayed occasionally into other ventures, such as the chairmanship of Sunderland Football Club.

**Extravagances**

Passionate Tory, which in Sunderland is an extravagance. Married twice with eight children.

Enjoys game shooting, walking and music, and wrote his own book, *The Tom Cowie Story*.

BUSINESSAGE LIBRARY

### Mick Jagger 51
### £75.5m (£69.5m)
### Music

(170) 159

**Source of wealth**

In 1963, an unknown rock band staged its first concert at the Railway Hotel in Deptford, after which the five original members split the £7 fee.

Thirty-one years later, Mick Jagger and the boys are about to hit the road again for a world tour that will earn them around £7 million each.

The Rolling Stones' latest album, *Voodoo Lounge*, was released in June, and Virgin is about to re-release a set of the band's original tracks on CD.

If that isn't enough to satisfy Jagger's bank balance, the grandfather of rock is also trousering £500,000 for a deal to market silk ties featuring his infamous lips.

We estimate Jagger's wealth has nudged up £6 million to £75.5 million in the past year, allowing for advance tour fees from sponsors Budweiser, and payments from

Virgin for completing the album.

**Personal style**

Although the music hasn't changed much, Jagger has learned to look after his money thanks to his personal financial advisor, the Bavarian aristocrat banker Prince Rupert of Lowenstein-Freudenburg. All his earnings are now diverted to the Channel island of Sark for tax reasons.

Once the baddest boy of rock, Jagger continues to move higher in society every year. In May, former Canadian Prime Minister Brian Mulroney tried to persuade him to buy his Ministerial plane, the "flying Taj-Mahal", for £36 million.

Jagger said no, on the advice of Prince Rupert. But the truth is he doesn't know, or really care, how much money he has. Asked recently if he was touring again for the money, he said "What about all the beer and all the girls in the front row?"

**Extravagances**

Palatial residences on the island of Mustique, France and Richmond in London means life is now lived at a more modest pace with wife, Jerry Hall and their three children.

much more comprehensible and promised the possibility of bigger profits. Weinberg believed that "since nobody buys insurance, you have to sell it", and set about marketing insurance in a most un-English way.

Weinberg founded Abbey Life, and after a two year struggle to survive got backing from America. Eventually it was bought by one of the backers, ITT.

The late Jocelyn Hambro had seen him in action and made the offer to set up Hambro Life with him. It was a success from the start. Hambro Life was floated after five years in 1976 – Weinberg took an initial £3 million cash – and it was acquired by BAT in 1984 for £664 million. In 1986 it was renamed Allied Dunbar. Weinberg left in 1990.

His third and current venture is the same, again in partnership with Lord Rothschild and called J Rothschild Assurance, but this time without his long time partners Joel Joffe and Sir Sydney Lipworth.

**Personal style**

Highly respected, he is the eternal outsider, even though through his second marriage – to Anouska Hempel, couturier and owner of Blake's Hotel – he became a member of the 'Princess Margaret set'. In 1986, his friend the Duke of Marlborough resigned in protest from the committee of the exclusive Corviglia Club in St Moritz after Weinberg was black-balled amid rumours of anti-semitism.

Weinberg likes to be his own boss and perhaps has a visionary streak. He had a 1967 plan to sell insurance in post offices. He invested in a Welsh gold mine and was sued for allegedly polluting a nearby river. He spent more than a decade developing a hand-held electronic personal organiser with a revolutionary keyboard. It was years ahead of its time but never caught on, and now the company has closed.

**Extravagances**

Only his work. He seems to hate his leisure time.

### Sir Mark Weinberg 64
### £75.5m (£71.5m)
### Finance

(163) 160

**Source of wealth**

Sir Mark Weinberg was born in South Africa in 1931, son of a Latvian emigré who died when he was two. The family had been "in insurance" and Weinberg fulfilled his

father's wish by emulating him. But first he qualified as a barrister, one of the brightest of a brilliant year at Witwatersrand University that included his future colleagues Sydney Lipworth and Joel Joffe.

Weinberg came to Britain in 1961, to an insurance industry shrouded in secrecy and controlled by actuaries. Existing life- assurance policies were fixed interest with bonuses. The new linked policies were

### Paul Hewson (Bono) 33
### £75m (£70 m)
### Music

(191) (165)

**Source of wealth**

Even before Paul Hewson signed a £130 million six-album deal with Polygram in June 1993, his group U2 qualified as very rich rockers indeed. Their breakthrough recording, *The Joshua Tree* (1987) sold 14 million copies – big league status in the rock world. Since then, the band has released two further albums, *Achtung Baby* (1991) and last year's opus, *Zooropa*. Both have been accompanied by apparently continuous – and highly lucrative – worldwide tours. Before the 1993 Polygram deal, U2's members were probably worth around £25 million each. Perhaps a third of that wealth crystallised with the sale of Island Records to Polygram in 1989. U2's 10 per cent stake in Chris Blackwell's company dated back to an earlier Island Records cash crisis which was only resolved when the band sacrificed royalties in return for equity.

Paul Hewson, who shares in a quarter of the band's income, used to live in a Martello Tower – one of Ireland's old seafront look-out stations of the kind portrayed by James Joyce in the novel *Ulysses*.

## Personal style

The band are currently at rest in Dublin, where they have investments in magazines, recording studios and a hotel. Anything but humble. Recently got into trouble for swearing at a televised music awards ceremony.

## Extravagances

Has re-opened the Clarence Hotel, overlooking the River Liffey; once a down-at-heel establishment, now a temporary home for musicians and Hollywood stars who choose to take advantage of Ireland's generous tax laws. His brother owns a late night eaterie down the road, the curiously named *Mr Pussy's*.

## John Stuart Bloor 50
## £75m (£85m)
## Construction

## Source of wealth

Despite investing millions in an attempt to revive the British motorcycle industry, John Stuart Bloor continues to make the *Rich 500* on the back of his construction interests. The last time accounts were filed for building group Bloor Holdings, for the year to March 1992, profits were a healthy £5 million on a £124.8 million turnover. No accounts have been filed for the latest year which may signal a leaner year and we have downgraded him by £10 million to reflect this uncertainty. His 95 per cent stake in Bloor Holdings would value him at £89 million, if it was a quoted company, but we think this is excessive in an industry only slowly rising out of recession.

His Leicester factory producing motorcycles is doing equally well, having captured 13 per cent of the market for bikes over 750 cc. By 1997, production at the factory is expected to treble but up to now it has been a cash drain.

## Personal style

Prefers to keep to himself and read motorcycle magazines in his spare time.

## Extravagances

Motorcycles (surprise, surprise).

## Anwar Pervez 60
## £75m (£70m)
## Retailing

## Source of wealth

Bestway was started by Anwar Pervez in 1976 as a shop in the Park Royal area of West London. It is now a highly computerised cash and carry operation. In the year to June 1993, turnover reached £472 million and the company returned to its 1991 pretax profit level of £14.5 million, having dipped below £12 million in 1992. Pervez owns just under half the shares.

Based on the strong property portfolio (worth more now than its £56 million

## Margaret Thatcher 68
## £75m (£63m)
## Literary

## Source of wealth

In retirement, Margaret Thatcher's appetite for secrecy is undimmed. Organisations that hire her as a speaker sign an all-encompassing non-disclosure statement. However, one organisation recently told *BusinessAge* that the former prime minister hires herself out for £40,000 per speech.

She routinely makes as many as 20 visits to the United States each year. She picked up a large advance from HarperCollins for her memoirs, which were published in October 1993. Worldwide television rights and a lucrative serialisation deal with Rupert Murdoch's *Sunday Times* followed. Curious, then, that the most recent accounts for the Margaret Thatcher Foundation in London (dated December 1992) show net assets of just £250,000.

Clearly, there is more to the foundation than that. In fact, Thatcher's organisation also has operations in the United States,

stated 1992 value) the company is worth about £160 million.

## Personal style

Pugnacious, no-nonsense Pervez is Pakistan's most successful export to the UK. Amid current uncertainty in food retailing, the Bestway chief has gone out of his way to reassure the small grocers and corner shops that are the company's lifeblood that he won't abandon their interests to serve the superstores.

## Extravagances

The richest Pakistani in Britain is gunning for Establishment status. He gave £140,000 to Prince Charles's inner city charity last year, and is tipped for the House of Lords.

Liechtenstein and Switzerland, following a plan drawn up by the West End law firm Glovers, and Lady Thatcher's PR adviser Tim Bell. In its first year of operation, 1991, the Thatcher Foundation set itself a target of £12 million in donations to meet operating costs. Further substantial sums may have been contributed by donors such as the Sultan of Brunei, said to have punted $5 million into the fund. Chinese industrialist Li Ka-shing added another million. The bulk of donations from the Middle East and Far East appear to be routed through Liechtenstein, where the Foundation has charitable status. The Liechtenstein office is the only one of the Thatcher Foundation's offices to offer the double advantage of secrecy and tax breaks to both donor and recipient.

When the Charity Commissioners turned down the Foundation's application for charitable status in 1991, the London branch was set up as a private company. Trustees included Mark Thatcher, former Conservative Party treasurer Lord McAlpine and Sir Geoffrey Leigh, head of Allied Land and once an energetic fundraiser for the Conservative Party.

Denis Thatcher's preferred option for the family fortune – an offshore trust – was turned down by advisers as being politically risky.

## Personal style

The Iron Lady denies she is worth anything like the figure we attribute to her. She denies she is even worth £5 million. But the elaborate tax smokescreen she has developed would not be worth it for that sort of money. We estimate that she can easily earn that amount in four months.

## Extravagances

She loves being busy and gets irritable on holidays. She is working and accumulating wealth to pass on to Mark. She dreams of a rich Thatcher dynasty. She has achieved her aim.

## Patricia Kluge 47
## £74m (£70m)
## Inheritance

### Source of wealth

Even a blockbuster specialist like Jackie Collins wouldn't have the nerve to incorporate Patricia Kluge's life story in sex and shopping novel.

Kluge – nee Patricia Rose – started out life as the penniless daughter of a British insurance manager and an Iraqi mother. Later in life, she became a soft-porn agony aunt, mixing words of wisdom with voluptuous full-frontal nude portraits of herself in men's magazines. Then she found the basis of her whole wealth, via marriage to the one time richest man in America, John Kluge. It didn't last long but it was lucrative. Currently, however, she is the beneficiary of a trust settlement – acquired courtesy of her divorce in 1990 from Kluge.

### Personal style

When in London, likes to get suits made up for herself at Bernard Wetherill, the bespoke tailors in Savile Row. No doubt wears them at board meetings of Kluge Investments back in the US. Meanwhile, she is grooming a 12-year-old son – John Jr – for a career on Wall Street. Appears to have lost money on a venture to produce sports cards adorned with top soccer stars but has fared better with a small Midlands based publishing house she funded.

Her post-divorce relationship with Douglas Wilder, the governor of the state of Virginia, turned heads. She lashed out a few million dollars on his failed bid for the Democratic presidential nomination in 1992.

### Extravagances

Many - and she can affford any she wants. She bought the Mar Lodge estate in Scotland – a forest with stags next to Balmoral – for £7 million.

## Michael Wates 59
## £73m (£70m)
## Construction

### Source of wealth

With his younger cousin Sir Christopher, Michael runs the construction side of the Wates empire and has a 4.77 per cent stake in the quoted property arm, Wates City of London.

The construction division faired well in 1993, coming back from the red to return a £2.2 million pre-tax profit despite poor trading conditions. Like his cousin, he hasn't suffered much from the lower valuation of the property business – just £145 million on the stock market. If anything, Michael's wealth, built up since he joined

the family business in 1959, is slightly up because of the improved performance of Wates Construction.

### Personal style

Unlike most counterparts in the rough and tough construction industry, Michael is better known as Mr Smoothie for his quite unassuming style. If customers don't pay him, he just says: "Please pay me."

### Extravagances

Very keen on racing, and was once the chairman of the British Bloodstock Agency and Thoroughbred Breeders Association. He successfully breeds horses himself.

## Richard Dunhill 67
## £72m (£72m)
## Inheritance

### Source of wealth

Richard Dunhill is the grandson of Alfred Dunhill, founder of the famous Dunhill company some 100 years ago. Alfred created the House of Dunhill, tobacconists to the rich. By 1930, he had moved into designer watches and pens. He gradually sold his shares to Rothmans.

### Personal style

His life has been blighted by the fact his playboy son, Christopher, was jailed in 1987 for drug-related offenses. Thanks to his grandfather, life otherwise has been rather pleasant.

### Extravagances

He lives in some style in Buckinghamshire.

## Lynn Wilson 54
## £71m (£62.75m)
## Construction

### Source of wealth

Lynn Wilson has the distinction of being chairman of one of the most successful construction companies of the past decade, Wilson Connolly. Ignoring the recession and the competition, the group returned £28.2 million pre-tax profits in 1993, up £11 million. The City is more than impressed, valuing Wilson Connolly at £369 million. Lynn Wilson's 27 million shares are now worth £54 million and he's just collected £770,000 in dividends. With past dividends and salaries, his current wealth is up to £71 million.

The Northamptonshire housebuilder was founded by his father, Connolly, before the Second World War, and passed on to Lynn and his brother Con. Con plays no role but holds a 10.2 per cent stake. Lynn is doing a good enough job on his own, with housing sales up a third and even the property arm of the group managing to break even.

### Personal style

Much of Wilson's success is down to the hiring of Mike Robinson in the late Seventies. Robinson made the housebuilding side the best known in Britain, by the savvy acquisition of land – a strategy still paying off today. Wilson himself concentrated on keeping overheads down, saying no to the helicopter and grand executive office that most building chairmen take for granted.

Robinson, who went on to become managing director, tragically drowned four years ago in Portugal. Since then, Lynn Wilson has shown he has what it takes to run the show himself.

### Extravagances

A keen member of the MCC, and chairman of Northamptonshire Cricket Club since 1990. Also likes golf, horse racing and shooting. Wilson lives in Northamptonshire with his two sons.

## Sir Bernard Ashley 68
## £71.5m (£85m)
## Retailing

### Source of wealth

Sir Bernard Ashley founded the Laura Ashley chain with his wife, Laura, 41 years ago. By 1979, the couple were multi-millionaires with a retailing and manufacturing empire that spanned the globe.

Laura died in 1985, and last year Sir Bernard stepped down as chairman. Over the past few years he has gradually cut his share stake, raising over £50 million. He is honorary life president of the group, and currently pursuing the development of Ashley Inns, a chain of upmarket hotels in Wales and America. With this in mind, we have slightly upgraded his wealth.

### Personal style

With his wife Laura, Sir Bernard founded what was originally known as Ashley Mountney. They struggled for 14 years to make it profitable, but eventually her creative talent for spotting designs and his sheer hard work paid off. Laura's death came on the eve of the stock market flotation, which meant she missed out on becoming one of Britain's richest women at the time. Without her input, the group struggled to survive, and only the appointment of a new chief executive saved the Ashley fortune. The cost was that none of the family, which in total is worth £200 million, has any input in the business.

The Ashleys have two sons, David and Nick, both worth over £40 million each, and two daughters – with £15 million each.

### Extravagances

Sailing and flying. He has a yacht in the Bahamas, and lives for most of the year in Brussels for tax reasons.

### David Wickens 74
### £71m (£65m)
### Motor Industry

## Source of wealth
Six years ago, David Wickens sold his company, British Car Auctions, for £182 million to Michael Ashcroft's ADT; the name was then changed to ADT Auctions.

Wickens had assembled the chain of auction houses by snapping up independents during the Seventies, including one of Bernie Ecclestone's operations. He also bought into the Lotus car company. Supplementing these mainstream ventures were a remarkable series of shares deals and investments, rarely confined to the UK.

## Personal style
Old rogue with a glimmer in his eye. Said to be fond of the odd cocktail. Used to boast a formidable temper when aroused. In these respects, he was not much different from his old pal and sometime partner, Denis Thatcher. A mainstay of the British business scene for many years, Wickens is now enjoying his retirement. He has recently been active in Gibraltar, and lives nearby in a villa outside Malaga.

## Extravagances
In business terms, few and far between. For a long time, Lotus looked like a self-indulgence. It wasn't. Wickens made a fat profit on its disposal to General Motors.

### David Ashley 39
### £70.5m (£70m)
### Retailing

## Source of wealth
David Ashley is the third Ashley family member to appear in the rich list. Like his brother Nick, it's entirely on the back of his inheritance from the Laura Ashley empire, founded by his parents at the time of his birth.

In the Seventies he had a major input in the group, pioneering its retail operations in America. As with the rest of the family, his mother's death in 1985 led to their severance from the business.

## Personal style
David divorced his first wife in 1984, a marriage break-up that was to have dire consequences on his late mother, who entered a Wiltshire religious retreat to get over the shock.

A year later he married the beautiful catwalk model, Caroline Pagano.

## Extravagances
David and Caroline are one of the world's super-rich couples, and they live in some style. But, like the other Ashleys, their priority is secrecy.

### Earl of Yarborough 31
### £70m (£65m)
### Aristocracy

## Source of wealth
The Earl of Yarborough is one of only two practising Moslems in the House of Lords. On his death in 1991, his father, the seventh earl, left his son an estate valued at over £60 million.

The family estate covers some 28,000 acres in Lincolnshire and South Humberside; its centrepiece is Brocklesby House, surrounded by parklands which contain grottoes and a temple. The Yarborough art collection includes works by El Greco and Reynolds.

## Personal style
Low-key; flowing robes and visits to the Mosque.

## Extravagances
That magnificent house.

### Apurv Bagri 34
### £70m (New entry)
### Business

## Source of wealth
Apurv Bagri, son of Raj Bagri, is now fully in control of the family commodity dealers Minmetco, which turned over £500 million worldwide last year. Raj, who started his career as a filing clerk in a Calcutta metals business, took his passage to England in the late 1950s and worked his way through the markets to the ownership of metal and commodity dealers Minmetco, which, if floated today, would be worth as much as £75 million.

To this can be added manufacturing companies (non-ferrous metals) based in Malaysia (which made 50,000 tonnes of copper products last year), Canada and India. Together with Minmetco they form the Metdist Group.

## Personal style
Raj Bagri has transferred his entire shareholding to his son although he still takes an active role in business and also chairs the London Metals Exchange. While Apurv is a full British citizen, both son and father talk of returning to India with their fortune and setting up metals businesses there. Apurv's sister, Amita, has made a dynastic marriage into the Indian business family, the Birlas.

## Extravagances
Both Raj and Apurv furiously deny possessing anything like the wealth popularly ascribed to them. Consequently neither leads a flashy lifestyle – Raj, for instance, lives quietly in St. John's Wood, London.

### Robert Iliffe 49
### £70m (£75m)
### Media

## Source of wealth
In 1975, Robert Iliffe, then a youthful 30 years of age, took over as chairman of the family newspaper group that included the *Birmingham Post & Mail* and the *Cambridge Daily News*. For several years now, Robert Iliffe has also chaired the Yattendon Investment Trust. Now he has inherited the fortune of his childless uncle, Edward Langton, the 2nd Earl of Iliffe, 75.

The company owns newspapers, marinas, healthcare businesses and hotels in Britain, the USA and Canada. Yattendon, which is named after the family seat, had another mediocre year in 1993 – its 5,000 berths at 17 marinas continued to suffer from slack business.

The controlling shares in Yattendon are held by the family, under a settlement made in 1969. In 1987, Yattendon sold a controlling share in its newspaper properties – including the *Coventry Evening Telegraph* and the *Birmingham Post & Mail* – to US publisher Ralph Ingersoll for £60 million. Robert Iliffe retained shares in the Ingersoll group. Yattendon continued to publish the *Cambridge Evening News* and other newspapers in the Herts/Essex area through its subsidiary, Iliffe Newspapers. These made a small loss on increased turnover in 1993.

The family also has shipping interests: in 1987, a Yattendon subsidiary purchased the Isle of Wight ferry service from Sea Containers for an estimated £110 million. Yattendon's investments in the USA centred on Bemrose Yattendon Inc, the advertisement printing firm, which was jointly owned with Bemrose Corp. In May, Bemrose announced its buy-out of Yattendon's 50 per cent share in the venture. Iliffe pocketed a small fortune from this transaction – a rare bright spot on the financial horizon.

## Personal style
Conservative gentleman. A question mark now hangs over his business abilities.

## Extravagances
Boats and (old) cars.

### Sir Ian Wood 52
### £70m (£64m)
### Business

## Source of wealth
Sir Ian Wood owns almost half the shares in Britain's largest independent oil services company – the John Wood Group.

Pre-tax profits for 1993 were up 3 per cent to £19.1 million, and Wood's stake in the group is now worth £70 million. The group has a healthy cash flow but Wood is not celebrating the increase. The company's growth is some way short of the 20 per cent a year he is targeting, and now plans to concentrate on overseas interests, notably gas turbine repairs.

**Personal style**

At long last, received a knighthood in the 1994 New Year honours list, for his contribution to building up the North Sea oil industry. The company is based in Aberdeen with operations on the East Coast, Texas, Oklahoma and Kuwait. It holds a five-year contract for design and engineering at three of BP's North Sea oil fields, which is worth £150 million.

**Extravagances**

Is reputed to travel economy class. Generally quiet except when it comes to debating the economic future of Scotland. Enjoys squash, hill-walking, reading and art.

## David Parker 54
## £70m (£66m)
## Business

**Source of wealth**

David Parker stood down as chairman and managing director of the Sherwood Group this year, 26 years after buying it for £12,000. But he is staying on as executive chairman and holding on to his 35 million shares in the quoted group, which are worth £47 million to him.

Sherwood Group was established in 1947, making glamorous ladies' lingerie, and now has the Burton Group and BHS among its clients. Floated on the Unlisted Securities Market in 1986, it moved to a full listing in 1993. Pre-tax profits in 1993 were up 9 per cent to £18.5 million on a £153 million turnover – also up. The company is performing well, despite the recession, and the purchase this year of the New York lace company, Touch, should add to bottom line profits, and Parker's wealth, next year.

Parker's personal wealth has slipped slightly because of the poorer stock market. But on top of his £47 million worth of shares, we have added past dividends and salaries, including £690,000 of dividends last year, putting him on £63 million. We feel this is an undervaluation, given the latest results and outlook. A fairer company valuation – what it would be worth if sold – puts his personal wealth at £70 million.

**Personal style**

An ambitious man who was once a Boots management trainee. He took over Sherwood in 1968 with a sleeping partner who has since left.

**Extravagances**

Jetting around the world to check out the latest trends in ladies' lingerie.

## Ronald Goldstein 57
## £70m (£68m)
## Retailing

**Source of wealth**

Ronald Goldstein holds £50 million-worth of Kingfisher shares as a result of selling his 300 store Superdrug chain in 1987 to the Woolworths company. He had more, but has sold some over the years, yielding a considerable sum in cash. His money is well protected from overly high rates of tax by Jersey offshore trusts. It was a stroke of genius to take the payment in Kingfisher shares, as it is the rise and rise of the share price which has made Goldstein such a very, rich man.

The genius has been somewhat offset by the fact that 1993 was a disastrous year for his investment in the Volume One bookshop chain. This went into receivership on Christmas Day. Goldstein is believed to have lost a few million in Volume One. We have, however, raised his wealth because Kingfisher dividends have far outweighed his losses. With dividends and share sell-offs we rate him at £70 million in 1994.

**Personal style**

Ronald Goldstein has always been more savvy than his younger brother Peter and therefore much wealthier. He is regarded as a wunderkind of retailing. Superdrug was an amazing conjuring trick on the British public. Although it was punted as a discount drugs store, in fact prices were exactly the same as the local chemist charged for many items. Ron Goldstein's trick was making it seem cheaper and there was no competition.

**Extravagances**

Life in the grand style now he is nearing sixty.

## Len Jagger 69
## £68.5m (£65.5m)
## Business

**Source of wealth**

Len Jagger sold his Yorkshire motor chain in 1972 to Thomas Ward, later an RTZ company, for a sum approaching £20 million. His share was £12 million. He then bought Rank Hovis McDougall's non-food interests and reversed them into a public company called United Engineering Industries. UEI bought brand names such as Quantel and Cosworth along the way. With Quantel came Peter Michael, the young entrepreneur who built the group up. Len Jagger sold out his stake in 1982 and Peter Michael then sold the whole group to Carlton Communications. The Cosworth and Quantel investments had

proved particularly inspired.

In 1983, Jagger, by then living in Jersey, met John Foulston, the entrepreneur, and invested in Foulston's fledgling Atlantic Computers. The rest was history. Under Foulston's tough management style the company prospered and went public. In 1987, however, John Foulston was killed in a motor racing accident at Silverstone. Jagger had invested in Foulston, and was glad to accept an offer from John Gunn, of British & Commonwealth, for his by then diluted stake. This deal netted him some £50 million.

His final profit from Atlantic was in the region of £40 million, and earlier gains and careful management have increased that to some £68 million.

**Personal style**

In his latter years, he was a passive investor who backed his hunches. He was happy to keep backing Atlantic while Foulston remained in charge but looked for an exit after he died.

**Extravagances**

Lives quietly in the Channel Islands and eschews the trappings of tycoonery.

## Peter Greenall 41
## £68m (£47m)
## Drink

**Source of wealth**

Things are beginning to settle down at the family brewers-turned-pub owners. The company, which can trace its ancestry back to Greenall & Co (established in 1762) is now incorporating JA Devenish, a West Country pub chain, into the new-look group under MD Peter Greenall. Greenalls now boasts more than 2,000 pubs.

Finally, the family has recently surrendered many generations of voting domination by allowing humble souls like City fund managers actually to exercise voting power with the shares which they have acquired: the non-voting 'A' shares were swapped into voting ordinary shares, heralding a new era in corporate governance in the realm of family-dominated business empires.

Profits last year improved 20 per cent to £68.3 million, as more people ate Greenalls pub food. Peter Greenall's own stake is worth £53 million. These shares generate an income of around £1.4 million, roughly equal to his salary. With wealth accumulated over the years (those dividends every year can't be bad), and a recent share sale, his worth is up to £68 million this year.

**Personal style**

The Eton and Cambridge-educated Hon Peter Gilbert Greenall, eldest son and heir to the Jersey-resident, 64-year-old 3rd Baron Daresbury, doesn't really look or sound like an aristocratic family business-man. But he does have solid business sense, and has been on the Greenalls board for ten years.

A London Business School graduate, he had no qualms about getting out of brewing: the Greenalls business was national retailing, not regional brewing, he concluded. Probably his biggest problem was in convincing his father, a former Greenalls chairman, of the logic of his strategy.

### Extravagances

When not working at Greenalls or spending time with his wife and four sons, he works as chairman of Aintree racecourse. Just don't mention the 1993 Grand National in his presence.

## Robin Fleming 62
## £68m (£26m)
## Banking

### Source of wealth

Robert Fleming – Robin to friends and family – is the chairman of the eponymous merchant banking group which was founded 120 years ago.

It's been a vintage year for Flemings. After-tax profits doubled to £145.7 million. The bank is mining a particularly rich seam through its Hong Kong joint venture, Jardine Fleming, which pitched up US$202 million profits last year.

On the current merchant bank sector average p/e ratio of 11, the company would be valued at a whopping £1.6 billion. Robin Fleming's personal 1.1 per cent stake in the family company is worth £22.5 million. He also controls a family trust of nearly 3 million shares (6 per cent), giving an annual income of £1.5 million, part of the 40 per cent stake controlled by the Fleming family. We have allocated a quarter of this trust to Fleming personally: for tax purposes the rest is likely to be in his children's names. As chairman he earned a salary of £147,000, and also £250,000 in dividends, before tax.

Dividend income plus Fleming's various inheritances and land holdings – and shrewd investment of his own cash – will have lifted Fleming's wealth to a total in excess of £65 million. He owns property in Bicester, Oxfordshire, and the Black Mount estate on the shores of Loch Tulla, near Bridge of Orchy, Argyllshire.

### Personal style

An Eton and Sandhurst man, and the son of an army Major, he served in the Royal Scots Greys between 1952 and 1958, at which point he left the army to join the family firm. He became deputy chairman in

1986, before taking over the top spot three years ago.

The first Robert Fleming Esq launched the investment trust movement in 1873 in Scotland as a means of investing the profits from his Dundee jute business. The company still counts fund management as a core business, particularly through its unit trust operation, Save & Prosper, but is now an all-round merchant bank, with a City securities arm as well as its corporate finance activities.

## Blanche Buchan 56
## £67m (£60m)
## Inheritance

### Source of wealth

Blanche Buchan is the second daughter of Lord Howard de Walden. She, like her sisters, has 25 acres around London's Harley Street which her father gave to her. In 1961 she married Captain David Sinclair Buchan, a Scottish landowner, and they live at Ellon in Aberdeen with a town house in West London.

She, with her three sisters, will become joint heiress to her father's title when he dies, the title being one of those which passes in the female line.

### Personal style

Married a seriously military man (Sand-

## John Apthorp 59
## £67m (£65m)
## Retailing

### Source of wealth

John Apthorp's company Bejam was taken over by Iceland, then a smaller company, in a bloody takeover battle in 1989. Surprisingly, Apthorp, with nearly a third of the equity, lost a takeover battle which he should have won.

But he did manage to exact a very high price of £240 million for the company.

Apthorp took involuntary retirement, as working with his old rivals was obviously impossible. His only consolation was that he was a lot richer than the Iceland Group's Walker brothers who bought the company. He invested his money in a couple of high profile ventures, International Data and Communication plc, the quoted lists supplier, and Majestic Wine Warehouses, a private company. Neither have been smooth rides but he doesn't seem to have lost a lot of money. He paid tax on a lot of his windfall, and we estimate his wealth today, with past dividends, at £67 million.

### Personal style

John Apthorp was one of the pioneers of frozen food retailing in Britain, building up

Flemings got into hot water last year for paying three of its London-based directors a total of £4.5 million - but City observers believe those salaries pale in comparison to the wads being trousered out in Hong Kong by Jardine Fleming bosses. Flemings also has the reputation of employing otherwise unemployable former Guards officers to act as executive gofers.

### Extravagances

He has stocked the Fleming HQ with an unrivalled collection of Scottish art.

DES O'NEILL

hurst, Berlin, Malaya, Singapore), but it is unknown whether she also shares her husband's apparent passion for needlework.

### Extravagances

A home in Marbella.

the Bejam chain which was eventually floated on the stock market. Ironically, the Bejam brand name – once the most famous in frozen foods – has now disappeared from the high street. It has been replaced by the Iceland fascia of the publicly-quoted former rival of Bejam, run by the Walker brothers.

### Extravagances

Likes dabbling in small companies with potential.

## Elliot Bernerd 49
## £66.5m (£32m)
## Property

### Source of wealth

We valued Elliot Bernerd cautiously and the *Sunday Times* valued him extremely optimistically when Chelsfield was a private company. Turned out the truth was somewhere in the middle.

He has a very clearly defined 45,515,506 shares in Chelsfield that were recently valued at £77.4 million – around 29 per cent of a company valued at £266 million. We believe that is the main source of Bernerd's wealth and he probably has some private borrowings that mitigate this. However, we are willing to take that value as fair even though the stock market appears content to value Chelsfield at five per cent more than its latest asset value. Including debts we make Bernerd worth £66 million.

No wonder Bernerd is nicknamed the patrician magician in the City. Two years ago things looked bad for his company. Profits of £16.7 million in 1991 dissolved into massive losses for the following two years.

The extraordinary gains from the Wentworth Golf Club development have helped to improve the picture, but there is not much other good news on the horizon.

Yet Elliot Bernerd survived the recession when many thought he wouldn't. He also managed to float a company that had suffered startling losses for the previous two years.

## Personal style

The patrician magician with slicked-back hair seems to take it all in his stride, just as he has the various controversies which have surrounded him over the years. Bernerd was born in the dying days of World War II and therefore missed out on the first great property boom of the Sixties. He was old enough, however, to fully indulge in the Seventies and emerge relatively unscathed from the bust of 1974-75.

He operates from a subdued head office in Brook Street with a glorious garden leading to a mews at the back which houses his staff. His reputation is as the man with an eye for the main chance. He is often in and out of deals at a profit where no one else can see an angle.

## Extravagances

Money and deals.

## James Moores 32
## £66m (£73m)
## Inheritance

## Source of wealth

James Moores holds around 4 million shares in Littlewoods, giving him an estimated worth of about £66 million including dividends paid over the years. Last year *BusinessAge* estimated that the Littlewoods empire would be worth £2 billion, if quoted on the stock market. We have downgraded James's wealth this year, as in our view, the advent of the national lottery will batter the Littlewoods business substantially. Accordingly we now rate the private empire at around £1.7 billion.

## Personal style

James Cecil Scott Moores is the great-nephew of Littlewoods founder Sir John Moores, and the eldest child of Nigel Moores, who was killed in a tragic car crash in 1977.

## Extravagances

He is hardly ever seen about town.

BUSINESSAGE LIBRARY

## Brian Souter 40
## £65.5m (£47.5m)
## Transport

## Source of wealth

The history of Stagecoach Holdings, Britain's largest independent bus operator, is one of phenomenal growth. The Perth-based company, formed in 1980 with capital of £25,000 and just two coaches, now operates three thousand buses – not only in the UK but overseas as well, in countries like Kenya, Malawi and New Zealand. Thirteen years after its birth, Stagecoach is worth £230 million on the stock market, with a turnover of £153 million in 1993. Souter's 32 million shares are worth £58.5 million. When the

## Michael Green 46
## £65.2m (£44.7m)
## Media

## Source of Wealth

If Michael Green's power could be quantified in money terms, we'd have to pitch his wealth at twice its current level.

Green has become the most powerful man in British television – too powerful some might say. He now controls over 30 per cent of ITV's advertising revenue, and the London weekday and Midlands broadcasting footprint has one of the most affluent and free-spending viewerships. Carlton also has stakes in GMTV and ITN, making Green the frontrunner for chairman of a possible agglomerated ITV plc.

But credit the City with some intelligence: the Central Television takeover at the beginning of the year was expected to push Carlton's market capitalisation well over £2 billion, adding a tidy £15 million to Green's paper fortune. Carlton is only worth about £1.9 billion at the moment, twenty per cent more than last year, valuing

company was floated on the stock exchange, it netted Brian Souter £4 million cash. He now controls 26.8 per cent of Stagecoach Holdings plc.

## Personal style

Brian Souter, an accountant who was a bus conductor in his student days, set up the company with his sister Ann Gloag. Their father donated the redundancy money he received after forty years as a bus driver.

The timing was ideal: government deregulation of the bus industry enabled private operators to enter business. In 1987, the National Bus Company was broken up, and Stagecoach began its spending spree. Its operations are now to be found in the north and east of Scotland, Cumbria and the Midlands – and in some pretty obscure parts of the world, too, like Malawi. But Stagecoach has set its sights still further afield: there are 32 remaining municipal bus operators and another ten companies within London Buses which the government has insisted will be privatised. If it ever happens, Souter will be first in line.

There has been one venture which defeated the company: the private rail experiment. In 1992 Stagecoach leased four coaches on the East Coast InterCity overnight service between Aberdeen and London, but the experiment proved unprofitable and subsequently folded.

## Extravagances

Winning is his extravagence. He usually does.

Green's 5.3 million shareholding at £47 million. It seems that analysts have finally added up all Carlton's equity and debt issues and come with a figure that's higher than the asset value.

Green's wealth is embellished by £10 million-worth of share sales and a significant art collection. He is also the sole shareholder in Tangent Industries Ltd, the holding company in which most of his Carlton shares are parked. Its assets (other than those shares) were worth £12 million in March 1993.

His 1993 income from Carlton was £1.2 million, up £200,000 on the previous year.

## Personal style

Green left school with just four 'O' Levels and joined a printing company as a compositor. By 1960 he had made his first acquisition, the loss-making Direct Mail Centre. He sold its headquarters and ploughed the money back in, renaming the company Tangent Industries.

Tangent moved into photography and mail order catalogues. Its growth was spurred on by Green's first marriage to Janet Wolfson, the daughter of Lord Wolfson, owner of Great Universal Stores.

In 1983 he reversed Carlton into financier Nigel Wray's Fleet Street Newsletter. (Wray still sits on the Carlton board). That year he also bought Mike Luckwell's Moving Picture commercial production company. Between the three of them they set in motion the development of Carlton into the huge media conglomerate that it is today.

### Mark Knopfler 44
### £65m (£57.5m)
### Entertainment

## Source of Wealth
As the lead man and songwriter with Dire Straits, Mark Knopfler has made a fortune. More an album band than singles oriented, their 1985 *Brothers in Arms* LP became the biggest selling UK album and CD of all time. And it set the CD ball rolling. Ironically, considering the great wealth the medium has brought him, Knopfler was one of the prominent musicians campaigning for cut-price CDs. As a side note, Dire Straits' manager and longtime Knopfler confidant Ed Bicknell was one of the

### Michael Rees 49
### £65m (£59m)
### Finance

## Source of wealth
Michael Rees owns about 8.75 million shares in the private Benfield group, a Lloyd's reinsurance broker. This represents an 18 per cent share in the company, making him worth nearly £65 million, including a payment which he received on selling his share in a similar business some years ago plus this year's dividends.

## Extravagances
Every takeover has precipitated a flood of new Carlton debt and equity. One day such largesse may catch up with Green. His extensive art collection, however, is rumoured to have been paid for with cash. He has a magnificent home in the country and London. He is seen most mornings in London in dressing gown and slippers retrieving the newspapers from his front step.

George Michael camp's star witnesses in the recent court action with Sony. Bicknell believes that had Michael won, Knopfler would have been several million better off from contract re-negotiations.

Dire Straits is an international force, and their 1985 album also went to number one in 24 countries. Knopfler continues to receive large royalty cheques, which amounted to just over £5 million in 1992, according to the accounts of his two companies, Chariscourt and Straitjacket songs.

Mark Knopfler has also made a substantial amount of his wealth from performing. Dire Straits undertook the biggest world tour in rock history, lasting a total of three years, and ending a couple of months ago. With a £10 million sponsorship by Philips, ticket sales alone were said to have grossed around £140 million. And that didn't include merchandising or album sales.

## Personal style
The ultimate unglamorous rocker, Knopfler's balding pate and croaky voice has always taken the backseat to his soaring guitar and songwriting skills. Recently he has become more of a movie soundtrack writer, following on from the surprising success of his *Local Hero* soundtrack in the early Eighties. His most recent album, *Screenplaying*, is a collection of his movie songs.

## Extravagances
Married with children, Knopfler used to keep a low public profile. Then earlier this year press reports linked him with a glamourous TV actress, with whom he was said to be setting up house in a £1.5 million Chelsea mansion.

Benfield had a remarkable 1992, making £30.6 million profit on turnover of £39.7 million. It followed up with the same performance in a difficult year with a £41.2 million turnover and profits of £31.2 million in 1993. Just launched a re-insurance company that will take on insurance risks itself, it is jointly funded by Benfield and venture capitalists to the tune of £50 million.

## Personal style
The oldest member of a remarkable team that run Benfield.

## Extravagances
Enjoys his money more than most.

### Adrian White 51
### £65m (New entry)
### Construction

## Source of wealth
Until May this year Adrian White was the controversial chairman of the Biwater Group, of one of the world's leading water technology and treatment companies. The last time accounts were filed, for 1992, White returned £16.5 million pre-tax profits on a £260 million turnover. The company operates in 30 different countries.

Valuing the company at £110 million on a modest p/e ratio, White's 28 million share stake is worth in excess of £70 million. However, he has resigned, reportedly to set up a Far East operation. We have therefore assumed a transfer on some shares to new chairman Leslie Jones, and value him at £65 million.

## Personal style
The former salesman started up Biwater from scratch in 1968 with £100 borrowed from his father. The company has always been acclaimed as the top performer in the water industry, winning four Queen's Awards for Export. But the past two years have not been pleasant ones for White. A group of his sub-contractors sent a document to the House of Commons in 1993 claiming Biwater had a great way of making money – not paying anyone. Biwater's many contracts won in Malaysia on the back of Government aid brought another headache after the Pergau dam affair. White announced his resignation in May, officially to work in the Far East, although he is not contactable there.

## Extravagances
A keen Tory, he is on first name terms with many ministers. White has donated over £70,000 to the party, a fact which is clearly unconnected with his role as chairman of the Epsom NHS Trust. White also owns Britain's biggest vineyard, selling 50,000 cases a year.

### Lord Palumbo 59
### £65m (£95m)
### Property

## Source of wealth
It has not been a good year for Lord Palumbo. First, there was family feuding – with his son, Jamie, launching a court action and complaining to the press about the financial terms offered to him by his father. Then, there was the deteriorating balance sheet at Rugarth Investment Trust – the vehicle that controls Lord Palumbo's inheritance from his late father, Rudolph Palumbo, the property developer who

famously destroyed part of St James's Square in the name of a similar combination of concrete and steel. In the year to March 1993, Rugarth's valuation slipped to £64 million. That's one-third down from last year's total. Meanwhile, the British public's hostility to the Palumbo family's mission to sprinkle the streets of London with thoroughly modernist architecture, remains unabated.

**Personal style**

Urbane developer placed under stress by the job of matching high falutin' Modernist ideals with the dirty practicalities of wheeling and dealing.

**Extravagances**

A fixture of the London social whirl. In terms of the great and the good who devote themselves to high art, his name is up there with that of Jocelyn Stevens.

## Anthony Crosthwaite-Eyre 62
**£65m** (£65m)
## Media

**Source of wealth**

Anthony Crosthwaite-Eyre made a fortune in 1987 when he sold his 37 per cent stake in Associated Book Publishing to International Thompson, trousering £65 million personally.

**Personal style**

A man of great timing – the sale was done a week before the stock market crash. The family used to own the Eyre and Spottiswoode publishing company before it was taken over by ABP in the 1960s, with Anthony becoming vice-chairman.

**Extravagances**

Anthony is one of only a handful of people who can trace his roots back to the time of the Crusades. The family has lived around the New Forest for 800 years.

## Duke of Beaufort 65
**£65m** (£55m)
## Aristocracy

**Source of wealth**

Valuing the assets of the Duke of Beaufort, whose home at Badminton is not open to the public (and who, incidentally, has not taken his seat in the House of Lords), is exceedingly difficult. The estate itself is 52,000 acres, enormous by English standards, but land prices have fallen by as much as 60 per cent in the agricultural sector and there is little demand for establishments as grand as Badminton.

The art treasures at Badminton have been valued at £8.1 million, equal to just two of his Canalettos. The Duke has operated over the years as a fine art dealer, which

suggests that both the assumption about what pictures he has and their value is wrong.

**Personal style**

He is married to an aunt of the present Marquess of Bath, who has recently raised money for charity by abseiling down the Royal Hospital in Gloucester. The Duke's eldest of three sons is known as the Marquess of Worcester, whose own son is known in turn as the Earl of Glamorgan.

Tall, thin and patrician he dabbles in business. Supporter of fox hunting – believes it offers practitioners "invaluable discipline". He teamed up with with master financier Sir James Goldsmith and Australian mega-millionaire Kerry Packer in the 1988 £13.5 billion bid for BAT.

**Extravagances**

Used to be a fine art dealer; truly appreciates both what he owns and what he would like to own.

## Earl of Radnor 66
**£65m** (£60m)
## Aristocracy

**Source of wealth**

Definitely not vulgar sightseers. The supremely patrician Earl of Radnor (full name: Jacob Pleydell-Bouverie) has refused for years to open his home, Longford Castle, near Salisbury, to the great British public. In 1976, he remarked: "The people who come around may be very nice. But you don't want to see or hear them all the time. I am told that you can even smell them and eventually your house becomes rather like a station." This comment provoked a Labour back-bencher to call for the Earl's abolition: "He will then be forced to get a job with all the other smelly mortals of the earth."

Admittedly, the Earl of Radnor doesn't need to let visitors poke into every corner of his home. The family owns two substantial freeholds just off Fleet Street, a large chunk of Folkestone, a heavyweight art collection and around 10,000 acres near Longford Castle.

**Personal style**

Old style land magnate. Went to Cambridge – but only for a degree in agriculture.

**Extravagances**

Wives – three of 'em so far.

## Israel Wetrin 47
**£75m** (£63.5m)
## Computers

**Source of wealth**

Israel Wetrin's computer group Elonex is prospering. Most recent accounts, to April

1993, show an after-tax profit of £6.2 million (up, thanks to a tax credit, from 1992's £5 million). This is success on any terms, but for an industry which has claimed many corporate casualties, it is particularly impressive.

Elonex is now planning a £5.5 million plant in Cumbernauld, outside Glasgow, which will manufacture up to 100,000 PCs a year, and perhaps twice that by 1996. So far, the company has a UK market share of around 5 per cent, making it the sixth-largest supplier.

A flotation on the stock market has long been mooted, and the company, 100 per cent owned by Wetrin, would likely be valued on a p/e of around 15. Wetrin's company might be worth something like £100 million. Viglen, a direct competitor, was sold to Amstrad recently on much less generous ratios. Therefore we value Wetrin cautiously at a current £75 million. High enough.

**Personal style**

Israel Wetrin, like all the best personal computer assemblers, started in a small flat – in his case, in Finchley, north London. Seven years on, he sells his Elonex computers direct to the public and corporate buyers through advertising and an in-the-field sales force. Wetrin is known as a man who runs a very tight ship, to the extent of personally vetting his employees' expenses claims – although he admits to paying his staff above-average rates. He uses graphology (handwriting analysis) to vet job applicants.

**Extravagances**

Few: he can hardly afford them. Wetrin took a paycut from £280,000 to £99,000 in 1992, but raised it to £120,000 in 1993.

## Earl of Inchcape 51
**£64.5m** (£62m)
## Inheritance

**Source of wealth**

In March, the current earl – known until then as Viscount Glenapp – succeeded his late father who closed out his career as life president at Inchcape plc, the global services and trading group which he ruled over as executive chairman from 1958 to 1982. The earl's death marked the end of the Mackay family's influence on the company.

The family's fortune was founded in the Far East. The first Earl of Inchcape created one of Britain's great colonial trading dynasties, and was elevated to the peerage in 1911 after a lifetime of toil in banking and shipping in India and Hong Kong. The late Earl's stepmother was the daughter of the British-sponsored Rajah of Sarawak (now Brunei); links to the oil business were prominent in the current Earl's career, which spans directorships of BP and Burmah Oil.

Inchcape is currently capitalised at £2.6 billion. Turnover in 1993 was up from just over £5 billion to £5.88 billion. Pre-tax profits were up around 10 per cent to £270 million. Some of the family wealth is now sunk into the Inchcape Family Investment Company, where the current earl became a director in 1985.

### Personal style
Former cavalry officer. Huntin', shootin' and fishin' type.

### Extravagances
Used to live in a modest home near Swindon. He has now inherited two stately homes – one in Scotland and one in Essex.

have upgraded him based on the sheer quality of the assets and the fact that we believe we have undervalued his father in the past.

### Personal style
The family's peerage is relatively new – only created in 1967. Business talent clearly runs in the family. But at the tender age of 25, the new Viscount has yet to prove himself.

### Extravagances
All that land.

### David Evans 33
**£63m** (£60m)
### Music

### Source of wealth
Although he is the originator of U2's distinctive guitar sound – the only thing, apart from wealth, that separates the group from hosts of competitors – David Evans remains a private man. Born in England, into a family of Welsh Methodists who later moved on to Dublin, he is the super group's technician.

U2 signed a £130 million six-album deal with Polygram in June 1993, but even before that he was probably worth around £40 million in common with his fellow group members. Perhaps a third of that wealth crystallised with the sale of Island Records to Polygram in 1989. U2's 10 per cent stake in Chris Blackwell's company dated back to an earlier Island Records cash crisis which was only resolved when the band sacrificed royalties in return for equity.

Evans also shares in a quarter of the band's income.

Dealing with U2's wealth has forced the Irish tax authorities to employ extra staff. Despite the Republic's punitive tax regime, U2's members, including Evans, appear content in their homeland – which may have something to do with the way in which successive Irish governments during the Eighties have offered tax concessions to artists and performers.

### Personal style
Far from living a late night rock'n'roll existence, he is more likely to be seen shepherding his three-strong flock of children around suburban Dublin on a Sunday afternoon.

Evans – who has taken the stage name 'The Edge' – is now separated from his wife and teenage sweetheart, Aislinn.

### Extravagances
In the basement of his large home in Dublin's Monkstown, where he moved after leaving his parent's home in the mid-Eighties, Evans has installed a £1 million recording studio.

### Peter Rigby 50
**£66m** (£38.25m)
### Computers

### Source of wealth
It's very difficult to value Peter Rigby in 1994. Ostensibly, for the record, profits at his company, Specialist Computer Holdings, are falling slightly year by year. In 1992-93 post-tax profits declined to £3 million. This is because of the launch of the Byte chain of computer retail stores which are being built all over England. At the last count Rigby had five open and each cost him around £3.5 million.

Valuing the private company at a shade over £35 million and the open stores at £7 million each (which we think that they are easily worth, such is the strength of the concept) then he is worth a shade over £70 million – up substantially from 1993. However, caution prevails and we have knocked £5 million off that, as Byte is still not generating profits although the performance of some stores is said to be phenomenal. If nothing else Rigby gets his timing dead right. He also seems to get just about everything else right as well.

### Personal style
In Byte stores, Liverpudlian Peter Rigby has had one of the best retail ideas of the Nineties. Already rich beyond his dreams Byte is his new dream.

### Extravagances
Opening more branches of Byte.

### Mary Czernin 59
**£63.5m** (£60m)
### Inheritance

### Source of wealth
Mary Czernin is the eldest of the four daughters of Lord Howard de Walden and his first wife, Countess Irene Harrach. Like her sisters, Mary was given 25 acres of London by her father. Most of the property, which came into the family via the eccentric fifth Duke of Portland (see Lady Anne Cavendish Bentinck), is let on long leases. She married Joseph Czernin in 1957.

### Personal style
Much charitable work.

### Extravagances
Enjoying her station in life.

### Viscount Wimborne 25
**£63m** (£40m)
### Aristocracy

### Source of wealth
Viscount Wimborne's wealth comes mostly in the form of a 32,000 acre estate and an investment portfolio tended by his grandfather, who was a successful Lloyd's underwriter. In the seventies, Wimborne's father was chairman of Harris & Dixon, the shipping and insurance company.

More than anything, however, the family's wealth derives from GKN, the metals and engineering group.

The current viscount inherited his title only recently, on the death of his father. We

### Larry Mullen 33
**£63m** (£60m)
**Music**

**Source of wealth**

Larry Mullen, U2's drummer, maintains a stony silence in the face of the superstar hysteria which surrounds the group. In fact, he was the band's founder – at Mount Temple school, Dublin, in 1977. Mullen had a new drum kit; he posted a note inquiring after fellow musicians and along came Bono (Paul Hewson): "I was in charge for the first 10 minutes until Bono came in," he later recalled. "That was it. He was in charge. It was his band and he organised it from then on."

The band currently has a £130 million six-album deal with Polygram. Discounting that, Mullen's other wealth probably came to around £40 million. A third of that amount would have come from the sale of Island Records to Polygram in 1989. U2 had a 10 per cent stake in the company, which dated back to an earlier cash crisis which was only resolved when the band sacrificed royalties in return for equity. He shares in a quarter of the band's income.

**Personal style**

On tour, and before journalists, Mullen plays the role of the band's silent conscience, a man with little time for schmoozing among the jet set. He is a devout Catholic.

**Extravagances**

Fast cars.

### Nick Ashley 37
**£63m** (£45.75m)
**Retailing**

**Source of wealth**

Nick Ashley has inherited most of his fortune from his late mother, Laura Ashley, co-founder of the world famous Laura Ashley Group. He has no significant role in the group, and is retained only for freelance design work. We have slightly increased his wealth to £63 million.

**Personal style**

Nick made the mistake of trying to emulate his mother's work as a designer, which he – like many others – failed to do. His life is more notable for another big mistake, giving an interview to the *Daily Mail* ten years ago. Although he always denies it, he was quoted as claiming Laura Ashley was subservient to his father. It caused a huge internal family rift and an even bigger one with the press. Nick married Arabella McNair-Wilson the same year, a wedding not attended by his parents for tax reasons.

**Extravagances**

After his disastrous press debut, he has not surprisingly kept any extravagances to himself.

### Michael Ashcroft 48
**£63m** (£55m)
**Business**

**Source of wealth**

Michael Ashcroft has set up a tortuous company structure which makes it difficult to quantify the exact extent of his wealth. His main business, ADT moved offshore several years ago and Ashcroft is rarely seen in this country, preferring instead the Florida sunshine of his Miami home.

Ashcroft spent part of his childhood in Belize which was then a British Crown colony. His master company there is Belize Holdings. It pays him huge personal dividends.

He owns Belize Bank, which claims assets of $80 million, a $6.5 million citrus processing plant, which handles almost half of Belize's citrus concentrate exports, and 11 per cent of Belize Telecom – bought for $3 million.

Five years ago Ashcroft could easily have had a claim to dollar billionaire status. But now he is relatively poor, after the recession and some poor investment decisions on which he has lost a lot of money. This year his fortunes have recovered somewhat.

**Personal style**

As a Boy Scout, he won 14 badges. An owlish and intense social climber.

**Extravagances**

He likes to make money but has a very grand yacht for holidays and the use of a private plane.

### Tony Clegg 57
**£63m** (£61m)
**Property**

**Source of wealth**

Tony Clegg turned out to have a genius for spotting the under-valued winners: in the 1980s, at Mountleigh he was beginning to be noticed in the City. One quick but lucrative deal, typical of Clegg, involved United Real Property, in 1986. Clegg bought it for £117 million, then almost immediately recouped millions by selling off the individual properties for a total of £140 million.

But, for most observers, Mountleigh's accounts might as well have been written in Sanskrit – the financing was intricate and the true function of off-balance sheet companies was never sufficiently clarified. Analysts occasionally became jumpy. In addition, the company dallied with Sasea, the giant Swiss trading combine that later collapsed amid a welter of murky allegations. Clegg's reputation was not helped by his directorship of the Netherlands Antilles-registered property and trading company United Dutch, which also entered bankruptcy – although after Clegg's departure.

In 1989, he sold his Mountleigh shares for £70 million: the American buyers were then bombed out as the property slump struck, and Mountleigh went under, losing all the shareholders their money – including J Paul Getty.

**Personal style**

Tony Clegg has always been an incurable workaholic. This has no doubt helped to make him very rich, but it also resulted in a brain tumour in 1988.

**Extravagances**

Clegg lives on an estate in Yorkshire, where one of his private passions is raising Highland cattle.

### Raymond Slater 60
**£63m** (£60m)
**Property**

**Source of wealth**

Raymond Slater made his fortune in 1985 when he received £40 million for his shares in Norwest Holst property group, after a management buy-out. He would probably be richer today but for a row with his partner, John Lilly, that prevented the company being floated. Slater went into tax exile in Guernsey and still has property, oil and gas interests in the USA.

**Personal style**

In his day, a ferocious, but patient, fighter – it took him eight years to gain final control of Norwest Holst in 1980. Five years later he had turned a £2 million loss into £6 million profit. Hard to believe he was once an estate agent.

**Extravagances**

Huddersfield-born Slater passionately follows Manchester United FC. Has spent a fortune restoring the former home of Olivia de Havilland in Guernsey, where he now lives.

### Earl of Derby 76
**£63m** (£58m)
**Aristocracy**

**Source of wealth**

The Earl of Derby's fortune stretches back to the 1400s; his lands total about 27,000 acres around the ancestral home of Knowsley House, near Prescot in Lancashire. Ancestors and relations have links with Rhodesia, South Africa and the famous City name, Montagu.

He succeeded his father in 1948; a large liability for death duties led to the sale of 12,500 acres of land over the next seven years.

The Earl attempted to maintain liquidity with a mix of sales and business ventures. In 1961, the Derby estate went into partnership with Rank Television. In the mid-Sixties, he sold a Rembrandt to the National Gallery. In 1970, the Earl sold the family's Stanley House stables at Newmarket, which had been home to some of Britain's finest thoroughbred racers since its foundation in the 1800s.

### Ann Gloag *52*
### £62.5m (£40m)
### Transport

## Source of wealth
Ann Gloag is managing director of Stagecoach, the hugely successful bus company which she founded with her brother Brian Souter. In 1980, she left her job in nursing as a theatre sister to go into business: by 1990 she was UK Businesswoman of the Year. By 1992 she was one of three European Women of Achievement. Starting off with just two coaches in 1980, the company made £9 million in the six months to last October, indicating it is on course for new profit highs for the full year. Gloag now owns 22.2 per cent of Stagecoach Holdings plc, worth £48.7 million at the current share price. She sold £9 million-worth in the March 1993 flotation.
## Personal style
How did it all begin? To supplement her income as a nurse, Gloag and her brother started hiring out buses and caravans. The

## Personal style
In 1784, the current Earl's ancestor gave his name to Britain's most prestigious flat race, the Epsom Derby. In 1983, perhaps as a consequence of this, the Earl of Derby – family name, Stanley – accepted the death of Shergar, the kidnapped racehorse, sooner than most.

He was part of the £10 million syndicate that raced the legendary thoroughbred. Two months after the nag's disappearance, Lord Derby sent his mares elsewhere. His syndicate investment, he says, was insured.
## Extravagances
The occasional flutter at racecourses.

pair soon realised that they could devote their full time attention to the business and so decided to set up Stagecoach, using their bus-driver father's £25,000 redundancy package. The business began with a cut-price service between Dundee and London, with tea and sandwiches being served.

This was followed by the introduction of services between the Scottish cities, and between Scotland and London. As the Thatcher government deregulated the bus industry, Stagecoach began to buy up local bus companies. In 1989, Stagecoach left the long-distance market, finding that increased congestion was making the business less profitable. Finding its niche in local bus services, Stagecoach spread its operations across Britain and beyond, as far afield as Hong Kong and New Zealand.

Stagecoach grew out of Thatcherite competition – and it was ruthless. Following the breakdown of her first marriage, Ann Gloag's former husband set up his own company, Highwayman, and tried to undercut her. Gloag easily won the day: she let her passengers travel free until Highwayman was broke.

Indeed, the classic Stagecoach philosophy has been to buy local bus companies, undercut all competitors until they go bust, then from a monopoly position hike the fares up and cut all but the most lucrative services. Gloag's had a few run-ins with the Monopolies Commission as a result.
## Extravagances
None. Work is the only thing. But spending some of that £9 million in cash must be a tempting prospect.

### Peter Wilson *62*
### £62.5m (£60m)
### Media

## Source of wealth
Peter Wilson made his fortune in 1990 when he sold the property magazine *Estates Gazette* to Reed International for £59 million. He turned down some lucrative offers to re-enter the world of publishing, choosing permanent retirement, and has not been seen in public for some time. Allowing for interest and a safe investment policy, we have slightly increased Wilson's overall wealth by £2.5 million.
## Personal style
Wilson's role in making *Estates Gazette* the leading journal in the commercial property market is beyond question. In his final year in 1989, he returned pre-tax profits of £7 million with £13.3 million reserves. Even better was his sense of timing – Reed paid him £59 million on the eve of the property crash. Although the journal is still Reed's flagship title, they would pay him less than half that today. Wherever he is, there is undoubtedly a huge smile on Peter Wilson's face.
## Extravagances
A keen sportsman with several country homes.

### Lady Teresa Rothschild *77*
### £62.5m (£58.5m)
### Inheritance

## Source of wealth
Lady Teresa Rothschild is the widow of Lord Victor Rothschild. There was a major row within the family when her husband's will was read. He left almost nothing to his three children by his first marriage, including his son, Jacob, who inherited his title.
## Personal style
Lady Rothschild herself had been a wartime special agent who was awarded the MBE for "dangerous work in hazardous circumstances". Her husband was a scientist, government adviser, but most controversially, an MI5 officer. She became his second wife in 1946. They have one son, who works at the family bank, NM Rothschild and married one of the Guinness family from the banking side.

Her husband had to be defended in Parliament against the charge that he had been involved with the Philby-Burgess-Maclean Soviet spy ring. She played a crucial role in warning of the existence of the spy ring. The prime minister cleared her husband of any wrongdoing.
## Extravagances
Travel and high living.

### Camilla Acloque 47
### £62m (£60m)
### Inheritance

**Source of wealth**

Camilla Acloque is the youngest daughter of Lord Howard de Walden, owner of about 100 acres of prime London property around Harley Street. Each daughter inherited 25 acres. Most of the properties involved are on nice income-earning 20-year-plus leases. The overwhelming majority of Acloque's assets are tied up in bricks and mortar. She is a caretaker for the next generation. It is one of the best managed and maintained estates in London.

**Personal style**

Acloque's father is holder of one of the oldest titles in the House of Lords. It was given to the fourth son of the fourth Duke of Norfolk in 1597. She married Guy Acloque in 1971 at the age of 24. She was quite a catch.

**Extravagances**

Country life and a home in London are her pleasures.

### Gordon Roddick 51
### £62m (£56m)
### Retail

**Source of wealth**

Body Shop, the skin and hair care retailer, was founded by Anita and Gordon Roddick in 1976 with a £4,000 loan from Ian McGlinn, who retains a quiet association with the company.

The 1994 annual report – printed on recycled paper, naturally – showed that Body Shop had a turnover in the year to February 1994 of £195 million, with profits improving to £28.6 million. Gordon Roddick, holding 13 per cent of Body Shop, worth £57.5 million, has dividends and other assets to bring his wealth up to £62 million.

Roddick and his wife cashed in £8 million worth of shares this year: £6 million will go to charity, £2 million to set up a film company to make films about threatened indigenous cultures.

**Personal style**

The Roddicks were always different: the City they described as "dinosaurs"; social and environmental causes they championed; but it was the company's stand against animal testing which was central to its ethos and appeal.

This year's annual report is relatively free of haughty enviro-conscious pronouncements, indicating Gordon's hand at work. The City too is back on side, placated by better profits of late. While his wife has taken the limelight with her publicity-generating stands on the environment, Gordon

has taken care of business. Orphaned at age seven, he was educated at Cirencester Agricultural College. A bizarre resolution passed at this year's AGM means that Body Shop directors must declare their "environmental interests".

**Extravagances**

If they have any they wouldn't dare tell.

*DAVID SHEPHERD*

### Gordon Stewart
### £62m (New entry)
### Leisure

**Source of wealth**

Gordon Stewart, or Butch, as he is universally known, founded the Sandals chain of holiday resort hotels in the Caribbean. He now has 12 of the luxury facilities open.

Before that he built the biggest industrial concern on the island of Jamaica and is its best known businessman. The ATL group is into cars and appliances. Stewart is, however, half British and this qualifies him for *Rich 500* membership.

The real estate value of his current properties stands at around $300 million. As an

example of his wealth, two years ago Stewart spent $16 million supporting the Jamaican currency which has constantly been under pressure. We have valued him at a conservative £62 million. We could be very wrong and don't be surprised at a big upward swing next year.

**Personal style**

At 27 years of age, he had $20 to his name and started selling and installing air conditioning in Jamaica. He built up a large industrial group and started Sandals in 1981. He knew nothing about hotels which enabled him to have a totally fresh start. The Sandals name came from his first site at the Sandals Inn at Montego bay.

**Extravagances**

Building hotels on beaches.

### Joseph Bamford 78
### £62m (£31m)
### Business

**Source of wealth**

The term JCB has now become almost generic and Joe Bamford claims to be the only man to have his initials in an English dictionary.

In 1946, Joe Bamford started a business in a lock-up garage, the manufacture of the famed JCB excavators.

Joe Bamford invented the mechanical digger, revolutionising the construction industry. Up until then, the alternative to digging a trench had been shovels. But his invention also halved employment in construction and increased efficiency. The JCB was a quantum leap for the construction industry, equivalent to the impact of the computer. Over the years, the business has grown into a world leader with turnover approaching £450 million. The lean years

of the recession have been replaced by boom times again, hence the big rise in Bamford's net worth.

**Personal style**

A tax exile in Switzerland, Joe Bamford handed over the business to his son, Sir Anthony, who was knighted for services to exports. Ironically, Joe Bamford himself was never honoured, although he was one of the most important industrialists in Britain in the 20th century. He is, hence, one of the richest and most significant UK industrialists to carry no title and is plain Mr Bamford.

Joe still maintains a house in the Midlands, a beautiful Jacobean manor which he bought on the borders of Staffordshire and Derbyshire. It is not owned by him for tax reasons, however.

**Extravagances**

He has call on the family helicopter and private jet when he wants. He can also languish in his son's magnificent west coast beachside house in Barbados.

## Lord Forte 85
**£61.5m** (£58.5m)
## Hotels

### Source of wealth
Lord Forte has 13,098,323 shares in Forte plc at 221 pence each these are worth £29 million. He also has personal assets of some £30 million, built up of dividends and other fine investments.

Any surplus shares have been moved to family trusts for his great grandchildren, who will be very wealthy indeed. Much of his wealth has already been passed on and he no longer sits on the board. His personal wealth still weighs him in at £61.5 million.

### Personal style
The Grand Old Man of British catering has fought hard to keep control of his company to pass to his son. The company he built is strong in every area of hospitality except New York where it has no really top class hotel.

### Extravagances
His family. He dotes on them and two are members of the *Rich 500*.

## Tim Vestey 32
**£61m** (£53m)
## Food

### Source of wealth
Tim Vestey is the anointed heir to the vast and troubled family meat business. He stepped into the breach in June 1991, and is widely credited as the man who recruited former Lonrho director, Terry Robinson, to pull the Vestey businesses out of the hole created by his father Edmund's lackadaisical management.

Union Investment's massive cattle stations and ranches in Australia are a thing of the past, and more than half of its 1,200 butcher's shops have been sold off. Tim himself has just finished his MBA at Cranfield and will shortly rejoin the business, probably taking over the chairmanship role from his father.

Tim's money comes from trusts set up by his father and grandfather Ronald Vestey.

### Personal style
Tim Vestey eschews the playboy lifestyle so enjoyed by his father Edmund. His crisis management skills are worth noting: he unseated Edmund to take control of the family firm, and before departing for his business degree he cut a "standstill" deal with the banks and put together a restructuring plan that effectively halved the size of Union.

### Extravagances
Since he carries the hopes of the Vestey dynasty he has a reputed £50 million life insurance policy, which took six months to place. Pays his executives well, but lunches on sandwiches and tap water. He owns a house in Pimlico and a house on the 11,000 acre Vestey estate in Essex. He showed his mettle when he ditched the company helicopter as part of the economy drive.

## Anita Roddick 52
**£61m** (£55m)
## Retailing

### Source of wealth
Anita Roddick, the simple girl from Hastings, who only wanted to run a small shop in the nearby town of Littlehampton, could hardly have guessed where her small ambitions would take her. She personally owns 12.7 per cent of the 1000-strong Body Shop chain of eco-friendly cosmetics stores, down from 13.8 per cent because of a share sale. Added to this is her now not inconsiderable liquid fortune from dividends (£515,000 this year) and investments, and she improves her net worth this year to £61 million.

### Personal style
Basing her approach on environmentally-friendly products at a time when the word "environment" meant little to anyone, she has turned what might have been a local beauty shop into one of the best known niche retailers in the whole world.

Anita and her husband, Gordon, oversee every single aspect of the chain's activities and spend much of their time travelling the world finding new and exotic products, naturally made, often by indigenous peoples whose way of life is threatened by modern civilisation.

Having been labelled a has-been by the City in the last two years, she has enjoyed watching them crawl back and beg forgiveness.

### Extravagances
Charity. Anita gave £230,000 to found The Big Issue, a newspaper sold by the homeless, and more recently she and husband Gordon took largesse to a new level by cashing in £8 million worth of shares (2.1 per cent of Body Shop's equity) and giving the money to a variety of causes.

## Jessica White 53
**£60m** (£60m)
## Inheritance

### Source of wealth
Jessica White's fortune is thanks to the 25 acres of land in London which her father, Lord Howard de Walden, passed on to her.

### Personal style
Her father was one of England's most important horse trainers, awarded the Steward of the Jockey Club on three occasions. His horse Slip Anchor won the Epsom Derby in 1985.

Jessica married Adrian White in 1966.

### Extravagances
Not so keen on her 25 acres of land in London – she lives in Oxford.

## Frank Brake 56
**£60m** (£67m)
## Food

### Source of wealth
With his elder brother, William, Frank Brake has run the frozen food distributor Brake Bros. for over thirty years.

He, too, owns around 25 per cent of the company, and sees his personal wealth slip, on the back of a lower stock market rating. The latest results for 1993 show a £19 million profit but like the City Frank is cautious and expects 1995-1996 to be the year for climbing up the *Rich 500*. By then, the so far costly launch of Larderfresh should be producing improved results.

### Personal style
Frank started the business from scratch at a pub, the Bull Inn, at Lenham, Kent, in 1958. The brothers began making money by killing and selling plucked chickens to the local community. They went to catering college together and were renowned, with their younger brother Peter who later died, for working 18 hour days.

### Extravagance
The single van grew to a huge fleet of trucks, and eventually flotation on the Stock Exchange in 1986. Frank himself, however, remains very much the same type of man, except that he doesn't have to chase chickens around the block anymore.

## Esmond Bulmer 59
**£60m** (£71m)
## Drink

### Source of wealth
Esmond Bulmer still personally controls over a quarter of the shares of the 106 year-old HP Bulmer cider company. He has been chairman since 1982 and had the good fortune to appoint a highly effective non-family CEO called John Rudguard. Rudguard has multiplied the family fortune a few times.

The group has been highly profitable over the past decade, concentrating on effective marketing and increasingly efficient production of its two main brands, Woodpecker and Strongbow, while still relying on apples grown in their own orchards. The family together still has a controlling 52 per cent stake, worth a shade under £100 million. The company has cashed in on the increasing popularity of cider: profits before tax and exceptionals were £21.5 million this year, up 10 per cent from 1992-93's £19.6 million on a turnover of £251 million.

The only bad apple in the barrel has been the company's disastrous pectin business, which cost £17 million in exceptional costs this year and has knocked the stuffing out of the share price. Bulmer's market capitalisation stands at £190 million, down from £223 million a year ago. Taking into account dividends and investments outside the cider business, we value Esmond at £60 million.

## Personal Style

Esmond wants to be the cidermaker that finally cracks the lucrative international market for what is, arguably, a much more marketable product than warm heavy beer. In 1992 the company purchased Belgium's leading cider maker, Stassen. A variety of new beverages are being test-marketed under the names Hockhams, Discovery, Black Jack's, Joe Bloggs and Brokov – the company is not committed to the future of any of them.

As the former MP for Hereford (1974-87), Esmond Bulmer isn't above a little political needling either: he wants the government to reduce cider duty, and recently accused "tied" pubs of overpricing their cider to halt declining beer sales and keep the parent breweries happy.

## Extravagances

The dominant family in Somerset, the Bulmers live the life of squires in an unassuming fashion.

### William Brake 62
### £60m (£67m)
### Food

## Source of wealth

William Brake is chairman of frozen food distributor Brake Bros., the company he founded with his two brothers Frank and Peter. The youngest, Peter, died in 1967, while Frank is currently managing director (and also in our list).

The group saw pre-tax profits rise 19 per cent to £19 million for 1993, largely thanks to the purchase of Country Choice Foods for £10 million last year. However, the City sees next year as the one for Brake Bros. to really take the market by storm, despite a 0 per cent increase in market share. The company is valued at just under £220 million on the Stock Exchange. William Brake's personal worth slips to £60 million as a result, after adding dividends and salaries.

## Personal style

Genuinely fascinated by the frozen food market, and generally snaps up anything going cheap.

## Extravagances

Worried about the impact a Labour government would have on the share price, he cashed in £2 million of shares just before the last election.

### Bernard Matthews 64
### £60m (£34.5m)
### Food

## Source of wealth

Bernard Matthews owns the turkey and food producer named after himself. After a few shaky years, Christmas has come early for Matthews, with profits in the first half of 1993 doubling to £4.64 million. The City is impressed, valuing the company at over £140 million. Matthews's 51 per cent stake, plus dividends, makes him worth £60 million.

## Personal style

In 1955 Matthews bought Witchingham Hall, an 80-room Jacobean mansion in Norfolk. Chicks were incubated in the dining room, turkeys reared in the bedrooms and processing done in the kitchen. The business grew and grew as turkeys became more than just a Christmas treat. By the Seventies, the business was indispensable and Matthews was famed for his TV commercials, whereby in his distinct Norfolk accent he would refer to his "bootiful" turkeys. In his latest adverts, he is desperately sought after by glamorous French housewives who want to taste his turkey. Never a stranger to controversy, in 1990 he paid fines for polluting two rivers with unusable turkey parts.

## Extravagances

Matthews is a local hero because he burns turkey droppings in a power station providing electricity for 12,500 Norfolk homes.

### Ronald Frost 57
### £59.5m
### (£36.25m)
### Business

## Source of wealth

Ronnie Frost runs a group of nearly 40 companies, called Hays, employing 6,000 people with sales of almost £500 million. Last year it posted £67 million profits. Half year figures of £38 million pre-tax indicate Hays is on course for £80 million plus profits this year.

The Hays acquisition juggernaut keeps rolling. The latest purchase was a data storage company, and Frost has become the dominant player in the supermarket distribution business. Frost's 20 million Hays shares have appreciated dramatically in the last year: they are worth £56.5 million at current market value.

## Personal style

Ronnie Frost boasts that he has made 25

employees millionaires. He has an uncanny ability to take small businesses and turn them into large, profitable ones, which has led to Hays being rated far above other service businesses on the stockmarket.

Ronnie joined a Smithfield poultry trader in 1960 and expanded it thirteenfold, while branching into frozen food distribution with his brother Derrick and their company Farmhouse Securities. They sold Farmhouse Securities to the Hays Group in 1981, and Ronnie Frost became chief executive of the Distribution Division. In 1983 he became group chief executive and MD, and in 1987 he led a management buy-out of the group from the Kuwaiti Investment Office, becoming chairman of Hays in 1989. In the same year the company was floated on the stock market, when the brothers' holding was valued at £30 million. It's now worth over £1 billion.

## Extravagances

Sailing and game shooting.

### Graeme Chilton 35
### £59m (£54.5m)
### Insurance

## Source of wealth

Graeme Chilton owns some 8,750,000 shares in the private Benfield Group, a Lloyd's re-insurance broker. This is an 18 per cent share in the company, making him worth nearly £59 million, including current and past dividends.

Benfield had a remarkable 1992, making £30.6 million profit, on a turnover of £39.7 million. It was followed up in 1993, with a similar performance, but in a more difficult year with a £41.2 turnover and profits of £31.2 million. It has just launched a re-insurance company that will take on insurance risks itself. The venture is jointly funded by Benfield and venture capitalists to the tune of £50 million.

## Personal style

Grahame Chilton is the youngest director of the remarkable Benfield company that has fellow directors, Matthew Harding, John Coldman and Michael Rees who are also on the list.

## Extravagances

Chilton is the youngest self-made member of the *Rich 500*.

### Earl of Airlie 68
### £58.5m (£60m)
### Aristocracy

## Source of wealth

The Earl of Airlie has been Lord Chamberlain to the Queen's Household since 1984. The basis of his wealth is 70,000 acres near Kirriemuir in Angus. If anything, his wealth is declining slightly.

## Personal style

Feats of derring-do have been second nature to the Ogilvy family since the 2nd Earl escaped from custody – and a parliamentary death sentence – in 1645, by dressing up in his sister's clothes.

From there, Airlie's career took a corporate turn.

## Extravagances

A rumoured liaison with Princess Margaret in the Fifties and tendency to go shooting with the Duke of Edinburgh.

### Sir Euan *28* Anstruther-Gough-Calthorpe
### £58m (£55m)
### Inheritance

## Source of wealth

The Harrow and Cirencester-educated third baronet inherited a large area of central Birmingham from his grandfather, the second baronet, in 1985. His father died too soon to inherit the title, hence the direct descent from grandfather to grandson and Sir Euan's relative youth. To confuse things further, his heir is his older uncle, brother of his father, who was trustee to Euan's fortune until he came of age. This has caused some confusion in other newspapers in the past, although the confusion isn't clear.

Nor is the title to Sir Euan's inheritance from his grandfather. Because of the mix of short and long leaseholds, the value of the land is uncertain, as is the actual ownership. There have been many rows about this, some in and some out of court. Now Sir Euan appears to have asserted himself as being in charge of the trusts, although the outcome of the court cases was private.

Sir Euan's fortune has almost certainly been overrated in the past, but has been saved from the ravages of the recession by being mostly sited in relatively prosperous Birmingham. He also inherited interests in Europe and America.

## Personal style

The youthful Sir Euan is one of the nicest baronets you could meet. He is so unassuming and pleasant that even close friends cannot believe he is so rich.

He was devastated recently by the closure of his old school Hawtreys.

## Extravagances

For all his wealth, Sir Euan does not seem to have much actual cash on hand.

### Adam Clayton *34*
### £58m (£55 m)
### Music

## Source of wealth

Adam Clayton is the poorest of the U2 band. He has the highest living expenses.

Fortunately, U2 signed a £130 million six-album deal with Polygram in June 1993, but even before that Clayton was probably worth around £40 million.

Out of U2's members, Clayton comes closest to living the glamourous high-life that might be expected of such well-paid stage stars. Recently linked with Naomi Campbell, the supermodel – long after his colleagues Bono and The Edge got hitched to partners who qualified as childhood sweethearts. Clayton, somewhat at odds with the band's other members, lives in a fortified mansion beyond Dublin's southern periphery. (The rest prefer less grand, if still expensive, accommodation nearer the city centre).

A third of his wealth crystallised with the sale of Island Records to Polygram in 1989. U2's 10 per cent stake in Island dated back to an earlier Chris Blackwell cash crisis which was only resolved when the band sacrificed royalties in return for equity. He shares in a quarter of the band's income.

## Personal style

Clayton was born into a military family, as the son of a former RAF pilot who finally settled in Dublin after acquiring work with the Irish state airline, Aer Lingus. As a teenager, he swapped ink blots and homework for a long sojourn around Pakistan, which left him with an advanced understanding, it seems, of "hippy ideals and paraphernalia." True to his reputation as a good-time boy, Clayton is well-known around the pubs and clubs of his native city.

## Extravagances

His mansion and his fast cars. The on-off romance with supermodel Naomi Campbell.

MATTHEW JOHN

### Duke of Roxburghe
### £58m (£47m)
### Aristocracy

## Source of wealth

Guy Inness-Kerr is a man who straddles three social worlds. First, since the age of 19, he has been the 10th Duke of Roxburghe, the holder of a title that goes back to the early eighteenth century, and which brought with it more than 50,000 acres of Scottish countryside in the borders region.

But the Duke of Roxburghe is also a businessman. He has invested time and money in a small number of private companies, teaching himself the business skills which, he told *BusinessAge* last year, he had never acquired through formal management or City training.

His proudest achievement so far, though, is Sunlaws, the 22-room country house hotel that he created ten years ago, out of an unused baronial mansion on his estate.

## Personal style

Hard-working aristocrat who plays with a straight bat.

He was once married to Lady Jane Grosvenor, sister to the Duke of Westminster. But last year he married Virginia Wynn-Williams, whom he met through his business contacts. She is an interior designer who has worked on a number of hotels and will no doubt be bringing her experience to bear at Sunlaws House. A friend of the Royals, and particularly the younger Royals: Prince Andrew proposed to Sarah Ferguson at Floors Castle, the duke's beautiful 200-room mansion on the estate which is open to the public six months of the year (even the lived-in bits!). The tabloids also announced recently that the Princess of Wales had been house guest there, along with her City banker friend, William Van Straubenzee.

## Extravagances

Good living.

### Peter Wood 47
### £58m (£45m)
### Insurance

## Source of wealth

Peter Wood's phenomenally successful Direct Line insurance business (part of the Royal Bank of Scotland) surged last year from £15 million to £40 million pre-tax profits. The company has now written 1.4 million motor insurance policies and is taking the household insurance market by storm. Wood's 1993 salary of £18 million was augmented by a £25 million buyout of his profit-related bonus contract. It made him Britain's best paid individual in 1993, but based on those profits he might be regretting taking that £25 million slug: in 1994 that could have been his salary.

## Personal style

Wood founded Direct Line Insurance in 1985, the motor and house contents insurance business, with backing from the Royal Bank of Scotland. In 1988, he sold his stake to the bank and negotiated for himself a superb growth-related bonus deal which has caused no end of press comment.

Always good for some original ideas, Wood's latest scheme's include a Direct Line credit card and a separate motor insurance company to offer Direct Line-type bargains to high-risk (young) drivers. He has called the life insurance business "the ultimate rip off" and recently served notice that his company will do there what it did with motor insurance.

He was sent a letterbomb earlier this year.

## Extravagances

Much to the annoyance of the press, Wood lives modestly and doesn't flaunt his wealth.

### Earl of Pembroke 55
### £58m (£50m)
### Aristocracy

## Source of wealth

The earl's wealth is based around an impressive art collection which includes works by Van Dyck and Rembrandt. In addition, he owns 14,000 acres of good land in Hampshire and previous valuations may have been too conservative.

We have upgraded his wealth considerably.

## Personal style

William Shakespeare and Koo Stark have both visited the Earl of Pembroke's 16,000-acre estate. The bard came to engage in conversation with the leading intellects of his day. Ms Stark came to bare all in the name of art, as the star of soft-porn film *Emily*, directed by the current earl on location at Wilton House. The earl is whippet-thin and handsome. Married twice. In the film business the present earl is better known by his nom de guerre, Henry Herbert.

## Extravagances

Horse racing.

### Leonard Steinberg 57
### £58m (£47.5m)
### Leisure

## Source of wealth

Leonard Steinberg's Stanley Leisure plc currently has a stock market value of £180 million – so Steinberg's stake of just under 27 per cent makes him worth about £46 million. Add past share sales and dividends, and Steinberg is worth some £58 million.

## Personal style

Leonard Steinberg's wealth comes from Liverpool-based Stanley Leisure, one of the largest bookmaking chains in the country, which he founded in Northern Ireland with his brother Gerald in the Sixties. His brother left in the early Eighties and cashed in £8 million in shares when Stanley went public. But Leonard stayed for the long haul, and has been highly rewarded.

## Extravagances

His family.

### Robert Sangster 58
### £58m (£55m)
### Business

## Source of wealth

Robert Sangster's chief claim to fame is that his wealth is as hard to calculate as the Queen's. His income stems from his horse-racing empire which has 1,200 horses across the globe. His grandfather founded Vernon's football pools, and a large part of the profits came from Sangster's racing interests, through his Swettenham Stud operation.

He sold the family pools company in the mid-Eighties for a pittance (around £80 million), and it was later taken over by Ladbrokes from the new owners at a much higher value, completely severing his family interests. After that, he focused on Australian bloodstock and currently owns 900 thoroughbreds. He also has mansion and estate which cost him £13 million.

To calculate Sangster's wealth, we have discounted for heavy losses from the collapse of the South African company Tollgate, in which he had invested. However, adding in prize money and other likely investments for the year – his horse Colonel Collins was third in the Derby but he had several other winners – we estimate he has gone up slightly to £58 million.

## Personal style

Sangster is generally associated with winning – in five separate seasons beginning in 1977 he owned the leading number of winning horses on the world circuit. Sangster was also a shareholder in the kidnapped horse, Shergar.

## Extravagances

Other than racing, plays golf regularly. Lives on the Isle on Man next door to Nigel Mansell's old house, but has been trying to sell the £3.5 million home all year. Maybe he's bored.

### Celia Lipton 67
### £58m (£58m)
### Inheritance

## Source of wealth

Celia Lipton, the ebullient daughter of the 1940s society orchestra leader Sydney Lipton, gets around £5 million in income a year from the estate of her late American husband, the prolific inventor and engineer Victor Farris.

Farris died in March 1985 of a heart attack, leaving his two Rolls-Royces, a seventy-foot yacht, and his ridiculously large fortune – estimated at more than £100 million – to his wife.

## Personal style

She has been dipping into her windfall ever since.

Part of the pile has been spent on worthy causes. While her husband was alive, Lipton raised well over £1 million by organising charity balls in Palm Beach, Florida where she and her husband lived. Since then her commitment to charity work has grown and in 1989 she personally gave £1 million to Elizabeth Taylor's Aids charity.

## Extravagances

Celia Lipton has also been keen to rekindle her past glories as a singer and actress. She was a household name in Britain when she was young. Her very first appearance was at the London Palladium when she was just 16 and she has also starred on Broadway.

But despite several records the planned comeback has not gone so well for her. In 1986 she was persuaded to part with £250,000 to make a record called *The London I Love*. However, there is a big question mark over just how much of that money actually went towards making the record – some say it was as little as £30,000. There is every indication that Lipton was seriously misled; the record went on sale in Harrods but sold very few copies, although she was led to believe that it had been a great success.

She still has a house in Palm Beach, Florida and a luxury apartment in Mayfair. Her living expenses and charity works means net worth has stayed even during the year.

## Colin Sanders 46
## £57.5m (£55m)
## Electronics

### Source of wealth
How much Colin Sanders is now worth depends very much on when he may have sold the Carlton shares and preference stock which he received in exchange for his UEI holding, which he in turn got for selling his dynamic recording electronics company SSL to them in 1986. Unless his timing was particularly bad when he sold the rest (Carlton shares dropped by almost two-thirds at one stage), he should still be worth £55 million, allowing for investment income from his huge windfall.

He finally parted company with SSL (and Carlton) earlier this year.

### Personal style
Whatever kind of music Colin Sanders plays on his sound system, it surely ain't the blues. He turned a hobby into a fortune through his ability to invent electronic recording systems. His first device was an electronic switching system for church organs, replacing the mechanical device which directed wind into the right pipe. He soon sold thousands – at £10,000 a time – with Westminster Abbey one notable client.

In 1975 he invented the world's first computerised recording mixer console for record studios, setting the standard for the music industry. His company, Solid State Logic (SSL), won a Queen's Award for Exports and he was awarded a CBE in 1986. Sanders was destined to take SSL to the Unlisted Securities Market with profits of £3.3 million on sales of £19 million. But then electronics group UEI ("a loose federation of companies," in Sanders' favourable view) offered Sanders more than £25 million of UEI shares for his business. And they wanted him to carry on running it.

Three years later, Carlton Communications took over UEI in a cash-and-shares deal. By then, Sanders's shares were worth £64 million.

### Extravagances
A wicked sound system. Insiders say he left SSL to spend more time with his money. He's an imaginative fellow: watch this space.

## Rory Guinness 20
## £57m (£51m)
## Inheritance

### Source of wealth
The Honourable Rory Michael Benjamin Guinness is the youngest son of the late 3rd Earl of Iveagh, who died last year. Under the terms of his grandfather's Will he inherits one quarter of his father's stake in the Will Trust set up in the 1920s. His mother, Miranda, is the daughter of an aristocratic Scottish family and is a prominent Irish socialite.

### Personal style
Too young, as yet, to have hit the headlines.

### Extravagances
Motorbikes.

## Lady Louisa Guinness 23
## £57m (£51m)
## Inheritance

### Source of wealth
Lady Louisa Jane is the youngest daughter of the late 3rd Earl of Iveagh, the last member of the Guinness family to head the drinks company which bears their name. Under the terms of her grandfather's Will she inherits a quarter of her father's stake in the Iveagh Will Trust Assets, which are worth over £2 billion in total.

The assets have appreciated significantly this year.

## David McMurtry 54
## £56m (£52m)
## Electronics

### Source of wealth
The recession may be over, but David McMurtry hasn't seen the benefits yet. His company, Renishaw, makes measuring probes for machine tools, and exports over 90 per cent of its production. Profits have halved since 1990 to £7 million, despite consistent sales of over £40 million, and McMurtry has only just escaped the wrath of the City by maintaining dividend levels by drawing on cash reserves.

### Personal style
Still has to find her feet and emerge from the shadow of the great Anglo-Irish dynasty.

### Extravagances
Clothes.

## Lady Emma Guinness 31
## £57m (£51m)
## Inheritance

### Source of wealth
Lady Emma Lavinia Guinness is the eldest daughter of the late 3rd Earl of Iveagh who died last year. Because of the British rule of male primogeniture, she did not inherit the title, which went instead to her brother. Under the terms of the trust, set up by her great-grandfather in 1923, she inherits a quarter of her father's stake in the assets and the income from them. She is a graduate of Lincoln College, Oxford.

Her share has appreciated significantly this year.

### Personal style
Laid-back low-profile Guinness heiress.

### Extravagances
Travel and shopping.

Renishaw shares have still languished below £3, though they've improved from last year: McMurtry's 18 million shares are worth £48 million. His dividend income last year was £1.2 million.

Renishaw makes electronic probes which test to see if a manufactured part has been built within its allowed measurement tolerances. The probes are also used to 'view' a mould so that robotic cutting machines can be programmed to mill a part to the exact dimensions required.

### Personal style
Engineering and entrepreneurial skills rarely mix. McMurtry is one of the exceptions: as a senior designer with Rolls-Royce, he invented his first probe to measure machining in the Concorde engines. In 1973, he and his partner, John Deer, set up Renishaw, but McMurtry had to convince Rolls to give him the patents. He didn't leave the company until 1976, and, with £200 start-up capital, began marketing his invention from his garage.

### Extravagances
Drives a Lamborghini, but still eats lunch in the staff canteen and is on first-name terms with all 200 staff at his Gloucestershire headquarters.

## John Haynes 56
### £56m (New entry)
## Motor Industry

### Source of wealth
Bounding back into the rich lists after a few leaner years John Haynes's fortune comes not from cars themselves but by showing people how to tear them apart and put them together.

After a hard few years the quoted Haynes Publishing is back in clover, selling £25 million worth of the car manuals - some written by Haynes himself - to a cult following of gearheads. Half the production is exported to the United States.

The results for the six months to last November showed continuing improvement: pretax profits up 30 per cent to £2.11 million, and predictions of £5 million plus when the full year results are released shortly. John Haynes controls 80 per cent of the shares, worth just over £55 million.

### Personal style
John Haynes worships the internal combustion engine the way that chefs worship food. His first book arose from the first car he ever bought, an Austin Seven, in the 1950s. He offered people a way to soup up the old British standby, and the 250 print run sold out almost immediately.

### Extravagances
With a personal loan from Singer & Friedlander, Haynes just dropped £700,000 on a 1931 Duesenberg. Only seven were ever built, and car fanatic Haynes bought it for his burgeoning car museum.

## Michael Stone 57
### £56m (£30m)
## Finance

### Source of wealth
Michael Stone is chairman of ED&F Man, one of the larger commodity trading groups now thinking about a flotation. The company is predominantly active in coffee, cocoa and sugar markets, but also has fund management and securities trading arms. The Swiss chocolate company, Jacobs Suchard, now part of US giant Philip Morris, bought a large stake in 1987.

Quite how much is anyone's guess: the ultimate holding company is in Bermuda, and the authorities there wouldn't let us see the share register. But it's clear that Stone still has a significant personal interest in the company that made after-tax profits of $39.7 million and paid $25.5 million in dividends in 1992. It has whopping debts however – unavoidable when buying future contracts for commodities – so a realistic value for the company would be its net assets: $245 million in the last accounts.

We estimate that Stone's remaining holding of about 25 per cent is worth £43 million. His paycheck of about £5 million after tax for the last three years has added about £13 million to his net worth.

### Personal style
Stone is more famous these days as the property developer behind the plan to tar-

## Tom Wheatcroft 73
### £56m (New entry)
## Construction

### Source of wealth
Tom Wheatcroft was a successful local builder who became obsessed with motor racing. It was to dominate almost the whole of his life.

Wheatcroft Developments expanded mightily in the Sixties under Wheatcroft, and dominated construction in the east Midlands.

Then he sponsored a young racing driver called Roger Williamson, and took him through to Formula One. Undoubtedly a future British world champion, Williamson was tragically killed in a fiery crash in 1975 at the Dutch Grand Prix in his first year of Formula One.

Wheatcroft's team-owning ambitions died with Williamson and he turned his attention to collecting vintage single-seater racing cars and rebuilding the Donnington Park racing circuit. All this he did

## Sean Lennon 19
### £55.5m (£47.5m)
## Inheritance

### Source of wealth
Sean Lennon is the youngest member of the Rich 500. When his father John Lennon's Will was read in 1980 it came to

mac large chunks of the Surrey Green Belt in order to build a feeder airport for Gatwick.

He's said to be bending the ears of several Tories on the Commons Aviation Committee to achieve his ends.

### Extravagances
Megalomania.

from his own resources.

Luck was on his side. At that time he picked up much of the land and the cars up for a relative song. Old Grand Prix chassis, complete with engines, could be bought for less than £20,000 even championship winning cars of that era. Little did Wheatcroft know that his hobby would become the fastest appreciating asset of the Eighties. Cars that Wheatcroft bought in the Seventies for £30,000 or less, are now worth between £500,000 and £1 million each. He bought so many that he decided to start a museum.

He doesn't own all the cars in his museum on the outskirts of the Donnington circuit, but he does own many of them.

We value the cars he owns in the museum at £25 million but we are having them professionally valued for next year's Rich 500, so expect a big leap in Wheatcroft's wealth then. In addition, the Donnington circuit is probably worth in the region of £11 million. But it has development potential, and could be worth far more.

With Wheatcroft's other assets at £20 million it comes to a very conservative £56 million.

### Personal style
Wheatcroft is now in his autumn years and looks and sounds like a country fellow. One would hardly guess that he is so astute and so rich. He is a private man but hospitable. He is in the middle of trying to get his biography written, as he has quite a few stories to tell.

### Extravagances
The museum and the racing circuit. Both his hobbies have made him millions.

some $30 million, despite bogus reports that it was worth between £150 million and £200 million. But it has increased many times since then, and BusinessAge had the estate of John Lennon valued at £145 million in 1993. This is because royalty payments have continued to flow: there were some massive hits with old songs immediately after his death, and his records have continued to be successful. The Lennon estate's income this year was around £5 million for his own material and £4 million from Beatles material.

We estimate that most of this will eventually go to Sean Lennon. Currently he has been endowed with half the fortune, and is therefore valued now at just under £56 million, after taxes.

## Personal style

He is half-American and half-British, as a result of being the son of the legendary John Lennon, gunned down in New York City in 1980 when Sean was barely five years old. Then, Sean would have been unaware that he was the son of a legend. Now it is his own calling card to fame.

In normal times, Sean would have shared this fortune with his half-brother Julian Lennon. But Julian was left a mere £70,000 when his father died and that has long been spent. He does feature in a trust fund which is split down the middle with Sean. The value of this is unknown, but may be no more than a few millions, and can only be paid out at the discretion of Yoko Ono.

## Extravagances

Very few. Sean lives with his mother in New York, leading as normal life as possible.

### Simon Draper 44
### £55.5m (£51m)
### Entertainment

## Source of wealth

Simon Draper, second cousin and one-time musical partner to Richard Branson, made £75 million from the sale of Virgin's music division to Thorn EMI in 1992. Branson made £320 million from the same deal, but Draper's ear for talent – he acted as talent-spotter – resulted in impressive growth for the company that released Mike Oldfield's Tubular Bells and the first album by the Sex Pistols. If Branson was the salesman, Draper was the musical adviser.

## Personal style

Cautious businessman. In 1984 Draper argued against starting Virgin Atlantic Airlines. He thought Virgin should stick to music – other schemes outside the area, like the notorious London listings magazine *Event*, had been spectacular failures. But caution shouldn't be read as corporate brown-nosing. He departed Virgin pretty quickly once the suits from Thorn EMI clambered on board. Branson and Draper are still firm friends. When the consortium headed by Virgin's founder lost its bid to run the National Lottery earlier this year, Branson trudged through the streets of Notting Hill to Draper's offices, looking for a shoulder to cry upon.

## Extravagances

A Ferrari Lusso, for which he paid £410,000 – just one part of his classic car collection. Not the best of investments, classic cars have probably placed a modest hole in Draper's fortune. Ventures since his departure from Virgin have probably evened out the losses.

### Jonathan Harmsworth 26
### £55m (£33m)
### Inheritance

## Source of wealth

Jonathan Harmsworth is the heir of one of Britain's only four billionaires.

He is gradually assuming control of that wealth as his father gets older. He is assuming as much as is possibly tax effective. His net worth has increased considerably this year, as a result of inheritances from his late mother who owned much of the family property.

## Personal style

It was a huge relief when Harold Jonathan Esmond Vere Harmsworth was born on 3rd December 1967, to Vere and Pat Harmsworth. He was their last child and the much needed male heir to the *Daily Mail* newspaper fortune. If Jonathan had not been born the empire would have reverted to Vere's brother's line.

He has already inherited from his mother's Will and various wealth from relations. But the big prize, his father's vast wealth, is still to come.

## Extravagances

The Rothermeres live a fine life with homes in London, France, Jamaica and Paris.

### John Beckwith 48
### £55m (£37m)
### Property

## Source of wealth

Last year, John Beckwith was below his brother, Peter, in the *Rich 500*. This annoyed and inspired him to seek new ventures, which have been so successful that he is at last ahead of Peter.

The brothers made £35 million each when they sold their property company, London and Edinburgh Trust, to SPP in 1990. After a quiet spell, the Beckwith's went into action together again last year with Riverside Holdings, a leisure company that plans to float this year. But John has parted from Peter for his main venture, Beckwith Holdings. He's snapped up a £25 million portfolio of offices and shops from Century Life, in partnership with Goldman Sachs. With some former colleagues from his LET days, John's also developing an office complex in Poland. Like Riverside

Holdings, he plans to float Beckwith Holdings, making him even more seriously rich.

## Personal style

John was in the shadow of his brother at LET, which explains why he's so busy now. Says a colleague, "John feels he has a lot to prove. He's a workaholic who loves making money."

## Extravagances

The only man who isn't satisfied with £37 million in the bank.

### Greg Stanley 50
### £55m (New entry)
### Retailing

## Source of wealth

The temperamental Greg Stanley owns Focus DIY, which recorded £3.66 million pre-tax profits in 1993, a jump of 57 per cent. This propelled him into the *Rich 500* for the first time. Stanley plans a journey to the Stock Exchange in the autumn, which will further increase his wealth. Focus, which he bought for just £4 million in 1987, has 50 stores, and has just purchased ten more from Do it All.

Stanley is also chairman of the worthless Brighton Football Club, which he wrote a £1.7 million cheque for last November, three hours before a winding up order was due to be served.

## Personal style

Stanley was born above his Dad's paint and wallpaper shop. He and brother Malcolm went into the family business, based in Bromley, taking over in 1962. The shop originally flourished following the post-war spending boom, and floated in 1972. By the Eighties, FADS, as it was known, was the top UK DIY retailer with 500 outlets. The brothers were offered the chance to buy B&Q for just £25 million, but, amazingly, Malcolm refused – B&Q is now worth £500 million. Greg, annoyed at the decision, sold most of his shares in the company, which was eventually sold to Ward White for £130 million in 1988.

But the brothers had the sense to take just £25 million of their proceeds in cash, the rest as shares. Boots later took over Ward White, and as a result, Stanley has a £10.5 million share stake in Boots.

## Extravagances

Brother Malcolm has retired and is living on a yacht. As for Greg, he is famed for wild drinking sessions at his mansion in Arundel, and the restaurant Hemmingways that he once ran. The neighbours would regularly call the police to stop the noise. Greg Stanley is one of the only entries in this year's *Rich 500* with a criminal conviction. In 1968, on the eve of a football match between Brighton and Doncaster, he got drunk and smashed a shop window, leading ➞

to a conviction for rowdy behaviour and a £250 fine.

He's matured now, but still upset with Malcolm about passing up the B&Q deal, which would have put him higher up the *Rich 500*.

### Clarice Pears 60
### £55m (New entry)
### Property

**Source of wealth**
Clarice Pears controls the family company, William Pears Family Holdings, which lifted profits to £9.5 million after tax in the year to April 1993 and had net assets of £126 million in the accounts.

Clarice controls 45 per cent of the ordinary share capital. The remainder is split equally between her two sons.

**Personal style**
Conservative, verging on the non existent. The company invests in safe city centre commercial properties. Its chief is rarely seen in public.

**Extravagances**
Who knows what goes on behind closed doors?

### Earl of Rosebery 65
### £55m (New entry)
### Aristocracy

**Source of wealth**
The Earl of Rosebery is a new entrant in the *Rich 500* this year. His place on the list is richly deserved. Our research turned up the fact that his family became intertwined with the Rothschilds in the mid-19th century – courtesy of a love match between the 5th Earl of Rosebery, the then prime minister, and the daughter of Baron Meyer De Rothschild. The union brought a number of treasures into the family home at Mentmore Towers, including a Rembrandt. This canvas was sold to an American collector in 1992. Similarly, the estate at Mentmore was sold off in 1977, three years after the current earl came into his inheritance, for a mere £6.5 million. The sale was forced by the need to pay death duties. But such asset sales foster a misleading impression. In fact, the family remains immensely rich in terms of art assets and land holdings. The current earl spends his time quietly in West Lothian, Scotland. We estimate the Earl is worth some £55 million.

**Personal style**
A quiet man committed to country pursuits, who has successfully shunned publicity for decades.

**Extravagances**
Among the earl's possessions is a rare portrait of George Washington, America's first president.

### Duke of Marlborough 68
### £55m (£49m)
### Aristocracy

**Source of wealth**
The duke isn't cash rich but he is not anywhere near as poor as the *Sunday Times* makes out.

His home, Blenheim, is impossible to value – simply because it is so valuable. The inheritance struggle centring on the drug-addicted Marquess of Blandford, heir to the Marlborough fortune, has focused attention on it. The stately home was constructed for John Churchill after his famous military victory of 1704. (Such was the importance of Churchill's victory at Blenheim that he was awarded the very un-English title, Prince of the Holy Roman Empire).

Tourism and related businesses at Blenheim these days generate an annual turnover in the region of £10 million. The duke's is one of the few active stately homes that appears to have successfully made the transition to self-sustaining business venture. Much of the credit for this must rest with the Duke of Marlborough himself and, in particular, with his canny way with balance sheets. The bulk of the fortune is tied up in trust.

**Personal style**
His life has been blighted by his son. But those who have viewed the behaviour of some offspring of the aristocracy are unsurprised. It is the most difficult job in the world to bring up children in those circumstances. The only solution is to be incredibly strict and to deprive them of any cash until the age of 30. Few can do this it seems, certainly not the Duke of Marlborough.

**Extravagances**
Three wives.

### Nicholas Forman Hardy
### £55m (New entry)
### Media

**Source of wealth**
Solicitors for Nicholas Forman Hardy wrote to the *Sunday Times* in 1991 informing the paper that their client was not rich. Well, I suppose it depends on your definition of rich. Forman Hardy certainly became very wealthy when his business, T Bailey Forman, which publishes the *Nottingham Evening Post*, was taken over by the *Daily Mail* for £90 million. This was double what most people thought the company was worth. As a result, we value him personally at £55 million, one of the highest new entries in the 1994 *Rich 500*.

**Personal style**
The Forman Hardy family is famous for its stand against the NGA print union in the

Seventies. Their company was one of the first newspaper groups to install cold-set computer technology and it employed a very tough chief executive, Christopher Pole-Carew, to get the job done. He fired all the NGA members and imposed new technology. This went virtually unnoticed nationally: the NGA handled the situation in a much more responsible manner than they did the Eddie Shah fiasco.

**Extravagances**
Plenty of money for extravagances now.

### Marquess of Bath 61
### £54.5m (£51.5m)
### Aristocracy

**Source of wealth**
The Bath family home, Longleat, is perhaps the most famous stately home in the country, made doubly famous when the late marquis invented the Safari park and populated it with the Lions of Longleat. The house itself is very old, going back to the time of Elizabeth I in the sixteenth century. It has a wonderful collection of treasures, though the valuation of £23 million put on the Will of the late Marquess seemed to reflect less than the whole of the assets. This may be because much of the wealth is tied up in trusts, which are essentially perpetual and there to preserve the estate from the tax man and indifferent heirs.

**Personal style**
A eccentric fan of Wessex nationalism, always happy to turn out a tale for the tabloids. Married to Anna Gael, the model and author, he has trailed a collection of girlfriends over the years. He refers to them as wifelets. For sixty years Alexander Thynne was merely the Viscount Weymouth. Then he finally acquired the marquessate and the fortune that went with it. He removed his brother from the management team, a job he had done for many years with great success.

**Extravagances**
Spent much of his years in waiting for the title as a painter of wild and erotic pictures, some of them as murals on the walls of his apartment in Longleat.

## Gordon Sumner (Sting) *42*
**£54m** (£52.5m)
## Music

### Source of wealth
No sign yet of the £6 million Sting says he was stung for two years ago. The pop star has lodged a £7.7 million claim against his accountants, claiming they didn't pay the money – mostly royalties – into his company Steerpike.

Regardless of that, Sting has more money than his lifestyle needs. As lead singer with the Police, he made around £30 million from touring and record sales. The group's final album *Synchronicity* topped the American charts for a record 17 weeks in 1983. Their singles, such as *Walking on the Moon*, *SOS* and *Every Breath You Take* are among the best selling ever in the UK.

Since going solo in 1985, the money has carried on rolling in. Two years ago he made around £10 million from touring,

and his most recent album *Ten Sum-moner's Tales*, topped the charts.

We have increased Sting's wealth based on royalties from this album, which is selling well in the USA, and deducted his sizeable living expenses.

### Personal style
Milkman's son Sting was a primary school teacher in Newcastle before finding fame as a rock star.

Since becoming famous, he hasn't missed out on the trappings of wealth and makes a habit of buying homes from people more famous than him. He has four homes – in Los Angeles, Manhattan, Highgate and Wiltshire, and previous owners include Billy Joel, Barbra Streisand and Sir Yehudi Menuhin.

### Extravagances
Sting went through a peculiar phase in the Eighties when he decided to save the Amazon rain forests and their inhabitants single handedly. He is still an avid charity worker, married to actress Trudie Styler and has five children.

## Sir Michael Bishop *52*
**£54m** (£45.5m)
## Business

### Source of wealth
Sir Michael Bishop's British Midland Airways is now the second-largest carrier to operate out of London Heathrow. The group now also includes Scottish airline, Loganair, and Manx Airlines, and flies more than 60 aircraft, ranging from twin-engine turboprops like the BAe Jetstream to the Boeing 737-400. Last year it flew nearly 6.5 million passengers, up 10 per cent on the previous year, and this year the company predicts an even bigger jump in traffic.

In 1988, SAS paid £25 million to acquire a 24.9 per cent stake in the parent group, Airlines of Britain Holdings, valuing it at

£100 million. In 1992, SAS raised their stake again, on terms which value the group at £165 million, buying £4 million worth of shares from Bishop in the process. SAS now has effectively 40 per cent of ABH.

1993 profits jumped to £1.1 million pre-tax, up from just £810,000 in 1992 on turnover of £400 million. The balance sheet still carries a lot of debt, and the airline's recently announced £275 million expansion will pile on the red ink. A link-up with another airline can't be ruled out.

British Midland has survived while Dan-Air, Laker, Air Europe and others have failed. A company which can survive this long in the face of such tough competition and difficult economics must be worth something: it would probably go for between £160 million and £200 million. Bishop's 28 per cent stake is worth around

£47 million.

### Personal style
He ain't no Richard Branson, but Sir Michael Bishop can stir up trouble just as effectively as his flamboyant fellow airline mogul.

British Midland has been described as the airline which forced Lord King's British Airways to serve coffee on the London-Glasgow shuttle, after BM launched a successful appeal to offer a competing service on that route. Simplistic, but it's a description which reflects Bishop's strongly competitive character: he is a vociferous campaigner for greater deregulation in the European airline industry, and has been particularly withering in his criticism of the proposed multi-billion franc bailout of Air France. He predicts another state-aid fiasco for Belgian carrier Sabena, who lost £90 million last year on the back of the hammering given to them by BM on the Brussels-London route.

British Midland started up sixty years ago, but the watershed in its history was when Bishop joined at the age of 22, becoming general manager just five years later. He was 28 when he joined the board, 30 when he became managing director and still only 36 when he became chairman in 1978, after leading a £1.8 million management buy-out with his two partners, John Wolfe and Stuart Balmforth. Since then, the airline has gone head-to-head against British Airways on Heathrow routes to Scotland, Belfast, Paris, Amsterdam and, most recently, Frankfurt. Four years ago, BM's revenues from non-domestic routes were just an eighth of turnover; now they represent almost half.

He was awarded the CBE in 1986 and knighted in 1991. He is currently chairman of Channel 4, and sits on the board of Airtours and Williams Holdings. Unmarried, his only family, he says, is the "4,000 employees who are directly affected by how well I run this business".

### Extravagances
He cares only about the company but has begun to enjoy life a little after cashing in some £4 million of his shares.

## Ian Skipper *57*
**£54m** (£50m)
## Business

### Source of wealth
Ian Skipper has made three fortunes. The first, when he sold his family's chain of Ford car dealerships, the second when he sold his stake in United Engineering Industries, and the third was his exit from Atlantic Computers when he sold his shares to British & Commonwealth.

The purchases and the sales were made →

with impeccable timing. That sense of timing has made Skipper a very rich man. Just how rich is difficult to quantify – his wealth is locked up in offshore trusts.

## Personal style

Skipper's father wanted him to become a vicar. But when he was just 20, his father left him to run the family motor business. The rest is history.

In 1984, Skipper won an award for his popular Jorvik Viking Centre in York. He set up Heritage Projects to develop similar themed museums in other parts of the country, and in 1987 was appointed a director of the English Tourist Board. He also helped Esther Rantzen set up Childline.

## Extravagances

Few and enjoys working on charitable projects nowadays.

## Lord Rayne 76
## £54m (£58m)
## Property

### Source of wealth

In 1993 London Merchant Securities, the property and leisure group, made after-tax profits of £20.8 million, up 20 per cent on its 1992 figure.

Net asset value also recovered from £294 million to £354 million, but the shares are still languishing. Its chairman, Lord Rayne, owns just over 18 per cent of the company, making him worth £54 million at the beginning of July.

## Personal style

The Rayne story begins in a tailor's shop in London's East End where Max Rayne, as he then was, worked for his father. The firm moved to Oxford Street, where Max discovered he could make more money letting his father's showroom than cutting suits. Realising his flair for property, Rayne's game plan looked easy. He purchased sites in unfashionable areas, renovated them, and waited for prices to rocket. They did, and remained valuable despite the recession. Now London Merchant Securities has diversified into oil and leisure interests, as well as property – LMS has a 14 per cent stake in First Leisure, where Rayne is also chairman.

Lord Rayne's son, Robert, is also a member of the board. His second wife, the former Lady Jane Vane-Tempest Stewart, is the daughter of the 8th Marquess of Londonderry.

He is also a keen patron of the arts, retiring after 16 years as chairman of the National Theatre in 1989, where he oversaw its stormy move to the South Bank.

## Extravagances

Two marriages and an obsession with fine art. Has also been seen playing bingo and ten-pin bowling.

## Robert Mills 43
## £53.5m (£47m)
## Business

### Source of wealth

Robert Mills is Britain's leading authority on plastic windows. It's lucrative too. He heads the PVC double-glazing windows and doors company, Regency International. In 1992, profits slipped 11 per cent to £5.3 million, and in 1993 still further to £4 million. But this doesn't mean Mills is getting poorer. Far from it, his salary is

## Bernard Holmes 51
## £53.5m (£51m)
## Business

### Source of wealth

Bernard Holmes sold his car-transport company, Silcock Express, to Tibbet & Britten in November of 1992.

He received £31.2 million for his stake and a further £21.4 million in stage payments. We have deducted the tax charge which only applied to the first tranche of money, and added previous dividends and interest to his wealth rating.

## Personal style

Holmes wanted to retire at the age of 50, and therefore a private sale was his only solution. The untimely recession and a lack of buyers for this type of business meant that he had to take a rather lower price than he would have got three years previously. He is now a tax exile and living in the South of France, in order to avoid a crippling tax bill on the money.

## Extravagances

None until he retired. Now everything is an extravagance.

## Lord Rotherwick 81
## £53.5m (£60m)
## Aristocracy

### Source of wealth

Our lower rating of Lord Rotherwick

around a million a year.

Profits are falling, because Mills is in the middle of a big investment period and has created a new company to manufacture windows for new houses that can be bought off-the-shelf from builders merchants. Mills estimates that the price can be the same as for a wooden window, if he's right then his wealth will be transformed in the next few years. Mills has substantial cash in the balance sheet. His stake in the business is worth well over £50 million. Add in his past salary and dividends and he is upgraded this year to £53.5 million.

## Personal style

Young Midlander who knows his industry like the back of his hand. Has revolutionised window making from the bad old days of aluminium. Only criticism is the lack of commitment from the window industry to increasing the security of its products. They say it can't be done, but the first manufacturer that does it will win big.

## Extravagances

Building new factories.

reflects the fact that the octogenarian is running his personal net worth down in his Autumn years. It does not reflect overall financial decline. Far from it.

The Rotherwick fortune was made in the days of the British Empire, when Charles Cayzer founded his own shipping line, the Clan Line, and with his wealth became a major landowner in Scotland. Charles' son-in-law Sir John Jellicoe became the first Earl Jellicoe of Scapa – a reward for his role as Commander-in-Chief of the Grand Fleet, taking the name from where he destroyed Germany's surface navy at the Battle of Jutland.

Following the Second World War, British shipping declined rapidly: by the end of the 1970s, the Cayzers no longer had any direct involvement in the industry. Family wealth was concentrated in the financial conglomerate British & Commonwealth, of which the present Lord Rotherwick was chairman.

## Personal style

Lord Rotherwick is a fully paid up member of the wealthy Cayzer family. He shares the political affiliations of his family and sits as a Conservative peer.

He has recently retired from the board of Caledonia Investments, the family company, along with his cousin, the former chairman, Lord Cayzer. Health reasons were cited.

## Extravagances

In the good old days, seafaring for leisure.

### Gilbert Greenall 40
### £53m (£42m)
### Drink

## Source of wealth

Gilbert Greenall has never really followed in his elder brother Peter's footsteps through the corporate hierarchy at Greenalls pub group.

Gilbert was appointed to the board of the family company in a non-executive role three years ago. His shareholding in the group is just slightly less than his elder brother's, and is worth around £48 million thanks to the company's steadily improving margins. His income last year was just over £1 million.

## Personal style

His doctorate is in medicine, not business, and his path has taken him into some of the world's hot spots – places where he may very well have often found that he could do with a pint. He is an adviser to the Overseas Development Agency and has served with them in northern Iraq. He was also the EC Taskforce chairman in war-torn Bosnia.

## Extravagances

A very reserved man who shies away from the limelight.

### Sir John Barlow 60
### £53m (New entry)
### Finance

## Source of wealth

The Barlow moolah came originally from the family's vast Malaysian rubber plantations. Those are now property of the Malaysian government, courtesy of a 1982 nationalisation. But the compensation was handsome and Sir John has since turned his old rubber company, Majedie Investments, into an investment vehicle to manage it. The results lately have been impressive, meaning Sir John gets membership of the *Rich 500* in spectacular style: the trust's net asset value has doubled in the last three years to 223 pence a share, valuing the company at £110 million. Though Barlow is listed as owning only four million shares personally, he controls another 20 million through trusts for his children and holding companies: the stake is worth £46 million at current market prices.

## Personal style

Barlow lets investment managers get on with it, and reaps the rewards. Majedie invests heavily in capital goods firms, and buys most rights issues.

## Extravagances

Sir John (the baronetcy was created for his grandfather in 1907) hunts and shoots in Cheshire, where he owns a large farm and is master of the local hunt.

### Robert Earl 42
### £52.5m (£41.5m)
### Leisure

## Source of wealth

Robert Earl got paid £20 million by Rank plc for building up their North American leisure and catering interests. It was the result of an incentive consultancy which he had negotiated with Mecca Leisure before it was acquired by Rank. Add that to the money he received for the original sale of President Entertainments, and his total wealth comes to £35 million. He has a share in a small, quoted restaurant chain in London.

But his real wealth and the reason for

### Tony Bramall 57
### £52.5m (£47.5m)
### Motor industry

## Source of wealth

Tony Bramall runs quoted Sanderson, Murray and Elder motor retailing group, valued at £60 million. He has a significant share in the business, worth some £20 million.

Sanderson bought 11 dealerships from Rio Tinto Zinc (RTZ) this year for £25.8 million. A rights issue raised most of the cash to pay for this. The purchase doubled the size of Bramall's new company, immediately enhancing overall earnings and so trebling its stock market value.

Before the rights issue Bramall had 52 per cent of Sanderson. Now he has 38 per cent, valuing his stake at around £20 million. He spent £4.6 million cash to take up his partial stake in the rights issue. His main source of wealth was his own motor retailing business, CD Bramall, which he sold to the rental company, Avis Europe, in 1987 for some £50 million.

this year's increase is the rising value of his investment in the Planet Hollywood restaurant chain. He owns most of the company with an American film producer. Smaller stakes are held by actors Arnold Schwarzenegger, Sylvester Stallone and Bruce Willis.

We estimate that this chain may now be worth as much as £60 million and that Earl has a 40 per cent stake.

## Personal style

Robert Earl founded a company called President Entertainments, took it public in the mid-Eighties and then sold it to Pleasurama. Pleasurama was then taken over by Mecca, which was in turn taken over by the Rank Organisation. Hence Earl went from being an entrepreneur to having four different bosses in as many years.

But Earl was really his own boss, and he negotiated a deal whilst at Pleasurama that saw him run the American catering interests – and he improved on the deal each time the company was taken over. He also took over the running of the Rank Hard Rock restaurant chain which he had bought when he was at Pleasurama.

To the chagrin of one of the founders of Hard Rock, Peter Morton, Earl then appeared to take the credit for creating Hard Rock. Be that as it may; he and Morton became sworn enemies and are now suing each other.

## Extravagances

A private jet is now necessary to transport him to his interests across the world.

Assuming tax was paid when he sold his original business and the investment he made to buy his way into Sanderson, plus past dividends and interest, we have rated him at £52.5 million.

## Personal style

Former estate agent, Tony Bramall, is a motor trader extraordinaire. Hailing from Sheffield, he is determined to build up a second fortune, not that he needs the money.

## Extravagances

Cars.

### Charlotte Morrison 39
### £52m (£47m)
### Inheritance

## Source of wealth

Like all truly great aristocratic fortunes, Charlotte Morrison's is less than easily understood. She is the only daughter of the 9th Viscount Galway, who died in 1971 leaving her a 3,000-acre estate near Doncaster. From her mother, Lady Teresa Fox Strangeways, daughter of the 7th Earl of

Ilchester, she received a 15,000 acre estate at Abbotsbury in Dorset and other properties in West London. The transfer took place before her mother's death last year and, despite the gift, her mother's Will disclosed additional assets of £41.2 million, most of which were left to her mother's second husband.

Charlotte's marriage to the Old Etonian art dealer, Guy Morrison, ended some years ago and her son, Simon, lives with her in Dorset.

## Personal style

She is joint master of the Cattistock Hunt and is active in local county affairs and in charities in the West Country. For years the *Sunday Times* propagated that she was Britain's richest woman when she wasn't even in the top ten.

## Extravagances

Male suitors and appearances in Nigel Dempster's gossip column in the *Daily Mail*.

### Isabel Goldsmith 40
### £52m (£49m)
### Inheritance

## Source of wealth

She is the eldest child of Sir James Goldsmith, but her great fortune came from her Bolivian grandfather, Senator Antenor Patino. The money she received two years ago, was part of a legacy of £75 million left to her grandfather in 1947. This legacy originated from Isabel's great-grandfather whose income from his tin mine in the Twenties was £100,000 a day, more than the government of Bolivia had to run the entire country – one of the poorest on earth.

## Personal style

Her mother, Isabel, eloped to Scotland in 1954 at the age of 20 and married the similarly-aged Goldsmith at Kelso. The couple were hotly pursued by her father, who did not approve of his daughter marrying the old Etonian tearaway and gambler. She was made a ward of court and an interim interdict was issued against the wedding. After a five-day court hearing the parents lost the fight. Tragically, four months later Isabel collapsed at a dinner in Paris and died of a brain haemorrhage. But the baby she was carrying was saved. Sir James gave the baby the same name in memory of her mother.

When she was nineteen, Isabel married Baron Arnaud de Rosnay, but the marriage was dissolved after two years.

## Extravagances

She has a large flat in London but her father must be the only man in the world whose Mexican estate includes not only lakes, mountains and a tropical forest, but an active volcano as well. She maintains a property on the Mexican estate.

### Stewart Milne 43
### £52m (£39m)
### Construction

## Source of wealth

Stewart Milne is a director of the 21-odd companies that make up the Stewart Milne Group. It has net assets of around £14.7 million and debts of £8 million. Its net profit is some £4 million a year on a £50 million plus turnover, but before that Milne pays himself a whopping salary.

The assets are believed to be understated, not having been revalued recently.

The company is investing now, at the base of the recession, and will emerge strongly. Last year it ploughed an extra £7 million into developing the business.

Milne owns an 85 per cent stake in the company, and this is reckoned to be worth some £52 million in the much healthier economic world of 1994.

## Personal style

Almost unheard of in England, Milne operates a Scottish-based diversified construction group which builds timber-framed houses and develops industrial parks and housing. Milne operates in the North East of Scotland.

North East Scotland was virtually unaffected by the recession, compared with the rest of the UK. This has tempted him south of the border to do a few projects.

## Extravagances

Rough and tough builder turned businessman. Only exists to construct things.

### Tony Travis 51
### £52m (£40.5m)
### Construction

## Source of wealth

After a rocky year, Tony Travis finally delivered the goods at builders merchant Travis Perkins plc, with pre-tax profits for 1993 almost doubling to £20.5 million. Travis became chairman in 1988, and his 12 million shares are now worth £40 million, thanks to the improved performance. With hefty dividends and salaries since becoming chairman in 1988, he is worth £52 million.

## Personal style

Tony Travis trained as a barrister before taking over the family business, Travis & Arnold, from his father Eric in 1970. It was a bed of roses until 1989, when he merged with Sandell Perkins after a bitter take-over battle, to create Travis Perkins. It was a shotgun wedding and it has taken five years for the bride and groom to get along and make a good return for shareholders. Tony Travis is still in shadows of his father who was a legend in the business.

## Extravagances

Making the merger work was exhausting and the time for extravagances is still to come.

### Lindsay Masters 61
### £52m (£28.5m)
### Media

## Source of wealth

Lindsay Masters is the publishing talent behind Haymarket, the privately-held magazine company that he developed in the Sixties and Seventies with Michael Heseltine, the President of the Board of Trade. We reckon that Heseltine, through nominees, holds around 50 per cent of the shares – with Masters holding the other significant shareholding of perhaps 30 per cent. It is difficult to be more precise given the group's complex structure. Because of the nature of its business, Haymarket is more sensitive than most publishing outfits to fluctuations in revenues from advertisers which buy space in the company's magazines. This year, ad revenue has recovered – and so, we think, has the potential value of the group, were it to be sold or floated. It could be worth as much as £200 million.

Both Heseltine and Masters took a substantial cash chunk out of the company when they sold a clutch of prestigious trade magazines including *Accountancy Age* and *Computing*, to the Dutch VNU publishing company in 1980. They were rumoured to have received £8 million each.

## Personal style

Masters remains at Haymarket as a colourful, eccentric and reclusive figure. He is reportedly fussy about his food: the company chef, for example, knows that Masters must never be served with English lamb. His relaxed habit of turning up for work clutching a carrier bag stuffed with documents endears him to employees and contemporaries alike. Even so, friends talk of a cultured and refined man. Masters separated from his wife, Marisa, only a few years ago. Rumours continue to circulate concerning the size of the separation settlement.

## Extravagances

He plays the trumpet, collects modern art and is a compulsive visitor to Spanish bull-fighting festivals.

### Jim Moffatt 74
### £52m (New entry)
### Leisure

## Source of wealth

When the Royal Bank of Scotland snapped up Jim Moffatt's travel agency in 1987 it paid him with 12 million RBS shares. Moffatt, who's now retired, has hung onto those shares, taking the £1.5 million annual dividend cheques and watching the shares appreciate. They are now worth £47 million.

## Personal style
Jim Moffatt founded the AT Mays travel agency in Saltcoats, Scotland, in the early Fifties. It became one of the North's largest travel agencies under his control. RBS has since sold the travel agency to a third party.

## Extravagances
A Jaguar. He lives with his 72 year-old wife Margaret.

### Marquess of Bute 35
### £51.5m (£47m)
### Aristocracy

## Source of wealth
The Butes, or rather the Crighton Stewarts, to give them their family name, made their aristocratic fortune from land. They own huge Scottish estates in Bute and Ayrshire. In the 19th century, they helped create the city of Cardiff. Currently, they own around 25,000 valuable acres in sun-kissed Marbella, the playground of the international jet set in Spain. The family home is Mount Stuart at Rothesay on the Isle of Bute. It houses a rare and valuable manuscript collection. The current marquess inherited his title last year on the death of his father.

## Personal style
The family are Catholic and the marquess was educated at top Catholic public school, Ampleforth.

## Extravagances
Formerly a fixture of the international racing circuit. Bouts of self-indulgence are few and far between – the Butes lack cash flow.

### Mark Thatcher 41
### £51.5m (£48.5m)
### Business

## Source of wealth
Mark Thatcher's name has been constantly connected with the international arms trade, from where he has made a fortune in commissions using his famous name to smooth paths and open doors. That marks his style: dubious people pay to use his name, which gives them respectability.

His connections with this murky world has inevitably caused him some problems socially, but not financially. Questions have been asked in the House of Commons about his alleged links with Saddam Hussein's weapons procurement network.

His links with a group of Arab expatriates closely linked with the Saudi royal family – and the £60 billion Al Yamamah arms deal – have also been noted.

## Personal style
One day he will be Sir Mark Thatcher –

compliments of the baronetcy controversially dished out to his father by John Major.

## Extravagances
Ultimate hedonistic lifestyle. Travels with a butler and other accompaniments of wealth.

### Michael Winner 58
### £51.5m (£47.5m)
### Entertainment

## Source of wealth
Michael Winner has two sources of wealth; property and film producing. He has his own small organisation, Scimitar Films Ltd, which runs his film productions. Nowadays, as he approaches his 60s, he makes one film every two years. Most of his serious money from films has come from the three *Death Wish* films he made, beginning in 1973. These have probably earned him a sum in excess of £8 million over the years. For the rest of his films, since *Death Wish*, he has averaged a million pound fee per film.

We calculate that Winner has earned £20 million from his film-directing career in the last 38 years. Additionally, Winner sold all his property holdings off for a sum believed to be £30 million in 1988. This foresight has made him £15 million richer than he would otherwise have been.

With total career gains of £50 million less tax, and the care that Winner takes of his money, we estimate that he is worth £51.5 million from real estate and films. Then there is also the value of his own home – and his small collection of art and furniture.

## Personal style
A few years ago Michael Winner was a little known film producer famous for the *Death Wish* films. Then he started writing as a restaurant critic for the *Sunday Times* at the behest of his good friend Andrew Neil, then editor. Since Michael Winner lists one of his recreations in *Who's Who* as "being difficult", he was entirely suited to the role of restaurant critic. His style was to round on the establishments with a vengeance. Few were praised and many were slated. It meant that his column became almost overnight, the best read page in the paper.

Recently, he has switched to overseas establishments which has taken the shine off the column away as people simply aren't interested, but overall Winner is now worth millions to the *Sunday Times* although he probably isn't paid much to do the job.

Winner, has a reputation for being a gruesome beast of a man. But when you actually meet him – providing you are not a fool, (the phrase "doesn't suffer fools gladly" was invented for him) – and penetrate his veneer, he is actually quite a nice

man. But the veneer is thick, and he doesn't care for it being penetrated.

## Extravagances
He is a man of exquisite taste, living in a Kensington mansion which is one of London's finest, unostentatious homes. However, he is constantly being burgled. Hence the security measures at his house – to keep burglars out, rather than to ensure his own personal security.

### Stephen Griggs 32
### £51m (£25m)
### Business

## Souce of wealth
Most people don't know Stephen Griggs but owe him a big thank you – Griggs manufactures Doc Martens boots. Once synonymous with Skinheads, the boots have become an essential fashion accessory in the UK and USA. This is reflected in the profits, rising to £10.75 million after tax in 1993, on a £76.6 million turnover. From the Northampton factory, 220,000 boots are produced a week.

The company would fetch well over £100 million if sold, and as chairman, Grigg's stake in the family business is now worth over £51 million.

## Personal style
The Germans take credit for designing DMs, and in 1959 the Griggs family answered a local newspaper ad seeking a UK producer. Their style of total quality control – easy to say but hard to achieve – is the backbone of the success. Each pair is checked five times before leaving the factory.

## Extravagances
The only company chairman who can get away with wearing DM's to work.

### David Lewis 69
### £51m (£46m)
### Retailing

## Source of wealth
David Lewis owns eight per cent of Lewis Trust, the parent of 300-store fashion chain River Island Clothing. The group made just over £14 million after tax in 1992, and we estimate his stake to be worth £27 million. He also has substantial property interests in the Israeli resort of Eilat – which locals refer to as 'Lewisville'. This increases his wealth to £51 million.

## Personal style
The son of an East End greengrocer, David Lewis was a navigator with Bomber Command during the Second World War, taking part in raids on Hamburg and Berlin. After the war, he opened his first fashion shop with his brother, Bernard, in Tooting in 1954. The Sixties brought a slew of

young people with disposable income, and David cannily metamorphosed his conservative Lewis Separates shops into the Chelsea Girl chain, which brought trendy fashion to the high street. Again sensing a shift in tastes, Lewis turned Chelsea Girl into River Island in the late Eighties.

## Extravagances

David Lewis is an accumulator, not a spender. Hence, perhaps, the River Island store credit card charging an astronomical 36 per cent APR on purchases.

### Duke of Rutland 75
### £51m (£47m)
### Aristocracy

## Source of wealth

The Duke of Rutland's land holdings cover 18,000 acres around his estates, Haddon Hall, Derby, and Belvoir Castle near Grantham, Lincolnshire. That sum is supplemented by art works by Poussin, Gainsborough and Holbein, worth around £20 million.

Belvoir Castle attracts a large number of tourists – as well as film production crews. But he remains keen on farming and would prefer not to have to raise timber on his lands. "I find the idea that the British farmer should become a sort of park-keeper totally unacceptable," he once said. The duke has two sons and one daughter, the one-time pop star wildchild, Lady Teresa Manners. His elder son, the Marquis of Granby, 34, who runs a firearms business, is the heir.

He backed the campaign to have Rutland recognised as an independent chunk of England once again – quite separate from Leicestershire.

## Personal style

Once described by an authoritative source (the novelist Barbara Cartland) as the most handsome man in England.

## Extravagances

Eccentricity.

### Con Wilson
### £51m (£45m)
### Construction

## Source of wealth

Con Wilson's brother Lynn Wilson is the chairman of Northamptonshire builder Wilson Connolly. Although Con doesn't appear in the boardroom, or anywhere near the offices for that matter, he holds a 10.2 per cent stake in the group.

His brother Lynn has done him proud this year. Wilson Connolly defied the recession and returned pre-tax profits of £28.2 million for 1993, up £11.4 million. The group is now capitalised at £389 million, and Con's stake a cool £39 million.

With past dividends and his many local interests, his wealth adds up to £51 million.

## Personal style

Con is rarely known as "Lynn's brother" in Northampton, where he is renowned for his chain of betting shops and former interest in Northampton Football Club.

## Extravagances

Still a keen football fan but watching from the stands these days. Much quieter than his brother but much more famous, at least in Northampton.

### Wensley 50 Haydon-Baillie
### £50m (£62m)
### Business

## Source of Wealth

The charismatic Wensley Haydon-Baillie may have resigned as chairman at the struggling Porton International pharmaceuticals company, but he still owns 35 per cent of its shares.

Set up in 1982 with £12 million of City backing, the company secured a controversial deal with the government's Centre for Applied Microbiology and Research at Porton Down three years later. The deal gave Porton International exclusive marketing rights over all of Porton Down's products. That same year, the company raised more money, selling 17.5 per cent of its shares for $100 million, valuing the group at £400 million (or about 1,000 times earnings). The company has worked on such products as human growth hormone, a treatment for a faster diagnosis of HIV, and a herpes treatment. In 1987, it looked like the company was heading for a stock market float which would value it at £1 billion or more. It predicted 1990 profits of £140 million.

But forecasting is always dangerous, especially when biotechnology is the issue. Some products have taken years longer to develop than originally expected, while the long-promised herpes treatment subsequently failed in clinical trials. And the Porton Down deal has been strongly criticised in Parliament; plans to privatise the government research centre and sell it to Haydon-Baillie's company have been scrapped.

Haydon-Baillie sold part of his shareholding in 1986 for £24 million; there is now no immediate prospect of the company being worth £1 billion, so this cash slug, plus investment returns, makes up a lot of his current wealth. Porton International might get away with being valued on a price/earnings ratio of something like 25 times latest earnings, but since after-tax profits fell again to £2.5 million in the year to December 1992 that would value the company at £60 million. Allowing for the

generous dividend payments over the years, Haydon-Baillie's wealth has only declined to £50 million.

## Personal style

Charismatic, verging on the roughshod. As well as overinflating its profit forecasts, Porton International has been accused of paying its directors and executives too much money for too few results. Haydon-Baillie's reputation as a dynamic entrepreneur has suffered as a result. He has also made a debut in the gossip columns this year with daring exploits regarding members of the opposite sex.

## Extravagances

All those six figure pay packets and the resulting lifestyle.

### Bill Rooney 53
### £50m (£58m)
### Business

## Source of wealth

Getting fired last year as chief executive of the company he founded, Spring Ram, was an excellent move for Bill Rooney. Yes, his wealth is down on last year, but the significant difference is the money in the bank.

Rooney was ousted in a shareholders revolt led by the Prudential, after announcing three consecutive profit warnings for the bathroom products producer. When he left in September 1993, his shares, totalling nearly 60 million through a family trust, were worth £47 million. The share price has since plummeted to 48 pence, with pre-tax losses of £36.4 million for 1993.

If Rooney were still there, his fortune would have dwindled. But he had the last laugh, selling almost his entire share stake for £34 million in April this year. Two months earlier, he sold the rights to take up 13.6 million shares (as part of a rights issue) for a cool £2.4 million. To rub salt in the wound for the new board at Spring Ram, Rooney was kept on as a consultant for £1,500 a month until March, although he had moved to Barbados. With past dividends and salaries, Rooney now has £50 million, and it's money he can spend today.

## Personal style

The £50 million doesn't mean he is about to retire. He founded Spring Ram after training with the Milk Marketing Board, and the company's shares peaked in 1991 at 181 pence. He found it hard to accept the criticisms following huge losses, and after a spell in Barbados thinking over his future, returned to Bradford earlier this year. He has started a rival bathroom producer, Full Circle Industries, with other former Spring Ram directors.

## Extravagances

Plenty of loot to do what he likes with. But at heart Rooney is married to his work.

## Thomas Trickett 62
## £50m (£44m)
## Business

### Source of wealth
Thomas Trickett is the brother-in-law of David Crossland, founder and chairman of Airtours. In 1972, when Crossland bought his first travel agency for £8,000, Trickett and his wife bought a third of the business to help relieve Crossland's debt burden. With the growth of the business and a few share sales, Trickett now holds just under eight million shares in the company, with a market value of £37 million. They add up to nine per cent of Airtours.

Trickett made an agreement with Crossland in 1988 that he would not sell eight million of his shares without Crossland's permission and – particularly interesting – also handed over the voting rights on these shares to Crossland. The agreement has been renewed until 1995.

In 1987, seven months after the company issued its flotation prospectus, Airtours had to announce to the stock market that it would not meet its profit forecast. Trickett and Crossland gamely offered to waive their dividend entitlements and even decided to exercise their warrants to buy more shares in the company, even though that would cost them twice as much as buying shares in the market. This impressive exercise in penitence cost Trickett around £500,000, so soon after he had pocketed £2 million on the flotation.

### Personal style
Hard to spot, as Trickett lives in the flamboyant Crossland's shadow. He owes his place on the board and his job as "product review director" – essentially reading the competition's catalogues to see what they're doing – to the canny investment of 22 years ago. The curious deal whereby Crossland controls his shares indicates a lack of ambition or independence.

### Extravagances
Few. Trickett lives quietly with his wife, and has effectively retired from Airtours.

## Cyril Stein 66
## £49.5m (£45.5m)
## Business

### Source of wealth
Cyril Stein, and his family, bought Ladbrokes in 1956 and it has been the source of all his wealth. We estimate share sales over the years have amassed him a personal fortune that is today worth £49.5 million.

### Personal style
At the age of 65, Cyril Stein was forcibly retired from Ladbrokes. He couldn't quite believe it. Cyril Stein bought the then private bookmaker Ladbrokes in 1956. Ten years later the company was floated on the London stock exchange. It weathered a casino scandal in the 1970s, when it lost its British gaming licence and developed its betting businesses. In 1987 it bought Hilton International for £645 million giving it a chain of 91 hotels throughout the world. The Hilton purchase was the highlight of Stein's career and banished all memories of the casino humiliation forever. The hotels were generally thought to be worth twice as much as he paid the day after he bought them. It was a genuine business coup and made up for the casino scandal.

### Extravagances
The turf. But nothing seems worthwhile anymore after the devastation of being fired from his own company.

*EVENING ARGUS*

## Nicholas van Hoogstraten 48
## £49m (£48m)
## Property

### Source of wealth
One of Britain's most notorious – or famous – private landlords, Nicholas van Hoogstraten owns around 100 commercial and residential properties in Brighton and another 40 in West London.

He also owns properties in Paris worth an additional £6 million. These assets are held through a network of offshore companies. ("I hide behind nominees," he once said. "I don't get involved in anything.")

The cash generated by his properties has enabled van Hoogstraten to move into other ventures. He maintains a keen business interest in Zimbabwe, where he has held a £118,000 stake in the Lonrho-controlled mining and cattle company, Willoughby's Consolidated. He used to hold a small stake worth, on paper, around £72,000 in a plantation company that has since gone into liquidation.

### Personal style
In Britain, van Hoogstraten lives in some style and for the past three years he has divided his time between here and a mansion in the South of France.

In 1967 Hoogstraten was jailed for four years for throwing a hand-grenade into the home of a Brighton synagogue official. The trial judge said: "This young man is a sort of self-imagined devil. He thinks that he is an emissary of Beelzebub."

### Extravagances
Apart from the home in the south of France, he has built an enormous country house worth £5 million in East Sussex.

## John Coldman 47
## £49m (£45m)
## Finance

### Source of wealth
John Coldman is managing director of the Benfield Group, a Lloyd's reinsurance broker. He holds slightly fewer shares than his colleagues on the board do – some 6,250,000 in total. This is a 13 per cent stake in the company making him worth £49 million with salary and dividends added.

Benfield had a remarkable 1992, making £30.6 million profit, on turnover of £39.7 million. Although followed by a difficult year, Benfield achieved a similar £41.2 million turnover and profits of £31.2 million in 1993. It has just launched a re-insurance company that will take on insurance risks itself. The venture is jointly funded by Benfield and venture capitalists to the tune of £50 million.

### Personal style
As the administrator of the star Benfield team, Coldman works in tandem with genius chairman, Matthew Harding.

### Extravagances
Just realising what it is like to be rich.

## Michael Gooley 57
## £49m (New entry)
## Leisure

### Source of wealth
The Nineties have been good for Michael Gooley and we can resist him *Rich 500* membership no longer. The hordes of young (and not so young) backpackers departing for long trips abroad have one thing in common: they've booked their odysseys through Trailfinders, the 24-year-old travel agency controlled by Michael Gooley.

The company's balance sheet would

make grown accountants weep: almost zero liabilities, a £23 million cash pile, and £3.6 million after-tax profits on £105 million turnover. The travel business is still in flux, however, and it's unclear whether Trailfinders' dominant position in its market niche will remain so lucrative. It is very much a personal business and with a price/earning ratio of 10, plus the cash values Gooley's 95 per cent shareholding at £49 million. He paid himself £300,000 last year and received £1 million in dividends.

## Personal style

Confirmed travel addict and ex-SAS man Michael Gooley set up the agency in 1970 to cater for the then-unusual business of long-distance leisure travel. From quiet beginnings Trailfinders has gone ballistic. Its reputation of going that extra mile to get its customers good long-haul flight deals - especially the increasingly popular "round-the-world" flights - has endeared the company to an entire generation of footloose Brits.

## Extravagances

That American Express advertisement, which is threatening to make him an Establishment figure.

### Sir Anthony Jacobs 63
**£49m** (£40m)
### Business

(302) 281

## Source of wealth

Last October's flotation of the British School of Motoring Group provided a hefty pay-day for Sir Anthony, who trousered over £7 million by reducing his share stake to 4.5 per cent. His remaining shares are now worth just under £2 million.

Most of his fortune was made in 1990, when he sold most of his shares in the business to the management for nearly £40 million. He still owns the Spud U Like chain and an aviation company.

## Personal style

Eton educated, trained as an accountant. Die-hard Liberal supporter, who stood as a candidate for Watford in the two 1974 elections, losing them both. Nevertheless, the Liberals still appointed him joint treasurer of the party for three years.

## Extravagances

Golf, opera, theatre, and writing to Paddy Ashdown.

### Earl of Mansfield 64
**£49 m** (£48 m)
### Aristocracy

(246) 282

## Source of wealth

The Earl of Mansfield's 37,000 acres surround Scone Palace, the family seat in Perthshire plus the contents, represents his wealth. There has been some appreciation

in both this year but the cost of maintaining the estate makes increases in the earl's wealth modest.

## Personal style

A true-blue Tory; in 1984, in his 50s, he retreated to his estate at Scone. The title came into the family in 1605, when James VI of Scotland rode south to become King of England. With him, the King took David Murray, the present earl's ancestor, who had the rank of Cupbearer, Master of Horse and Captain of the Guard. In London, Murray was given the title Lord Scone.

The earls of Mansfield have steered clear of affairs of state for 200 years. After a brief turn in Malaya in the late Forties, the current earl went into politics via law, working for the Tory Party successively in the European Parliament, the House of Lords front bench, the Scottish Office and the Northern Ireland Office.

## Extravagances

The earl is asset-rich but less flush in terms of cash.

### Stanley Cohen 67
**£49m** (£95m)
### Retailing

(116) 283

## Source of wealth

Betterware plc, the direct selling consumer goods quoted company, has turned Stanley Cohen into a very rich man although not as super rich as he was last year. Last year we described the Betterware story as, "What a difference five years makes". This time it is in the negative and we say "What a difference a year makes".

Last year Betterware was worth some £260 million and Cohen and his son Andrew owned 65 per cent, just over 30 per cent each. They reduced their holding by 7.5 per cent each last Summer, raising £15 million each. A few months later the share prices crashed in half and then by another third and the company today is valued at less than £100 million.

The Cohens didn't reveal, when they sold their stake, that growth had stopped and sales had actually shown signs of declining. They then kept on denying and denying that something was wrong but the City clearly didn't believe them. It was right not to. At the last results, they finally admitted year-on-year sales were actually down. Clearly, Betterware was a child of the recession and when times boomed again consumers turned off the cheaper goods sold door-to-door. Cohen is one of the biggest losers in this year's *Rich 500*.

## Personal style

Stanley Cohen has been a long-term investor in British companies for most of his life. Through his investment company,

Queensway Securities, he has made many great investments and just a few bad ones. One of his other public successes was the Platignum pen company where he made a few millions.

## Extravagances

Boats.

### Derek Crowson
**£49m** (£47m)
### Business

(280) 284

## Source of wealth

Derek Crowson chairs, and owns, Derek Crowson Ltd the holding company for Crowson Fabrics, which designs and distributes furnishing fabrics.

With annual sales of £34.5 million the last time accounts were filed for the year ending December 1992, Crowson returned just £1.55 million profit. But with considerable liquid assets, the company is worth closer to £40 million on the market. Derek Crowson himself collects an average £2 million salary each year.

## Personal style

An unknown quantity except to the residents of Uckfield in East Sussex where the firm is based.

## Extravagances

A £32,000 donation to the Conservative Party in 1992.

### Clive Smith 45
**£48m** (£54m)
### Finance

(222) 285

## Source of wealth

The wealth of Clive Smith preoccupies many, including the Serious Fraud Office. The affairs of this wealthy man are indeed unusual. In early 1993, Smith applied for a voluntary arrangement to circumvent impending bankruptcy proceedings. His creditors claimed some £20 million. In response, Smith – the first man in Stoke-on-Trent to own a helicopter – estimated his assets at a mere £1.7 million.

Much of the proceeds from his deals in the Eighties, it is reckoned, were ploughed into offshore trusts registered in the names of close relatives. Clive Smith is currently under investigation by the SFO, even though he is in voluntary arrangement with his creditors owed over £20 million-worth of debts. We rate his wealth lower this year because putting it into hiding has been expensive and it is being spread amongst others.

You may think the story of Clive Smith is remarkable. And you would be right. It is.

## Personal style

Smith is a Midlands entrepreneur whose name has cropped up in connection with the collapse of half-a-dozen quoted natural resources companies in the past decade. He is superficially suave and complex financial deals come naturally.

Smith got his start in the meat trucking business in the Seventies. He had inherited the business from his father, a local businessman of some repute in and around his hometown of Stoke-on-Trent. Ultimately, Smith sold out his transport business to Unilever. In time, he diversified into mining, taking charge of small scale local minerals operations in the Midlands.

In the Eighties, Smith's name appeared in connection with companies such as Far East Resources and Butte Mining. Large promoters' profits on the sale of highly-priced mining properties in the United States were a recurring factor.

### Extravagances
Lives in a lavish house considering what he tells his creditors. Renowned as the first man in Stoke-on-Trent to own a helicopter.

### Richard Biffa 55
### £48m (£50m)
### Business

### Source of wealth
Rubbish has always had a sweet smell for Biffa. The fortune started with the family waste disposal business, Biffa Ltd, which Richard joined in 1958. BET bought the family out in 1971, but Richard stayed on and in 1985 organised a buyout of Rechem, BET's hazardous waste unit. (BET sold Biffa's old company for £212 million to Severn Trent Water in 1991).

Three years later, Rechem was floated, and in 1990 it was merged into waste disposal rival Shanks & McEwan. Biffa's Rechem stake was valued at £40 million by the takeover, and he still holds just under five per cent of Shanks & McEwen, whose shares have underperformed in the last year. His stake is currently valued at £7.5 million, some £2 million less than last year.

### Personal style
His life seems to have revolved around rubbish, and with that he has found it difficult to create a personal style. But who cares? Biffa proves the truth of the old adage that where there's muck there's brass.

### Extravagances
A £5 million country estate and a luxury yacht. A private jet cannot be far off the horizon despite this year's slight drop in his net worth.

### Gerald Weisfeld 56
### £48m (£50m)
### Retailing

### Source of wealth
Gerald Weisfeld and his wife, Vera, made a mint from discount retailing in Scotland and the north during the Seventies and

Eighties from their chain of stores, What Everyone Wants. In 1991, 20 years after founding What Everyone Wants, Weisfeld sold the chain to Philip Green's Amber Day for a lavish £50 million.

After taxes, but adding back past profits and salaries, and discounting the investment in Celtic and merchant banking fees from the abortive bid, we reckon Weisfeld at £2 million lower than last year.

### Personal style
Gerald and Vera aren't too happy right now. They had their comeback all planned out: riding to the rescue of Brown & Jackson, the debt-ridden retailer behind the Poundstretcher discount chain, waving a £6 million cheque. Unfortunately, a rival suitor showed up, in the form of South African retailer Pepkor, offering £20 million. The shareholders opted for the latter.

Gerald's particularly peeved because rumours that old enemy Philip Green is somehow connected with Pepkor, just won't go away. Green tried to make the What Everyone Wants business "sweat" a bit more money and the Weisfelds resigned from the Amber Day board in disgust.

### Extravagances
Like many rich people with more money than sense, Gerald has sunk a portion of his wealth into a football club. In this case it's Glasgow's Celtic, and the club is rapidly turning into a financial black hole for the directors.

### James Gulliver 63
### £48m (£52m)
### Business

### Source of wealth
James Gulliver didn't bite the dust when Lowndes Queensway went bust. He never had more than a few millions in the project, and financially he came away unscathed, even if the deal broke his spirit.

Nothing has been heard of Gulliver for the past three years; but just because he is quiet doesn't mean to say he is poor . Far from it . We estimate that careful management of his money has increased his worth. He has turned from doer to investor, finding it more lucrative for his skill patterns in the Nineties. But he hasn't had a particularly good year, investment wise and we rate him down slightly at £48 million.

### Personal style
It is doubtful that Jimmy Gulliver will re-emerge in the public eye: he is too battered for that, and getting old. After all, why should he expose himself again? He has all he wants.

He has a few interests in some public companies and private leisure ventures.

His nemesis was losing to Guinness in the battle to take over Distillers Company. If he

had won that prize he would still be a powerful man, and Argyll would be valued at twice its current market capitalisation. Instead, he lost, and his colleagues forced him out of Argyll. Some say he only bought Lowndes Queensway to show them they were wrong. He merely showed them that they were right. Sir Alistair Grant, the man who fired him, said he was devastated when it was revealed that Gulliver had lied about getting an MBA from Harvard University in his entry in *Who's Who*.

### Extravagances
Luxurious houses and women.

### Judah Binstock 65
### £48m (£46.5m)
### Finance

### Source of wealth
Judah Binstock began his career by making a mint out of small company shares. But as he headed toward the big time, he fell foul of both the Inland Revenue and the Treasury. At issue, there were alleged breaches of exchange controls worth around £20 million. The transactions stemmed from a Seventies dollar premium fraud centred on EIC Eurosecurities and shares in the Hong Kong and Shanghai Bank.

He qualified as a solicitor, and ran a flourishing practice in the late Fifties in London's Marylebone. Observing how his clients were making a fortune from property deals, he decided that he could do even better. Armed with the inside knowledge he gained in this way, he got in on Britain's first great property boom.

This was how he came to meet men like Sir Eric Miller, the famed Peachey Property boss who committed suicide one summer in the late Seventies.

In the end, Binstock had got into too many doubtful deals and fled the country – to Marbella, where he lived in comfortable exile, courtesy of the lapse of extradition laws between Spain and the UK in 1978. In 1977 Binstock was said to be worth £15 million. But leading the life of a fugitive proved an expensive business. However, he has made money on the Continent on property deals during his years in exile. When he left Britain he transferred all his money into Swiss Francs at six times the value of today.

### Personal style
In his pension year Binstock hasn't changed overmuch. He is still married to Josie, his very attractive French wife who is buying a house in London. Binstock prefers to stay at the St James Club where he books in under assumed names (usually American wild west characters such as Bill Hickock and Jesse James), so that , he claims, previous acquaintances can't contact him

to borrow money.

However, it is far too easy to meet people in London who do not hold Binstock in high regard. A surprisingly high number of people will testify to being at the wrong end of a Binstock deal.

**Extravagances**
Maxim's in Paris and caviar.

### Arnold Clark 66
### £48m (New entry)
### Motor Industry

#### Source of wealth
Arnold Clark owns all the shares in Scotland's biggest motor trader, the Arnold Clark Organisation and has elbowed his way into the *Rich 500* on the basis that, in 1992, his company returned profits of £4.6 million after tax on a £247 million turnover. We value the company, taking into account its brand name, at over £45 million. Clark himself is one of Scotland's best paid executives.

#### Personal style
Clark knows all about starting from scratch. Originally a mechanic in the RAF in 1955, he saved enough money to buy a used-car showroom in a converted shop in Glasgow to begin trading.

#### Extravagances
Passionate sailor, who hit the headlines in 1987 when he bought Simon Le Bon's yacht, Drum, for £250,000.

### John Chedzoy 71
### £48m (New entry)
### Business

#### Source of wealth
John Chedzoy is an accountant who distributes cigarettes for a living. He's quite good at it too: his company, Palmer & Harvey Holdings, turned over £1.35 billion in 1992, and made £16.8 million and that was after corporation tax. It is one of the largest private companies in Britain by turnover. Chedzoy's 17 per cent stake would net him around £42 million if P&H were sold today, valuing the company at £250 million.

#### Personal style
He's an accountant.

#### Extravagances
Paid himself £2.4 million in 1992, just behind Rocco Forte (£12 million) and David Sainsbury (£35 million) in the accountants-who-take-home-lucre stakes.

### Noel McMullen
### £48m (£60m)
### Business

#### Source of wealth
Noel McMullen and brother, Max, generate annual turnover of around £170 million

via their privately-held company, Maxol.

The Seventies oil shock generated windfall profits for the McMullens, who subsequently diversified into construction via their Castletown Homes subsidiary. Much of their wealth was based on a situation familiar in many sectors of the Irish economy: control by a few individuals of key industries or trade franchises. But the recent worldwide oil glut has seen their profits tumble. Neither has the savage recession in the Republic's property market

### Paula Brown 41
### £48m (New entry)
### Inheritance

#### Source of wealth
The source of Paula Brown's wealth was her late husband, Sir David Brown, an engineering genius who built up a worldwide engineering business, producing tractors and Aston Martins alike, after

### John Ray 45
### £47.5m (New entry)
### Business

#### Source of wealth
John Ray owns 100 per cent of Rigblast, the Scottish oil services support group, which had a record year to December 1992. Pre-tax profits were around £6 million on turnover of £85 million. We value Ray's group at £45 million. Borrowings are low, and the company has positive cash flow.

#### Personal style
Curmudgeonly, John Ray, has little time for grand titles or high profiles, but he did see fit to reward himself with wages and dividends totalling over £1 million last year.

#### Extravagances
Who would have thought he had a soft heart? Ray gave £70,000 to charity last year, putting larger (and publicly listed) Scottish companies to shame.

done them any good. Accordingly, we have marked down his net worth somewhat this year to £48 million.

#### Personal style
Quiet businessman: not much sighted amid the Dublin social scene. In a nation with limited natural gas resources, Maxol oil pumps supply heating oil to a large swathe of rural Ireland.

#### Extravagances
Not yet known as a racehorse owner – the typical pastime of most Irish tycoons.

the Second World War. At one stage, the company owned Vosper Thorneycroft and qualified as a famous name in the British engineering industry, with subsidiaries dotted around the Commonwealth. In the Seventies, the industry and the company alike entered into terminal decline.

In 1978, Brown left for tax exile in Monte Carlo. Twelve years later, he died, leaving one son and one daughter by a previous marriage. In the same year, 1990, the company he founded was sold off by the family to an MBO consortium for £46 million. Since then, the company has prospered. On its flotation in April last year, it was valued at £90 million.

#### Personal style
As Sir David's secretary, and from 1980, as his wife, Paula Brown guided the old engineering genius through his twilight years in tax exile.

#### Extravagances
Sir David was a hardy old entrepreneur, more devoted to generating good ideas than conspicuous consumption. His wife is cast in a similar mould, and, although still in her 40s, leads a quiet life.

### Jim Raper 66
### £47.5m (£49.5m)
### Finance

#### Source of wealth
Despite his crookedness, Jim Raper is very wealthy. Strangely, the *Sunday Times* has never included him on its list, but on 6th March 1988 the newspaper estimated his wealth at £50 million. Adding up his crooked haul, we agree with that figure. When he left Britain, the whole of his gains were transferred abroad. Behind him, he left a trail of financial destruction. Fortunately for investors he now seems to have retired, and shows no inclination to return to Britain, where he would be arrested on sight. We rate him lower as the cost of being a fugitive is high.

#### Personal style
Jim Raper was a businessman of some talent. But his activities were of a distinctly

unsavoury nature. First, there was the scandal of his acquisition of mining company St Piran in 1980 which he cleared out of funds. Then he stuffed Westminster Property Group shareholders after St Piran bought it.

The DTI stumbled about in a bid to nail Raper. Finally, it roundly condemned him in a 1988 report. But he was long gone by then, and reportedly laughed his head off. Apparently, he never even bothered to read the report. The list of Raper's victims include investors with the Isle of Man-based Savings and Investment Bank, which crashed in 1982. Raper borrowed £5 million from the bank, which was never repaid. All in all, Raper's timing was impeccable. He knew when to leave the country for good and count his loot.

He is a fitness fanatic and entered for the 1988 London Marathon – until he found Scotland Yard looking for him, after a two-year sentence was imposed for contempt of court. He based himself in Cannes, France, realising that he could not be extradited from there for a contempt of court offense. He is also wanted in Singapore for offenses. Last heard of in the South of France, living the life of a millionaire, with a 'ravishing' Filipino girl.

## Extravagances
Parties and women.

### Peter Vardy 47
### £47m (£35.25m)
### Motor Industry

## Source of wealth
Peter Vardy has the biggest smile north of Watford. The quoted Reg Vardy car-dealer group, which he chairs and owns a substantial proportion of, saw pre-tax profits jump 92 per cent to £8.4 million for 1993. With turnover approaching £300 million, the City is more than impressed, valuing the company at £90 million.

With past dividends and salaries, Peter Vardy is now worth £47 million.

## Personal style
Vardy is the eternal optimist, never accepting the recession could affect his sales. He's not a bad businessman either, snapping up the plum Mercedes dealership in Kelvinside last year, which greatly contributed to profits. With land disposals under way, things may get even better.

## Extravagances
Too busy dreaming up new ways of making money for any extravagances. Earlier this year he physically pulled out all the "Vardy" stickers on the back of the company's Cavaliers, replacing them with "Vauxhall." When bemused staff asked why, he explained Vauxhall were paying him for each sticker displayed.

### Peter Beckwith 50
### £47m (£42m)
### Property

## Source of wealth
Peter is the elder of the famous Beckwith brothers, who trousered £35 million each in 1990, when they sold London and Edinburgh Trust to Swedish property investor SPP for £491 million. Peter is now dabbling in the property business, again with his brother John, through a new company Riverside Leisure Holdings. The company is building a chain of quality health clubs around Europe and plans to float later this year. We have added £5 million to his wealth, and it will increase substantially if the flotation is a success.

## Personal style
Peter Beckwith was the star of the property business in the Seventies, building up LET and surviving the 1974 property crash. His timing in selling to SPP was perfect – just before the 1990 crash. Beckwith stayed on the board as SPP slowly sunk, resigning appropriately on bonfire night in 1992.

## Extravagances
The desire to make serious money has gone, despite the Riverside venture. He prefers raising money for Cambridge University, and has many theatre interests.

### Peter Thomas 51
### £47m (£42m)
### Food

## Source of wealth
In 1988 brothers Peter and Stan Thomas sold the family pie and sausage business to Grand Metropolitan for £75 million, perhaps the largest sum ever paid for a private business in Wales. Peter's share was a straight £30 million and his sister got £15 million, making the whole family worth a sum today approaching £90 million.

Peter's shares in Grand Met and various property investments have appreciated since then.

## Personal style
Peter's Savoury Products was the second goldmine for the Thomas family. Stanley Thomas Senior started a pies and savoury snacks company in 1952 in the heart of the South Wales coalfields. In 1965, it was sold to the Avana group but five years later Stanley Jr launched Peter's Savoury Products which again produced solid fare for the coal-mining community.

After the takeover by Grand Met, Peter has stayed on to run the business.

## Extravagances
He lives in a large house surrounded by 16 acres in Merthyr. He enjoys sailing, golf and flying, but must enjoy work most of all

because with all those millions in the bank, work is the one thing he could afford to give up.

### Harry Solomon 57
### £47m (£36m)
### Business

## Source of wealth
Harry Solomon's personal wealth comes from his original share stake in quoted Hillsdown Holdings, which he co-founded in 1975 with David Thompson. The recovery in Hillsdown's share price and other investments meant his wealth has risen substantially this year.

## Personal style
The fall of Hillsdown as a City glamour stock during his reign at the helm, hit him very hard and this is thought to be the reason for his resignation from the company he loved. He had co-founded the group in 1975 with partner David Thompson. Then Thompson left and Solomon was in charge.

Now Solomon has left and is the executive chairman of a Hillsdown clone called Princedale, a USM-quoted marketing services company. Solomon has invested £600,000 in Princedale which bought three unrelated businesses from Hillsdown for £7.65 million. The deal quadrupled the size of Princedale.

Harry Solomon retired at the age of 55. He is paranoid about having his photo taken and has gone into business again. Harry Solomon doesn't talk to the press much either although he is actually an approachable and very likeable man.

## Extravagances
Since he has never been photographed, only sketched, he is hardly going to let on about is personal extravagances.

### Lord Margadale 87
### £47m (£45m)
### Aristocracy

## Source of wealth
Lord Margadale's family were in the textiles retailing business, and he inherited half a million pounds at the tender age of 21. But the lord's luck didn't stop there: in the Sixties, he was given one of the last hereditary peerages to be created. The head of a political family, his son Sir Peter Morrison was junior minister at the DTI in the mid-Eighties and, in 1990, was PPS to Margaret Thatcher before her resignation. Another son, Sir Charles Morrison, was MP for Devizes from 1964 to 1992.

## Personal style
Lord Margadale himself was the MP for Salisbury from 1942 to 1964, and was once described as the richest MP in Parliament. He was chairman of the powerful 1922

Committee in the government of Harold Macmillan. His daughter, Mary Morrison, has held the title of Woman of the Bedchamber to the Queen since 1960. He owns the Fonthill House estate in Salisbury, Wiltshire, and another one in Argyll, Scotland.

## Extravagances

Fox-hunting used to be a major preoccupation. He was master of foxhounds in Wiltshire for over 30 years until 1965.

### John Newsome 60
### £46.5m (New entry)
### Business

## Source of wealth

John Newsome owns 78 per cent of Mottram Group plc, the PVC windows group. The company made £3.98 million after tax profit from a turnover of £48 million in the year to December 1992. On a sector p/e of 15, this values the company at just under £60 million should it ever hit the market. Newsome's shares are worth £46.5 million by this calculation.

## Personal style

Newsome and partner Ken Symonds founded Gradus Ltd, a PVC products company, 28 years ago. They merged it into their other company, Mottram, last year. "Mottram is considered particularly strong in PVC extrusion and injection moulding," said *Carpet and Floorcoverings Review* last year.

## Extravagances

An undying love for things plastic.

### Tim Mahony
### £46.5m (£45m)
### Business

## Source of wealth

Tim Mahony runs one of Ireland's more successful car import operations. On the back of his car deals, he has launched Killeen Investments, which boasts engineering and automotive operations – many of them based on Mahony's original success as a trader plying between Ireland and Japan.

Killeen has busied itself setting up joint-ventures with Japanese partners – such as Munekata, which manufactures plastic casings for electronic equipment – engaged in industrial operations in Ireland. Turnover on the Toyota brand-name in Ireland in 1991 came to around £132 million. Allowing for the fact that the basis of his business empire is tied to Toyota's marketing plan, Mahony's car business plus other investments are worth £45 million.

## Personal style

Supreme salesman. Devotee of all things Japanese.

## Extravagances

A subsidiary, Killeen Trading House, set up in 1988, has taken a few hard knocks over the years – mostly from over-ambitious attempts to imitate Japanese business methods.

### Nigel Mansell 41
### £46m (37.5m)
### Sports

## Source of wealth

In 1985 Nigel Mansell was a pauper. Nine years later he is Britain's richest sportsman. The first sign of things to come emerged in 1986 when he earned £500,000. Not until 1987 did he enter the big league, when he received £3 million for that record-breaking season – every race he entered he started on the front row of the grid. In 1988 Mansell received £5 million in his least successful season, when his best result was a second place as the Williams team lost their Honda engines.

He was hired by the high-rolling Ferrari team in 1989 and was reputedly paid £10 million for one season's work, his fee supplemented by Marlboro cigarettes. He repaid the faith shown by Ferrari and Marlboro by winning the first race of the season. In 1990 he continued to earn the same sort of money, easily eclipsing what the world champion, Ayrton Senna, was then earning at McLaren.

Frank Williams tempted him back for the 1991 season with a £7 million payment for two seasons and the most competitive car on the circuit. Then, after becoming world champion in 1992, he was lured to Indianapolis racing, in the United States, for a base fee of £3.25 million. Lucrative Stateside endorsements added another £1.5 million to that sum.

His arrival has transformed the worldwide appeal of Indy Car racing. As series champion, his reward is a total pay-packet, including endorsements, of more than £10 million. In addition, he will probably pick up a further £4 million from Williams for guesting at four Grand Prix races this year.

He is likely to be back at Williams next year for a retainer approaching £8 million. He is worth every penny.

## Personal style

Mansell is a national class golfer and could have made a living in that sport. He is married and has three children. His business interests are restricted to ventures which exploit his name, such as videos and car retailing.

His income from these unrelated ventures exceeds £1 million a year in profits and royalties. His own income from sponsorship and helmet advertising is worth

£500,000 a year to him personally.

Only Nick Faldo challenges him as Britain's richest sportsman, but golf lacks the universal appeal of motor racing, and the sheer amount of money that fans will pay to see their heroes in action.

His presence is worth around £10 million in gate receipts for the British Grand Prix alone.

## Extravagances

Mansell has spent his money wisely. His few luxuries include boats, supplied free of charge by British manufacturer, Sunseeker, and a personal jet aeroplane. He lives in a beautiful waterside castle in Florida which set him back £2 million, plus restoration costs.

Mansell's net worth is eroded by his considerable living expenses and the taxman. The taxman has given him few problems since he moved to the Isle of Man and even fewer in Florida.

### Nigel Alliance 59
### £46m (£44m)
### Business

## Source of wealth

Nigel Alliance is the younger brother of Sir David Alliance, chairman of Coats Viyella, the textiles combine. What binds both men together is the fate of N Brown, the fourth largest mail order clothing catalogue house in the country.

Nigel joined the company in 1969, a year after his brother. Around the same time, David Alliance reversed his own mail order business into N Brown, taking effective control of the group.

Today, the Alliance brothers own 55 per cent of the quoted company. As chairman, Sir David – busy with Coats Viyella much of the time – now earns only £24,000 in salary.

Meanwhile, Nigel, an executive director, gets by on the dividends generated by a stake in the N Brown group that is valued by the stock market at £42 million – around 10 per cent up on last year's figure .

The N Brown Group is known for its newspaper mail order service and fashion catalogues typically aimed at women over 35. Sales and profits both rose strongly through the recession: turnover last year was up to £186.8 million, generating £22.5 million in pre-tax profits.

Nigel Alliance is involved with a number of private companies, in addition to his responsibilities at N Brown. All in all, he is worth a good £44 million.

## Personal style

Quiet younger brother of the more famous Sir David.

## Extravagances

The rag trade is his life.

### Robert Gavron 63
### £46m (£44.5m)
### Business

## Source of wealth

Robert Gavron used to own a healthy slab of shares in St Ives, Britain's most successful printer, which is capitalised at £300 million. He held 10 per cent of the company until he resigned this year and sold off much of his stake to go into retirement. He has other book publishing interests, and past share sales and dividends have seen him build a net worth of £44 million.

He is expected to sell off the rest of his shares in St Ives soon.

## Personal style

He was always one of the more eccentric type of public company chairmen and that probably explains his abrupt departure in 1993. His ability was never questioned however, and he did more than anyone to change the British magazine printing industry. His competitors are resting far more easily now he has gone.

## Extravagances

Retirement.

### Lord White 70
### £46m (£42m)
### Business

## Source of wealth

This year Lord White all but retired from Hanson, the company he co-founded with James Hanson. White has been running the US arm Hanson Industries since the late Seventies, although never officially a director or board member at Hanson plc.

His wealth therefore stems largely from his salary – £1.5 million basic at the last count. His shareholding has never been transparent but certainly over £30 million.

The young Gordon White and James Hanson became friends in the late Fifties, eventually going into business together. The legendary strategy of stalking out companies at the bottom of their cycle, then taking them over, was very much White's, though Hanson often took the credit. When White got fed up with Britain twenty years ago, he took just £3,000 to start an operation in America.

The latest results at Hanson plc show the two men are still a formidable team, with half year profits of over £600 million. We have increased White's wealth based on his salary and dividends, though it may well be his last. He can at last start drawing his huge pension.

## Personal style

Like his chum, Lord Hanson, White Knight was once as big a player on the night club circuit as the boardroom. Former girl-

friends include Elizabeth Taylor and Marilyn Monroe. When Californian model Victoria Tucker, 40 years his junior, ditched him for a younger man offering a four-carat diamond ring, he wooed her back with eight carats.

White is no stranger to controversy either. In 1992 he had to publicly apologise

### Bernie Taupin 43
### £45.5m (£43.5m)
### Music

## Source of wealth

Only in the past two years has Bernie Taupin begun to receive the recognition he deserves as Elton John's lyricist, having penned all but one of John's albums.

Taupin won't be too bothered as he is a multi-millionaire in his own right, taking half the royalties from all John's songs. He also took a huge slice of the £26 mil-

### Nigel Wray 44
### £45m (£28m)
### Property

## Source of wealth

Nigel Wray's main income source is through his chairmanship of property group Burford Holdings. The share price rise at Burford means the group is now capitalised at £315 million, and his Burford stake worth £37 million. The group made the year's biggest property transaction, snapping up London's Trocadero from the receiver for £94 million, three months after buying Ladbrokes's property portfolio for £103 million. With plans to turn the Trocadero into a theme park, Wray's wealth looks set to rise further.

This year Wray also took control of the Carlisle Group after injecting £2.7 million

for saying that "Hitler was a great provider of jobs." Earlier this year *BusinessAge* readers voted him Foreign Secretary if the government was made up of businessmen.

## Extravagances

Enjoys riding, skiing, tennis and flying. He holds a helicopter licence. Lives in a £6 million Los Angeles home.

lion deal Elton John signed with Time-Warner in 1992. Taupin co-owns Big Pig Music Ltd with Elton John, and also collected £5 million after winning a court case against their first publishing company Dick James Music.

However, while John has seen his wealth rise to £7 million in the past year on the back of touring, Taupin has had to rely on royalties. Elton John's continuing popularity means Taupin's added another £500,000 to his account.

## Personal style

Bernie Taupin has always been the quiet man behind Elton John throughout their 30 year partnership. Their personal relationship has often been strained, and the work relationship always bizarre. Elton John would, and still does, sit in one room creating tunes on the piano, while Taupin sits in another, putting down the words. Classics such as *Your Song*, *Candle in the Wind* and *Yellow Brick Road* were all written this way.

In 1993 a special album of other artists performing their songs was released, appropriately titled *Two Rooms*.

## Extravagances

Compared to his partner, none. A private man, who lives in Los Angeles with his second wife, Toni Russo, and their two children. Taupin receives additional income from the stylish restaurant Cicada which he runs.

following a rights issue. The group has just returned interim pre-tax profits of £1 million, the first time it's been in the black in two years.

His total wealth nudges up to £45 million on the back of two other interests, Carlton Communications and merchant banking group Singer Friedlander.

## Personal style

Wray's sense of timing and ability to spot a good deal, and a fair bit of luck along the way, is legendary in the City. He tried desperately to sell Burford after the 1987 stock market crash, with no success. So he just sold off the bulk of its property – just before the property crash. Once the market bottomed out, he started buying again, and of course piling up his fortune.

Wray's first job was as a trainee with Singer & Friedlander. In 1976 he bought the share tipsheet *The Fleet Street Letter*

(FSL), quickly making it cash positive.

Seven years later he persuaded Michael and David Green to reverse Carlton into *FSL*, to form Carlton Communications, giving him shares worth over £1 million.

Wray later bought the quoted Gilbert House for just 16 pence a share, increasing the value by seven times then buying property group Centrovincial for £48 million. Gilbert House was used to purchase Singer & Friedlander for £148 million, and he became deputy chairman.

Wray gained control of his real cash cow, Burford, in 1988.

### Extravagances

Buying and buying companies. Wray knows how to play the stock market better than most, and you may be advised to think twice if he tries to sell you something.

## Tommy Sopwith 54
## £45m (New entry)
## Inheritance

### Source of wealth

Not including Tommy Sopwith as a *Rich 500* member before has clearly been a act of negligence.

Quite what was the value of the large estate Sir Thomas Sopwith left to his former playboy, but now highly respectable, son, Tommy, is a matter for speculation. But it's becoming clear that at his death in 1989, aged 101, Sir Thomas wasn't short of a few bob. The legendary founder of what became Hawker Siddeley left behind him a castle on the Scottish Isle of Harris, a Hampshire estate called Compton Manor, which was sold in 1990 for £12 million, and large houses in Yorkshire and the Bahamas.

We estimate that his property holdings alone were worth £70 million, and on top of that he had considerable investments. Son Tommy can perhaps lay claim to half this wealth after other bequests and probate, so we value him (conservatively, since the younger Sopwith likes spending money) at £45 million.

### Personal style

Tommy Sopwith has played up the prodigal son image. When he's not been powerboat racing, Sir Thomas's son and heir has been racing E-type Jags and swanning in the Mediterranean and Caribbean on large luxury yachts.

### Extravagances

You name it, he's done it. Curiously, though, he's a bit slow to buy a round: sailing pal Sir Max Aitken once tried to set up the Sopwith Drinking Club, with membership restricted to those for whom Tommy had bought a drink. It produced just three applicants. Otherwise aeroplanes and helicopters absorb his wealth.

## Derrick Frost 59
## £45m (£30m)
## Business

### Source of wealth

Derrick joined his brother, Ronnie, to found Farmhouse Securities, their frozen foods distribution company, in 1965. Within two years of their company's 1981 takeover by the Hays Group, Ronnie was chief executive and Derrick was on the board. Derrick retired as commercial director of Hays in December 1992. His brother's continuing diligence at Hays has improved Derrick's shareholding value to £45 million.

### Personal satyle

Derrick Frost is the older of the Frost brothers, but has not been the leader in their joint activities.

### Extravagances

He is retired, and lives quietly.

## Earl of Lonsdale 71
## £45m (£51m)
## Aristocracy

### Source of wealth

The Earl of Lonsdale was forced in the mid-Eighties to turn over his estate to commerce – in this case, developing a 150-acre amusement park on his lands. In 1988, he reportedly sold the business to two circus clowns from Blackpool.

It was a characteristically colourful move by the earl, whose family has spawned some of Britain's more intriguing peers. His great uncle, who scandalised the nation by dancing with a London pearly queen, was the man who dreamed up the idea of awarding Lonsdale belts to champion boxers.

His wealth centres on a 72,000 acre estate in Cumbria but we think the family fortune is now declining.

### Personal style

An eye for grand gestures and a passion for making his estate commercially viable. The current Earl of Lonsdale, four times married, is one of a growing number of British aristocrats to have benefited from the sale of the subsidiary titles that are hidden beneath the central title of peer-of-the-realm in *Debrett's*. In 1989, he sold 30 subsidiary aristocratic titles for around £500,000. Among the titles he attempted to sell was the Lordship of Calder – a patch of his estate that happens to include the Sellafield nuclear complex.

The earl is one of Britain's cash-poor blue-bloods. But you cannot fault him for trying. In 1982, for example, he claimed ownership of oil and natural gas reserves beneath the Irish Sea, off the coast from his 72,000 acre estate in Cumbria. The earl's claim relied on an 1860 grant, but was rejected by the courts. At least the earl retained the right to profit from extensive forestry operations on his estate.

### Extravagances

In 1981, he attempted to settle a mountainous tax bill by offering to the nation the 2,847ft peak of Blencathra on his estate.

## Mickey Duff 64
## £44.5m (£42m)
## Entertainment

### Source of wealth

Mickey Duff – real name Morris Praeger – has spent most of his life making money from boxing bouts.

The son of a rabbi who fled from Poland as anti-Semitism boiled over in 1936, Duff became a fighter himself at 16. He entered the ring 65 times before turning manager, staging his first fight promotion in London in 1952.

Duff has always worked in partnerships – with Jarvis Astaire, the late Harry Levene and more recently, Terry Lawless. For 20 years he has been one of the controlling influences on the British boxing scene. Despite the best efforts of Frank Warren and Barry Hearn, Duff's business, National Promotions, remains in tip-top condition.

### Personal style

Relatively modest. Lives in a £500,000 flat in West London and drives a Ford Sierra. Married happily for 42 years. His own suggested epitaph: "Boxing couldn't have existed without him."

### Extravagances

Not many, apart from his home in California. Not keen on small talk or social occasions. He has said: "If there's one thing I have an aversion to, it's men who wear bow-ties during the week."

## Leonard Lewis 40
## £44m (£39.25m)
## Retailing

### Source of wealth

Leonard is a member of the Lewis family, who control the Lewis Trust Group. His father Bernard is chairman, and his uncle decides the strategy of the company. With an equal 13 per cent shareholding to his brother Clive, Leonard is worth almost £40 million.

### Personal style

Can you remember as a teenager the embarrassment of buying a pair of jeans in Concept Man and walking out with a Chelsea Girl carrier bag? This social embarrassment was ended by Leonard Lewis, when he revamped the Chelsea Girl chain into the more right-on River Island

Clothing Company.

**Extravagances**

The company just launched a expedition-style package holiday operation, said to be Leonard's baby. Travel agents are sceptical of its prospects.

### Dr Philip Brown 58
**£44m** (New entry)
### Publishing

**Source of wealth**

The journals *Scrip*, *Pharmaprojects* and *Animal Pharm* don't sound like obvious money spinners, but through his company PJB Publications, Dr Philip Brown has found a cash cow. The market research, financial information and journals published by PJB are vital to the growing bio-sciences industry. This fact is reflected in the £4.25 million post-tax profits returned for the year ending August 1993. In the previous two years, in excess of £2 million profits have been made.

On a moderate price/earnings ratio, PJB is worth around £40 million. Dr Philip Brown, who chairs the company, holds half the shares, the other half is held in his wife's name. His annual salary is a moderate £84,000, but he trousered £3 million in dividends last year. With regular dividends of over £2 million, we value him at £44 million.

**Personal style**

Dr Brown is one of a handful of academics breaking into the *Rich 500* for the first time, cashing in handsomely on their medical expertise.

**Extravagances**

Highly intelligent. He must have realised that working for the NHS is not the best way to make the *Rich 500*.

### Peter Jones 59
**£44m** (New entry)
### Construction

**Source of wealth**

Nearing the age of 60 Peter Jones makes his *Rich 500* debut via the dramatic increase in profits at Emerson Holdings, a Northwest-based builder and developer.

The company has been particularly involved in developing parts of Moss Side in south Manchester, but also owns retirement homes. Pre-tax profits for the year to March 1993 showed better-than-average margins some £6 million made from over £50 million turnover.

There are good prospects for builders surviving the recession and we value Emerson conservatively at some £40 million given the low prices achieved for private companies in the construction industry and the high debts in the balance sheet. With

past dividends and personal wealth this puts Jones at £44 million.

**Personal style**

Jones, a former brickie, doesn't forget his roots: his mansion near Macclesfield, Cheshire often hosts fiercely contested snooker games. His leading position in Northwest power circles has ensured that large construction projects have come his way, and his sharp eye for a bargain has always served the company well.

**Extravagances**

Emerson still has a big debt hangover from the Eighties, but unlike more unfortunate family firms (Costain springs to mind) Jones has managed to placate the banks long enough to produce the goods.

### Lord Tanlaw 60
**£44m** (£43m)
### Aristocracy

**Source of wealth**

Lord Tanlaw's wealth is accumulated through his chairmanship of the Fandstan Group of private railway engineering companies for the past twenty one years. Prior to that, after serving in Malaya, he joined the quoted Inchcape group in 1959, where he eventually rose to the post of managing director.

**Personal style**

Known to his chums as Simon Brooke Mackay, Lord Tanlaw became a life long Liberal Peer in 1971. He is a half brother of the 3rd Earl of Inchcape, and married with two children to Rina Siew Yong Tan.

**Extravagances**

A member of the consultative panel, the Horological Institute. He also has a stake in Covent Garden's Poons restaurant. Lord Tanlaw lists his recreations in *Who's Who* as "normal", which probably means wine, women and song.

### Nat Somers 86
**£44m** (£43.75m)
### Business

**Source of wealth**

In 1961, John Nathaniel Somers - known to all simply as Nat - bought Southampton Airport from the city council. The few hundred thousand pounds he and his wife, Phyllis, initially spent plus the money invested in building a concrete runway in 1966, have paid off handsomely. In 1988 Somers sold the airport to financier, Peter de Savary, for £52 million. Somers had spotted the airport's potential long before anyone else, and now it has excellent motor and rail links to London.

Fortunately for Somers, they were well prepared for the huge profits from the sale of their beloved airport. Practically every-

thing was declared by the Jersey-based holding company, Saipur Investments, as profit, with only £7,000 paid in UK tax. The rest went with the Somers' to Jersey, where both had become residents in the Seventies. Over the years, Somers had built up a substantial fortune of some £20 million. Between this and the profits from the 1988 sale split between husband and wife, Nat Somers is worth about £43 million.

**Personal style**

Although he says he hated selling it, he is probably enjoying his retirement as an extremely rich tax exile in Jersey. It's all a long way from the event that first led him to Southampton. He was 14, and had run away from home on his bike, to try to get work at sea. It took him three days to get there, and then he discovered that there was no work to be had. After being picked up by the police and spending the night in the cells, he was sent back home.

**Extravagances**

The Somers's live in a large but unostentatious Jersey home.

### Clive Lewis
**£44m** (£39.25m)
### Retailing

**Source of wealth**

Clive Lewis is the son of the reclusive chairman of Lewis Trust Group, Bernard Lewis. This is a case of wealth coming before age: Bernard has transferred the bulk of his holdings to his son, and Clive now holds 13 per cent of the company. With after-tax profits up nearly 40 per cent to £14 million in 1992, Clive Lewis is worth £44 million.

**Personal style**

Trained as an accountant, he takes responsibility for the banking operations of the group.

**Extravagances**

In common with the dour Lewis family tradition, Clive doesn't flaunt his wealth.

### Sheena Easton 35
**£43.5m** (£39.5m)
### Music

**Source of wealth**

Sheena Easton is the most financially aware pop star there is. Her financial worth is five times what would normally be expected of a pop singer of her talents. This is because of some canny contract arrangements and the fact that she took personal charge of her affairs. She also invested her income in California property and sold out at the height of the boom.

She has also made plenty from pop music. She linked with Prince in 1987 and the album *U Got The Look* was a global record-breaker and topped her previous successes, including *9 to 5* and the theme from the James Bond movie, *For Your Eyes Only*. A stint on the TV series *Miami Vice*, which is still running in ever-more remote parts of the globe, has not been followed by any similarly successful series. But Easton, who made the big move to Hollywood ten years ago, is not resting on her laurels.

## Personal style
She comes from a very poor background, something she often refers to in her press interviews. She was only ten years old and the youngest of six children when her father died. Her mother took up factory work to support the children. Easton has repaid the debt she owes to the woman she calls her role model by buying her a home of her own.

Despite the tales of hardship, Easton went to Glasgow University from where she graduated at the end of the Seventies. Easton married at 19 but that marriage ended in divorce, as did her second one, to Hollywood agent Bob Light. Easton denies the extent of her wealth – as do most artists who consider it bad for their image to be deemed rich.

## Extravagances
As a rich single woman in the high-profile world of pop music in Hollywood, she has to keep a low profile.

## Rocco Forte 49
**£43.5m** (£38.5m)
**Hotels**

## Source of wealth
Rocco Forte controls in his own right some 12,688,586 shares which are currently worth £27million. Much of the Forte family wealth has been moved to tax efficient trusts to benefit their heirs, and the principal members of the family have left themselves with as much as they will ever need in their lifetimes. With past dividends and a large salary, Rocco Forte weighs in at £43.5 million in 1994.

## Personal style
Rocco Forte is a fully trained accountant who entered his father's business as director of personnel in 1973, at the age of 28. He has never looked back, and last year became chairman of hotels group Forte.

His birthright was not always assured, as his father, Lord Charles Forte, had to fight hard to retain control of the hotel chain over the years. And, for many years, Rocco has had to fight off phantom takeover bids which have mainly existed only in the minds of journalists.

## Extravagances
He is mindful that he is only a caretaker for the next generation of Fortes. Work is now his extravagance.

## Nigel Raine 48
**£43m** (£27.25m)
**Food**

## Source of wealth
Basildon Dairy Foods and Raine's Dairy Foods together had profits of £6.7 million in 1992-93. Nigel Raine owns 50 per cent of Basildon Dairy Foods, which had the lion's share of those profits, £4.8 million after tax (1991-92: £2.8 million) and was cash positive to the tune of £6 million. He also owns 24 per cent of Raine's Dairy Foods, which had profits of £1.9 million in the same period. Using the same earnings multiple as last year (15), we value Raine at £43 million.

## Personal style
Nigel Raine has done astonishingly well, considering the margins squeeze on food producers in general, and dairy products in particular during the supermarket price war.

## Extravagances
Nepotism. Styles himself after Garry Weston.

## Mickie Most 55
**£43m** (£41m)
**Entertainment**

## Source of wealth
Rejected time after time when he brought recordings of his bands to mainstream record companies, Mickie Most set up his own record company, RAK Records, in the early Sixties, and had made his first million by the time he was 24.

Most took groups and performers like *The Animals, Suzi Quatro, Hot Chocolate* and *Kim Wilde* under his wing, acting as talent scout, producer and PR man. He was spectacularly successful. In the 20 years to 1984, his company sold 400 million discs in Britain and the US alone. Then he sold out to EMI for £20 million. He still maintains a recording studio near Regent's Park in London – the freehold property itself is worth a million or two. On further investigation, we've upped Most's wealth this year.

## Personal style
Knows his onions. Not afraid to let anyone know. Once said: "finding a good accountant is like finding a virgin in Bangkok." Said recently: "The people at the top of this business are bluffers. They wouldn't know a crochet from a hatchet." Hangs out with Sixties friends, Jackie Collins and Michael Caine.

## Extravagances
His house in north London, believed to be worth around £10 million and equipped with 30 rooms, a 40 metre swimming pool

and fitness and sports complex (with underwater stereo music system). The garage houses a £500,000 collection of veteran cars.

## David Samworth 58
**£43m** (£52m)
**Food**

## Source of wealth
Samworth Brothers, the East Midlands meat products group, made £4.47 million after tax in 1992. The company may be worth £67 million. David himself controls about half the shares. Samworth's fortune is augmented by the money from the sale of his previous business, Pork Farms, to Northern Foods. We value him slightly less this year at £43 million.

## Personal style
After military service in the Middle East, David Samworth joined his father in 1956, selling pork wholesale to butchers. Just over ten years later, armed with a degree from Harvard Business School, Samworth became chairman and managing director of the flourishing business and bought Pork Farms from Garfield Weston. In 1971, the group was floated, and in 1978 was sold to Northern Foods with Samworth going onto the Northern board. The sale reportedly netted the Samworths £10 million. In 1984, he was back in business with his two brothers – using part of the Northern Foods cheque as startup capital – in a high-quality food manufacturing business called, aptly, Samworth Brothers Ltd, of which he is chairman.

He is an enthusiastic non-executive director of Thorntons, the quoted chocolate manufacturers and retailers.

## Extravagances
Joint master of the Cottesmore hunt in Leicestershire. Chocolate.

## Leon Litchfield 61
**£43m** (£28m)
**Construction**

## Source of wealth
The Derby-based, family-owned LB Plastics Ltd have prospered through the recession. Turnover at the plastic windows and doors group was up to £40 million and profits to £7 million.

More remarkable for a company of this size (and in this business) is the burgeoning cash pile – £26 million in the latest accounts. Leon Litchfield has just under a third of the company, which would value him at about £31 million. He seems to have plenty of other resources to hand however. Last year he spent an estimated £15 million to buy the 20,000 acre Tulchan estate in Morayshire, Scotland. Meanwhile he only reduced his shareholding by 3 per cent.

## Personal style

PVC windows are not exactly aesthetically pleasing, but they give Leon Litchfield some spending cash. He may be applying for industrial tycoon status with his Scottish purchase: Tulchan was once owned by Jim Slater.

## Extravagances

That Morayshire estate again. It boasts seven miles of prime salmon fishing along the River Spey.

### Dame Barbara Cartland 93
### £43m (£40m)
### Literary

## Source of wealth

According to the *Guinness Book of Records*, Barbara Cartland is the best-selling living author in the world with more than 500 million copies of her works sold around the globe. She says that she has been published in every language on the planet – the Chinese language deal came through this year, where the books are apparently selling extremely well.

She was initially launched to stardom by the late newspaper tycoon, Lord Beaverbrook, with whom it was rumoured she had a brief affair. Beaverbrook had first paid her to write when she was in her mid-twenties.

Her books are essentially romantic fiction, with titles such as *Who Can Deny Love*, *A King in Love*, *Revenge of the Heart*, and so on.

Until very recently, few of her stories made it to the silver screen but in the last two years she has had offers of over £6 million for the film rights to some of her novels.

She also receives author's royalties of 10 per cent, and even at just 10 pence per book her revenues to date will have comfortably exceeded £50 million.

## Personal style

Dame Barbara Cartland is the step-grandmother of the Princess of Wales. She is also the most published authoress in English with 600 books to her credit, a Dame of the British Empire and she was voted "Achiever of the Year" in 1981 by the National Home Furnishing Association of Colorado Springs, USA.

These charming facts come from her own obituary which she herself wrote and sent to *The Sunday Times* after the paper had awarded her a £20 million entry in its 1990 Rich List. It must be one of the very few accolades which this enchanting and eccentric lady has ever balked at.

Born in 1901, a fact which she discreetly omits from her *Who's Who* entry – which is, in fact, the longest single entry in that prodigious book – there is very little that Barbara

Cartland has not attempted or done, apart from, perhaps, actual front-line combat.

The daughter of a militia captain who was killed in action in 1918, she married an army captain herself and, though later divorced, it was the daughter of that marriage, Raine, who became Countess Spencer and step-mother of the Princess of Wales. Dame Barbara is at pains in her obituary to point out that, through her second husband, her sons are related to the Spencers and "thus the Princess of Wales".

Her two brothers were killed during the retreat and evacuation of Dunkirk in World War II. She was a captain in the Army Transport Service during the war. In 1984, she was honoured in the USA for her part in developing the air-towed glider, which the Allies used (at great cost) in the recapture of the continent from the Nazis.

## Extravagances

Her 93rd birthday was celebrated in some style earlier this year, with guests (and of course Cartland herself) wearing bright pink in her honour. She swears by a very expensive anti-wrinkle treatment that is only available from Harrods. She has two sons and a daughter. They will inherit the much-denied fortune – eventually.

### Paul McGuinness
### £42.5m (£40m)
### Entertainment

## Source of wealth

From his base in Dublin, Paul McGuinness is the management dynamo behind the world's most successful rock group, U2. His expertise is marketing – particularly in the context of the band's constant concert tours, which represent a valuable earnings stream.

U2's tour of the USA in 1992 grossed £68 million, at a time when less remarkable, but better-known, acts were playing to half-empty stadium audiences. Resembling a banker rather than a promoter, McGuinness typically ensures sold-out stadiums by making tickets hard to obtain. Outside U2, however, his other business ventures seem to have lacked sparkle.

## Personal style

Studied anonymity; never, ever, talks to the press.

## Extravagances

Fast cars and good food.

### Lady Anya Sainsbury 61
### £42m (£46m)
### Retailing

## Source of wealth

Lady Anya Sainsbury still has the poise and looks of the prima ballerina that she once was. Married to Lord John Sainsbury of

Preston Candover, the recently-retired chairman of food chain J Sainsbury plc, she holds £40 million-worth of the company's shares, the nearest thing to cash after a five pound note in the UK. The shares are somewhat off their peak of last year and that accounts for a slight fall in net worth, but her dividend income alone exceeds £1 million a year.

## Personal style

Born in Manchester in 1933, the daughter of George Charles Eltenton, a scientist, she went with her family to the Soviet Union soon after she was born. All around them, Stalin's terror was claiming the lives of millions of people, but just before the Second World War broke out, her father was posted from the misery of the Soviet Union to the warmth of California. There, her dancing potential was recognised, and she spent some time as a pupil with Kosloff, the great ballerina Pavlova's partner, who was then living in Hollywood.

After the war, she auditioned for the Sadler's Wells Ballet School and by 1955 danced the role of Swanilda in *Coppelia*. By the late Fifties she was being tipped as a possible successor to Dame Margot Fonteyn, one of the greatest ballerinas of her era and the prima ballerina of the Royal Ballet for many years. She danced all the great roles, including that of Odette in *Sleeping Beauty*. In 1958 she married an American violinist, Igor Tamarin, but they were divorced in 1962.

In 1963 she married the Hon. John Sainsbury, the eldest son of Lord Sainsbury of Drury Lane. She has three children; two sons and one daughter. Her son John is married to the daughter of Dame Butler Schloss, sister of the late Attorney General, Lord Havers, whose own son is the actor Nigel Havers.

Even after her subsequent marriage into the Sainsbury family and the birth of their first child, Lady Anya continued to dance.

## Extravagances

Her major extravagance is persuading her husband to give so much to the arts. Lady Anya is a major patron of both the Royal Ballet and the Royal Opera. She enjoys all the trappings of being married to the head of the Sainsbury dynasty.

### Michael Noble
### £42m (New entry)
### Leisure

## Source of wealth

Michael Noble, with his brother Philip, is the driving force behind the Noble Organisation, one of the largest but least well-known leisure companies in Britain. Among other things, the company owns Brighton Pier, the most successful pier in

Britain. Michael Noble bought it for £600,000. It is now thought to be worth £8 million.

But the company's best asset is the Sun Valley chain of amusement arcades. Michael Noble, together with his late brother, Barry, who founded the business as Barry Noble Ltd, pioneered luxury amusement arcades which became a trend in certain sites.

The Noble Organisation is worth upwards of £90 million if it ever came up for sale.

## Personal style

Michael Noble already had a sizeable business when his brother died early in life from a heart attack. His amusement arcade chain passed directly into the hands of his brothers rather than to his wife, Josie and her son. He gave Barbados hotel owner, Michael Pemberton, his start and taught him how to make money and find good sites for amusement arcades.

## Extravagances

None.

### Philip Noble
### £42m (New entry)
### Leisure

## Source of wealth

Philip Noble is a partner, with his brother Michael, in the Noble Organisation, Britain's biggest operator of amusement arcades – and certainly the most profitable.

They took over the business when their elder brother, Barry, died of a heart attack at Isle of Man airport in 1985. Barry Noble was a legend in the industry. The business passed straight to his brothers and bypassed his wife and young son.

It is thought that the Noble family shares are worth just under a £100 million. His share is £42 million.

## Personal style

Philip Noble came good after his brother's death and kept the family fame alive. Barry Noble had achieved fame by bidding to buy Blackpool Tower and announcing he would paint it yellow. Fortunately, it was bought by First Leisure and remained black until recently when it was painted gold. He lives quietly in the north east of England and keeps a low profile.

## Extravagances

A Caribbean holiday here and there – but little else.

### George Harrison 51
### £41.5m (£32m)
### Music

## Source of wealth

Some Beatles fans would argue that George Harrison was the most talented of the Fab Four. If it's any consolation to him, he collected a massive cheque this year after selling his film production company Handmade Productions to Paragon Entertainment for $8.5 million. The company, which he founded with Denis O'Brien, was initially a success story, delivering films such as *Life of Brian* and *Time Bandits*, which between them grossed $67 million.

But the company flopped at the turn of the decade, and Harrison was delighted by Paragon's generous offer for what many saw as an insolvent business. This year he returned to the recording studio with Paul McCartney and Ringo Starr for the first time in 24 years, and may collect a £20 million cheque if rumours of a come-back concert in New York are true. His share of the ongoing Beatles earnings this year was £5 million thanks to the compact disc sales of old albums.

## Personal style

Always in the shadow of McCartney and Lennon, Harrison surprised the music world with his first solo effort in 1970, *My Sweet Lord*. It became one of the all time best selling singles, and is requested in music stores even today. The lyrics reflect his conversion to the Hindu religion, a movement with which he has been closely involved ever since.

## Extravagances

Harrison lives with his second wife Olivia in a £6 million Henley-on-Thames mansion. He has holiday homes in Australia and Hawaii.

### Sir Sydney Lipworth 63
### £41.5m (£38.5m)
### Insurance

## Source of wealth

Sydney Lipworth is the quiet member of the remarkable triumvirate of Mark Weinberg, Joel Joffe and Lipworth, South African lawyers and friends who led the UK insurance industry for nearly 30 years.

His fortune came with the flotation of Hambro Life in 1976, and was multiplied when the company (by then renamed Allied Dunbar) was bought by BAT for £664m in 1984. Lipworth joined the board of BAT and was also a director of J Rothschild Holdings.

His two per cent stake in Allied Dunbar netted him at least £15 million when BAT bought it, in addition to the original flotation proceeds.

## Personal style

Mark Weinberg persuaded Lipworth to come to England because "...if he was going to grind himself into the ground he should do it for us." He joined Weinberg as legal director of the infant Abbey Life, and left with him in 1970 to found Hambro Life, later Allied Dunbar. Their highly-trained direct sales force sold new unit-linked policies to a middle-class audience which was buying insurance for the first time.

He resigned as deputy chairman of Allied Dunbar in 1988 to become chairman of the Monopolies and Mergers Commission. He was knighted in 1990 and retired from the MMC in 1992. Once tipped for the post of deputy chairman of the BBC, he is now chairman of the DTI's Financial Services Task Force. Will it be enough of a challenge?

His secret, perhaps, is that he needs no more than two hours' sleep a night, often working until four o'clock in the morning at home, and returning to the office before nine. No-one has ever been known to say a bad word about him.

## Extravagances

He refutes claims that he's a workaholic, enjoying parties, art galleries and his own art collection, and the deputy chairman-ship of the Philharmonia Orchestra. He drives a five-year-old Ford Fiesta.

### Bruce Robertson 41
### £41m (£40m)
### Retailing

## Source of wealth

Bruce Robertson owns 75 per cent of Trago Mills discount stores. The three branches at Liseard, Falmouth and Newton Abbott are each run as separate companies, offering everything from cheap furniture to Des O'Connor tapes.

The last time accounts were filed, for 1992, profits were £5.57 million, valuing the group at just over £50 million. We have made no significant changes to Robertson's wealth given that new accounts are unavailable, and we do not foresee any significant improvement in the profitability of Trago Mills.

## Personal style

Unfortunately for Bruce, he is better known as the son of Mike, founder of Trago Mills. Having started the business in 1964 with a £2000 loan, Mike became notorious for using every trick in the book to flog his goods: Des O'Connor tapes were priced at 49 pence because this made them cheaper than buying blank tapes, and photographs of shop-lifters were posted on his shop windows.

Robertson would also go to any lengths to increase productivity, including trying to convert his staff to Islam so they would work on Sundays.

## Extravagances

Compared to his father he is rather boring, thank goodness.

### Stanley Thomas 53
### £41m (£38m)
### Food

## Source of wealth
He and his brother Peter sold their pies and sausages business to Grand Met in 1988, in a £75 million deal, one of the largest cheques ever written for a private Welsh company. Stan and his brother took a £30 million slice each, though Stan has enjoyed it a bit more than his brother. Consequently, he is valued at only £41 million.

## Personal style
After the sale of Peter's Savoury Products to Grand Metropolitan, Stanley Thomas announced: "I've just ordered a Bentley and I wouldn't mind a little sailing yacht." Unlike his brother who stayed on with Grand Met, Stanley has pursued other interests. The family, including his sister Mary, is now worth well in excess of £100 million.

## Extravagances
That Bentley and yacht, for starters. Stan also enjoys buying golf courses.

### John Aspinall 58
### £41m (£36.5m)
### Leisure

## Source of wealth
John Aspinall's long-term partner in his gaming ventures has been Sir James Goldsmith. Their coup, and the main source of Aspinall's wealth, came in 1989 when they sold their Aspinalls Club complete with freehold for £90 million, taking half each. The deal included some gaming interests in Australia.

He later bought back the assets and the name of the club for less than £5 million. Deducting expenditure on the zoos, plus the set-up costs of the latest casino and adding back some capital value for the new venture, Aspinall is worth some £41 million.

## Personal style
John Aspinall has founded four casinos in his lifetime and two zoos. He debuted with the Clermont in 1962, Aspinalls Club in 1978, Aspinalls Curzon Club in 1984 and his new Aspinalls club only last year. He opened Howletts Zoo in 1958 and Port Lympne Zoo in 1973.

He is one of the gaming industry's pioneers, and he won a key 'interpretation of the legislation' legal battle with the Home Office in 1958.

He has been married three times and has two sons and one daughter by two of his wives. He is now married to Lady Sarah Courage, the widow of brewing heir Piers Courage, who was killed driving a De

Tomaso racing car at the Dutch Grand Prix in 1970.

## Extravagances
He is one of the few men who lists his business interests in *Who's Who* as also being his recreation. In Aspinall's case, the business is wild animals and gaming – although, of course, he is strictly unable to gamble in his own casino, under Gaming Board regulations.

### Greta Fenston
### 59
### £41m (£39.5m)
### Inheritance

## Source of wealth
Greta Borg's husband, Felix Fenston, died in 1970, leaving the then considerable fortune of £12.6 million to his wife. Together, the couple had built up Kyle Stewart, the construction group, which was sold for about £50 million.

## Personal style
A woman with a head for figures. Nowadays she runs the two family trusts, investing the proceeds shrewdly.

## Extravagances
Fenston and her husband managed to buy Devonshire House, formerly the London residence of the Duke of Devonshire, when post-war reality finally caught up with the

### Lord Hanson 70
### £41m (£39m)
### Business

## Source of wealth
Dubbed "the oldest swinger in town", Lord Hanson surprised the City by announcing half year profits of over £600 million at Hanson plc. This is a sharp turnaround from the first ever quarterly loss announced two years ago. His six million shares are now worth in excess of £14.5 million, in a company worth over £12 billion. He trousered an extra £5 million last year from a share sale.

The Hanson family made a fortune when their haulage and transport interests were nationalised in 1948 by the Labour Government. The young James Hanson used the cash to build up a successful haulage business in Canada.

However, it was an introduction, through his younger brother Bill, to Gordon White in the late 1950s that was to change Hanson's life. Bill died of cancer aged just 29, after which Hanson and White became close friends – virtually brothers. They went into business together thirty years ago, with a now legendary strategy: staking out companies at the bottom of their cycle, stalking them and then buying them. Gordon White, now Lord

White, runs Hanson's American operation.

Hanson's reputation grew into that of the most feared corporate predator in the world but, surprisingly, it is not matched by his wealth which is mostly an accumulation of salaries and dividends over the past 30 years.

## Personal style
Never afraid of a fight, with scars from many fierce take-over battles, notably the chemical and typewriter maker SCM in the Eighties, and the raid on ICI.

## Extravagances
Six foot four Yorkshireman with a love for powerful cars and racehorses. He has a country house, a London house and holiday home in Palm Springs. In his younger days he was better known as an international playboy – once engaged to Audrey Hepburn. Married (in 1959) and is still married to Geraldine. Endless list of powerful connections in the Tory party, to which he has regularly donated. Watch out for the take-over of the decade before he bows out.

### Ron Dennis
### £41m (£25.5m)
### Sport

## Source of wealth
Grand Prix motor racing can barely be described as a sport any more. It is big business. Five members of the *Rich 500* who have made fortunes from it.

Dennis owns 40 per cent of the Tag McLaren Group. It includes the team, an electronics company, the motor car collection and the sports car manufacturer. The group can hardly be valued by a profits multiple, asset value seems more fitting. It only makes a couple of millions profit a year. But it owns assets that are easily worth £50 million in the shape of the collection of historic McLaren racing cars. The team generates around $50 million in sponsorship every year and the last two years are believed to have been very profitable.

We rate the value of Tag McLaren at £80 million. Add in personal assets and his 40 per cent share and we rate Ron Dennis at £41 million.

## Personal style
Ron Dennis is a fanatical motor racing team owner, and arguably the most successful of all time, with only legendary (and very rich) American Roger Penske coming close to matching his record.

Dennis bought McLaren in 1980 for himself with the aid of Marlboro cigarette money. He hasn't looked back since. Originally in partnership with John Barnard, he built the first carbon fibre Grand Prix car. The Eighties and early Nineties gave him seven world championships with Nikki Lauda, Alain Prost and the late Ayrton

Senna. It caused the team to be labelled 'unbeatable' until the last three seasons.

Dennis shares ownership with Mansour Ojjeh of the Tag Group, the Paris-based company behind Heuer watches. He is regarded as one of the most capable business managers in Britain. Despite not winning much lately McLaren is still regarded as the best managed and run grand prix team.

**Extravagances**

The new McLaren sports car was an extravagance but will be wildly profitable. The mark up is believed to be 100 per cent. As it is regarded as the best sports car in the world, helped by an expert PR campaign on launch, it is selling very well. He has a lovely country home in Kent and dotes on his wife and young family.

### Michael Peagram 50
### £40m (New entry)
### Business

**Source of wealth**

The April 1993 flotation of Holliday Chemicals ("very professionally accomplished," conceded Peagram in its latest annual report) crystallised Michael Peagram's wealth at £40 million, based on his 17 per cent stake in the company, the £2 million he trousered at flotation, and the £1.2 million dividends paid him in the last two years. The shares have significantly outperformed the market in the last six months, giving him membership of the *Rich 500* for the first time.

**Personal style**

Shareholders were mighty disappointed when Peagram issued a profits warning a mere eight months after flotation. The shares plummeted, knocking £10 million of his net worth alone. They've since returned on the back of better-than-expected £12.1 million pre-tax profits for the year to December 1993. Holliday recently spent £52 million acquiring Reckitt & Colman's pigment business.

**Extravagances**

Yet to flex those eight-figure financial muscles. Peagram hotly denies he's about to buy a yacht and retire to the Mediterranean. He's promised the City he won't reduce his substantial shareholding until next year.

### Keith Richards 50
### £40m (£38m)
### Music

**Source of wealth**

Keith Richards is often credited as being the creative force behind Mick Jagger. He writes most of the Rolling Stones's songs with Jagger, and takes a decent slice of the

cash too. Like all the band members, their fortune was spent as quickly as it came in the Sixties.

But their fame has survived, and Richards has been able to stash up his wealth again thanks to lucrative touring – the band earned $1 million a night for a sell out tour of America in 1989.

Richards' wealth increased greatly after the £50 million deal the band signed last year with Virgin. We estimate his wealth has nudged up another £2 million with advance payments for the forthcoming world tour (already sold out). As a guide, their *Urban Jungle* world tour grossed £25 million. The new album *Voodoo Lounge* topped the UK charts in the summer. More significantly, Richards is picking up royalties from the large number of re-issued Rolling Stones albums currently on sale.

**Personal style**

Richards and Jagger seemed to spend years competing for the title of "wildest man in rock", causing much tension over the years. It virtually defies belief that the two are still together, though friends suggest neither can perform without the other. Jagger's attempts at a solo career have been spasmodic, and Richard's brief effort a disaster.

Having blown most of his Sixties earnings, Richards has become more financially astute second time round, using the same financial adviser as Mick Jagger, Prince Rupert Loewenstein.

**Extravagances**

Drugs are now behind him, he insists. Richards has properties in London, Paris, New York and Jamaica, but prefers to live in Connecticut for tax reasons.

### Robin Lodge 51
### £40m (£39m)
### Computers

**Source of wealth**

Robin Lodge made his fortune in 1985 when he sold his software company Metier to the US aerospace giant Lockheed for £100 million, trousering £30 million himself. Lockheed made a huge loss when it sold the company to Lucas five years later.

In 1987 Lodge and his business partner Brooke Johns invested in Nesco Investments, a small software company. Lodge is now chairman, and has increased his stake in the group. We have, therefore, slightly increased his wealth to £40 million.

**Personal style**

Lodge was accustomed to the big time at Metier, supplying software to NASA. But he seems to prefer the quiet life – Nesco is worth just £3 million and has pulled out of a major operation in Nigeria to concentrate

purely on the IT business.

**Extravagances**

Thankfully he can now afford his expensive hobby of buying and racing vintage cars. He married the second daughter of orchestra conductor Sir Charles Grove in 1976, and has three daughters.

### Viscount Coke 62
### £40m (£38m)
### Aristocrat

**Source of wealth**

Apart from 26,000 acres and the remarkable Holkham Hall, most of Lord Coke's cash flow comes from his art collection – bits and pieces of which are regularly put under the hammer in a bid to raise badly needed funds.

In the early Eighties, he sold a Leonardo da Vinci manuscript for £2.2 million to Dr Armand Hammer. Lord Coke pleaded poverty: "Certainly, on paper, I am a wealthy man. But I have not got the cash," he announced. At the time, death duties were the main burden.

Even while trying to pay off the Inland Revenue, Coke has been hampered by other departments in Whitehall. In 1991, for example, he tried to sell18 of Holkham Hall's old master drawings. The price was settled at £3.26 million at Christie's. But the drawings were impounded by the government to allow British museum bosses the chance to bid for them.

**Personal style**

Once hit the headlines when he received a £2,947 home improvement grant from King's Lynn and West Norfolk borough council. Coke has two sons and one daughter. His marriage was dissolved in 1985.

**Extravagances**

None, he just lives quietly, dreading the day when he might have to think about selling off more than just a canvas or two.

### Ron Hickman 62
### £40m (£38m)
### Business

**Source of wealth**

Ron Hickman is the man who came up with that fatal encouragement to DIY adventurers, the Workmate. Since 1973, over 30 million Black & Decker Workmates have been sold – and Hickman has earned three per cent royalties on each and every one. This has helped him amass a fortune of some £40 million over the years – not bad for a product which Stanley Tools originally said would sell "dozens rather than hundreds".

But Hickman has had to spend over £1 million on legal fees to protect his fortune, fighting patent infringement suits against the huge US retailer Sears Roebuck (thereby winning 11 per cent royalties on their 'Workbuddy') and around 30 other would-be imitators. He also claims to have blown a couple of million working on inventions which never had any commercial success.

## Personal style

Father's Day hasn't been the same, thanks to Ron Hickman. The South African-born, Jersey-retired inventor was toiling away in Essex in the 1960s when, after accidentally sawing the leg off a chair, he crossed a workbench with a vice in order to make a tool which would prevent him from destroying any more furniture. Eventually, after plenty of rejection letters from tool manufacturers and a short spell manufacturing and marketing the thing himself, he managed to sell the idea to Black & Decker.

## Extravagances

Hickman's 79-room Jersey home – a DIY enthusiast's dream with a vast range of labour-saving gadgets – was featured on Jersey postage stamps some years ago. He now spends much of his time researching his family history, and says he can trace his ancestry back to a Norman knight who came across with William the Conqueror. Of the Workmate and his struggle to get it launched in the market, Hickman told the *Mail on Sunday*: "I hope I never invent something so implausible again."

# Portia Kennaway 28
## £39.5m (£45m)
## Inheritance

## Source of wealth

Portia Kennaway – née Moores – is the great-niece of Sir John Moores of Littlewoods fame, the gigantic football pools and mail-order empire. Her father was the tragic Nigel Moores, who died in a car accident in 1977, when she was only eleven years old.

Last year *BusinessAge* estimated that the Littlewoods empire would be worth £2 billion, if quoted on the stock market. We have downgraded her wealth this year, as in our view, the advent of the national lottery has devalued the Littlewoods business substantially, and we now rate the private empire at around £1.7 billion.

With shares totalling some 2.5 million, she has a paper wealth of about £39.5 million.

## Personal style

Portia Kennaway is one of the 30 Moores heirs who own the private company. She keeps her life exactly that – private.

## Extravagances

Although very wealthy on paper, dividends are relatively slight, leaving little room for extravagances.

# Lawrie Lewis 46
## £39.5m (£37m)
## Business

## Source of wealth

Lawrie Lewis attended more than 150 exhibitions in the 1970s in the UK and abroad, and saw an opening. In 1979 he set up Blenheim Dresswell, specialising in fashion fairs and clothes shows. Blenheim expanded from five to 36 exhibitions a year. In 1986, the company was floated on the Unlisted Securities Market. The shares went up by nearly 1,000 per cent in the next three years, and Lewis sold his stake to American publisher Ziff Davies for £28 million in 1991.

He now rates his wealth at £40 million and we agree. He is currently enjoying life.

## Personal style

Lawrie Lewis now lives in Monte Carlo wondering what to do next at his relatively young age.

## Extravagances

A large yacht.

# Chris Wright 50
## £39.5m (£34.5m)
## Business

## Source of wealth

Chris Wright has had a bumper year as things start to go right at Chrysalis and it is reflected in the share price, which has more than doubled since last year – then considerably dented by the disaster that has occurred in its amusement machine division.

In last year's profile we said that we expected the share price to double this year. This was based on information we possessed about developments at the company, and the previous debilitating effect of the amusement division – now closed. It has done more than that.

We discounted this rise and therefore Wright's net worth has only risen by £5 million. Wright owns half of Chrysalis which is now valued at a more realistic £46.5 million.

But his share stake is not Wright's only source of wealth. He has a considerable cash pile of his own from share sales and dividends. He also owns considerable property, plus an art collection of Impressionist paintings worth some £5 million.

## Personal style

Chris Wright has been through the mill. His life as a millionaire has not been smooth and only now, as he reaches his fiftieth year, are things going more smoothly. The man who pads around his office barefooted, often in his three piece suit, is resting more easy these days.

## Extravagances

Houses and horses including a 450-acre stud farm in Gloucestershire, a large London home and holiday homes in Antigua and Cap d'Antibes.

# Louise White 30
## £39m (£45m)
## Inheritance

## Source of wealth

Louise White is the child of Nigel Moores, and great-niece of Sir John Moores, who founded the Littlewoods empire. Her father was killed in a car accident when she was thirteen.

Last year *BusinessAge* estimated that the Littlewoods empire would be worth £2 billion, if quoted on the stock market. We have downgraded her wealth this year, as in our view, the advent of the national lottery has devalued the Littlewoods business substantially, and we now rate the private empire at around £1.7 billion. We estimate her wealth – some 2.5 million Littlewoods shares – at about £39 million.

## Personal style

The extremely attractive 30 year old is the estranged wife of theatre impresario, Michael White. She married her much older husband in 1985, when she was 21 and he was 49. She couldn't tame the sophisticated White but they had a son and split up soon after. They remain great friends and she is friends too with his new girlfriends.

## Extravagances

She loves London life.

# Duchess of Roxburghe 39
## £39m (£35.5m)
## Inheritance

## Source of wealth

The Duchess of Roxburghe was born into the vastly wealthy Grosvenor family, based in Ulster. In 1977, she married the Duke of Roxburghe, then an officer in the Household Cavalry, just 12 months after meeting him at a party in Belfast.

But it wasn't to last. They divorced 12 years later. However, the duchess kept hold of her own considerable slice of the Grosvenor family wealth. As with most Grosvenor daughters, she is said to receive income from 5 per cent of the entire fortune, which was tied up in trusts by the 2nd Duke of Westminster.

## Personal style

No illusions about men. As she told the *Daily Express* when her divorce came through: "Boys will be boys". She has three children.

## Extravagance

Country life, i.e. gardening.

### Benzion Freshwater 46
### £39m (New entry)
### Property

## Source of Wealth

Benzion Freshwater bounds into the *Rich 500* for the first time as a result of the dramatic share price increase of the family firm. The Freshwater wealth comes from Freshwater family's 80 per cent grip on Daejan Holdings plc, which is capitalised at £250 million: Benzion's own shares are worth about £12 million. His share of the family holdings we estimate to be a shade under £30 million.

The fortune originated with Benzion's father, Osias, who built up a portfolio of nearly 20,000 residential properties in the Fifties and Sixties, and used the supposedly tenant-biased Rent Act of 1965 to double and sometimes treble rents on his properties after he'd bought them at knock-down prices. Today Daejan, the Freshwater company, owns mostly commercial property and has rebounded quickly from the recession. It made £13.2 million after tax last year (up 10 per cent), and its net asset value is £194 million. Most of the shares are held in trust, with Benzion as sole trustee. His income last year was just over £1 million.

## Personal style

Benzion has taken Daejan into commercial property and run down his father's interests in residential flats since he took over in 1976. This to great effect.

## Extravagances

He lives in one of his father's old investments, which cost him £27,000 in 1978.

### Rod Stewart 48
### £39m (£39.5m)
### Music

## Source of wealth

Rod Stewart has trousered over £100 million since he released the now legendary track *Maggie May* in 1971. His relative poorness, if you can call it that, is down to two reasons: free spending and fast women. Although currently happily married to model Rachel Hunter, who is expecting their second baby, he forks out £500,000 a year in child support to his former wife Alana Hamilton. Former partner Kelly Emberg is lurking in the wings hoping to cash in later.

We have slightly downgraded his wealth because of this. In fact, Stewart would have lost more were it not for his recent revival in the pop charts. On top of a string of hit singles in the past year, the album *Unplugged and Seated* is still riding high.

## Personal style

Stewart began his career as part of The Faces. After limited success he went solo, and the crokey soul voice on soft ballads made him the star he is today. Unfortunately, by the late Seventies, he tried to change his musical image with songs such as *Do You Think I'm Sexy*. They too were hits, but his big market – the USA – gave a thumbs down. He has returned to recording ballads lately, a move reflected in the surge in his popularity. Stewart headlined this year's Brit Awards, teaming up after 25 years with The Faces again.

## Extravagances

Rod Stewart lives with wife, Rachel Hunter – a model – in a $13 million Beverley Hills mansion, but visits Britain regularly, staying in his £1.6 million Essex home. The wild days are over, this is said to be the influence of his new wife and Stewart is now even very strongly anti-smoking.

### Charles Dobson 49
### £39m (New entry)
### Business

## Source of wealth

Charles Dobson makes his first appearance in the *Rich 500*, thanks to the steady growth of his quoted signmaking company Spandex. Spandex's biggest income is through distributing and servicing computers and signmaking equipment made by Gerber. In May 1994, the share price soared to 643 pence – more than four times the value when floated in 1986 – after Dobson announced £3.44 million post-tax profits on a £60 million turnover.

With his wife, Mary, Dobson owns six million shares and more than half the company, capitalised at £73 million. We value him at £39 million, taking into account past dividend payments, which amounted to £420,000 in 1993 alone.

## Personal style

Dobson never misses a trick. The day after the Berlin Wall came down, he pushed his way through the crowds to set up a distribution network for Spandex in the former East Germany.

## Extravagances

Mainly admiring his own equipment, particularly the new three dimensional signs which allows him to see his wealth in 3-D.

### Barbara Taylor Bradford 52
### £39m (£35.5m)
### Literary

## Source of wealth

In 1985, the Channel 4 TV serialisation of her book *A Woman of Substance* was shown in America and in some places drew an even bigger audience than Dallas did, which was then at the height of its popularity.

In 1992 she signed a deal with her new publisher, Rupert Murdoch's *Harper Collins*, which almost exactly doubled her wealth, putting her ahead of Jackie Collins. The advance she took totalled £17 million, and now that she has delivered the second of the three books she has £10 million in the bank. The deal put her in the *Guinness Book of Records* as the highest-paid author of all time, until she was surpassed recently by John Grisham.

Additional income has come from film, serial and paperback rights, which have amounted to some £12 million over the course of her writing career. She receives royalty cheques every year for at least £2 million for sales of her older titles.

## Personal style

Her books are a mixture of romance, business and power, defying precise categorisation. They are blockbusters, selling in all the world's major languages, although they are all set in Britain. The most popular so far, and the best known are; *A Woman of Substance*, *Hold the Dream*, *To Be the Best* and *The Women in his Life*.

She was born in Yorkshire, in the Armley suburb of Leeds.

She did not publish her first work of fiction until 1980. This was *A Woman of Substance*. It has so far sold 15 million copies in 40 countries and 22 languages.

## Extravagances

Her husband manages and produces the TV mini-series based on her books.

They live in an exquisite apartment on the 47th floor of a Manhattan apartment block overlooking Central Park.

### Martin Copley 54
### £39m (New entry)
### Insurance

## Source of wealth

Martin Copley owns a sixth of consumer good warranty insurers Domestic & General plc. He also chairs the Wimbledon, south London-based company, whose pre-tax profits may break the £10 million barrier this year on the back of recovering appliance and consumer electronics sales. The shares have performed well and are now worth £27 million. Add in share disposals worth £12 million after tax in the last two years and his worth puts him well into the *Rich 500* for the first time.

## Personal style

Copley has aggressively pursued the extended warranty market, and has teamed up with big players like Philips and Sony, to offer across-the-board coverage.

## Extravagances

Copley cuts quite a high profile in a relatively unknown corner of the insurance industry. He's seen as a bit of a maverick among grey men.

## John Zochonis 65
**£39m** (£38.5m)
## Business

### Source of wealth
The name of the family company, Paterson Zochonis, is hardly a household word: better known is their major product, Cussons Imperial Leather soap. John Zochonis retired in December last year, having been chairman since 1970, handing over the job to nephew Anthony Green. His 7.5 million shares were worth just over £37 million at the beginning of July. Including his large annual dividends (£500,000 last year after tax) we think he is worth £39 million.

### Personal style
Zochonis, who has never married, is the grandson of the Greek side of the partnership. Educated at top public school Rugby, he is chairman of the council of Manchester University and a freeman of the City of London.

The company started out as an Anglo-Greek partnership trading in West Africa and Nigeria, in 1884. In 1975 Zochonis bought up Cussons, which brought with it the famous soap. Manchester based, John Zochonis owns around 22 per cent of the share capital of a company which gets little publicity.

It has tended the Imperial Leather brand well, investing millions in it, which has depressed the share price. The company is considerably undervalued on the stock market.

### Extravagances
Long soapy baths in the morning, now that he has more time on his hands.

## Robin Phillips 61
**£38.5m** (£35.75m)
## Business

### Source of wealth
Robin Phillips is the largest shareholder in quoted Warner Howard, with 48.3 per cent of the equity. At the beginning of July this was worth £37 million. He also received £800,000 in dividends. Warner Howard flourished on the new product phenomenon of the Eighties, the warm air hand dryer, which replaced paper towels in most public conveniences. It rents out hand dryers and is the dominant supplier. Profits for the year to February 1994 were £6.8 million.

### Personal style
An LSE graduate and qualified chartered accountant, Robin Phillips started off in the Sixties working for Coinamatic in Canada. He was sent to London to manage the British offshoot, which at that time rented out coin-operated washing machines. By 1980, the Canadians' attention seemed to be elsewhere and a management buy-out was launched with the aid of a venture capitalist. A year later, Warner Howard was bought and the combined operation was renamed after it. From then on the company prospered, and was floated in 1987. Phillips is non-executive deputy chairman, but not as involved in the business as he once was.

### Extravagances
Ill health has forced Phillips to give up any hope of a fast lifestyle.

## Lord Weinstock 70
**£38.5m** (£41m)
## Electronics

### Source of wealth
Lord Weinstock's announcement that he will stay on as managing director of GEC for another two years may be his first badly judged move in thirty years at the helm.

Coupled with the lower than expected £866 million profits for 1993, up just £3 million, the City knocked eight per cent off GEC's share price the next day. Thankfully for him, he has gradually passed on the bulk of his share stake to his son and potential successor, Simon, leaving himself with a less than 0.5 per cent holding, worth only £27.5 million. With salaries and dividends, his personal wealth stands at £38.5 million, down slightly because of the drop in the value of his shares.

### Personal style
The institutional shareholders that want him out are being harsh. He may be 70 years old, but Lord Weinstock was still voted one of the most powerful men in business by a *BusinessAge* survey in 1994. And rightly so – his legendary meanness with cash means there is £1 billion sitting in the bank at GEC, but he would argue there hasn't been a worthwhile acquisition to spend it on. If anything, he showed he has lost none of his fighting spirit by offering Ferranti one pence a share. When the shareholders refused, he took the best bits from the receiver anyway. As a manager, he scares the hell out of his staff if they don't come up to scratch. In his book, coming up to scratch includes remembering to turn the lights out at night.

Lord Weinstock's obsession with numbers originates from his days as a statistics undergraduate at London School of Economics. His big break came from his father-in-law Sir Michael Sobell, who put him in charge of Sobell's Radio & Allied Holdings in the Fifties. Two years later GEC bought the company in a reverse take-over.

### Extravagances
Obsessed with classical music.

## Derek Thomson
**£38.5m** (£27.5m)
## Media

### Source of wealth
After the chairman Brian Thomson, Derek Thomson is the second most powerful director at DC Thomson & Co Ltd, the Dundee-based family publisher. But he is the biggest shareholder, with 320,799 shares – 5.3 per cent of the company. On after tax profits of £23 million (up from £17 million in 1992), Derek Thomson is worth £38.5 million.

The company did particularly well out of Carlton's takeover of Central. The deal valued their 19 per cent stake at £150 million - about fifteen times the purchase price. Because we reckon the Carlton windfall has made a huge difference to the balance sheet we have added another additional £5 million to Thomson's wealth this year. We believe some of this cash will find its way directly to shareholders soon.

### Personal style
The Thomson family has more individual millionaires in its ranks than any other family in Britain. There are few trusts, and the shares are registered in family names.

### Extravagances
Fishing and single malt whisky.

## Paul Slater 35
**£38m** (£45m)
## Retailing

### Source of wealth
Paul Slater is the managing director of Glasgow's best known shop Slaters' Menswear. The shop in Howard Street, created by his father, Ralph, has become a Scottish institution for low price and high quality.

The last time accounts were filed, for 1992, Slaters' returned a £2.3 million post-tax profit on a £25 million turnover, making the company worth well over £35 million, taking into account one of Slaters' key assets – its name. Paul Slater owns 95 per cent of the company, but we have downgraded his wealth slightly because of fierce competition on the high street.

### Personal style
Slater's style, apart from wearing his own suits, is for every browser that walks into his store to walk out with a suit. Not a front man himself, he concentrates in the backroom on keeping the prices low enough for his style to work.

### Extravagances
The shop once had an entry in the *Guinness Book of Records* as the largest store in the world selling only men's suits and accessories.

### Ray O'Rourke 47
### £38m (New entry)
### Construction

**Source of wealth**

O'Rourke runs and owns Britain's most profitable private construction company, named after himself. Despite being in the country's most depressed industry, he returned a staggering 14 per cent profit margin on a £46 million turnover, mainly by employing all the 500 staff directly rather than sub-contracting and employing as many of his own family as possible. Brother Hugh is vice-chairman, and even the secretary, Bernadette, is his niece. He owns over half of the £80 million valued company, but is likely to face a serious drop in profits this year.

**Personal style**

Extremely secretive, both in business and private. Known as the "tough guy" of Britain's toughest industry, O'Rourke never loses cash because of late payment from clients. Reneging on a deal with Ray O'Rourke is not a good idea. Goes to extraordinary lengths to hide his wealth, regularly setting up shell companies.

**Extravagances**

None – too busy working. Even a pint of Guinness is a rarity.

### Everard Goodman 62
### £38m (New entry)
### Property

**Source of wealth**

Tops Estates, the quoted company in which Goodman has a 48 per cent stake, is the source of much of his wealth. It controls property with a 1993 market value of £190 million, and produced after-tax profits of £2 million last year. The company's debts are still piled high however: it paid £9 million in interest on debts totalling £120 million.

The properties, which include Corby Town Centre shopping arcade and the Bond Street Centre, Leeds, may well be worth more this year as the commercial property market emerges from its prolonged recession. The shares are trading near their low for 1994 (but are far ahead of their 1993 value), giving Goodman a value of £40 million and putting him on our list for the first time.

On the strength of consistent dividends that have netted Goodman £500,000 a year for the last five years, a £5 million controlling interest in the Trust of Property Ltd (an associated investment company) and the almost-certain re-rating of the shares, Goodman could enter at slightly under £50 million. We don't like the high level of

indebtedness however and have valued him more conservatively.

**Personal style**

Goodman is another one of these "secretive" rich, but he employs few of the disguises – he even gives press interviews on occasion.

The company is worshipped by property analysts, who love Goodman's low profile and long-term outlook.

**Extravagances**

He lives modestly in a flat in the West End, his home for the last twenty years. He gives substantial sums to charity. He has two sons.

### Duke of Richmond 64
### £38m (£40m)
### Aristocracy

**Source of wealth**

The Richmond estate, Goodwood in Sussex, includes 12,000 acres and a famous race course. Art treasures supplement the family's fortune – including some remarkable pieces by Canaletto and Reynolds. We have marked down the duke's fortune on the basis of poor performance of his business interests this year.

**Personal style**

Unusually for a blue blood, the Duke of Richmond is a chartered accountant. He is also a devout Anglican, and much involved at senior levels in the Church of England. This makes for a contrast with the family's history. The male line was founded in 1672 by the bastard offspring of Charles II's liaison with a French countess.

**Extravagances**

Women. Once said to have paid £10,000 to a former mistress who fell ill. The tabloids got wind of the story, the duke confessed and got a public pasting from his ex-lover into the bargain.

### Sir Adrian Cadbury 65
### £38m (£36m)
### Food

**Source of wealth**

Sir Adrian Cadbury will be remembered for turning round the family confectionery business after its merger with J Schweppes in 1969. In 1974, he retreated to the post of chairman. The Cadburys continue to hold a small stake in the company– apparently well under 1 per cent. Currently, the company's shares are looking anaemic: 418p as opposed to the high for the year of 545p. We have edged Sir Adrian's wealth downward to reflect the change.

**Personal style**

Dry and austere, Sir Adrian has sat on the board of the Bank of England for the past 24 years. The Cadbury Committee has left

him with something of a reputation as a philosopher, a man much exercised by ideas like structures and responsibility – plus an odd but welcome tendency, in one so obviously well-connected, to rail against the power of the City's Old Boy network.

He has a personality to match the role of high priest for corporate governance. Tends to criticise the Old School Tie syndrome, but is himself remarkably well-connected.

**Extravagances**

Probably a good book at bedtime.

### Gordon Baxter 77
### £38m (£48m)
### Food

**Source of wealth**

W A Baxter & Sons is the company everyone wants to buy – a quality image, a profitable concern, careful but steady expansion – Scots' virtues of which the company is proud and which it has no intention of relinquishing.

Baxters has no borrowings and a name which is worth much more to a purchaser than the bricks and mortar.

The company's value is somewhat academic, however. Elder statesman, Gordon Baxter, has repeatedly stated he won't sell the company, and is now transferring his holdings either outright to his children or into trusts. While the company's theoretical value (anything from £80 million to over £100 million, depending on how you value brands) has risen lately, Gordon's holdings have fallen to just over a third of the equity.

**Personal style**

Gordon Baxter has spent 47 years with the firm since war service, but in a sense has been working for Baxter's for 70 years, as he first got up in the wee small hours to take the factory keys to the manager, and glued the labels on the jamjars after school.

Executives of the nearly 200 companies that have offered to buy the business are well entertained by him and his wife in their home near the factory at Fochabers, but well watered with the local whisky and usually entertained with fishing on the local river, they're all sent away empty-handed.

**Extravagances**

All those rebuffed takeover bids merit a mention in the *Guinness Book of Records*. Gordon is apparently at work on a memoir entitled *200 Not Out*.

### Ronald Diggens 82
### £38m (New entry)
### Property

**Source of wealth**

Ron Diggens owns 15.4 million shares in

Slough Estates. The spectacular performance of the multinational property group's shares in the last 18 months, despite the recent correction, have nearly doubled Diggens's holding, propelling him back into the ranks of Britain's seriously wealthy people after a few years out of the running. Based on the share price in mid-July, Diggens's shareholding is worth £37.5 million.

## Personal style

From a pound-a-week surveyor's mate in 1922 Diggens has built a mighty fortune. He built bridges in the Second World War and invested heavily in commercial property in the Fifties and Sixties. He is now retired.

## Extravagances

The octogenarian is living out his remaining years as one would expect – very quietly.

### Tom Walduck
### £38m (New entry)
### Leisure

## Source of wealth

Tom Walduck is one of those people whose wealth you can never quite pin down. He acts like he's got money – but where's it from? The answer can't be found in the accounts of his family's hotel group, Imperial London Hotels. They give the company's net asset value at a mere £12 million.

The company's true value is somewhat different. In addition to hotels like the Imperial, Mediterranean charter boat operations and a package holiday company, it owns large chunks of Russell Square and the surrounding area. A door-to-door check reveals that Imperial is the landlord for at least £100 million worth of property in the area.

The accounts carry debts of £7 million, and assets have been listed at book cost and then depreciated. The company's true value (it made after tax profits of £19.7 million in 1991) would be more like £200 million. Walduck has 25 per cent of the company, giving him a potential net worth of £50 million. But we believe his stake may be less than that now.

## Personal style

Six generations of Walducks have been in the hotel business. Tom runs the company he inherited from father, Stan, and uncle Norman, with his brother Richard.

## Extravagances

Parties. Socialite Tom and his family pop up regularly in the pages of *Hello!* magazine.

### Richard Desmond 46
### £37.5m (£44.5m)
### Media

## Source of wealth

It's been an interesting year for Richard Desmond, chief of Northern and Shell Group, the company that publishes two of Britain's better known soft porn magazines, *Penthouse* and *Forum*.

On fundamentals, the group's newly formed holding company, Equalcentre, seems to have performed well. On turnover of £13.5 million, operating profit before taxes, minority interests and exceptional items came to £2 million. But the company's profit and loss account was transformed by the addition of £16.5 million exceptional item – payment from United Newspapers for 10 of Northern and Shell's music and cycling titles. This was a remarkably steep price to pay. But United Newspapers seems to have handed over the cash after a complicated legal wrangle over distribution services.

Flush with cash, Desmond now has several options. He could reduce very high borrowings. Alternatively, he could syphon off some of the cash through large dividend payments or proceed with the rumoured launch of a no-nudes men's title, which would push his company further into "respectable" territory.

There's little that Desmond would like more than to become a respectable media mogul. At 46, he's got all the time in the world. We have reduced his worth because of those high borrowings.

## Personal style

A mainstay at Variety Club. Still lacks an entry in *Who's Who*, however.

## Extravagances

Desmond takes home a millionaire's salary – and lives on Millionaire's Row (Bishop's Avenue) in Hampstead. Last year he paid himself wages of £1 million.

### Sir John Hall 61
### £37.5m (£38.5m)
### Property

## Source of wealth

Metro Centre was developed by Sir John Hall's company, Cameron Hall Developments, before being sold to institutions and netting Hall some £60 million in the process. Since then he has done nothing. Hall is a one-deal tycoon.

Cameron Hall is losing money. A turnover of only £823,000 meant a loss of £4.4 million in 1992, the glory days of Gateshead long behind it. But these losses are actually making Sir John richer as he is clawing back previously paid corporation tax on profits. But Hall's company still has net assets of £42.6 million to fall back upon, and he is developing Wynard Hall, a 4,000-acre estate, into an upmarket leisure development.

He has also pumped some £6 million into Newcastle United Football Club where he owns 88 per cent of the shares, and scored huge success by recruiting Kevin Keegan to manage the club. Although Sir John Hall's high-handedness almost lost him at the beginning, fortunately Keegan has proved to be a fine manager. Hall may also score financially from the development of the Newcastle sports stadium.

Despite a property recovery, we rate him a fraction lower this year.

## Personal style

In 1983 John Hall was quite literally a nobody. He was a man with a big idea and he was trying everything he knew to get tenants interested in his planned Metro Centre in Gateshead.

Eight years later he is an elder statesman of the property business, having scored a huge success with Metro Centre and made himself a huge cash pile as a result.

## Extravagances

Good living and football.

### Dick Francis 73
### £37.5m (£35.25m)
### Literary

## Source of wealth

The Queen Mother's favourite writer lives in Florida. Second only to Catherine Cookson in terms of popularity with British library book readers, he typically completes a new book every year. Since 1962, he has produced 34 titles, which have been translated into 23 languages.

## Personal style

Francis describes himself as "just a jockey with a story to tell." But in the flesh he's about as communicative as that other jockey with stories to tell, the stony-faced Lester Piggott. Every year, the press turn up at the London launch of a new Dick Francis novel. And every year they find less to write about. But the man's fans couldn't give two hoots. The Queen Mother, for example, sends a congratulatory note each time Francis publishes a new book. Francis himself remains a realist: "People come up to me and say: 'Gee, Dick, I enjoyed your book. I read it last night in three hours.'"

## Extravagances

Lives quietly among Fort Lauderdale's flourishing ex-pat community of Brits.

### Sir Nicholas Bacon 40
### £37m (New entry)
### Aristocracy

## Source of wealth

The ninth baronet of England, Sir Nicholas Bacon owns two estates in Norfolk and Lincolnshire covering over 14,000 acres, worth £30 million. The more valuable of the two is Raveningham Hall in Norfolk, built over 200 years ago by the Bacon family, where Sir Nicholas lives with his wife Susan. He also has arguably the best collection of English watercolours, and the John Staniforth Beckett collection, valued at £7 million.

## Personal style

The son of England's premier baronet Sir Edmund Bacon, Sir Nicholas was Page of Honour to the Queen, a job he was forced to retire from at the age of sixteen because he was too old. So he went to Eton and took up mixing in the right circles for a living.

## Extravagances

Apart from the art collection and magnificent homes, Sir Nicholas is a keen gardener. He says, "I'm rather a tree man. I'm very interested in woodland trees especially." How interesting.

## Countess of Lichfield 45
## £37m (£35.5m)
## Inheritance

## Source of wealth

The countess grew up in Fermanagh, Northern Ireland, the daughter of the Fifth Duke of Westminster. As a member of the Grosvenor family, she has an interest in the vast property holdings controlled by the family. She married society photographer Lord Lichfield in 1975; ten years later, the marriage ended.

The countess held on to her own wealth, of course. That fortune, like Lichfield's, is based on trusts, and on a provision traditionally made for female heirs of about 5 per cent of the main family wealth. This makes her worth £37 million.

## Personal style

While married to Lichfield, she lived in a small part of a grand house that was otherwise rented out to the local council for use as a museum. Apparently, this did not sit well with the countess, who was used to living on a grander scale.

## Extravagances

As a younger woman, the Countess of Lichfield lived life in the fast lane – almost as fast as her former husband.

## Mary Foulston 46
## £37m (£27.75m)
## Inheritance

## Source of wealth

Mary Foulston inherited most of John Foulston's fortune, then valued at around £70 million. But it was a paper fortune in the quoted Atlantic Computers plc. By sheer good fortune, John Gunn, who was then running the go-go conglomerate British & Commonwealth, came along and

offered £550 million for Atlantic Computers. Gunn paid twice as much as it was worth and seemed happy to do so. It was the luckiest day of Mary Foulston's life. An investment which would be absolutely worthless a year later netted the Foulston family around £50 million cash. John Foulston had also arranged his tax affairs nicely and little was paid to the Inland Revenue – the cash went straight into some Jersey trusts for Mary and her children. Her share was around £40 million, plus some other property and a stake, again held in trust, in the Brands Hatch chain of motor racing circuits.

Some £10 million is in trust for each of her daughters but Mary has doggedly held onto the rest. We overestimated the amount that had been passed on to the daughters last year hence Mary's net worth has risen considerably. The Foulston family is at war as although daughter Nicola runs the family motor racing business, it is owned by Mary. The two often do not speak although there was a reconciliation of sorts when Nicola was married last year.

## Personal style

Mary Foulston lost her husband, computer leasing magnate John, very suddenly in the autumn of 1987. He died testing a vintage Indianapolis McLaren at Silverstone. For Atlantic Computers, the company which Foulston founded and took to the stock market, his death was also a disaster. Atlantic was a one-man business run by the genius of the leasing industry. Without him, it almost immediately floundered. John's genius had been in personally masterminding and calculating every piece of business which Atlantic did. It was the classic one-man success story.

## Extravagances

The money pales into insignificance against the loss of her husband, a hugely dynamic man who raced cars, flew helicopters and planes and did everything in life at 10 times the pace of others.

## Lady Sheila Butlin 62
## £37m (£35m)
## Inheritance

## Source of wealth

Billy Butlin, later Sir Billy, built up an organisation, the famous Butlin's holiday camps, which was eventually acquired by the Rank Organisation. He met Sheila Devane who had worked for Butlins since 1947 and she became his companion.

Sheila Devane and Sir Billy Butlin went to live in Jersey in the early Seventies at a time when the *Daily Mirror* estimated his fortune at just £2 million. At that point he

said he was worth £4 million but had given £2 million away to charities (for which he was knighted) and had decided to live in tax haven Jersey, "to safeguard what I have." At that time, tax rates in the UK were running at 98 pence in the pound, at the top end of the scale. She later married Sir Billy and became Lady Butlin in 1976.

Sir Billy retained a stake in the company, however, and when he died in 1980 he is thought to have been worth up to £100 million, including various charitable trusts that he set up.

## Personal style

Lady Butlin lives very quietly in Jersey and, apart from her appearance at the launch of her autobiography, she has not given any interviews. She has played a major role in maintaining and looking after the range of charitable trusts which her husband set up and is reckoned to have doubled the money originally left to fund them. She has one daughter.

## Extravagances

Tax exile in Jersey is not a lot of fun.

## Lady Juliet De Chair 65
## £37m (£35m)
## Inheritance

## Source of wealth

In 1979, Lady Juliet de Chair inherited the Earldom of Fitzwilliam, which brought with it Wentworth Woodhouse, the largest house in England, with 365 rooms. Her own father, the eighth earl, had died in an air crash in France in 1948.

At the time of her father's death the media made much of the fact that she would inherit £200,000, about £4 million in today's terms, when she was 21. "Enough to live on independently," was her comment at the time. She only really came into the big money after a series of cousins died unexpectedly. Her wealth is boosted by some remarkable works of art, such as Foggini's *Samson and the Philistines* and canvases by George Stubbs, the famous English equestrian painter.

## Personal style

In her younger days, she was a headstrong heiress. At the age of 24 she married the Marquess of Bristol against the wishes of her elderly male cousin, who then held the Fitzwilliam earldom. Fortunately for her, he could do nothing to alter the trusts which bequeathed both her mother's home in Coolatin, Ireland, and Wentworth Woodhouse to her. She and the Marquess of Bristol were divorced in 1974; they had one son. She then became the fourth wife of Captain Somerset de Chair, a colourful soldier, writer and former Conservative MP for south west Suffolk.

**Extravagances**
Lives in some style, dividing her time between Kent, Essex and New York.

### Duke of Wellington 79
### £37m (£35m)
### Aristocracy

**Source of wealth**
The present Duke of Wellington, Arthur Wellesley, is the eighth successor to the Iron Duke who defeated Napoleon at Waterloo in 1815. The basis of his wealth is Stratfield Saye, the beautiful estate of 7,000 acres given to his ancestor by a grateful nation and Parliament in return for his victory at the Battle of Waterloo which ended Napoleon's domination of Europe. In fact, most of Europe showered titles – and possessions – on the 1st duke. In Spain, he was created a grandee first class, a title which brought with it another estate of 2,300 acres. In Portugal, Wellington became Duke of Victoria. In Belgium, he was made a prince. In London, the family still own Apsley House on the corner of Hyde Park.

**Personal style**
A professional soldier, like the first Duke, he retired as a Brigadier General, having served in a number of senior positions including that of Silver Stick in Waiting to the Queen.

**Extravagances**
Wildlife conservation and chairmanship of the Pitt Club – a very rowdy supper club for wealthy and titled Cambridge undergraduates.

### David Hood 46
### £36.5m (New entry)
### Electronics

**Source of wealth**
David Hood's owns 31,000 of the 50,000 shares issued in Pace Micro Technology, the data communications and satellite dish manufacturer that holds 50 per cent of the British dish market and posted after-tax profits of nearly £3 million in the year to August 1992.

Dish sales have spiralled upwards since then, and Pace's British-made dishes have made further inroads into Amstrad's market share. (Pace may make and sell over 1 million dishes this year) We value the company at £58 million, and Hood's 63 per cent stake at £35 million.

**Personal style**
You know when you're successful because Alan Sugar sues you for libel. Hood joined this exclusive club last year, in the wake of a Pace satellite dish ad campaign which asked "which would you prefer: a British

dish or an oriental one?", a disparaging reference to Amstrad's imported satellite receivers.

**Extravagances**
Hood paid himself £855,000 in 1992.

### Earl of Halifax 50
### £36.5m (New entry)
### Aristocracy

**Source of wealth**
The Land Registry reveals a figure of 14,000 acres for the Earl of Halifax, the figurehead of one's of Britain's most blue-blooded, aristocratic families. On his death, the previous earl left a small estate of £2.5 million. But the rest of the family's wealth was – and remains – tied up in trusts. With an impressive collection of art included, we value the earl at £35 million. His high Tory connections are evident from his connections with Hambros Bank, where the earl has been a director since 1978. In his younger days, he was also close to the Royal Family. He is married, with one son and one daughter.

**Personal style**
Recently seen waving the flag for York Minster. Early in life, as plain Lord Irwin, when he had yet to inherit the family's riches, he tried his hand as a Conservative candidate, but was turned down by the local selection committee in Bridlington.

**Extravagances**
Horse racing, a passion that runs in the family. The earl's father was one of the country's leading bloodstock owners.

### Edwin Boorman 59
### £36.5m (£35m)
### Media

**Source of wealth**
Edwin Boorman joined the Kent Messenger Group 34 years ago, taking just three years to become chief executive. Well, he took over from his father. As chairman and owner today, his 240,000 shares value him at £36.5 million – a few million up on last year.

**Personal style**
Like his father, the HR Pratt Boorman who took over the group after only five years as a journalist, Edwin Boorman thrives on responsibility and power. Most notably in 1985, he sacked 114 printers when they refused to adopt new technology. The results show the benefit: two out of every three people in Kent read one of the group's publications each week.

Keen on keeping it in the family, his daughter already works in the newspaper industry. Watch out for son Henry in about

ten years' time.

**Extravagances**
Deep sea fishing is the family's second favourite pastime, closely behind running a publishing company.

### Viscount Hambleden 64
### £36.5m (£34.5m)
### Inheritance

**Source of wealth**
Viscount Hambleden and his relatives control – if not actually own – one of Britain's biggest companies. WH Smith is one of the few companies that retain the antiquated two-tier share structure with the voting shares being dominated by the family.

Viscount Hambleden is the current head of the family. He controls nearly 20 per cent of the 'B' voting shares of WH Smith, the news, stationery, music and computer retailers worth just over £30 million. He also has significant property assets.

The voting structure may well not survive until the end of the century, as the company will in all probability enfranchise the 'A' shares, ending family control. Hambleden does not sit on the board of directors.

**Personal style**
Viscount Hambleden is the fourth baron of the line and has extensive farming interests adjoining the manor house at Hambleden, near Henley-on-Thames. His mother, a daughter of the Earl of Pembroke, has been lady-in-waiting to the Queen Mother since the Thirties, and he himself is a close friend of Princess Margaret.

**Extravagances**
A magnificent estate in Oxfordshire.

### Bevitt Mabey
### £36.5m (£40m)
### Construction

**Source of wealth**
Bevitt Mabey owns most of the shares in Mabey Holdings, which makes specialist support equipment (mainly steel) for the construction industry. Post-tax profits for the year to September 1993 were down to £3.1 million, largely because of re-organisation costs. Turnover was up £6 million, to £62 million.

However, the company has substantial investments in land and property worth over £7 million. We value the company at £35 million, and Mabey's stake at £31 million, plus his personal assets.

**Personal style**
Awarded a CBE. More a back seat driver, who has been cleverly diversifying the company from making heavy steel for bridges (which, because of foreign subsidies is not

profitable for British firms) into property investments, while competitors keep moaning about the recession.

## Extravagances

Regular donations to the Tories, with another £1,000 added this year. It's less than half the regular hand-out but enough to get on John Major's Christmas card list.

### Andrew Cohen 40
### £36m (£75m)
### Retailing

## Source of wealth

Last year we got Andrew Cohen all wrong. It was at the peak of his fortunes that his value was assessed. Almost from that moment onwards, it was downhill all the way.

As an example of how high he was riding a year ago, we said: "It's a 50-50 bet that one day Andrew Cohen will be on the *BusinessAge* billionaires list." Well, that won't happen now. The City will never forgive him for the second fiasco in his short stock market career. (The first was a botched flotation).

Last year, Betterware was worth some £260 million and Cohen junior owned just over 32 per cent. He reduced his holding by 7.5 per cent last summer raising £15 million.

A few months later the share priced crashed in half and then by another third and the company today is valued at less than £100 million.

Cohen didn't reveal when he sold his stake that growth had stopped and sales had actually shown signs of declining. He then kept on denying and denying that something was wrong through his official mouthpiece, chairman Walter Goldsmith, but the City clearly didn't believe him. They were right not to. After the last results he finally admitted year-on-year sales were actually down.

The City marked the shares down by a third and Betterware is worth under £100 million although the yield has gone up considerably.

One would have thought Andrew Cohen would take the opportunity to buy back as many shares as he could at these prices. Not a bit of it. His purchases have totalled a mere token 8,000 shares.

## Personal style

Bombastic. Open when he wants to be, secretive when he doesn't. Can be naive at times although he has an excellent business brain.

## Extravagances

Busy spending the £15 million when he cashed out. Collects old film posters, paying ridiculous sums of money for them.

### Maria Phillips 48
### £36m (£36m)
### Inheritance

## Source of wealth

Maria Phillips inherited the Luton Hoo estate in Bedfordshire after the death (by asphyxiation in his car) of husband Nicholas, grandson of the great art collector Sir Harold Wernher.

## Personal style

She is the daughter of an Austrian Count, Paul Czernin. Luton Hoo was left to her late husband, Nicholas Phillips, by his grandfather, Sir Harold Wernher. When he inherited, Nicholas did not have the problem of heavy estate duties to pay: his grandfather had seen to that. But tragedy struck when Nicholas started an ambitious development scheme on the 4,000-acre estate. He died in a fume-filled car there. The coroner, finding no evidence of suicide, recorded a verdict of accidental death. Phillips's will was probated at £19 million, but Maria has now taken over the running of the museum and estate, part of which was developed at a cost of £100 million in the Eighties.

## Extravagances

Maria has a sober lifestyle by all accounts - so far, she has not had to sell any of the major works of art, but the art treasures market is still sluggish. There were rumours that a Constable was to be auctioned for £2 million but it was withdrawn. She has two children.

### Keith Chapman 51
### £36m (£41m)
### Business

## Source of wealth

Keith Chapman is chairman of Fine Art Developments, the Bradford-based business which manufactures and sells greeting cards, stationery and educational accessories.

Most of the selling is by mail order. Chapman has over 6 million of the 79 million or so shares, and an option on another 300,000.

The group is capitalised at £470 million on the stock market, making Chapman worth £36 million with other accrued wealth. That is down considerably from last year.

## Personal style

Keith Chapman is Bradford born and founded Fine Art Developments plc. He made it into one of the top ten gift manufacturers in Britain.

## Extravagances

Work and more work.

### Michael Luckwell 51
### £36m (£37m)
### Media

## Source of wealth

Michael Luckwell trousered £25.6 million in 1986 when he sold his stake in Carlton Communications. Prior to that he had, with Michael Green, taken Carlton from a £16 million, third division outfit to a £300 million Premier League side. He would therefore argue that he is not lucky to be rich, as his rivals often joke.

After leaving Carlton he bought a small stake in TV-am for £4.6 million which he later sold for a £2 million profit. Luckwell also invested heavily in the West Nally Group, before quitting the chairmanship for £2 million. He also managed to offload his speculative interest in the shares of quoted marketing services group, WPP, before the shares crashed.

Luckwell has a 17 per cent stake in HIT Entertainment PLC, and teamed up in early 1994 with property gurus, John and Peter Beckwith, to build up Riverside Leisure Holdings. We have slightly downgraded his wealth as a result of this latest investment, but Riverside is planning to float in December, which should help Luckwell climb back up the *Rich 500*.

## Personal style

Luckwell's first job was as a junior dealer on the Stock Exchange, which obviously taught him how to spot a good deal. After quitting the City in 1970, he entered the media business, setting up the mould-breaking Moving Picture production company. It was bought by Carlton in 1983 for £13 million and Luckwell became managing director.

## Extravagances

Too restless to concentrate on any extravagance.

### Adrian Berry 57
### £36m (£41m)
### Media

## Source of wealth

Adrian Berry must be the richest journalist in Britain. His wealth springs from the newspaper he works for – the *Daily Telegraph*, which was once owned and managed by his father, Viscount Camrose.

Camrose sold out his newspaper interests to Conrad Black in 1985 for a bargain basement price. These days, as the family's representative at the Telegraph Group, Adrian Berry combines the roles of non-executive director and science correspondent on the *Daily Telegraph*.

The family wealth is held in trust – the

Telegraph Newspaper Trust, to be exact. This trust contains two major assets: shares in the Telegraph Group and the cash (around £45 million) that the family received from Black for their newspapers.

Shares in the Telegraph Group are significantly depressed following a falling-out between Conrad Black and City analysts. Accordingly, we have valued the shares in which Berry and his relatives have an interest at £28 million.

The family wealth is divided between several individuals. Adrian Berry's share in the trust comes to £36 million all told.

## Personal style
Related by marriage to the Sulzberger family, which controls *The New York Times*. With his father, Berry sits on the board of the Telegraph – and is said to get on famously with Conrad Black. The Canadian publisher may have pulled off the deal of the decade when he bought the group so cheaply. On the other hand, he also managed to save the newspapers which the Berry family had run for so long.

## Extravagances
Like the rest of the family, Adrian Berry shies away from the limelight, maintaining a stiff upper lip.

## Peter Moores 62
### £36m (£31m)
### Retailing

## Source of wealth
As the younger son of Sir John Moores, Peter Moores was one of the major heirs to the huge Littlewoods fortune. He owns a small share in the company, having passed most of it on to his son and daughter. He inherited a few millions when his father died but in typical style the money has all been passed to the next generation - avoiding inheritance tax being the aim.

Last year *BusinessAge* estimated that the Littlewoods empire would be worth £2 billion, if quoted on the stock market. The advent of the national lottery has devalued the Littlewoods business substantially but this has not affected Peter Moores' wealth rating.

## Personal style
Like his brother John Moores II, his education – Eton and Oxford – was very much geared towards preparing him for the family business. When a public row between his father and brother led to John Moores II walking off the executive, it was left to Peter to move into the spot of heir-apparent within the business in 1977.

He was given a rough ride as profits plummeted from £49 million in 1978 to £11.5 million in 1980. He was forced to give way to his father who came out of

retirement to restore profits and has been far less active since then. He is tipped to be the future chairman of the Royal Opera House.

He is known for his original methods of funding, buying first-time opera-goers their seats, or buying would-be stars tents to help them tour the great Italian opera houses cheaply. His protégés include Placido Domingo, Dame Joan Sutherland and Sir Colin Davis. He was awarded the CBE in 1991.

## Extravagances
Like his father before him, Moores is a major patron of various trusts and charities. He lives well at Parbold Hall near Wigan.

## Bill Ruffler 83
### £36m (New entry)
### Leisure

## Source of wealth
Bill Ruffler made his first fortune by putting vending machines in council flats that supplied one cigarette for the price of 5p. After the war he operated and sold jukeboxes. Such was the scale of his business in 1947, that he placed the biggest jukebox order ever seen than. It was valued at £7,000.

With partner Fred Walker, he distributed amusement machines under the Ruffler and Walker banner. That company eventually became Associated Leisure, which is now owned by the Rank Organisation.

When the founder sold Ruffler and Walker for millions he acquired a licence to accept deposits and started a hire purchase business, Lordsvale Finance. He took deposits and lent money and made another fortune. We value him now after a long career – and few mistakes – at £36 million.

## Personal style
Bill Ruffler started out as a milkman. However, in subsequent years he liked to describe his first job as "working for the Milk Marketing Board." The business is now run by his son, Roy.

## Extravagances
Not ever retiring.

## Robert Hanson 33
### £35m (£34m)
### Business

## Source of wealth
The reason his more famous father Lord Hanson isn't higher up the *Rich 500* is because young Robert, aged 33, has been handed many of his father's personal assets. His visible assets are 3.75 million

shares in Hanson PLC, worth just over £9 million, slightly more than last year. But he has been passed much of the family's investments in the last few years as his father reaches the age of 70.

## Personal style
Following closely in his father's footsteps, with a seat on the Hanson board and recently, the chairmanship of Hanson's Hong Kong operation – Hanson Pacific, in addition to responsibilities for Europe. Slight complex problem given his family connections in the company.

## Extravagances
None, preferring to stay within his father's shadow. Still based in London despite chairing Hanson Pacific. Loves throwing parties and is still single meaning he is a magnet for pretty girls.

## Sarah Bathurst 36
### £35m (£34.5m)
### Inheritance

## Source of wealth
The Hon Sarah Bathurst resides at Eastnor Castle, near Ledbury in Herefordshire. She is the second-eldest daughter of Viscount Ingleby, a prominent landowner in North Yorkshire.

The castle was built in 1812 and boasts one of the finest stately home interiors in Britain. Her husband is a direct descendant of the Somers family, who owned vast tracts of rich farmland in Worcestershire, Hereford and Gloucestershire. Once these lands generated the equivalent of £800,000 a year in revenues. Much of the land seems to be intact and in the hands of the family. They have two children and live on the estate.

## Personal style
The family have no reputation for ostentation, but lead a quiet existence.

## Extravagances
A large portion of Bathurst's wealth comes in the form of artefacts and art works, including some very fine Italian old masters and some of the best works of James Watts, the English master painter.

## Chris Evans 36
### £33m (New entry)
### Business

## Source of wealth
Chris Evans is the dapper, dynamic young bio-boffin behind two recently floated biotechnology companies, Celsis and Chiroscience. He owns more of the former (26 per cent) but is chief science officer of the latter. Recent products from both companies have included a detector for salmonella ➤

in food and a safer organic anaesthetic.

Current market values put Evans's Celsis stake at £12.5 million, and his Chiroscience one at just over £3 million. His previous company, Enzymatix, was wound up in 1989 due to problems at its major backer, Berisford International, but Evans is reputed to have made £11 million out of the company.

The two recent flotations netted him an estimated £8 million.

## Personal style

A scientist by training, Evans got his microbiology Phd from Hull University within three years. Business sense came from his impecunious youth in Port Talbot, South Wales, where he would sell bilberries door-to-door, picking up perhaps £16 a day.

He says he's always been fascinated by bugs, and admits he needs to be working on at least half a dozen projects at once. For fun he designs car security products. He's also a bit of a venture capitalist on the side too, investing his burgeoning wealth in a number of startup companies, and it is rumoured he breathes, eats and sleeps too. He remains unmarried.

## Extravagances

Chris Evans shouldn't be confused with his television presenter namesake. Both may drive snappy cars (our boy owns a Mercedes 500 SL, whereas the Big Breakfast's Chris drives a Testarossa) but there the comparison ends.

Boffin Chris enjoys doing elaborate biotech experiments at odd hours of the night. Considering his ability to come up with world-beating solutions, no one's complaining.

## Marquess of Normanby 40
## £35m (New entry)
## Aristocracy

## Source of wealth

The Marquess inherited his title and a 15,000 acre Yorkshire estate from his father, who died earlier this year. His mother, now in her 70s, is transferring property assets to her son to avoid death duties.

She falls off the list as a result, and the young aristocrat takes his rightful place among the nation's richest.

## Personal style

The Normanby estates have been a curious exception to the rule of declining aristocracy. In the last forty years their property holdings have in fact expanded ninefold, and now encompass nearly 57,000 acres.

## Extravagances

Fashion shows and parties: Normanby's wife, Nicola, also happens to be *Vogue* editor Alexandra Shulman's sister.

## David McErlain 43
## £35m (£33m)
## Motor Industry

## Source of wealth

Just 12 months ago David McErlain was the safest bet to soar up this year's rich rankings, but he barely scrapes in with £35 million. His motor dealer chain Chatfields was all set to be reversed into Sterling Gate in return for £20 million cash. Weeks before the deal went through, City institutions blackballed the whole idea leaving McErlain to contemplate life in the lower echelons of the *Rich 500*. His wealth has increased slightly because of the improved performance of his motoring chain, with 11 dealerships and a £100 million turnover.

## Personal style

That he nearly finagled victory with the Sterling Gate deal is an achievement in itself. Just five months earlier, in May 1993, he was forced to resign as chairman of the debt-laden Anglo-United energy group after disastrous losses during the recession. But McErlain is probably still smiling – he earned millions in his years at Anglo-United, channelling the money into Petrogate, his Swiss based Private Trust. Better still, he bought Chatfields from Anglo-United two years ago, when he was still chairman, for just £6.5 million. Six months later, a revaluation of Chatfields showed the net assets were worth £6 million more. McErlain also collected a £500,000 pay off after getting the boot.

## Extravagances

Allowing himself too much time contemplating ways to move up the *Rich 500*.

## Peter Kane 47
## £35m (New entry)
## Business

## Source of wealth

The flotation of Business Post last July was the culmination of 22 years of Peter Kane's labour. The Slough-based overnight delivery service is now worth £55 million, valuing Kane's stake at £33 million. He and his brother pocketed £1 million each at flotation, and in its first year as a public company Business Post made £5.3 million on £42 million sales.

Peter Kane drew £150,000 in salary and received just under £1 million in dividends during the year.

## Personal style

Hard-nosed business sense in a hopelessly crowded market have helped Peter Kane survive (and begin to prosper) as a public company. The shares dived in November

when the City caught a whiff of unfulfilled prospectus predictions. Conservative MP Dudley Fishburn sits on the Business Post board.

## Extravagances

After years of hard work, Kane has some cash to spend at last. A novelty.

## Marquess of Douro 48
## £35m (£30m)
## Aristocracy

## Source of wealth

Lord Arthur Charles Valerian Wellesey, heir to the 8th Duke of Wellington, is one of the few aristocrats in Britain to have proved himself in business. Since 1991, he has been chairman of Dunhill Holdings plc. His other directorships include: Transatlantic Holdings plc, Global Asset Management worldwide Inc., Rothmans International plc and Sun Life Corporation plc. From his father, he will one day inherit the title that brings with it the family pile, Stratfield Saye in Hampshire, and Spanish estates presented to the Iron Duke for doing rather well at Waterloo.

## Personal style

In 1977, he married the very beautiful Princess Antonia von Preussen – a Guinness heiress whose wealth outstrips his own. They have five children.

The only apparent disappointment in his career has been his failure to get into Parliament. In 1974, at the age of 29, he got the hopeless job of contesting the Labour stronghold of Islington North in London and lost. Five years later, he became a member of the European parliament, where he stayed until 1989.

Friends describe him as an old fashioned millionaire who is intensely private. His social set includes the Prince of Wales and Camilla Parker-Bowles.

## Extravagances

His CV reads like that of a workaholic. In the Douro household, an extravagance would mean daddy going on holiday with the kids.

## Vivien Duffield 48
## £35m (£38.5m)
## Inheritance

## Source of wealth

Vivien Duffield, daughter of the late retail and property tycoon, Sir Charles Clore, is best known known for her extraordinary battle to prevent the taxman taking a £67 million bite out of her father's legacy. He died in London when he was domiciled in Monaco for tax purposes; the assets, mostly in property and Sears shares, were in England. She lost the battle but managed to keep £57 million: her brother, Alan, having been disinherited by their father.

## Personal style
Despite her treatment at the hands of the Inland Revenue, Vivien has almost tried to compete with the Sainsburys in terms of her gifts to the arts in the UK. The Clore Gallery at the Tate was built with a £6 million gift from her. More recently she has taken the lead in campaigning to raise £45 million for the Royal Opera House renovation. She is a very prominent figure in London society, along with her daughter Arabella, and lives with Jocelyn Stevens, who is a director of English Heritage; marriage is not said to be part of their plans.

## Extravagances
She still keeps a home in London, and bought the Brechin Estate from the trustees of the Earl of Dalhousie in 1987, at a cost of more than £2.5 million. Like her father, she has made Switzerland her legal domicile and recently splashed £250,000 on Jocelyn Stevens's 60th birthday party.

## Margaret Barbour 54
**£35m** (New entry)
**Business**

### Source of wealth
Everyone from hip Italian young men to the terminally snobby American preppies are wearing waxed Barbour jackets, so long the symbol of the British establishment.

J Barbour & Sons chairman, Margaret Barbour, isn't complaining: 1993 profits dwarfed the previous year's. Turnover is up 40 per cent to £53 million, and after-tax profits are up over 50 per cent to £6.6 million. Her 25 per cent personal stake would be worth at least £33 million if the company ever came to market. She also paid herself £660,000 last year.

### Personal style
Two Queen's Awards for Export on the trot, and half the production going abroad might smack of aggressive marketing. But like all successful British products overseas, Barbours have almost sold themselves. The original design dates back to 1894. Margaret took over the company when her husband died in 1972 and has seen its sales take off in the Eighties.

### Extravagances
Margaret Barbour keeps her head down. She was awarded a CBE in 1991.

## David Kirch 57
**£35m** (New entry)
**Property**

### Source of wealth
David Kirch's fingers are in many pies. He has stakes in Flagstone, a penny-share property and leisure group, and Clark Nicholls & Coomb, a sweets-to-property combine, which together are worth about £5 million. He also owns 20 per cent of Nycal, a mining group, which bought the Lands End and John O'Groat's Company from Peter de Savary. His main vehicle is Channel Hotels and Properties, which he bought control of in 1984 for £5 million. It now lists assets of £50 million. Our valuation however is based on how much a buyer would be willing to pay for Kirch's holdings: the answer, we believe, is not very much.

### Personal style
Kirch started with a £5,000 inheritance, and has wheeled and dealed his way to a property fortune.

A £350,000 under-the-table-and-into-the-Swiss-bank-account payment to Harry Lapidus when Kirch bought his shareholding in Channel Hotels in 1984. It landed him in court, where he was fined £10,000 for making a false statement in connection with the takeover.

### Extravagances
Limited on Jersey apart from the usual mansion and boat.

## William Benyon 64
**£35m** (New entry)
**Inheritance**

### Source of wealth
In Who's Who, Bill Benyon lists his occupation as "farmer (since 1964)". This much is true: but what marks Benyon out for *Rich 500* membership is the fact that in 1964 he inherited from a cousin not just a farm, but a enormous estate, on the borders of Reading in Berkshire.

Before coming into his inheritance, he had served a ten year stint in the Navy and toiled away at Courtaulds Ltd for a similar length of time.

As a Conservative MP from 1970, latterly for Milton Keynes, he was a junior minister and government whip under Edward Heath. His son, Richard, may follow in his footsteps: recently he offered himself as a Conservative candidate to contest the by-election at Newbury, but was rejected by the selection committee.

### Personal style
Politically, he's a wet – spoke up in Parliament against the poll tax in 1988.

Since his retirement from Parliament, at the age of 62, in 1992, Benyon has devoted himself to charitable work and a cellar stocked with expanding quantities of fine wine.

### Extravagances
Wine.

## Mark Birley 64
**£35m** (£24.5m)
**Leisure**

### Source of wealth
Marcus Oswald Lecky Birley had the good fortune to open Annabel's nightclub in Berkeley Square in 1963 – the year of the Profumo Affair, when sex was invented and London started, officially, to swing.

In the three decades since then, he has made millions brightening up the leisure hours of the upper classes. Should he ever write his autobiography, it will prove a rattling good read. If nothing else, Annabel's is a hotbed of high grade, high society gossip.

Later, Birley expanded by opening Mark's Club and Harry's Bar, which is much favoured by the international jet set. In 1988, he opened for business at the Bath and Raquets club next to Claridge's. The membership fee was £2,000 per year. The same year Birley celebrated Annabel's silver jubilee with the three-week import of a samba troupe from Rio. We have updated Birley's wealth this year to take account of successful ventures in the property market. We have also attributed some value to the Annabel's brand name. Hotel owners such as Donald Trump are showing increased interest in licensing the name.

### Personal style
Raffish, even roguish, but gentlemanly. Through the exclusive Clermont Club, a gambler's paradise, Birley was associated with both John Aspinall and Lord Lucan. Annabel's was named after Birley's then wife, sister of the Marquess of Londonderry. The couple were divorced in 1975. For 10 years, she had been the mistress of his good friend Sir James Goldsmith. His personal life has been marred by tragedy. His elder son Rupert vanished in 1986, while on a business trip to Togo. The younger, Robin, was mauled as a teenager by one of John Aspinall's tigers.

### Extravagances
Work.

## George Williams 67
**£35m** (New entry)
**Business**

### Source of wealth
George Williams is attempting fortune number two, having sold his Anglian Windows business in 1984 to BET for £25 million. Naturally he's trying to strike gold in the same spot with a double-glazing business that competes head-on in Norfolk with Anglian, now a public company worth £180 million. Giving Aspen Windows (his new concern) a nominal value of £10 mil-

lion, we rate Williams at £35 million giving him membership of the *Rich 500* for the first time.

## Personal style
Williams spent much of the late Eighties in the tabloids, when it was revealed his wife had run off with her son-in-law and got married. Williams himself is now married to 35 year-old beauty, Alex, and is back where he feels most comfortable: running a double-glazing sales force (incidentally, many of the top salesman he poached from Anglian to run the new Aspen Windows business: Anglian is suing).

## Extravagances
A massive estate in Norfolk, featuring a 14th century manor house, a holiday home in the Virgin Islands, a farmhouse in Pennsylvania, and for good measure a home in Devon. For tax purposes he resides in Jersey.

### Sir Leslie Porter 74
### £35m (£32m)
### Retailing

## Source of wealth
Young Leslie Porter had the good fortune to marry Tesco heiress, Shirley Porter, in 1949. He had started off in life as a car mechanic and salesman, but by the late Fifties, he was doing business with Tesco, and acting as a consultant. He helped found the company's Home 'n' Wear division, which achieved sales of £75 million within 12 years. In the meantime, he also developed his father's old firm into a thriving textiles concern. Ultimately, he became chairman of Tesco, retiring in 1985. He still holds a substantial amount of shares in the company.

## Personal style
In his younger days, Sir Leslie fought off constant efforts on the part of the family to involve him at Tesco. He was determined to make it on his own. There have been reports that he has recently suffered with ill health.

## Extravagances
Not so many.

### Viscount Leverhulme 79
### £35m (£35m)
### Aristocracy

## Source of wealth
The Leverhulme family fortune rests upon the profits generated before the First World War by sales of Sunlight soap. Ultimately, this wildly successful brand was parlayed into Unilever, which was founded by the present Viscount's grandfather.

The peerage was granted by Lloyd George in 1917. At this point, the first Lord Leverhulme also set up the family's trusts, which now control nearly £500 million in investments – including Unilever shares.

A member of the Order of St John of Jerusalem, Viscount Leverhulme controls several thousand acres of prime farming land adjoining the family home in Cheshire. These land holdings, together with bloodstock interests and holdings in Unilever, appear to be the basis of his wealth.

In the past, doubts have been raised over the size of the family fortune. When the present Leverhulme's father died in 1949, many wealth-watchers thought the estate to be worth around £15 million (£190 million in current values). But only around £400,000 (£5 million in current values) was passed on to the male heir the current Lord Leverhulme.

Appearances can be deceptive. In fact, the second Viscount distributed much of his wealth before his death in 1949. Once again, careful tax planning saved the day. The Viscount has added to his holdings substantially over the years.

Even so, at £35 million we have valued his estate generously.

## Personal style
Military background; usual Leverhulme high moral standards.

## Extravagance
Horse racing.

### Lord Home of the Hirsel 91
### £35m (£35m)
### Aristocracy

## Source of wealth
Lord Home's inherited wealth is tied up in 50,000 acres in Lanarkshire and the Borders, and some prime salmon fishing rights. But it is as Sir Alec Douglas-Home that he is better known. Home's career as a politician – from 1931 – kept him constantly in the public eye: at Munich with Chamberlain in 1938, as Macmillan's foreign secretary from 1960 to 1963, and then as prime minister. (To get the job, he had to renounce his inherited title: a decade later he was granted a life peerage.) After his failure at the 1964 election, he stepped down as Tory leader in 1965. But Sir Alec was far from finished, and served again as Foreign Secretary under Heath.

## Personal style
The only man alive who has met Hitler, Mussolini, Stalin, Khrushchev, Truman, Eisenhower, Kennedy and Johnson – and that's just the dead ones. He once described his ancestors as "a bloodthirsty lot – robber barons, really."

## Extravagances
Receiving accolades from Scottish towns and cities. He has been granted the freedom of Edinburgh, Coldstream and Selkirk.

### Joe Bollom
### £35m (New entry)
### Leisure

## Source of wealth
Joe Bollom built his fortune in the amusement industry. He had the UK agency for Atari games in the early Eighties and prospered mightily when Atari boomed. Then he got out before the ensuing bust. He was an investor in First Leisure with Lord Delfont and ran the private companies Ingersoll, Ameco and Arlington Leisure.

Bollom was also among the pack of entrepreneurs who roamed the market in the Seventies when opening amusement arcades was very easy, very cheap and very, very profitable. The half dozen people who spotted the opportunity are all now multimillionaires. Joe Bollom was one of them. He still sits on the First Leisure board and has just joined the board of Tring, the discount CD maker.

## Personal style
His main company, Arlington Leisure, is now run by son Michael and runs eight amusement arcades including the biggest arcade in Blackpool.

## Extravagances
British seaside resorts: he wants to buy them all.

### John Delaney
### £35m (£30 m)
### Inheritance

## Source of wealth
John Delaney now owns 1.3 million shares in Securicor, not the 4 million attributed to him in the *Sunday Times* this year. The holding is still worth just under £20 million, and he appears to have sold the balance in the last year.

## Personal style
In 1966, John Delaney married Denise Pigott, the heiress to the Securicor fortune who controlled nearly half the voting shares of the group. Her father and uncle had bought, and built up the armoured vans security company so successfully that by 1979 it was carrying £38 billion of cash around the country.

Denise sat on the board and John was also given a seat. Denise died in 1980, leaving John to watch over the family interests. During the Eighties, the company's worth was transformed when, in partnership with

British Telecom, it won the licence to operate the Cellnet mobile phone service in Britain. If only Cellnet had been as profitable as Vodafone, then Delaney would have joined the ranks of the mega-wealthy.

**Extravagances**
Takes the concept of low profile to a new level.

### John Draper
### £35m (New entry)
### Business

## Source of wealth
John Draper took over as chairman of Britain's best known tools company, Draper Tools Group, in May this year after the death of his father, Norman. As a result, he makes his first appearance in the *Rich 500*.

At the end of 1993, turnover was £34 million and profit after tax up to £4.4 million. Customer stockholding is down. However, John's stake in the business with his family is currently worth £35 million, given the improved trading conditions and no borrowing.

## Personal style
Little is known about Draper – and he wants to keep it that way – he plans to let his power tools do the talking.

## Extravagances
None – too busy looking through his tool box.

### Tim Rice 50
### £34.5m (£32m)
### Entertainment

## Source of wealth
Timothy Rice is incredibly wealthy as a result of his lyric-writing prowess over the years. These days he has tapped Hollywood, and is on some lucrative contracts after winning an Oscar for Walt Disney's smash hit *Aladdin*.

He has a very lucrative three-year contract with Disney to write lyrics for several projects on stage and screen, which is said to be worth £4 million alone.

## Personal style
Taller than people think, he is probably better known for his passion for cricket than he is for his work. He doesn't regret not earning the mega-bucks of his former partner, Sir Andrew Lloyd Webber. He said in 1993 in an interview with *You* magazine: "If you want mega-bucks you have to have a positive interest in the business aspect of show-business. I'm not particularly good at money but I'm lucky – I made a lot so it doesn't matter." Indeed.

## Extravagances
Only cricket.

### Sir Julian Hodge 89
### £34.5m (£35m)
### Banking

## Source of wealth
Sir Julian Hodge is a man of many parts, for a time the dominant shareholder in Avana Foods and Commercial Bank Of Wales and the Hodge Group.

He sold Hodge Group in November 1973, Avana in September 1981 and Commercial Bank in June 1986, before retiring to Jersey. In the Seventies, Hodge Finance Ltd was the most aggressive supplier of hire purchase finance, and made a small fortune as a result. Sometimes it was just a little too aggressive for the establishment.

Each sale netted him millions and with careful management Hodge has turned the £30 million he got for his shares in all three companies into £64 million today. He had paid little tax, due to careful management. Hodge founded the Jane Hodge charitable foundation 41 years ago in memory of his mother. Much has been given to charities – so much so that this particular charity has an annual income of £1.5 million, indicating that Hodge has endowed it with at least £25 million. It has recorded assets of nearly £20 million. We rate Hodge personally at £34.5 million.

## Personal style
Sir Julian Hodge is one of the grand old men of British business. An accountant by training, he gave a number of famous entrepreneurs their first break, including Sir Tom Cowie. Few of his contemporaries are still alive but he rests quietly in Jersey, still enjoying life.

## Extravagances
Gazing out to sea, remembering some extraordinary times.

### David Gold 57
### £34.5m (£31m)
### Retailing

## Source of wealth
David is the second half of the Gold brothers duo, who between them are the sole shareholders in A & P Roberts, Ann Summers Sales and Gold Star Publications. Their principal activity is merchandising, but *Hustler* and *Parade* are published by them, in collaboration with David Sullivan, the pretender to Paul Raymond's position as the king of soft-porn publishing.

The Golds also have a 25 per cent stake in Sullivan's Sport newspapers. Despite the high turnover of the companies, profits in last year's accounts are miniscule. Both brothers have other interests, including property.

## Personal style
He is a former professional footballer with the savvy daughter, Jacqui, who runs the Ann Summers party plan retail business, now believed to be the biggest money earner for the family.

## Extravagances
Not having their photo taken.

### Tom Walkinshaw
### 34.5m (£30m)
### Sports

## Source of wealth
Tom Walkinshaw 's TWR Group is lucky to be still in business. Over expansion meant it nearly went under in the recession. But some nifty financing deals by Walkinshaw enabled it to stay afloat and prosper. External investments have substantially underpinned his net worth. TWR owns a host of vehicle industry interests. The car dealerships have been hit by the recession and have since been restructured.

As part of a solution to his problems he sold a half share in his motor dealer business to Silverstone Circuits for £5.3 million. Silverstone is owned by members of the British Racing Drivers' Club, who objected to the decision and forced Walkinshaw off the Silverstone board of directors in 1992. He later bought the stake back for half price.

In recent years, Walkinshaw has done two deals with the Italian Benetton clothing company. He has bought one-third of the Benetton Grand Prix team while Benetton has bought a 50 per cent stake in his master company TWR Group Ltd. The considerations for either of these deals have never been revealed, but would undoubtedly indicate the value of the Walkinshaw wealth. It looks as though cash, to the tune of £50 million, has been injected into the company in recent years.

We value TWR at around £100 million and it has annual turnover well over a £100 million but miniscule profits. Based mainly on his involvement with Benetton we value Walkinshaw at £33 million.

## Personal style
Tom Walkinshaw is one of the best engineering/financial brains that Britain has ever seen combined in one man. He was undoubtedly in trouble at the end of the Eighties but got out of it in Houdini style. His deal with Silverstone was a lifesaver but it cost him his reputation amongst the establishment of British motor racing and caused the whole of the BRDC board to be fired by its members an absolutely unprecedented move.

## Extravagances
Walkinshaw travels the world in an experi-

mental Beechcraft aeroplane that has propellers but the performance of a jet. He leases the machine from Beechcraft for a rumoured $40,000 a month, maintenance included. He has a couple of mansions in Oxfordshire where he is believed to enjoy an unconventional family existence: i.e. he has more than one of them.

## Jackie Stewart 55
## £34m (£32.75m)
## Sports

### Source of wealth
Jackie Stewart earned a million dollars a year for the final four years of his driving career – until 1973. When he retired from the sport he was worth a comfortable £5 million. But that was only the start, although, at the time, he thought his big earning days were over. In his last year he was supported by Goodyear tyres, Elf, Ford, ABC, Rolex and Moet et Chandon. All of these sponsors retained their business with him in retirement and he found his earnings didn't change.

Stewart has admitted that he currently earns $3 million a year and has accumulated total wealth of some £34 million. Of course, much of his sterling and dollar earnings were converted to Swiss Francs when the exchange rate was 12 francs to the pound, rather than the two of today. This boosts the value of his original fortune still further. With very careful planning, he has paid very little tax. Stewart is very loyal to his sponsors and he gives good value. His other business interests include his own profitable racing team, based at Silverstone, and a shooting school in Scotland. He commentates for ABC television in America.

Stewart is managed by Mark McCormack and the original deal, where McCormack takes 25 per cent of his non-sports activities, endures today. As we said, Stewart is very loyal, and over the years has made £10 million for his manager. Stewart is known to think it money well spent.

### Personal Style
Stewart was arguably the greatest racing driver of all time. He crossed the line in first place in a staggering one-third of all the Grand Prix races he entered. He had scheduled his retirement to coincide with his 100th Grand Prix, going out as the reigning world champion. It never happened. His retirement was marred by the death of his team mate, François Cevert. He actually went out after only 99 races, as the team was withdrawn by owner Ken Tyrell after Cevert's death at the United States Grand Prix.

For 17 years Stewart held the record as having won the most Grands Prix races, an accolade inherited from another Scottish driver, Jim Clark. However, his record has been overtaken in recent years by Alain Prost, the late Ayrton Senna and Nigel Mansell. Their successes are attributable to the sheer number of Formula One races that are now held.

Stewart said he retired in 1973, at the ridiculously young age of 34, because he was bored with racing and because of the number of close friends who had been killed over the years. In those days motor racing was very dangerous, and the odds were against a successful driver, racing at the front, surviving more than 50 races. He saw Jochen Rindt, Piers Courage and Bruce McLaren die in one year alone and he, and his wife Helen, often picked up the pieces for their families. He was only too aware that it could have been himself, rather than François Cevert, who crashed and died during his very last race.

### Extravagances
Stewart enjoys an expensive lifestyle. He keeps a permanent suite at the Grosvenor House Hotel in London and travels, first class, 400,000 miles every year. Last year, he made 43 trips to the US, mostly on Concorde.

He also uses helicopters extensively. No expense is spared to ensure his family's well being. When in Britain he is chauffeured around in a Ford Scorpio with the number plates 1 JYS. He always sits in the front seat, conscious that he should never be considered a remote celebrity, and is invariably talking on one, or both, of the car's two cellular phones.

He lives in a lakeside villa in Geneva with his wife, Helen. It was purchased in 1970 for a few thousand pounds. Now, it is worth a few million.

## Ralph Gold 56
## £34m (£31m)
## Retailing

### Source of wealth
Ralph Gold owns half of the Gold Brothers empire, which straddles an interesting mix of pornography and other sex-based merchandise. The empire is based upon a company called A & P Roberts Holdings Ltd. This company, through which they distribute on behalf of American and Scandinavian publishers, has turnover of almost £60 million. But profits are miniscule indicating the Golds have an aversion to paying corporation tax.

### Personal style
Ralph Gold, the younger brother, is an ex-professional wrestler. It was reputedly his idea to buy the Ann Summers retail chain,

now the biggest earner in the group through its party plan activities, run by Ralph's niece, Jacqui.

### Extravagances
Never having his photo taken.

## Bill Wyman 57
## £34m (£32m)
## Music

### Source of wealth
Bill Wyman's decision to quit the Rolling Stones two years ago has cost him dearly, with the band embarking on a lucrative world tour and having just released a number one selling album. He's probably not too bothered as he still collects half the Jagger-Wyman song royalties. Ironically, the surge in popularity of the Rolling Stones has led to many of the old albums being reissued on compact disc, and Wyman adding to his wealth.

Wyman spent most of his earnings from the band in the Sixties, and only really became rich after touring in the Eighties. He runs a West End restaurant, Sticky Fingers, which adds around £100,000 a year to his income. The divorce from Mandy Smith cost him a relatively low £580,000. Interestingly, Smith is now rumoured to be penniless.

Taking into account royalties and the value of his restaurant, we have slightly upgraded Wyman's wealth to £34 million.

### Personal style
Always regarded as the serious man of the Rolling Stones, fans would take bets on whether Wyman, who played bass guitar, would shake any part of his body on stage. Mick Jagger nicknamed him Mr Formica because he had such bad taste.

### Extravagances
He claims 1000 women know his style intimately. The figure is unlikely to rise as he is married to Californian actress Suzanne Accosta. He has a penthouse Chelsea flat, a property in Venice, and Gedding Hall, a medieval mansion near Bury St Edmunds.

## Ian Hutcheson 63
## £34m (New entry)
## Food

### Source of wealth
Ian Hutcheson founded the edible oils and fats manufacturer Acatos and Hutcheson in 1966 with just £21,000. The group, now quoted on the Stock Exchange, is capitalised at £93 million and Hutcheson's 37 per cent share stake values him at £34 million.

He would be worth more were it not for the 50 per cent rise in the prices of edible oils during 1993. The company, which supplies oils to supermarkets, returned interim profits of £5.59 million before tax in April 1994.

## Personal style

Hutcheson's claim to fame is that he was the first person to import lard in bulk tankers from America, in the Fifties. He also hit upon the idea of producing margarine with a 10 per cent butter content.

## Extravagances

A keen Liberal Democrat, Hutcheson is one of several industrialists drafted in by Paddy Ashdown to advise on employment policy. This is an inspired choice by Paddy Ashdown, seeing as Hutcheson is closing down his Merseyside factory in December 1994, making 250 people redundant.

### Lady Edna Samuel 86
### £34m (£33m)
### Inheritance

## Source of wealth

Lady Edna Samuel married property developer, Harold Samuel, in 1936. Her husband went on to develop Land Securities into the biggest metropolitan landowner in Britain. At his zenith, Samuel eclipsed even such legends as Jack Cotton and Charles Clore.

The empire began with purchases of derelict and bombed-out sites during the war. Deals were often struck with major landlords like the Westminsters and the Portlands. Samuel went on to thrive in the office construction boom that followed in the Fifties and Sixties.

## Personal style

Edna's husband was made a peer with the title of Lord Samuel of Wych Cross. He died in 1987, a legend. The former Edna Nedas has two children, Carol and Marion.

## Extravagances

Lives in Hampshire.

### Harry Shipley
### £34m (New entry)
### Leisure

## Source of wealth

Harry Shipley owns National Leisure Ltd which owns and operates amusement arcades.

In the Seventies, opening amusement arcades was easy, cheap and very profitable. Harry Shipley, one of the small number of people who spotted the opportunity, is now very rich as a result.

Harry and his brother, John, were two of the most successful. Their original company, HJM Caterers Ltd, was split between the brothers a few years ago when they ami-

cably went their separate ways.

## Personal style

Quiet, charming and for the most part unseen, Harry Shipley is one of the most powerful men in the leisure industry. He aspires to be president of the amusement machine trade association BACTA, a very important position. He is well on the way. In a flashy industry often ruled by greed, Harry Shipley is a breed apart, recognised as a gentleman.

## Extravagances

His quest to make amusement arcades more socially acceptable.

### John Shipley
### £34m (New entry)
### Leisure

## Source of wealth

John Shipley is the owner of HJM Caterers, a long established company operating amusement arcades. There was a propitious time in the Seventies when opening amusement arcades was very easy, very cheap and very, very profitable. The half dozen people who spotted the opportunity are all now multi-millionaires. Shipley is one of them.

He started the company with his brother Harry and some help from their father, Jim Shipley. A few years ago, the company was split into two. John Shipley retained the original company name. Currently, he is one of the richest men in the leisure industry and our valuation is very conservative.

## Personal style

The Shipleys were an old family of travelling showmen. But their father sent them to public school. He owns and lives at Drayton Manor near Tamworth, a leisure park. Shipley senior is a wealthy man in his own right. John keeps a very low profile and lets brother, Harry, take all the limelight.

## Extravagances

Has just found time to enjoy his family.

### Richard Gabriel 38
### £33.5m (£40.5m)
### Business

## Source of wealth

Richard Gabriel became rich when his Interlink express parcels company went public in 1986. Then he sold Interlink Express to Australian transport multinational, Mayne Nickless, in 1991. Their 71 per cent holding was worth just over £50 million. Gabriel has less than that, due to a significant stake being the possession of his mother, Rose.

Since selling, he has dabbled in cars via a

stake in the Healey Motor Car Company, building replica vintage sports cars, and owns salmon farms in Scotland and Eire which he is attempting to turn to profit.

We have marked him down slightly as these ventures mark time and the larger stake held by his mother than we originally thought.

## Personal style

Starting as a motorcycle courier, Richard Gabriel built up the Interlink Express courier business with his mother, Rose Bugden. Beginning in 1976, they concentrated on computer data deliveries between building societies and supermarkets, delivering at night when the roads were clear and employing agents to complete the local delivery during the day.

## Extravagances

Cars. And finally getting married.

### John Thornton 50
### £33.5m (£30.5m)
### Food

## Source of wealth

John Thornton, chairman of chocolatemakers Thorntons, is teetering on the brink of the *Rich 500* for a second year, although ironically his wealth has gone up despite continued haemorrhaging at his company's French operations. But such is the way of the City: having got the pain out of the way (£9 million exceptional charge in the accounts) the shares have been re-rated.

Thornton seems to have control of just under 30 per cent of the equity, and that is his total wealth: we rate him at a shade under £34 million.

## Personal style

He is a third generation leader and the first since the company went public, meaning that the Thornton family wealth is being split between umpteen members of the family.

## Extravagances

That French folly.

### Vicountess Linley 24
### £33m (£30m)
### Aristocracy

## Source of wealth

Last year, Serena Stanhope married Viscount Linley, son of Princess Margaret. Their wedding matched Linley's bloodline (son of Princess Margaret, 12th in line to the throne) with the fabulous wealth, centred on properties in west London, of the Stanhope clan.

Her father, Viscount Petersham, is heir to the Earl of Harrington, who went into tax exile in the Irish republic in the Sixties. ➤

Later the Earl of Harrington signed over the bulk of his fortune to Petersham. These are seriously rich folk. When Serena's father got married, for the honeymoon, he bought a 102ft yacht and spent 880 days sailing the long route (35,000 miles) around the world.

Property values rising has boosted her net worth but married life is more expensive.

**Personal style**
Increasingly fawned upon by the media as the older Royals find their tiaras tarnished. Her husband, Viscount Linley, is 12th in line to the throne. Could it be that the Palace wants to push forward younger personalities into the limelight?

**Extravagances**
Expensive couture outfits.

### David Padley 39
**£33m** (£30.25m)
**Food**

**Source of wealth**
David Padley runs GW Padley (Holdings) Ltd, the Lincolnshire-based poultry and vegetables processor. That may not sound spectacular, but the company has substantial assets and is consistently profitable. In the year to July 1993, pre-tax profits were up £1 million to £4.6 million. If sold today, Padley would trouser £33 million for his 75 per cent stake.

**Personal style**
David took over the firm seven years ago after his father was killed in a car crash in Majorca. His mother, seriously injured in the same crash, started the company by buying and selling poultry from the back of a truck. The cash began to flow after an automated chicken plucking line was bought in the late Sixties.

**Extravagances**
Very much a family man carrying on the traditions of his late father.

### Olga Polizzi 43
**£33m** (£32m)
**Hotels**

**Source of wealth**
The Hon Olga Polizzi has 9.1 million shares in Forte plc, valued on the stock market at almost £2 billion. A director since 1983, she heads the Building and Design department. With dividends over the years, including nearly £500,000 last year, her wealth moves up to £33 million.

**Personal style**
The eldest daughter of Lord Forte, she married the Marquess Polizzi of Sorrento in Italy in 1966. He was killed in a car crash in

1975 and Olga was left to bring up two daughters on her own. She eventually began working in the Forte hotel empire and currently has over 100 new projects under her belt.

**Extravagances**
Hasn't re-married. A councillor for Westminster City, she enjoys walking, ski-ing and opera.

### Frank Williams 51
**£33m** (£26.5m)
**Sports**

**Source of wealth**
We moved Frank Williams off the *Rich 500* when Ayrton Senna was killed but have since reinstated him.

The reason that we did this was that he had to pay Senna's salary for the full two years of his contract, whether he drove or not. Then we discovered that Senna was insured, and Williams sponsors stayed with the team after Senna's death. It was business as usual. Gruesome as it may be, Williams has actually made money out of Senna's death in the short term because his driver retainers are now under a million a year. Williams was very unsuccessful until Patrick Head, the designer, joined his team on 28th February 1977, Williams has never looked back. Soon Head was given equity in the team Williams Grand Prix Engineering Ltd, and his cars started winning regularly from 1979, averaging five wins a season since then, and dominating the sport for the past three years.

From 1980 onwards, Williams has earned over £1 million a year since that time. Both he and Patrick Head have become multi-millionaires. He shares ownership of the team with Head, but has the majority share. The team today is worth some £50 million and if it were measured as a normal private company, would probably show a surplus of £5 million a year. It is worth £50 million if you include the now priceless collection of Williams grand prix cars in the asset list. These are worth an average of £350,000 apiece and the team has kept many of them for the past 14 years. With his private assets and his share of the team Williams is worth some £33 million.

**Personal style**
He survived a car accident in the South of France in 1986, which caused paralysis from the neck down, to come back and lead his team to more success. He has been looked after faithfully by his wife, Virginia, since then.

**Extravagances**
Re-employing Nigel Mansell, for a rumoured £1 million per race.

### Deverok Pritchard 54
**£33m** (New Entry)
**Business**

**Source of wealth**
Dev Pritchard paid the ultimate price of success this year. Fourteen years after founding the successful nursing homes provider Takare, his fellow directors decided they had enough of his "shoot from the hip" style and fired him.

Pritchard promptly disposed of his 12.5 million shares, trousering £30 million. With past dividends he has £33 million.

**Personal style**
For the past fourteen years he thought he had great style, taking Takare from scratch to a £14.9 million pre-tax profit in 1993, a 26 per cent rise. The group is valued at £300 million. Pritchard founded it with his close friend Keith Bradshaw. So close that they would share the same office and secretary. Unfortunately by last year whispers were spreading about Takare's accounting policies. Bradshaw says Pritchard was too much of an entrepreneur and didn't know how to delegate. So the directors unanimously decided to fire him. (Unanimous that is except for Pritchard).

**Extravagances**
Noted for ending telephone conversations by saying "Take Care." Maybe that's why he really got fired.

### Lindsay Bury 54
**£31m** (£26.5m)
**Finance**

**Source of wealth**
Lindsay Bury, who runs the Sharp Technology Fund, is one of the unsung heroes of venture capital. His most conspicuous success was the former Apricot Computers company, ACT. He chaired it for many years and made a considerable sum of money from it. His wealth has increased this year with flotations and sheer appreciation of the venture capital sector.

**Personal style**
He sits on the boards of many companies, reflecting his venture capital roots.

He is married with a son and a daughter.

**Extravagances**
A magnificent walled estate in Shropshire, called Millichope Park.

### David Blackburn 62
**£33 m** (£75m)
**Motor Industry**

**Source of wealth**
David Blackburn tumbles down the *Rich*

*500* not because his company's doing badly – indeed, profits at Colt Car Company rose to £16.7 million after tax for the year to March 1992 – but because we've got better idea of his shareholding this year. He personally owns 15 per cent of the company, and Mitsubishi has a 50 per cent stake: the remainder is tied up in a labyrinthine series of nominee companies which Blackburn is said to control. An informed source in Guernsey now tells us that Blackburn has assigned his beneficial interest in the bulk of the nominee companies to his four children. Valuing Colt at £220 million, his visible wealth comes to £33 million.

## Personal style
David Blackburn spent much of the Fifties and Sixties working for Mercedes Benz and BMW, leading their drive into the British luxury-car market. Then, in 1974, he went into partnership with Mitsubishi to distribute its cars in Britain.

## Extravagances
Cars, cars and cars: BMWs, a gaggle of vintage Rolls Royces. A large house in the Turks and Caicos islands.

### Alan Clark 66
### £33m (£30.25m)
### Inheritance

## Source of wealth
Quite aside from his inherited wealth and the phenomenal success of his *Diaries*, it emerged this year that Alan Clark was, and is, quite a player on the stock markets.

Meanwhile, Clark owns Saltwood Castle, an estate of 27,000 acres, three other country homes, a property in Switzerland and an art collection valued at £12 million (bequeathed by his father, the art historian, Lord Clark.) Apart from investment successes, and his income as a writer (six books in total) his wealth is inherited.

## Personal style
He describes himself as "Genghis Khan – only richer." What some would call political realism is a strong point. Among Clark's mottos: "Dirty tricks are part of government," and "Lie, if necessary." Politically, Clark will be best remembered for his role in blowing open the trail of Matrix Churchill directors who were indicted for their part in selling munitions to Saddam Hussein. But the man's indiscriminate frankness is accompanied by a disturbing side-order of eccentricity, if not unpleasantness. Clark, who feels that "no man could refrain from admiring" Adolf Hitler, once attended a party thrown by Nazi apologist, David Irving. Drinks were served with swastika cocktail sticks.

## Extragances
Women, women and more women. Skirt-

chasing looms large in his diaries and Clark's reputation as a womaniser led MI5 to tail him for many years. ("Why the sex police had to spy on Alan Clark", was one of last year's more entertaining tabloid headlines.)

### Earl of Harrington 71
### £33m (£30m)
### Aristocracy

## Source of wealth
Some years ago, the colourful Earl of Harrington signed over to his son a large part of the family fortune – including a large slice of residential west London. His son, Viscount Petersham, took over the burden of running the estate.

The Earl of Harrington, meanwhile, has lived quietly in Co Limerick, Ireland, for 30 years. Before leaving Britain, in 1963, Harrington also sold up 4,500 acres in Derbyshire for £1 million. Though occasionally troubled financially, his activities in the bloodstock business have produced modest returns on investment over the years.

## Personal style
The holders of Irish noble titles – and there are many of them – rarely live in Ireland. In a pleasant reversal of the trend, the Earl of Harrington chooses to live in Ireland even though he doesn't hold an Irish title. In 1965, two years after his arrival, he became an Irish citizen. At the time, this was a serious matter. As the *Daily Telegraph* informed its readers, the Earl's move didn't mean that he had become "an alien" or that he had "in any way ceased to be a British citizen showing allegiance to the Her Majesty the Queen."

## Extravagances
The earl lives amid a 700-acre estate, Greenmount, in Limerick.

### Rodney Webb
### £33 m (New entry)
### Business

## Source of wealth
Crest Packaging, the cartons business Rodney Webb and his fellow managers bought out from Bowater in 1985, came to market last year among a flurry of new issues. Initially valued at £54 million, the company's share price has slid ever since: it is now worth £40 million. Webb's 62 per cent share is now worth only £26 million, but fortunately for him he netted £7 million (after tax) off the flotation, and so makes his debut on the *Rich 500* at £33 million.

## Personal style
As with many management buyouts, the

true value of the company only emerged when it was in its managers' hands. Bowater must be kicking itself for letting all that property (the main reason Crest could invest without borrowing) slip through its fingers.

## Extravagances
Give Webb time: that £7 million will be burning a hole in his (very large) pocket.

### Baron Inverforth 28
### £32.5 (£35.5m)
### Inheritance

## Source of wealth
The young Baron Inverforth appears to be in a lot better position than he was last year. He owns most of the shares in Andrew Weir & Company, an ailing shipping, brokerage and one-time insurance broker. He inherited from his father who died when he was only 16. Losses of the last two years, that totalled £27 million, have subsided to less than £2 million. Inverforth appears to own around 60 per cent of the shares.

Net assets are still some £70 million, including a chunk of cash and we have valued the company at no more than its current net asset value. The continuing losses, albeit much reduced have caused us to slightly downgrade Inverforth's net worth to £32.5 million, unlike the *Sunday Times* which, for some inexplicable reason, trebled the family's wealth last year. Beats us.

## Personal style
Whilst young Inverforth was coming of age, his fortune was minded for a while by his uncle The Hon John Vincent Weir. Weir retired as chairman in January 1991. Although at 59 he is approaching retirement age, he is the young Lord Inverforth's heir as the baron has none of his own, which creates some confusion especially as the *Sunday Times* which is still listing Inverforth's heir as holding the fortune.

The company is now chaired by Lord Runciman and the share register is just about the most confusing we have seen.

## Extravagances
Not having to worry so much about the family business anymore.

### Ken Follett 44
### £32.5m
### (£24.25m)
### Literary

## Source of wealth
Ken Follett is now one of the top fiction writers in the world. His wealth and status have jumped considerably during the year.

In 1990, the US-based Dell Publishing Company reportedly agreed with Follett a £7.2 million deal to publish two unnamed, unwritten, unplanned novels. Remarkably, this sum was agreed in exchange for publishing rights in the United States alone. Carole Benn, president of Dell, argued that the key to Follett's financial appeal lay in the fact that he was "one of the few thriller writers that appeal to women." For Dell to recoup its investment, Follett's first novel for the imprint would have had to sell 4 million copies in paperback and 500,000 in hardback.

Follett's first novel, *Eye of the Needle*, reached the top slot in American bestseller charts in 1977. Paperback rights were subsequently auctioned for £500,000 – not bad for a 28-year-old junior publishing executive previously accustomed to getting by on a £7,000 annual salary.

Adding up Follett's book sales and royalties plus advances, and deducting tax, means Follet again just makes it into the *Rich 500*.

## Personal style
Glimmers of Follett's wealth emerge continually. In 1986, he announced that he would return to live in London, despite an annual tax burden in the region of £500,000.

## Extravagances
As many as he can afford. Despite being a socialist he has said many times he really enjoys being rich.

### Jeffrey Archer 54
**£32.5m** (£26.5m)
**Literary**

## Source of wealth
In 1974, Jeffrey Archer nearly went bankrupt when the family of Joe Bamford (of JCB fame) reputedly called in his guarantees on shares sold to them. Archer subsequently realised that he had been unwittingly caught up in an investment scam. The shares were worthless and he was forced to pay up. Later, he noted he was "so low" at the time, that he would have "sold fake Gucci bags on street corners." This wasn't necessary. Instead, Archer carved out a career as a novelist.

His first novel was *Not A Penny More, Not A Penny Less*, published in 1976. His next blockbuster, *Shall We Tell the President?* (1977), earned him around £1 million in the USA alone. A third novel, *Kane and Abel* (1980), garnered several millions in hardback, paperback and film rights in Europe and the United States.

Successive novels brought in ever larger amounts. In 1990, Archer told the *New York Times* that a US publisher had offered him £11.5 million for world rights, excluding Britain and Japan, to three successive novels. Sniffily, Archer announced that he

had rejected the offer.

In 1992, he switched from his old UK publishers, Hodder & Stoughton, to Rupert Murdoch's imprint, Harper-Collins. The rumoured bidding for Archer's signature on the contract started at £14 million and went up to £18 million. Advance sales for *Honour Among Thieves*, published last year, totalled £3 million. Archer has also earned very large sums in Japan.

## Personal style
A born fighter – and likeable, as a politician, because of his willingness to get involved in an old-fashioned argument rather than stonewall interviewers with platitudes.

His career as a novelist ran parallel to his elevation within the Conservative Party. In the Seventies, he was one of the youngest MPs in Parliament. By 1985, he was deputy chairman of the party – a post offered in return for access to his prodigious fund-raising skills. Subsequently, despite his fierce loyalty, his political career has petered out.

Archer's hospitality at Conservative Party conferences – Krug champagne flows freely – has acquired the status of legend.

## Extravagances
A huge penthouse on the top of a redundant office block on the south side of the Thames. Arguably the best views in London.

### Sean Connery 64
**£32.5m** (£26.75m)
**Entertainment**

## Source of wealth
A one-time French polisher in Edinburgh, Sean Connery now commands fees of around £3 million per film. His earning potential only recently scaled such pinnacles. Admittedly, he earned top money (£1 million per film then) for the *James Bond* series of films. But a price had to be paid, and in Connery's case, he later suffered from a bad case of typecasting for much of the Eighties. Accordingly, he was only able to ask around £500,000 for appearing on the silver screen in between Bond projects.

In 1987, at the age of 57, his prospects were transformed overnight with a groundbreaking supporting role opposite Kevin Costner in *The Untouchables*. This was followed by a run of successes: *The Hunt for Red October*, *The Russia House*, and more recently *Rising Sun*, plus a significant role in the last *Indiana Jones* film.

## Personal style
Connery has a reputation as a hard-headed businessman, and has sued many studios

in his time. He once sued his former financial adviser, Kenneth Richards, and reputedly won a settlement of £23.8 million. *Forbes* magazine estimates his earnings between 1989 and 1992 at £30 million.

He has been married twice, first to actress Diane Cilento, a union that produced his now almost as famous son, actor Jason Connery, who played Bond creator Ian Fleming in a recent movie about the novelist's life. Connery is now married to a fiery Italian, Micheline.

While his ability as an actor has never been seriously questioned, he seems curiously unable to alter his startling American-Scottish brogue – even, for example, when he was required to play a Russian submarine commander in *The Hunt For Red October*.

## Extravagances
Golf and sunny villas abroad.

### Joseph McWilliams 74
**£32.5m** (New entry)
**Business**

## Source of wealth
Joseph McWilliams owns 59 per cent of Zortech International's 100,000 issued shares. The group is based in Droitwich and makes high temperature thermal insulation material. McWilliams is also Chairman of the group. After-tax profits for 1992 were £6.3 million (up 50 per cent), and turnover was £74.5 million, compared to 1991's £62.4 million. Net assets were £26 million, but this includes property that, according to the annual report, is worth far more than its listed book value. On a realistic price/earnings ratio of 12, we value McWilliams at £35.5 million. Just enough for this new member of the *Rich 500*.

## Personal style
New Zealand-born McWilliams runs a tight company, and has managed an astonishing profit growth through the recession. Recently introduced production techniques have helped the company keep costs low. Borrowings are minimal.

## Extravagances
His Kiwi heritage prevents him from the kind of largesse that £1 million plus annual dividends can buy.

### Nick Faldo 37
**£32m** (£28m)
**Sports**

## Source of Wealth
Nick Faldo has amassed a personal fortune of £32 million which is soundly managed by Mark McCormack's IMG organisa-

tion. Last year, he won £2 million in prize and appearance money. His off-course earnings were £5 million. Faldo's main sponsor is sweater manufacturer, Pringle. This year his total earnings are widely predicted to reach £10 million. At the age of 38, he is nearing the height of his powers.

Faldo is nicknamed "the man for all seasons" because of his remarkable ability to market himself and adapt to the needs of any sponsor. He manages to fit in commercial activities, for which he can sometimes expect to earn £100,000 a day, around the 30 weeks he spends away from home during the golf season.

His commercial success stems from the fact that he is tall and good looking, and wears clothes perfectly. Pringle is said to pay him at least £500,000 a year to be its frontman. His golf club contract is worth the same, and there is another £2 million where all that came from - courtesy of a host of secondary sponsors and one-off deals ably sewn up by John Simpson of IMG. So much so that Faldo candidly states today that he has no idea how much money he has.

## Personal Style
Faldo is very interested in commercial success and earning money. "I expect that to put another '0' on the end of the my fortune" he said, after his first British Open success.

He was helped by the standard McCormack performance clauses in each contract. The more successful he became, the more his sponsorship commitments earned him. The biggest immediate spin off from his first Open victory was a £1 million contract just for wearing Stylo shoes. One other factor that drives his income upwards. After a certain level, Faldo gets a royalty on jumpers, shoes and golf clubs sold.

He is the best and most consistent golfer Britain has ever produced. Major tournament successes have included winning the British Open in 1987, 1990 and 1992; the US Masters in 1989 and 1990 and the French Open three times.

But it was not always so. When Faldo first started out, he had £350 in the bank and lived in a rented house in Welwyn Garden City. He claims that worrying about money affected his game and the standard of his play has improved as the money worries have receded.

He married first wife Melanie when he was young, got divorced and then married his present wife, Gill, in 1986. They have a son and daughter. He attributes his golfing success, since 1986, to the joy of his second marriage. He was awarded the MBE in 1988. His recreations outside golf include fly fishing, DIY, snooker and motor sports.

## Extravagances
Faldo lives at Ascot, Berkshire. His Porsche with distinctive registration plate, NAF 911, is a familiar sight along the county's country lanes.

## Dave Stewart 41
## £32m (£31m)
## Music

## Source of wealth
When the Eurythmics first found fame, the music world was in awe of Annie Lennox's stunning looks. Dave Stewart was widely regarded as a decent backing guitarist. How wrong. Stewart soon became recognised as not only the best musician/producer in the business, but a pretty good businessman too.

With Lennox he set up DnA Ltd, channelling all their royalties and touring fees. A string of other companies were set up to disperse their incomes, and Stewart swapped his guitar pick for a calculator. By the late Eighties, the company was turning over £5 million.

After the band split Stewart launched his own band Spiritual Cowboys, with limited success. But it was his production skills that the industry sought, leading him to set up his own studio – The Church, in London.

In the past year The Church has gone through a rough patch, sacking five people and keeping on just two staff. The main problem is the studio is in London. We estimate Stewart has added £1 million to his fortune by producing records for other artists around the globe, mainly in America. He is believed to be among the world's ten highest paid record producers. Like most pop stars his living expenses are high.

## Personal style
Stewart comes across more as a businessman than rock star, carrying a briefcase to work each morning. He has stopped wearing sunglasses at night and the goatee beard has been stylishly trimmed. Married with two children to ex-Bananarama star Siobhan Fahey, for how much longer no one knows.

## Extravagances
The usual ones of a pop star.

## HRH Princess Anne 44
## £32m (£29m)
## Royalty

## Source of wealth
Princess Anne owns the 1,000-acre Gatcombe Park estate in Gloucestershire. On her marriage to Captain Mark Phillips in 1973, the Queen signed over the estate to Anne. Her husband's name didn't appear in the agreement. Today, long after their divorce, he manages the estate, and hands an annual rental fee over to Buckingham Palace.

In addition, Anne has been the beneficiary of a series of bequests within the Royal family and will eventually inherit part of her mother's cash wealth, her share of which will be £15 million.

As the second child of Queen Elizabeth II, the Princess Royal used to receive the tax-free sum from the public purse, via the Civil List, of £4,423 per week. Now, however, the Queen bears the cost of supporting her daughter.

She has two children, Peter Mark and Zara Anne, and is now married to the former Queen's Equerry, Royal Navy Commander Tim Lawrence.

## Personal style
Princess Anne carries out a very wide range of Royal functions. She is eighth in line to the throne and in recent years has been conspicuous by her support for the Save the Children fund. Once unpopular because of her perceived lack of the common touch, she is now only slightly less favoured in public opinion polls than the Queen and the Queen Mother.

## Extravagances
Horses and Gatcombe.

## Marquess of Hartington 50
## £32m (£30m)
## Aristocracy

## Source of wealth
The Marquess of Hartington is heir to his father, the elderly Duke of Devonshire. In his own right, he already lays claim to two stately piles: Bolton Abbey (plus 30,000 Yorkshire acres); and Lismore Castle (with 8,000 acres in County Waterford, Ireland). On the death of his father, he will inherit Chatsworth, probably Britain's best-known stately home.

## Personal style
Low profile aristocrat. But with an inheritance like Hartington's, who needs a profile?

## Extravagances
Horse-racing. He is chairman of the British Horse-racing Board.

## Duncan Davidson 53
## £32m (£28m)
## Construction

## Source of wealth
Duncan Davidson set up Persimmon Homes in 1972 with his wife, Sarah. Since flotation in 1986, the company has had a

bumpy ride but always been known as a quality homes builder. It appears to be emerging out of the housing market slump, and is valued by the City at £292 million. With his 10 per cent stake, and share sales along the way, Davidson's wealth goes up to £32 million.

## Personal style
Davidson is one of many former trainees at construction giant George Wimpey that have made it big in their own right. He set up his first company Ryedale in York in 1965 before selling it to London Merchant Securities for £1 million, saying he needed the cash to finance Persimmon.

## Extravagances
A cousin of the Duke of Norfolk, but thankfully he doesn't use that as a conversation starter on building sites.

### Jackie Collins 54
### £32m (£31.5m)
### Literary

## Source of wealth
Not many authors can still command a seven-figure advance, now that the recession has really hit book publishing, but Jackie Collins remains part of this select bunch of scribblers. In 1988, she took the world record by getting a £10 million advance for just three books. She did this on the back of the sales generated by her previous 12 books, which together have sold over 100 million copies throughout the world. By doing so she easily topped the £2 million advance which her sister, Joan, got for her attempted blockbuster, *Prime Time*.

Royalty and rights payments (after the advance has been earned out) have netted Collins a cumulative £12 million over the years. She's said to be close to delivering the final manuscript in the three-book deal, at which point her agent will no doubt argue for a Barbara Taylor Bradford-size contract, which could pay her £7 million per book – or about £65 a word. But until that shows up, her wealth does not change significantly.

## Personal style
Jackie Collins lives in Hollywood, but was born and brought up in London, one of the three children of Joe Collins, a successful theatrical agent. She says that she and her sister are not rivals: they have collaborated on various film and other projects. Her best known books are *The Stud* and *Hollywood Wives*.

## Extravagances
Hasn't been seen wearing a skirt for about twenty years. Jackie claims not to live the life of her fictional characters – women who live hard, love hard, and spend their massive bank balances. Good thing too: for a

start, she'd have permanent back strain from trying to keep up with her characters' sexual antics.

### Sam Whitbread 57
### £32 m (£27m)
### Business

## Source of wealth
The Whitbread family, headed by Sam, control over £100 million worth of the eponymous brewing company's shares. Sam personally controls only £8 million worth, but has a beneficial interest in a £16 million trust. Add in his property and art holdings and his net worth improves to £32 million.

## Personal style
If ever there was a reluctant businessman, Sam Whitbread is he. A full-time job in the family brewing firm has always been his for the asking, but he has always been much happier with his Bedfordshire farming and forestry business. He was a director of Whitbread for a dozen years, but in a non-executive role. Then, in 1984, there was a vacancy which he was asked to fill – right at the very top of the company. A succession gap led to Sam Whitbread agreeing to act as a temporary chairman; the job actually lasted eight years. Only in 1992 was he able to step down, although he did keep a seat on the board.

## Extravagances
His large Bedfordshire house – "which I remember spending millions on" he told *BusinessAge* last year – and his art collection. He is, at least, a man who clearly enjoys his riches.

### Julie Andrews 59
### 32m (£30m)
### Entertainment

## Source of wealth
In 1989 Julie Andrews gave her daughter Emma Walton, also an actress, a $2 million Los Angeles mansion. This reflects the sort of wealth which Julie Andrews has accumulated in her forty-odd years in the business.

For much of her career she has been guided commercially by her husband, film director Blake Edwards. He saw how his great friend, Peter Sellers, got rich from being an actor and he applied the same methods very successfully with his wife. The film that really put her on the road to riches was *The Sound of Music*, the most watched and the most shown movie of all time. But her career was launched with *Mary Poppins*, another all-time favourite all over the world.

Although immensely successful by the 1970s, a second wind to her career came with more mature roles, most controversially in *Victor, Victoria*. And she melted the hearts of many with her performance opposite Omar Sharif in *The Tamarind Seed*. Nonetheless, she has so far steered clear of the American TV mini-series cult despite being offered $7 million to star in *War and Remembrance*. That was just a step too far after *Mary Poppins*, according to her husband. But it showed her earning power.

We estimate her wealth at £32 million this year as her career winds down as she approaches her 60s.

## Personal style
In 1969 she married Blake Edwards, a successful Hollywood producer-director whose best known films are the *Pink Panther* series, starring Peter Sellers. She had been married before (to Emma's father, Tony Walton) and so had Edwards. Between them she and Blake have five children, two of them are adopted. The marriage of Edwards and Andrews is one of showbusiness's most successful and remarkable.

At 58 years of age, Julie Andrews still looks in her early 40s.

## Extravagances
Doting on her daughter and homes in Malibu, California, England and Gstaad, Switzerland.

### Henry Hoare 62
### £32m (£36m)
### Banking

## Source of wealth
The chairman and chief executive of Britain's poshest private bank, C Hoare & Co, retains his *Rich 500* membership again, thanks to over 7,000 elite customers – some of whom have held family accounts with C Hoare throughout its three century history.

Net assets are £326.35 million but Hoare's customers have had a more difficult year than him as many are also Lloyd's names. We have downgraded Henry Hoare's worth slightly to reflect this.

## Personal style
Extremely secretive, as has been the entire Hoare family for 300 years. Does not publish accounts. The closest he came to revealing profits was a rare interview last year, saying "we did fairly badly in the second half of the nineteenth century."

## Extravagances
Passionate conservationist, and member of The English Trust that bid £5 million for a 42,000 Scottish estate. Owns Luscombe Castle in Devon, and is married to Camilla, his second wife.

## HRH Princess Margaret 62
### £32m (£30m)
### Royalty

### Source of wealth
Princess Margaret's personal wealth was inherited from her father, King George V. She, the Queen and the Queen Mother split £20 million when he died. In turn, Princess Margaret will inherit a considerable fortune from her mother when she dies. Until 1992, she received a grant from the public purse of £4,230 per week, tax free. These days, she gets pocket money direct from her sister, Queen Elizabeth II.

Despite being the Queen's sister, Princess Margaret is only 11th in line to the throne and has no formal role under the constitution.

Charitable work takes up some of her time: she is colonel-in-chief of several regiments and president of innumerable organisations including Dr Barnardo's, the Girl Guides and the Royal Ballet.

### Personal style
Once, in the Fifties and Sixties, lived life in the fast lane. Only now are stories of that time starting to emerge, further damaging the once untouchable aura that protected the Royal family. Meanwhile, her private life has been unhappy. She indicated that she wished to marry Group Captain Peter Townsend, her sister's former equerry, in 1955.

Nigel Dempster quotes her as saying: "It was Peter who said no." But both Townsend and the Princess came under enormous pressure to abandon the match. The Establishment won.

In 1960 she married Anthony Armstrong-Jones, the photographer, who was later ennobled as the 1st Earl of Snowdon, entitling him to sit in the House of Lords. They were divorced in 1978, the first divorce in the House of Windsor.

There are two children from the marriage, Viscount Linley and Lady Sarah Armstrong-Jones both now happily married.

### Extravagances
Caribbean islands.

## Roger Moore 66
### £32m (£25.5m)
### Entertainment

### Source of wealth
A little bird (who should know) told us we had underestimated Roger Moore's wealth last year. He is one of Britain's evergreen actors. But if he hadn't become James Bond in 1973, he wouldn't be very rich at all.

Apart from Bond, he has appeared in a string of mediocre films, and probably earned less than £500,000 each time. But once he'd settled in, Bond was different, and after the first two films he demanded – and got – £7 million apiece for the rest from producer, Cubby Broccoli. Moore knew that Broccoli needed him, and Broccoli knew it too. The negotiations sometimes lasted right up to the beginning of shooting the film, and the drama was played out in the newspapers as well as on set, particularly for the last two Bonds.

Moore made seven Bonds, from 1973 to 1985, earning a total of over £40 million. We now think Moore has earned a shade over £60 million in his entire career. Take off tax (not much), and fees to managers and so on, and he has let just over £32 million stick to him.

### Personal style
He has been a surprisingly active actor, starring in two or three films a year since the mid-Fifties. His television work too has been prolific, as *The Saint* and in *The Persuaders*, with Tony Curtis. He has been married three times, and has two sons and one daughter with his third wife, Luisa.

### Extravagances
Dotes on his family especially his children. Lives good life in Geneva and Hollywood, although he is now showing signs of old age.

## HRH Prince Philip 73
### £32m (£30m)
### Royalty

### Source of wealth
The Duke of Edinburgh is a relatively poor man, at least in terms of the circles in which he moves – or even in terms of his immediate family. But the impressive machinery of the Royal household cloaks the Duke's poverty.

He gives four addresses, including Buckingham Palace, but has not registered any landed estates in the UK in his own name, although he is understood to have had several opportunities to do so. His real wealth is never likely to be known, as his will, like all Royal wills, will be sealed and remain private. While having no obvious commercial positions, he is the beneficiary of a series of trusts, some inherited, some created by his wife, and some by his friends.

### Personal style
Over the years, he has both publicly and privately developed a life and career of his own. Intriguingly, out of the older generation of Royals, he remains one of the few to be relatively untouched by scandal.

Nonetheless, the satirical magazine *Private Eye* irreverently refers to him as "Phil the Greek" because he was born in Greece, in 1921.

It's an old jibe. Yet Prince Philip is directly descended, via his mother, from Queen Victoria. The Englishness goes further: after education at Dartmouth, he became a British naval officer, serving throughout World War II.

In latter years, he has been prominent in a variety of charitable outfits, including the World Wildlife Fund.

### Extravagances
Roving eye.

## Catherine Cookson 87
### £32 m (£30.5 m)
### Literary

### Source of wealth
Although she is classed by some as the ultimate rags-to-riches story, there is much more to Catherine Cookson than the kind of story-line that might leap off the page of one of her novels. At 87, and too frail any longer to answer the innumerable begging letters which she gets, she remains one of the most successful female authors this century. Her books have sold more than 100 million copies in 30 or more languages, with several successfully adapted for TV.

### Personal style
She was born in South Shields in 1907, the daughter of a barmaid and a father who was never identified. Her working class family lived in conditions that now seem unimaginable. When she was seven she made the shattering discovery that the person she thought was her sister was actually her mother and that she was illegitimate. From South Shields she went south with her mother, by then an alcoholic. In 1943, she married her husband Tom, a school teacher five years her junior. Four miscarriages drove her to a nervous breakdown. Again, writing acted as therapy.

### Extravagances
She is known to have given away large sums of money and, until she collapsed recently, Tom would reply on her behalf to the begging letters. Most of her donations have been to medical charities.

## Gemma Maughan
### £32m (£30m)
### Business

### Source of wealth
Gemma Maughan's Gowan Group distributes Peugeot and Honda vehicles in Ireland.

In 1989, profits were £6 million. Overall, the Gowan Group may have been worth £25 million at the time, perhaps slightly less now. Its subsidiary, Gallic Distributors, now sells Citroens, too.

## Jimmy Thomas
### £32m (New entry)
### Leisure

### Source of wealth
Jimmy Thomas is one of the half dozen self-made members of the *Rich 500* who have made their fortunes from the amusement industry.

There was a propitious time in the Seventies when opening amusement arcades was very easy, very cheap and very profitable. The half dozen people who spotted the opportunity are all now multi-millionaires. He built a chain up called Showboat which was a mixture of instant bingo and fruit machines. He virtually invented instant bingo when he opened the Beacon in Loughborough. He also pioneered the placement of AWP-type small jackpot fruit machines in bingo halls, when only two high paying jackpot machines had previously been thought viable.

His wealth has been punctuated by sell-offs and the more openings. Early in his career he had to sell off two arcades to pay a big tax bill and then sold half his chain to Rank Organisation for £16 million, five years ago. We estimate him at £32 million for his *Rich 500* debut.

### Personal style
The scion of Jack Thomas - a travelling showman. His claim to fame is inventing the bingo blower which he called Bambi. Aspires to join the establishment.

### Extravagances
Loves to flaunt his wealth with his gold door-handled white Rolls Royce number plate JT1 parked in the most conspicuous places in London. Has expensive penthouse in Chelsea harbour and expensive yacht in the Med. Likes to have the Home Secretary round for dinner.

## Kaveh Alamouti 38
### £31.5m (New entry)
### Finance

### Source of wealth
Iranian turned Briton, Kaveh Alamouti was the highest paid City trader two years ago, picking up a staggering £9 million salary for his job as head of arbitrage trading at Tokai Bank in London. Playing the bond and currency markets, Alamouti made Tokai a fortune thanks to Black Wednesday, and they handsomely rewarded him. We estimate Tokai has kept up his salary level. In fact, Alamouti has been raking it in since his first big job, with Salomon Brothers in 1983. He became the first person to trade gilt and option warrants on sterling proprietary trading, after

which the Bank of England gave Salomon the go-ahead to start trading contracts. They rewarded him heftily too.

### Personal style
Friends describe him as a "walking computer" or "consummate rocket scientist" who plays the entire stock market like a movie in his head. For a bet, he once stood up at a clients' seminar and offered to quote two-way prices on any share option his audience cared to mention. He won the bet.

### Extravagances
Father of four, Alamouti lives in a £900,000 home in London's Maida Vale. Despite five cars parked in the driveway, he keeps a very low profile, preferring home cooked meals to expensive restaurants, lounging around the house in a tracksuit watching Queens Park Rangers FC. According to wife Wendy, he is "no smoking, no drinking, no butter and no milk in his coffee – pretty boring actually."

## Ringo Starr 48
### £31.5m (£27m)
### Music

### Source of wealth
Ringo Starr still pockets a decent slice of the never-ending income from the Beatles days. This year that was nearly £5 million before tax. He teamed up with Paul McCartney and George Harrison earlier this year to record the music for a new TV documentary.

Starr is also a shareholder in the Britt Allcroft Company, which owns the rights to Thomas the Tank Engine. It plans to float this year on a valuation of £50 million.

Rumours continue that the surviving Beatles will release an album next year and perform a one off concert in New York, worth £20 million to each of them. In the meantime, he'll have to make do with £31.5 million.

### Personal style
As the drummer with the Beatles, the opportunities for a solo career were limited but he still managed a solo number one, with "*Your Sixteen*." After that his only hit was the bottle, but he's now a reformed alcoholic.

### Extravagances
His beautiful wife, Barbara Bach.

## Eric Clapton 49
### £31.5m (£26m)
### Music

### Source of wealth
One of the world's guitar doyens, Clapton has surprisingly accumulated most of his

wealth during the last five years. Always a musician's musician – he has collaborated with icons such as Bob Marley, John Lennon and George Harrison – it has been his transition from musician to singer/songwriter that has brought in his millions.

The accounts for his company, Marshbrook Ltd, reflect his changing financial success. In 1985, he only received a salary of £94,000 with the company turning over £180,000. However, the figures improve, boosted no doubt by the 1986 release of his bestselling album *August* (produced by Phil Collins), and his successful 1990 album *Journeyman*. By 1990, the company was turning over a massive £11 million, netting him a salary of £5,097,000, and in 1991, a turnover of £6 million, giving him a salary of £3,867,000.

Performance royalties have made him a mint. His world tour in 1990 accounted for the exceptionally high company income of that year. In the last three years, he has held a "residency" at the Royal Albert Hall, playing for 18-24 nights a year. And they have been complete sell-outs.

### Personal style
Alcohol and drugs took its toll on Eric Clapton mid way through his career. By 1974, Clapton was on the verge of bankruptcy, having to sell not only his houses and cars, but even some of his guitars.

A year or so later, however, he was back on his feet financially, when he released a solo single, *I Shot the Sheriff*, co-written with Bob Marley, which went to number one in America and stayed near the top of the charts in the UK. It established him as a solo artist, but it took a few years for him to see some real income.

Clapton has had a somewhat tempestuous love-life, fuelled by his obsession to have children. He has admitted to paying maintenance for another child since 1985, and is being pursued by other women claiming child maintenance. Tragically, his son Conor died in a freak accident by falling to his death from a high rise building in New York two years ago.

### Extravagances
Girls. Although he lives alone in his mansion Hurtwood Edge, in Surrey.

## Sarah Davidson 52
### £31.5m (£27.5m)
### Construction

### Source of wealth
Sarah Davidson helped form Persimmon plc, the housebuilder, with her husband David in 1972. She remains a non-executive director with a 10 per cent stake. The

improved outlook for the housing market has seen the value of her stake rise, putting her total wealth at £31.5 million.

## Personal style

The Davidsons are a rare husband a wife team in construction. While David learned all about the building industry, she learned the more important things – building a fortune.

## Extravagances

Making money in the housing market.

## Peter Goldstein 54
## £31.5 (£35.5m)
## Business

## Source of wealth

In 1983 Peter Goldstein helped his brother, Ronald, float Superdrug on the stock market. In 1987, they sold the company to what was then Woolworths (now Kingfisher plc) for a tiny sum of money, but with 300 stores. But wisely, they took nearly 16 million Woolworths shares in payment.

Ronald Goldstein took the lion's share of the payment, but Peter's wealth is still healthy. Some is wrapped up in trusts in Jersey. Peter left the Kingfisher board and didn't keep his shares as long. Today Superdrug has almost 600 stores.

Last year was a disastrous year for Peter, however, as the Volume One bookshop chain went into receivership on Christmas Day. He is believed to have lost around £4 million on this venture. His brother also lost money.

Goldstein held around 40 per cent of the equity of a company that in 1992 had a turnover of £21.5 million and lost £1.6 million but net assets were then £4 million. In 1992 alon,e they had to pump nearly £4.5 million in to keep it afloat.

We have therefore lopped that off his fortune, but by adding other income he just retains membership of the *Rich 500* at £31.5 million.

## Personal style

Less savvy than his older brother. He is only half as rich and nearly lost his membership of the *Rich 500* this year.

## Extravagances

It was books and that probably led to the Volume One disaster.

## Andrew Knight 54
## £31.5m (£29.5m)
## Media

## Source of wealth

Andrew Knight made a straight £14 million out of share options granted to him when he worked at the *Daily Telegraph*.

This was much to the chagrin of proprietor, Conrad Black, who describes how they were acquired in his recent biography. He negotiated himself a similar-sized deal with Rupert Murdoch's News Corporation when he joined them. The lot has gone tax-free into Jersey.

According to the *Sunday Times*, which in this instance should know, he sold some £10 million worth of shares last year. We have upgraded Knight to £31.5 million this year.

## Personal style

From being a relative pauper 10 years ago, Andrew Knight has made a great deal of money. He is living proof that journalists can get rich, and by other methods than fiddling their expenses. But he made his own luck. He observed the problems at the *Telegraph* and put then Canadian small time newspaper proprietor, Conrad Black onto the best deal of his life. The rest is history.

In 1990 the relationship between Black and Knight deteriorated (so far only Black has given his side of that story) and Knight took control of all News Corporation's interests in Europe steering the company through the very traumatic period in which Rupert Murdoch's empire nearly went bust. But Knight cut costs brilliantly and kept the lid on expenses. The profits submitted by the Wapping newspapers literally kept Murdoch's group afloat. Knight was rewarded when the value of his share options soared afterwards.

But a few months ago, he was out on the streets as he resigned from News International and is now resting at home.

Knight is met with jealousy from other journalists who do not like what he has achieved. A typical quote, reputedly from a Wapping colleague in a profile two years ago in *The Guardian* said: "Andrew's quality is to ring Rupert Murdoch in the morning and tell him how wonderful he is. He used to do it with Conrad Black, and now he's doing it with Rupert."

But there must have been more to it than that. No one can deny that during his stewardship of both *News International* and the *Telegraph*, wonderful things happened to both companies and grudgingly it seems both proprietors credit them to Knight.

## Extravagances

He enjoys money but does not have a lavish lifestyle.

## Sir Freddie Laker 72
## £31.5m (£25.5m)
## Business

## Source of wealth

Sir Freddie Laker built up a large aviation

group in 1960 and then sold it for a sum approaching a million pounds. That would be worth £30 million in today's money, and Laker has invested his money shrewdly. When he started Laker Airways in 1966, after a short retirement, he put in hardly any of his own cash.

He lost all his investment in Laker and – indicative of how rich he was – in 16 years he never took a penny in salary or dividends out of the business. Everything was ploughed back. He didn't need to pay himself: his investment income was huge. If Laker had survived, Sir Freddie would probably be worth at least £250 million today, with the subsequent rise in aircraft values and the Eighties boom. He was to get another windfall after his lawyer, Bob Beckman, won him £8 million compensation from the world's largest airlines, after he alleged that they had conspired illegally to put Laker out of business.

Today he runs Laker Airways Bahamas, with three Boeing 727s flying from American cities to Freeport, and back. Last year, we were too cautious on valuing Sir Freddie. This year we have put that right.

## Personal style

Sir Freddie was everyone's favourite businessman, until his airline went broke in 1982. Bitter recriminations followed, as Laker accused British Airways and Midland Bank of being responsible for putting him out of business. He has suffered tragedy, with the loss of his eldest son Kevin in a motor accident in the Sixties. He has been married and divorced three times, and his present wife is Lady Jacqueline, after whom he named his boat.

## Extravagances

Laid back Sir Freddie has many. He has homes in Miami and a farm in Sussex. His apartment in Miami is on the prestigious Fisher Island, which is reached by a 24-hour ferry and attended by uniformed guards who would look more at home in the British Governor's residence in Bermuda. His large motor yacht is moored right outside his front door.

## Doris Thompson 91
## £31.5m (£28.5m)
## Leisure

## Source of wealth

Doris Thompson, née Bean, is the active octogenarian chairman of one of the biggest leisure companies in Britain, Blackpool Pleasure Beach plc, which her family has run since the turn of the century.

It was a big gamble when her family acquired their particular stretch of the Blackpool beach frontage, as the site is slightly off the main run. However, the

Bean family were showmen extraordinaire and they established themselves quickly. Doris married a Thompson and her son, Geoffrey, is now the managing director. The company now has leisure operations all over the world.

All the shares are held by her and her family and, as well as benefiting from the company's steady profits, the family owns property acquired long before the recent boom and slump.

## Personal style

Doris Thompson is now equivalent to Royalty in Blackpool and still goes into the office almost every day. Up to a few years ago, she even tested the rides herself. Many regular visitors to the entertainments know her personally and her involvement as the head of the company is described as "very active."

## Extravagances

The equivalent of the Queen Mother in Blackpool.

### Eric Norman 47
### £31m (£32.25m)
### Business

## Source of wealth

Eric Norman, chairman of Panic Link plc, the parcels carrier company based in Lount, Leicestershire, says he is worth £40 million. That's a bit hopeful, but Norman is a classic example of one of the money success stories of the Eighties.

Last year the company turned over only £13 million, and made £690,000 after tax. Panic Link has also built up assets worth £7 million since 1987.

Norman, who owns 100 per cent of the company, could arguably be worth as little as £20 million today. But capital expenditure is proceeding apace – a new £3 million hub in south London opened in January, and the ambitious "eurohub" at Lount is currently under construction. Based on the improving economy and the company's low cost base, we value him at £31 million.

## Personal style

Redundancy motivated him to set up Panic Link in 1987 together with his wife Pauline, now managing director. She takes an active role in the business, and Eric admits he wouldn't have succeeded without her.

The trick with Panic Link has been its franchising: in six years Norman has built a 1,200-strong international network of parcel delivery companies carrying the Panic Link logo, at negligible cost to himself.

## Extravagances

Eric Norman travels by chauffeur-driven Rolls, number plate PAN 1C. He sports a year-round tan and sharp designer suits, and owns a mansion in Guernsey.

### John Cleese 52
### £31m (£26.5m)
### Entertainment

## Source of wealth

John Cleese received nearly £10 million when his Video Arts company was sold out to its managers just before the recession. Before that, he had taken large dividends, a high salary and fees from the highly profitable company which he founded with Sir Anthony Jay of *Yes, Minister* fame. That in itself has not made Cleese a member of the *BusinessAge Rich 500*.

That achievement belongs to the film *A Fish Called Wanda*, one of the few genuinely British films that has ever really done well in America. Few realise that Cleese actually owned the property, and has therefore netted around £12 million from its success so far. It cost only £3.5 million to make and grossed £22 million in America in its first seven weeks. And there is an ongoing ownership in the negative of the film: that will earn money for years, and probably even stand a re-release or two.

His best year was in 1989 as he sold Video Arts and cashed in on *Fish* in the same year. He earned nearly £20 million that year, but paid some tax as well. Fortunately he had cashed out in a year of low taxation.

He reputedly gives 10 per cent of anything he earns to charity. Despite that, thanks to his prodigious work rate and another good year for his property and investments Cleese is currently worth £31 million.

## Personal style

Like fellow successful British actor Christopher Lee, John Cleese has had to make his way in life being over 6'4" tall. He has overcome the handicap by creating his own niche in the comedy acting world. He made it into a very big and profitable niche indeed.

But the thing he is probably most famous for is the epic 12-episode *Fawlty Towers* series, which made him less than £1,000 an episode. Without his commercial activities he would never have been able to afford to make *Fawlty Towers*.

## Extravagances

Palatial, almost billionaire-class home in Holland Park.

### Dame Shirley Porter 62
### £31m (£28m)
### Inheritance

## Source of wealth

Dame Shirley Porter's shareholdings in Tesco remain intact. She is one of two daughters of Sir Jack Cohen, the founder of Tesco and discount food retailing. She inherited her fortune after it passed from Sir Jack through to her mother, Lady Sarah Cohen. Those Tesco shares have been hit by the retail sector's general price slump this year.

But the daughter inherited much of Sir Jack's canniness as well as his money. Hence the political career she undertook, encouraged by her father.

The family fortune is estimated at around £60 million shared by her husband, Sir Leslie Porter and her son and daughter.

## Personal style

It's not been a nice year for Dame Shirley Porter. The report of the district auditor into events at Westminster Council, which she lead in the Eighties, was chock-full of serious allegations – among them that votes had been bought for the Conservatives with taxpayer's money. A public inquiry into the Westminster Council allegations later this year may lead to a demand that Porter and other former councillors hand back to the taxpayer the millions they are alleged to have spent for party political purposes. News of that particular bombshell was followed by the demise of LBC, the local London radio station chaired by Porter herself.

Most former officials of Westminster Council interviewed by the media this year have said they lived in fear of their leader. She also appeared to have a remarkable hold over senior Tory figures at a national level.

## Extravagances

Large donations to an Israeli university in recent years.

### Harry Patterson 65
### £31m (£29.5 m)
### Literary

## Source of wealth

Jack Higgins (real name: Harry Patterson) has been described as a Belfast-born Scots-Irish Yorkshireman.

Higgins has earned much of his fortune from US sales. His books are also available in 42 languages, including Polish and Chinese. He has published 52 novels; around a quarter of them have spent substantial amounts of time at the top of bestseller lists worldwide. The newer stuff doesn't sell quite so well, but his publisher can usually bank on shifting at least 100,000 hardback copies, something few authors can do these days. Royalties from backlist books and new advances keep his wealth ticking along at £31 million.

## Personal style

He hates the Inland Revenue, enjoys tax exile status in Jersey, has never voted Conservative and describes himself as a socialist, which he defines as respecting hard work and achievement.

As the best-selling British novelist of his generation, Higgins has spent much of his career fleshing out thriller plots that tend to fall somewhere between understanding the impulses of Irish nationalism and glamourising the gunmen of yesteryear (the Forties-style IRA man played by Donald Sutherland in *The Eagle Has Landed* is a case in point).

Like Ken Follett, Higgins has little love for Rupert Murdoch, who took over the Collins imprint in the late Eighties. Yet Higgins's disdain for News International doesn't preclude commercialism in his own work.

## Extravagances

Relentless self-promotion, among other things. Higgins recently caused a major traffic jam in West London's Cromwell Road by staging a mock battle to publicise his latest book *Thunder Point*. He also enjoys wine-filled dinners at St. Helier's La Capannina restaurant.

### Angela Yeoman 66
**£31m** (£44m)
### Construction

## Source of wealth

Angela Yeoman controls about 40 per cent of Foster Yeoman, the West Country quarrying firm. It still trades at a loss (£713,000 in the latest accounts to May 1992), but long-term prospects are better. We value her stake at a lower £31 million this year.

## Personal style

Not many pensioners go direct from the Post Office to the executive suite of a company with turnover of £10 million a year.

But Angela Yeoman is an unusual pensioner. In 1987 she was forced to step into her late husband's shoes as chairman, at the quarrying company, Foster Yeoman. At the time the firm had just brought onstream a huge new project in Glensada in Scotland, and was still engaged in major investments at its home base quarry at Torr in Somerset. The company is run by herself, her two sons and her son-in-law. The Yeomans are very much the "big family" in their quiet corner of Somerset.

## Extravagances

An environmental conscience.

### Roger Baker 53
**£31m** (New entry)
### Food

## Source of wealth

Although he is one of the richest men in the county of Northamptonshire, Roger Baker is virtually unknown within its boundaries.

No one, it seems, has heard of him.

Nonetheless, he runs FW Baker, a meat processors. The company is quite valuable even though its profits are patchy. In 1991 it made nearly £5 million pre-tax. Last year that figure was cut in half. Overall, however, FW Baker is a strong attractive company. We rate Baker at £31 million including past dividends. This figure propels him into the *Rich 500* for the first time.

### Robert Rayne
**£31m** (£25.5m)
### Inheritance

## Source of wealth

The Hon Robert Rayne is the son of Lord Rayne, chairman of both London Merchant Securities (with interests in property and investment) and First Leisure, the quoted entertainment group. The Rayne fortune was made in the post-war years when Max Rayne, as he was then, bought up property in unfashionable areas of London and then waited until prices soared to make his fortune. Robert Rayne is a director of both LMS and First Leisure, and Rayne senior is now transferring assets to his son to minimise inheritance tax.

## Personal style

Robert is listed as "Investment director" in the LMS accounts. His record is unenviable: the investment in Cullens supermarkets (where Robert is chairman) has gone sour, with a loss of £674,000 in 1993. Ditto Jazz FM, which Robert also chairs. Unlike high flying Classic FM, Jazz has failed to break £3 million sales after three years on air, and has lost a cumulative £5 million since 1990. The station has also come under fire from jazz lovers, since jazz makes up only 20 per cent of the playlist. They've even changed the station's name.

### John Reid 43
**£30.5m** (£27.5m)
### Music

## Source of wealth

John Reid earned his loot through managing Elton John and in the process has become almost as famous. Through his company John Reid Enterprises, he is putting together John's world tour and has been behind the star's surge in popularity this year. As usual, Elton John has rewarded him handsomely for his services, pushing his wealth up to £30.5 million.

## Personal style

By the age of 25 he was a millionaire, running companies turning over £40 million. A confessed homosexual, he was once described by the tabloids as the "Evil Poof of Pop." This hasn't stopped big names like David Essex, Queen and Kiki Dee asking

him to manage their affairs.

## Extravagances

Has seen and done everything associated with the music industry. Last October, he was reportedly the only man who knew where Michael Jackson was hiding.

### Cliff Richard 54
**£30.5m** (£28.5m)
### Music

## Source of wealth

It's hard to believe that Cliff Richard is the same age as Railwaymen's Union leader, Jimmy Knapp.

Cliff Richard would be much richer had he made it big in the USA or had he not decided to donate half his earnings to Christian Charities in the Third World. Nevertheless, his 35 year career has produced sales of 150 million records, including the now customary Christmas number one. In 1990 his "From a Distance" tour grossed £12.6 million in concert tickets and merchandising alone. His still receives hefty royalties from the songs he made in the Sixties.

In 1994 Richard announced spectacular plans to stage the musical *Heathcliff* playing the lead role himself. He put his own money into the venture but it has been shelved for a year. But £3 million worth of advanced bookings have been taken so he is not out of pocket. In fact, it may have been a good thing – the stages that were to be used for the show will instead be used for his own concerts celebrating 35 years in pop, netting around £2 million.

### Leigh Webb 55
**£30.5m** (£25m)
### Food

## Source of wealth

Between them, the Webb family owns more than 80 per cent in Webb's Country Foods, the Lymington-based food group whose main activity is processing poultry. Leigh Webb, who is on the board, owns almost half of the shares. Turnover for the year to September 1992, reached £74.8 million, and profits, after tax, were just over £3 million. The company is a prime target for many international food groups, and has been valued at more than £60 million.

## Personal style

Webb is in an expansionist mood. Another processing factory, a feed mill and 19 farms were bought in July 1992, at a total cost of £9 million. Borrowings stand at about £17 million, more than half of which is secured by a floating charge over all the assets.

## Extravagances

A large yacht in Lymington harbour. Otherwise lives quietly.

### George Michael *31*
**£30m** (£35.5m)
**Music**

#### Source of wealth
George Michael's true wealth is one of the most hotly disputed subjects in the music industry, but his recent High Court battle with Sony confirmed some of the rumours. His only two solo albums, *Faith* and *Listen Without Prejudice*, have earned him £16.89 million in royalties; in 1988, Michael received a £15.6 million salary from his investments company Nobby's Hobbies Holdings; he pocketed £11 million instantly for signing with Sony records.

When asked to reveal in court his wealth, he said: "I'd rather not. It's quite shocking."

But the shock is how relatively small Michael's fortune actually is. Most of his earnings, since leaving the pop duo Wham!, have been channelled into his investment company Nobby's Hobbies Holdings. In the year ending 1988, the solo move had paid-off handsomely with the world-wide success of his album *Faith* selling 14 million copies. As chairman of Nobby's Hobbies, he collected £15,547,140 making him Britain's highest paid director that year.

But after that, slump has set in. Much of the 1988 income was thanks to Sony's £11 million signing-on fee. Michael holds six other directorships, but Nobby's Hobbies accounts for earnings from the two recent albums, concert tours and promotions. By the end of 1989, Michael trousered a meagre £1,007,753, falling to £770,960 a year later. In 1991, he barely topped £1.3 million, falling to £390,000 by the end of 1992. In total, therefore, since going solo, his declared earnings are just £19,039,853. No wonder he is unhappy at making only £1.33 from every CD he sells, compared to Sony's £3.38.

Michael's five years with Wham! did, however, generate over 60 million in record sales and three major tours. Wham! is still the most successful pop duo ever, ahead of Simon & Garfunkel. We estimate Michael's share from Wham! at £8 million. Add to that his investments and property, and continuing royalties, and his wealth approaches £35 million. However, taking into account the hefty legal bill from his court battle, he is left with £30 million.

Michael has effectively kissed goodbye to the outstanding £39 million Sony promised him over the next ten years to record again. One saving grace may be a rumoured job as the new lead singer of Queen for a world tour, said to be worth a staggering £25 million.

#### Personal style
Described in the High Court as "articulate and intelligent", has done a complete U-turn since his Wham! days when he placed shuttlecocks down his boxer shorts during live performances. Now wants respectability for his music rather than be worshiped as a sex symbol, but in danger of getting neither.

#### Extravagances
Three homes, worth £6.2 million, in Santa Barbara, Los Angeles and Hampstead. Despite being Elton John's best friend, Michael is not flash with cash, and owns just two cars – a Mercedes and a Range Rover. Prefers spending on black Versace T-Shirts. Linked with several top models, but still lives alone with his pet Labrador, Hippy, which has lead to rumours about his sexuality.

### Audrey Baxter *33*
**£30m** (New entry)
**Food**

#### Source of wealth
Soup and jam company WA Baxter and Sons has a lot going for it. Its brand name has bigger players drooling with envy, it's a very profitable business, and family members know how to nurture it. The mantle of control is now passing from the older generation (Gordon and Ena) to the children, particularly Audrey, recently appointed managing director. She personally controls a sixth of the company, which on profits of £3.8 million last year would easily fetch £80-100 million at auction.

Around 200 takeover offers have been rebuffed. The pledge is to keep the company "private, and in Scotland".

#### Personal style
Having cut her teeth at Kleinwort Benson in the Eighties, Audrey is the ideal candidate to take the sweet, if sleepy, Baxter business to the next level. She enlivened an Institute of Directors' conference earlier this year when she and her father presented a history of the company.

#### Extravagances
Being a Baxter is a duty rather than a means of enjoying wealth.

### Ross Warburton *35*
**£30m** (New entry)
**Food**

#### Source of wealth
Warburtons, the family bakers headed by Ross (who owns 25 per cent of the company), made £7.98 million after tax in the year to September 1992, off a £149 million turnover. On an earnings multiple of 12, Ross's stake is worth £24 million. Net worth is about £30 million, just enough to qualify for *Rich 500* membership.

#### Personal style
Ex-fund manager Ross should take this sleepy business by the scruff of the neck.

#### Extravagances
Fast cars, a legacy from his Eighties City days.

### Natalia Duchess of Westminster *35*
**£30m** (£25.25m)
**Inheritance**

#### Source of wealth
Natalia Phillips did not have to marry one of the richest men in England to make herself rich. She is the grand-daughter of Sir Harold Wernher, who left about half his enormous fortune to her mother. Nor did she lower the level of blue blood in the Grosvenor family. She is a direct descen-

dant of Tsar Nicholas I of Russia. Her grandmother was the daughter of the Grand Duke Michael of Russia.

**Personal style**

She has three children, two daughters and a son who will inherit the Duke of Westminster's name and fortune. The Duchess has closely followed her husband's return to his family roots in the Chester area. Her children go to local schools in Cheshire where she is a very popular local figure.

**Extravagances**

She is well-known at the local jewellers.

### Allen Lloyd 45
### £30m (£28m)
### Retailing

**Source of wealth**

Allen Lloyd was delighted when last year's flu season came earlier than expected, helping push interim profits in Lloyds Chemists plc to £26 million. His nine million shares are now worth £28 million and, with dividends, salaries and property interests his wealth nudges up to £30 million.

Group sales for 1993 are expected to have almost doubled to £800 million. Lloyd paid £10.5 million for the Daniels Pharmaceuticals Group in May 1994, a move that will help build his manufacturing base – and his wealth.

The share price is back over 300 pence, despite a slump when the NHS reforms were first announced.

**Personal style**

Lloyd founded the company in 1973 at the age of just 24, after training as a pharmacist with Boots.

**Extravagances**

Another of those health conscious people who never has a hang-over, but gives good advice on how to cure one.

### Robert Murray 47
### £30m (New entry)
### Business

**Source of wealth**

Robert Murray got out of Spring Ram, the bathroom fittings company he founded with Bill Rooney 12 years ago, in 1990. He cashed in his shares for £25 million after tax, and has invested the money, generating enough returns for membership in the *Rich 500*.

**Personal style**

Murray got out just in time. Partner Rooney was still sitting on a pile of shares when Spring Ram's accounts imploded. He is now a relative pauper with only £15 million worth to his name.

**Extravagances**

He may yet make good on his plans to dive into the home products business again.

### Richard Palmer 47
### £30.5m (New entry)
### Business

**Source of wealth**

Richard Palmer stands behind European Motor Holdings, the car dealer which has shown stellar profits growth over the last two years. Profits rose 50 per cent, to £5.15 million, in 1993-94. The company was losing £1 million a year in 1992. It recently bought rival Normand Ltd for £12 million.

This is just the latest success for Palmer, who led a management team into Western Motors in 1987 for £5.5 million, and sold the company for £100 million to Tozer Kemsley in 1990. The fat rewards from Western, estimated at £10 million profit for Palmer alone, and the value of his shares in EMH (plus options and properties) put him well over £20 million. We value him at £30.5 million.

**Personal style**

Now on his third enterprise, Palmer is the darling of every City scribbler. His uncanny ability to make the right buys at the right time (such as concentrating on north of England BMW and Audi dealerships just as the recession there was ending) now allow him to raise as much cash as he wants. Palmer's success at Western came from an unlikely source: the unloved Lada car. He managed to sell thousands of them, at unheard of margins because the then Soviet Union was so grateful for the hard currency. Recently he has begun selling Land Rovers to Russia.

**Extravagances**

Former show off Palmer drives a BMW 5 series. Used to own three Bentley Turbos, but "people kept scratching their car keys along the side when it was parked," he says.

### Malcolm Walker 48
### £30m (£29.5m)
### Food

**Source of wealth**

Malcolm Walker co-founded Iceland Foods with Peter Hinchcliffe. The City is still cautious despite the 571 stores. On top of his share stake, Walker's dividends and salaries nudge his wealth up to £30 million.

**Personal style**

"He who dares wins" is Walker's motto. In 1989 he made a daring bid for Bejam, far bigger than his company, and managed to take it over. Bejam's John Apthorp, who owned 30 per cent of the shares, was booted out along the way. But the irony that Apthorp is personally much richer than him, is not lost on Walker.

**Extravagances**

His freezer is never empty.

### Peter Waterman 48
### £30m (£32.5m)
### Music

**Source of wealth**

"Dom Dom Daa Daa Dom Dom" is the bass line that Waterman used to launch the careers of Rick Astley, Kylie Minogue and Jason Donovan. As part of the writing/producing trio Stock, Aitken and Waterman, he was behind 90 top 40 chart hits, which account for much of his fortune.

In fact, Waterman has earned far more than £30 million but has been carefree with the money. His company, Peter Waterman Ltd, has turned in a £2.5 million loss, but this is compensated by a new joint venture deal with Warner Records.

Waterman's earnings in the past year, a few million, have been wiped out by the £10 million he personally splashed out in May to buy the Charter and Special Train Unit. Through his other company Flying Scotsman Services, he will charter the trains for football supporters next year. He still scrapes into the *Rich 500* thanks to his collection of 20 vintage locomotives.

**Personal style**

Waterman confesses to being a "rail nut", and his ambition is to re-create the era of rail travel in 1950s. This stems from his days as a BR-fireman in Wolverhampton. With a partner, he spends more time these days admiring his trains than producing Kylie Minogue records, which is probably a good thing for most people.

**Extravagances**

Was into fast cars and women but now into marriage, fatherhood and train spotting.

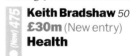

### Keith Bradshaw 50
### £30m (New entry)
### Health

**Source of wealth**

Keith Bradshaw is one of the few to benefit from the Government's NHS reforms, scraping into the *Rich 500* for the first time. His company Takare PLC, the nursing home operator, achieved full stock exchange listing in 1989 and has seen its profits rise consistently ever since, up 26 per cent in 1993 to £14.9 million. As chairman, Bradshaw's 12 million shares are worth over £26 million, and with dividends and interest in the past five years, is valued at £30 million.

**Personal style**

Not one to be detracted from making money, he sacked his managing director, Dev Pritchard, last year after disagreeing on the way forward.

**Extravagances**

Praising the NHS reforms.

## Trevor Burke 51
## £30m (£25m)
## Computers

### Source of wealth
Trevor Burke has a 58 per cent stake in PhoneLink PLC, the information services company recently floated on the Stock Exchange at £110 million. On paper, at least, that should mean he's worth £64 million. But PhoneLink is banking heavily on its new Tel-Me service to maintain the high 310 pence share price. Burke needs to return £4 million profits in the next year to realise his wealth. Although the City is gambling on him, our own technology experts doubt that Tel-Me can tell him to retire. A more realistic valuation of Burke's share stake is £30 million and that is what we estimate his worth at.

### Personal style
Highly technically minded. Probably a better computer programmer than business guru, but an excellent salesman none the less. Every company he has run and owned has been in partnership with wife Heather.

### Extravagances
Still can't believe his luck. Has to pinch himself every morning to make sure the company is really valued at £110 million.

## Bryan Morrison 52
## £30m (New entry)
## Entertainment

### Source of wealth
Bryan Morrison's second fortune comes from polo. The first came from music publishing: during the Seventies he controlled The Bee Gees and Pink Floyd publishing rights.

Now out of the music business, his 25 acre Royal County of Berkshire Polo Club, just down the road from crusty Smith's Lawn, Windsor, hosts tournaments and charges members a £3,500 sub.

### Personal style
Morrison has never been short of drive, or cheek for that matter. Making the blue-blood sport of polo accessible to the hoi polloi was a great move.

### Extravagances
Employed Fergie's dad, Major Ronald Ferguson, at the club until the stench of scandal was too great.

## Michael Pemberton 52
## £30m (£100m)
## Leisure

### Source of wealth
1993 saw Mike Pemberton suffer his first major reversal. Something went wrong with his third hotel, the Grand Palazzo on the Virgin Island of St Thomas. It went into receivership in October 1993. The American bank that financed it foreclosed and it was put into receivership. The bankruptcy hearing took place on 28th July, a humiliating day for Pemberton. Rock Resorts are poised to take over management for the bank.

Pemberton is thought to have dropped some £20 million personally as a minimum. And it has all been kept very quiet. The foreclosure has destroyed his carefully cultivated reputation although he is still said to have ambitious expansion plans in Cuba and Spain.

Then it was revealed that although he owns the freehold of Glitter Bay he has sold off the individual rooms to owners and rents them out on their behalf.

As a consequence we have cut Pemberton's value by 70 per cent.

He is therefore one of the biggest percentage losers in this year's *Rich 500*.

### Personal style
Pemberton and his wife Lynne have leapt from obscurity to fame in the last 18 months – the result of a carefully executed public relations campaign which has seen them in gossip columns and the glossy mags.

### Extravagances
Pemberton's billionaire lifestyle has been curtailed somewhat by the Virgin Island reversals . He lives in billionaire style, jetting back and forth between London and the Caribbean by Concorde.

## Robert Johnson 53
## £30m (New entry)
## Food

### Source of wealth
Robert Johnson owns the listed mail order and food processing group Farepak, which makes most of its money through Christmas hamper sales.

He just scrapes into the *Rich 500* for the first time in 1994 after selling £6 million – worth of his shares in 1993, in addition to the £24 million stake he has in the group, now valued at over £80 million.

Pre-tax profits were £6 million in the year to April 1993, and the prospects are brighter with the purchase of Littlewoods' hamper division for £8.5 million. This has given Johnson three million new names to add to his customer database.

### Personal style
Johnson is competing head-on with the Park Food Group, which holds most of the market. It's a fierce battle which Johnson is losing on a personal level. His namesake and opposite number at Park Food, Peter Johnson, is much higher up the *Rich 500*,

worth £130 million.

### Extravagances
Likes surrounding himself with rich and successful people. Rentokil chairman Clive Thompson, who trousered £2.8 million in a share sale last year, is on the board.

## Douglas Gregory 54
## £30m (New entry)
## Business

### Source of wealth
Fitted kitchens firm, Symphony Group, made £2 million after-tax profits in the year to September 1993. Douglas Gregory founded the company in 1971. On a price/earnings ratio of 15, he breaks into the ranks of the nation's richest with a net worth of £30 million.

### Personal style
No-nonsense Yorkshireman Gregory runs a tight ship – so tight, in fact, that creditors have to wait months to be paid while debtors are persuaded to pay up right away.

The resulting cash flow has seen the company ride out the kind of storm that engulfed competitor Spring Ram recently.

### Extravagances
Gregory lives modestly with his wife, near Harrogate.

## David Horrobin 54
## £30m (New entry)
## Health

### Source of wealth
Dr David Horrobin makes a first appearance in the *Rich 500* after successfully floating his pharmaceutical company Scotia. The company's research into lipid technology (constituents of membranes surrounding cells), diabetes and pancreatic cancer generated huge interest in the flotation, which was oversubscribed five times and raised £37 million. Chief executive Horrobin has an 18 per cent stake in the company, worth £30 million.

First year results showed a £6.5 million loss, but the company has invested over £8 million in research, making it one of the top 100 research spenders in the UK. One possible pitfall is a pending European court ruling involving rival Norgrine, over the licensing rights to one of Scotia's key products.

### Personal style
Dr Horrobin is probably the most academic entry in the Rich 500. Has held senior academic posts at Magdalen College in Oxford and St Mary's Hospital Medical School.

### Extravagances
He is said to be too health conscious for any major extravagances.

## Marquess of Zetland 56
**£30m** (£28.5m)
**Aristocracy**

### Source of wealth
Despite his strong links with the world of horse racing, the likeable Marquess of Zetland remains far from the traditional image of horseback aristocrat. He has tried to fend off the traditional aristocratic problem of cash poverty in any number of ways. He has been a lumberjack, wine dealer and banker, and busied himself with a small chain of upmarket toyshops before coming into his inheritance four years ago. ("It's all part of turning unearned income into earned income," he once told reporters. "Tax is vicious. But if I had not had a private income, I don't know how we would have kept going.") The family owns substantial lands around the ancestral home at Richmond in Yorkshire.

### Personal style
There is a trace of discomfort over his status: he reportedly rarely signs letters as "Zetland" in the correct manner.

### Extravagances
The owner of Redcar race course is no shrinking violet when it comes to one of Britain's underprivileged minorities – the trainers and owners of British thoroughbred horses, whose cause he has championed in speeches at the House of Lords and in press interviews.

## Princess Alexandra 58
**£30m** (£27.5m)
**Royalty**

### Source of wealth
In 1992, when the Royal tax arrangements were recast, it was revealed that the costs of supporting the Dukes of Gloucester, Kent and Princess Alexandra ran to £630,000 annually. They hardly needed the money, especially Princess Alexandra who is wealthy in her own right.

### Personal style
Princess Alexandra is related to current or former royal families in Germany, Denmark and Russia. She is the daughter of a Greek princess and a British prince (born in 1936 to the Duke and Duchess of York), and granddaughter of King George V.

"Elegant and serene" (*Daily Star*). At school she was regarded as a troublemaker, the leader of St Trinians-style gang. Princess Alexandra is generally reckoned to have been the first Royal ever to go "walkabout" during a public engagement.

### Extravagances
Sailing. During Cowes Week, which the Queen never attends, she has acted as hostess on the Royal yacht, *Britannia*.

## Michael Caine 61
**£30m** (£28m)
**Entertainment**

### Source of wealth
Michael Caine currently commands around £1.5 million a film, if he is lucky. But he would rather take £500,000 than not work at all. After all, he has a relatively expensive lifestyle to maintain.

He owns shares in the company that controlled Odin's and Langans in London. He has also punted money into an eaterie in Chelsea Harbour, the troubled 1980s residential development on the banks of the River Thames.

### Personal style
Despite appearing merely as himself – cheeky chappie, laid-back Cockney – in over 60 films, he has nurtured the impression that talent, rather than just hard bloody work, lies behind his success. But his connection with the US has deepened over the years. Resenting British taxation rates, he moved to the USA in 1979, buying a £10 million mansion in Beverley Hills. He eventually returned to Britain in 1987 and bought a £2 million residence in Henley-on-Thames, which he shares with his Indian wife, Shakira, and two daughters.

### Extravagances
Luxurious homes, socialising and big cigars.

## Alf Gooding 61
**£30m** (£31m)
**Electronics**

### Source of wealth
Alf Gooding's main source of wealth is the Gooding Group where he holds 90 per cent of the equity. Race Electronics, employing 1,200 people, is the main component. He recently acquired Grundig's loss-making television business in an £18 million deal, and now markets a satellite decoder under the Grundig label.

The most recent Gooding Group accounts, to December 1992, show a £3.9 million loss on £70 million turnover. However, the company is expected to return to profitability this year, so we have only downgraded Gooding slightly.

### Personal style
Alf Gooding would be a popular prime minister of Wales. In the last few years, this millionaire son of a Rhondda miner has brought hope and jobs to the valleys.

### Extravagances
He'd rather work than spend money. "I wouldn't be happy staying home all day with millions in the bank," he told *Business-Age* earlier this year. His one indulgence is travel in his chauffeur's Escort XR3i.

## Viscount Weir 61
**£30m** (£28.5m)
**Business**

### Source of wealth
Profits improved for the 10th successive year at Weir Group, the quoted Scottish-based engineering firm headed by Viscount Weir, to £39.2 million before tax. Weir controls 6.5 per cent of the shares, worth just under £30 million.

### Personal style
Scion of a Scottish industrial dynasty ennobled by Lloyd George, an English-accented Conservative peer and vocal supporter of the Union, Viscount Weir is highly regarded by colleagues and competitors as an effective and serious leader of British heavy engineering.

### Extravagances
Three marriages, and a large Ayrshire estate.

## Mary Mackinnon 64
**£30m** (£40m)
**Drink**

### Source of wealth
When her husband Norman died a few years ago, Mary Mackinnon took over the running of the company that makes the scotch whisky liqueur Drambuie. Lately the company has fallen on hard times: it plunged to a £5.6 million loss in 1991, and slipped further into the red in 1992 with a £6.7 million deficit. Mary Mackinnon resigned as chairman in 1992, and both her sons were replaced by non-family managers in the business. They promised £2 million profits in 1993, but until the accounts come out no one will know for sure.

Strictly speaking the company is only worth £30 million at present, with Mary's estimated 30 per cent share worth less than £10 million.

But the value of the brand to a major company such as Guinness would be closer to £70 million. Also Mary has outside property interests.

She drops to £30 million this year, and just scrapes into the *Rich 500*.

### Personal style
The formula for Drambuie remains a secret, given, it is said, to the Mackinnons by Bonnie Prince Charlie for their loyalty during the Jacobite Rebellion of 1745. Drambuie is one of Scotland's major exports and, to remind overseas visitors (and locals) of the source of their success, the Mackinnons have decorated a conference room in the style of the wardroom of a French man 'o' war, after the ship that took the Prince "over the water" into permanent exile.

## Extravagances

Mary's biggest extravagance was indulging her family and putting her sons in charge.

### Miriam Louisa Rothschild 86
### £30m (£27.75m)
### Inherited

**Source of wealth**

The venerable Miriam Rothschild inherited her wealth, in trust, from her father, the first Lord Rothschild, head of the family merchant bank group NM Rothschild. She married George Lane, a holder of the Military Cross, during World War II. They have two sons and two daughters but the marriage was dissolved in 1957. Like her brother, the late Lord Victor Rothschild, she is a scientist and a most eminent one – a Fellow of the Royal Society, one of the world's oldest and most venerable scientific bodies. Of its 1,100 Fellows, she is one of only 60 women.

**Personal style**

Miriam Rothschild is the world's foremost authority on the humble flea. Her publications include six volumes, written between 1953 and 1983, which catalogue the Rothschild Flea Collection at the British Museum.

**Extravagances**

She lives relatively modestly in a beautiful country cottage in Northamptonshire and watches butterflies for pleasure.

### Michael Brinton
### £30m (New entry)
### Retailing

**Source of wealth**

Michael Brinton took over from his father Topham as chairman of Brinton Carpets three years ago, and has a sizeable stake in the company. The UK market remains dead, but Brinton scooped a prestigious and huge order for the MGM Casino in Las Vegas. In the past year, 100 new staff have been taken on and turnover in at £70 million, with export sales up.

Given the company's quality name and tradition, it is worth over £50 million, and Michael joins the *Rich 500* at £30 million.

**Personal style**

Michael has a lot to live up to – he is the eighth Brinton to become chairman of the group since it was formed as a family business in Kidderminster in 1783.

**Extravagances**

Michael invited fashion queen, Vivienne Westwood, to his factory last year to check out his carpet designs, suggesting she should use the patterns for her garments. She duly obliged. Heaven help the next person who buys a Westwood garment and goes gambling at the MGM Casino.

### David Doyle
### £30m (£40m)
### Business

**Source of wealth**

There is no doubting David Doyle's wealth, despite the fact that the late PV Doyle left only £4.7 million in his will. The rest of his assets had already been passed on to him.

**Personal style**

Hard driving son of a tough entrepreneur. Until recently, David Doyle ran one of Ireland's leading hotel and construction businesses, the creation of his late father, PV Doyle. The family's private company owns the Berkeley Court Hotel in Dublin, which has been through an expensive facelift in recent years. The group also owns a couple of hotels in Washington DC.

However, the past 12 months have proved difficult for Doyle. An internal family dispute has seen him edged out of the company. Rumours indicate that the row developed over whether the company should look for outside equity partners.

Utterly devoted to his work – at a meeting with staff to announce his resignation as chairman, he failed to choke back the tears. Doyle's money remains tied up in shares: a settlement will have to be devised before he can launch new ventures.

**Extravagances**

Spending more time with his family.

### Richard George
### £30m (New entry)
### Food

**Source of wealth**

Richard George is the chairman and largest shareholder in Weetabix. The company made £16 million after tax on sales of £184 million in the year to July 1992: strictly speaking the company is only worth £230 million, but with almost no borrowings, a conservative balance sheet (that wonderful brand isn't even valued), the company could fetch over £300 million at market. George's 10 per cent stake is therefore worth at least £30 million.

**Personal style**

Richard George took charge of the Food and Drink Federation last year. "The food industry must project a more positive attitude about its immediate prospects," he said earlier this year, in the face of continuing pessimism from supermarket price wars, mad cow disease, and vanishing margins. The family business employs 2,000, and has one of the most cast-iron brands in the business.

**Extravagances**

A poster advertising campaign which boasts of Weetabix's laxative qualities.

### Chris Lazari 47
### £29.5m
### (New entry)
### Property

**Source of wealth**

Now a naturalised Briton, Chris Lazari fell through cracks last year, as his wealth failed to the clear the *Rich 500* threshold. This year with the rise in commercial property values he just sneaks in at £29.5 million.

He started making dresses in a firm called Christy Fashions. At the very base of the Seventies property recession bought property. He has made £18 million from this and Christy makes about £2 million a year. We have valued him at £29 million.

**Personal style**

The very distinctive looking Greek-born entrepreneur is the real surprise of the list.

**Extravagances**

Buying more factories.

### Sir Lawrie Barratt 66
### £29.5m (£28m)
### Construction

**Source of wealth**

Sir Lawrie Barratt has never been a member of the super rich. He sold far too many shares, far too early in the business which he founded – his sale of 850,000 shares for £1.7 million in 1981 was typical. But he easily qualifies as a member of the *Rich 500* for the wealth he has accumulated over the years from share sales, dividends and personal property investments. He now owns 1.3 million shares in Barratt Developments, the company he returned to rescue in 1991. The shares have more than doubled since then.

**Personal style**

The old stager has once again produced the goods. Barratt doubled its profits in the six months to December 1993, and predictions of £32 million pre-tax in the full year figures (out in September) are floating around the City. The company was losing £100 million in 1991.

Barratt's secret is his rare combination of moneyman and salesman. The company now sells higher margin upmarket homes, and Sir Lawrie has 13,000 plots in reserve to take advantage of the housing upturn.

**Extravagances**

A country pile in Yorkshire, which he bought for £1.5 million in 1981 and is now worth many times that.

### Alan Elliot 57
### £29m (£27.5m)
### Electronics

**Source of wealth**

Alan Elliot controls 6.6 million shares of

Blick, the clocking-on devices group he chairs. At the beginning of July, they were worth £27.7 million, and with a steady dividend income stream of £600,000 or so, he is worth £29 million.

**Personal style**

Elliot has spent his entire working life at Blick, the last 22 years, as executive chairman. His wife Tara – also a major shareholder – is deputy chairman.

**Extravagances**

Huntin', shootin' and fishin'.

### Sir Ernest Harrison 67
### £29m (£27m)
### Electronics

**Source of wealth**

Sir Ernest Harrison has created three public companies out of the Racal Group: Racal Electronics plc, Vodafone plc and Chubb Security plc, making himself very wealthy in the process.

Sir Ernie has shares in all three. All told, these shares are worth a cool £23 million. He de-merged Vodafone in 1991, and Chubb in 1992. He could make several million more today by cashing in his Racal options. Since 1988 he has more than trebled Racal shareholders' money.

**Personal style**

If *The Guardian* newspaper was still awarding its Businessman of the Year award it would have been wise to send it to Sir Ernest Harrison.

**Extravagances**

Racehorses (he owns a few) and football.

### Earl of Cawdor 29
### £29m (New entry)
### Aristocracy

**Source of wealth**

The young Earl of Cawdor inherited his title last year on the death of his father. The family's huge Scottish estate rambles around Cawdor Castle, over about 56,000 acres in all. The family fortune received a considerable boost in the last century when members of the family profited from the great railway boom. From this episode, the family acquired a Welsh estate of 36,000 acres. In 1976, these lands were sold to pay death duties. In recent years, the family fortune, based on land, art treasures and other investments, has been badly hit by the collapse in land prices.

**Personal style**

The current earl's mother, known as Countess Angelica von Bukowa before her marriage, has done much to develop tourist business around Cawdor Castle.

**Extravagances**

Not many. Liquidity is a constant problem, and the family maintains a low profile.

### Stanley Kalms 62
### £28m (£28.5m)
### Retailing

**Source of wealth**

Kalms has few shares in Dixons, the electrical retailer that embraces Currys white goods stores, having sold an average of a million shares a year to bring his stake down to 3.1 million shares, worth £6 million. With past dividends, 1993 income of over £1 million, Kalms is worth £28 million slightly down on last year. He is a big giver to charity.

**Personal style**

In 1948, Stanley Kalms virtually founded Dixons. He was appointed to the board of this one-shop company in 1951, and was clearly destined for great things. It is now a huge high street retailer dominant in both brown and white goods.

In addition, there is a property development arm. This year Kalms finally got rid of US electronics retailer Silo, the disastrous investment that led to a massive £210 million write-off in this year's accounts, plunging Dixons to a £165 million loss.

**Extravagances**

American follies and expensive takeover bids.

### Joel Joffe 61
### £28m (£27.5m)
### Insurance

**Source of wealth**

South African lawyer, Joel Joffe, made a fortune with his boyhood friend, Sir Mark Weinberg, joining him in the ground-breaking insurance company, Abbey Life, and later moving with him and Sir Sydney Lipworth to the phenomenally successful, Hambro Life, now Allied Dunbar.

Hambro Life was sold to BAT in 1984.

**Personal style**

Joel Joffe was Nelson Mandela's solicitor in the notorious Rivonia trial in 1963. He left South Africa the same year and was allowed to return only once, on compassionate grounds, until Mandela's release in 1990.

After retiring as deputy chairman of Allied Dunbar, Joffe surprised the insurance world in 1992, by criticising the sales practices of the insurance companies. He said that 50 per cent of policies sold were inappropriate, and that high commissions "increased the incentive for a salesperson to sell an insurance policy rather than a rival savings product, regardless of the consumer's needs". Eyebrows were raised since Abbey Life and Allied Dunbar had been profiting greatly from these practices,

and had virtually introduced direct selling to the UK insurance industry.

**Extravagances**

Biting the hand that fed him.

### Christopher Marshall 54
### £27.5m (£35m)
### Construction

**Source of wealth**

Christopher Marshall owns 92 per cent of the shares in the property company Marshall Holdings Ltd. Principal activities are developing and managing property, and building contracting in the north of England. Profits for the year to December 1992, declined again to £2.1 million, down more than 50 per cent on 1990. Based on current uncertainty in the property development market the company is probably worth only £30 million (net asset value is £25.7 million). We value Marshall at £27.5 million.

**Personal style**

Marshall's reputation as the canniest property developer in the north east is suffering. Where other developers have climbed out of the property recession, Marshall Holdings still languishes.

**Extravagances**

Overstretching the company in the Eighties.

### Bryce Alexander 76
### £27.5m (£25m)
### Business

**Source of Wealth**

Bryce Alexander is a director of the chemicals and fertiliser company, Tennants Consolidated, and is the largest single shareholder, with a 15 per cent stake. The company was founded in 1930, by Brig Gen Sir William Alexander MP and two partners. The latest set of accounts, covering the year to December 1992, show that the company turned over £115 million and made £8.5 million after tax profits.

In the last four years Bryce Alexander has trousered nearly £4 million personally, in the form of dividends and special cash distributions from the firm. Given its consistent profits and the strength of its balance sheet – it owes the banks a mere £2 million - Tennants' auction-block price would comfortably exceed £150 million. On that basis Bryce's stake is worth £23 million; brother Kenneth Alexander, the chairman and CEO, has shares worth about £15 million.

**Personal Style**

Little evidence of any. The company runs itself, and Kenneth makes most of the decisions.

**Extravagances**

Could use some.

# Part Four
## *Wealth Rankings*

| Rank | Name | Wealth(£m) | Rank | Name | Wealth(£m) |
|------|------|-----------|------|------|-----------|
| 1 | Paul Raymond | £1650.00 | 47 | Martyn Arbib | £195.00 |
| 2 | David Sainsbury | £1380.00 | 48 | Alexander Grant Gordon | £195.00 |
| 3 | Sir Evelyn Rothschild | £1350.00 | 49 | Paul Channon | £190.00 |
| 4 | Lord Rothermere | £1220.00 | 50 | Andrew Brownsword | £189.00 |
| 5 | Duke of Westminster | £900.00 | 51 | Eddie Healey | £188.00 |
| 6 | Lord Rothschild | £775.00 | 52 | William Brown | £187.00 |
| 7 | Sir James Goldsmith | £730.00 | 53 | Malcolm Healey | £186.00 |
| 8 | Viscount Cowdray | £700.00 | 54 | Simon Sainsbury | £185.00 |
| 9 | Richard Branson | £650.00 | 55 | Lady Grantchester | £185.00 |
| 10 | Garry Weston | £650.00 | 56 | Frederick Barclay | £184.00 |
| 11 | Galen Weston | £630.00 | 57 | Sir David Alliance | £181.00 |
| 12 | Bruno Schroder | £503.00 | 58 | Robert Madge | £180.00 |
| 13 | Paul McCartney | £482.00 | 59 | Patricia Martin | £179.00 |
| 14 | Lord Cayzer | £400.00 | 60 | Duke of Buccleuch | £175.00 |
| 15 | Sir Adrian Swire | £390.00 | 61 | John Asprey | £171.00 |
| 16 | Ronald Hobson | £350.00 | 62 | Henry Keswick | £170.00 |
| 17 | Sir Donald Gosling | £335.00 | 63 | Bernie Ecclestone | £167.00 |
| 18 | Jack Walker | £325.00 | 64 | David Sullivan | £166.00 |
| 19 | Simon Keswick | £320.00 | 65 | Trevor Hemmings | £165.00 |
| 20 | Edmund Vestey | £320.00 | 66 | Martin Bromley | £165.00 |
| 21 | Sir John Templeton | £315.00 | 67 | John Madejski | £164.00 |
| 22 | Earl of Iveagh | £310.00 | 68 | David Crossland | £160.00 |
| 23 | Chryss Goulandris | £300.00 | 69 | David Barclay | £160.00 |
| 24 | Lord Vestey | £300.00 | 70 | Kenneth Morrison | £160.00 |
| 25 | Sir Andrew Lloyd Webber | £290.00 | 71 | Sir John Swire | £160.00 |
| 26 | Cameron Mackintosh | £286.00 | 72 | HM The Queen | £158.00 |
| 27 | Stephen Rubin | £275.00 | 73 | Felix Dennis | £155.00 |
| 28 | Harry Hyams | £270.00 | 74 | Lord Ashburton | £152.00 |
| 29 | Duke of Devonshire | £268.00 | 75 | Duke of Atholl | £150.00 |
| 30 | Tom Jones | £265.00 | 76 | Lady Elizabeth Nugent | £148.00 |
| 31 | Lady Brigid Ness | £265.00 | 77 | Duke of Northumberland | £146.00 |
| 32 | Viscountess Boyd | £235.00 | 78 | Matthew Harding | £145.00 |
| 33 | Tony O'Reilly | £230.00 | 79 | Mark Lennox-Boyd | £145.00 |
| 34 | Robert Edmiston | £225.00 | 80 | Paul Sykes | £145.00 |
| 35 | Patrick Murphy | £221.00 | 81 | Sir Humphrey Cripps | £145.00 |
| 36 | Donatella Moores | £218.00 | 82 | Prince Charles | £142.00 |
| 37 | Jack Dellal | £218.00 | 83 | John Moores II | £140.00 |
| 38 | Steve Morgan | £216.00 | 84 | Prince Nicholas von Preussen | £140.00 |
| 39 | Paul Hamlyn | £215.00 | 85 | Marquess of Northampton | £136.00 |
| 40 | David Wilson | £212.00 | 86 | Phil Collins | £135.00 |
| 41 | Francis Chamberlain | £210.00 | 87 | Viscount Portman | £135.00 |
| 42 | Tiny Rowland | £208.00 | 88 | Ken Scowcroft | £132.00 |
| 43 | David Thompson | £206.00 | 89 | Ian McGlinn | £131.00 |
| 44 | Graham Kirkham | £204.00 | 90 | Viscount Petersham | £130.00 |
| 45 | Lord Wolfson | £200.00 | 91 | Peter Johnson | £129.00 |
| 46 | Albert Gubay | £198.00 | 92 | Marquess of Tavistock | £128.00 |

| Rank | Name | Wealth(£m) | Rank | Name | Wealth(£m) |
|------|------|-----------|------|------|-----------|
| 93 | Martin Naughton | £127.00 | 144 | Prince Rupert von Preussen | £86.50 |
| 94 | Alan Lewis | £126.00 | 145 | John Moores III | £86.00 |
| 95 | Maurice Hatter | £125.00 | 146 | Earl Spencer | £85.00 |
| 96 | Lord Sainsbury | £124.00 | 147 | John Menzies | £85.00 |
| 97 | Michael Smurfit | £123.00 | 148 | Thomas Mackie | £85.00 |
| 98 | Sir Anthony Bamford | £122.00 | 149 | Earl Cadogan | £85.00 |
| 99 | John Murphy | £121.00 | 150 | Peter Kindersley | £83.00 |
| 100 | Jacques Murray | £120.00 | 151 | Jarvis Astaire | £83.00 |
| 101 | Alan Sugar | £119.00 | 152 | Charles Hambro | £82.00 |
| 102 | Sir Peter Michael | £118.00 | 153 | Marquess of Salisbury | £82.00 |
| 103 | Chris Blackwell | £116.00 | 154 | Christina Foyle | £82.00 |
| 104 | Timothy Sainsbury | £115.00 | 155 | Sir Chrisopher Wates | £80.50 |
| 105 | Noel Lister | £112.00 | 156 | Evan Cornish | £78.00 |
| 106 | Sir Terence Conran | £110.00 | 157 | Michael Hollingbery | £76.50 |
| 107 | Sir Jack Hayward | £110.00 | 158 | Sir Tom Cowie | £76.00 |
| 108 | Bernard Schreier | £110.00 | 159 | Mick Jagger | £75.50 |
| 109 | Simon Weinstock | £109.00 | 160 | Sir Mark Weinberg | £75.50 |
| 110 | Terry Curry | £109.00 | 161 | Paul Hewson (Bono) | £75.00 |
| 111 | Leon Tamman | £109.00 | 162 | John Stuart Bloor | £75.00 |
| 112 | Lady Virginia Stanhope | £108.00 | 163 | Anwar Pervez | £75.00 |
| 113 | Michael Heseltine | £108.00 | 164 | Baroness Thatcher | £75.00 |
| 114 | Peter Dawson | £107.00 | 165 | Patricia Kluge | £74.00 |
| 115 | Ben Dunne | £106.50 | 166 | Michael Wates | £72.00 |
| 116 | Willoughby de Eresby | £106.00 | 167 | Richard Dunhill | £72.00 |
| 117 | Lady Cavendish Bentinck | £105.50 | 168 | Lynn Wilson | £71.00 |
| 118 | Marquess of Chomondeley | £105.00 | 169 | Sir Bernard Ashley | £71.00 |
| 119 | John James Fenwick | £105.00 | 170 | David Wickens | £71.00 |
| 120 | Margaret Heffernan | £104.00 | 171 | David Ashley | £70.50 |
| 121 | Abe Jaffe | £103.00 | 172 | Earl of Yarborough | £70.00 |
| 122 | John Whittaker | £102.00 | 173 | Apurv Bagri | £70.00 |
| 123 | Englebert Humperdinck | £102.00 | 174 | Robert Iliffe | £70.00 |
| 124 | Charles Saatchi | £98.00 | 175 | Sir Ian Wood | £70.00 |
| 125 | Colin Shepherd | £96.00 | 176 | David Parker | £70.00 |
| 126 | Felix Grovit | £95.00 | 177 | Ronald Goldstein | £70.00 |
| 127 | Fred Walker | £95.00 | 178 | Len Jagger | £68.50 |
| 128 | Pamela Harriman | £95.00 | 179 | Peter Greenall | £68.00 |
| 129 | Michael Cornish | £94.00 | 180 | Robin Fleming | £68.00 |
| 130 | Kevin Leech | £94.00 | 181 | Blanche Buchan | £67.00 |
| 131 | Laxmi Shivdasani | £94.00 | 182 | John Apthorp | £67.00 |
| 132 | James Sherwood | £92.00 | 183 | Elliot Bernerd | £66.50 |
| 133 | Countess of Sutherland | £92.00 | 184 | James Moores | £66.00 |
| 134 | David Moores | £91.00 | 185 | Brian Souter | £65.50 |
| 135 | Sir Philip Harris | £91.00 | 186 | Michael Green | £65.20 |
| 136 | Marchioness of Douro | £90.00 | 187 | Mark Knopfler | £65.00 |
| 137 | Prince Andrew von Preussen | £90.00 | 188 | Michael Rees | £65.00 |
| 138 | Princess Victoria von Preussen | £90.00 | 189 | Adrian White | £65.00 |
| 139 | Duke of Argyll | £90.00 | 190 | Lord Palumbo | £65.00 |
| 140 | George Moore | £90.00 | 191 | Anthony Crosthwaite-Eyre | £65.00 |
| 141 | Lord Laing | £90.00 | 192 | Duke of Beaufort | £65.00 |
| 142 | Earl of Stockton | £88.00 | 193 | Earl of Radnor | £65.00 |
| 143 | Elton John | £87.00 | 194 | Israel Wetrin | £64.50 |

| Rank | Name | Wealth(£m) | Rank | Name | Wealth(£m) |
|------|------|------------|------|------|------------|
| 195 | Earl of Inchcape | £64.50 | 246 | Earl of Rosebery | £55.00 |
| 196 | Peter Rigby | £64.00 | 247 | Duke of Marlborough | £55.00 |
| 197 | Mary Czernin | £63.50 | 248 | Nicholas Forman Hardy | £55.00 |
| 198 | Viscount Wimbourne | £63.00 | 249 | Marquess of Bath | £54.50 |
| 199 | David Evans (The Edge) | £63.00 | 250 | Gordon Sumner/Sting | £54.00 |
| 200 | Larry Mullen | £63.00 | 251 | Sir Michael Bishop | £54.00 |
| 201 | Nick Ashley | £63.00 | 252 | Ian Skipper | £54.00 |
| 202 | Michael Ashcroft | £63.00 | 253 | Lord Rayne | £54.00 |
| 203 | Tony Clegg | £63.00 | 254 | Robert Mills | £53.50 |
| 204 | Raymond Slater | £63.00 | 255 | Bernard Holmes | £53.50 |
| 205 | Earl of Derby | £63.00 | 256 | Lord Rotherwick | £53.50 |
| 206 | Ann Gloag | £62.50 | 257 | Gilbert Greenall | £53.00 |
| 207 | Peter Wilson | £62.50 | 258 | Sir John Barlow | £53.00 |
| 208 | Lady Teresa Rothschild | £62.50 | 259 | Robert Earl | £52.50 |
| 209 | Camilla Acloque | £62.00 | 260 | Tony Bramall | £52.50 |
| 210 | Gordon Roddick | £62.00 | 261 | Charlotte Morrison | £52.00 |
| 211 | Joseph Bamford | £62.00 | 262 | Isabel Goldsmith | £52.00 |
| 212 | Gordon Stewart | £62.00 | 263 | Stewart Milne | £52.00 |
| 213 | Lord Forte | £61.50 | 264 | Tony Travis | £52.00 |
| 214 | Tim Vestey | £61.00 | 265 | Lindsay Masters | £52.00 |
| 215 | Anita Roddick | £61.00 | 266 | Jim Moffat | £52.00 |
| 216 | Jessica White | £60.00 | 267 | Marquess of Bute | £51.50 |
| 217 | Frank Brake | £60.00 | 268 | Mark Thatcher | £51.50 |
| 218 | Esmond Bulmer | £60.00 | 269 | Michael Winner | £51.50 |
| 219 | William Brake | £60.00 | 270 | Stephen Griggs | £51.00 |
| 220 | Bernard Matthews | £60.00 | 271 | David Lewis | £51.00 |
| 221 | Ronald Frost | £59.50 | 272 | Duke of Rutland | £51.00 |
| 222 | Grahame Chilton | £59.00 | 273 | Con Wilson | £51.00 |
| 223 | Earl of Airlie | £58.50 | 274 | Wensley Haydon-Baillie | £50.00 |
| 224 | Sir E A-Gough-Calthorpe | £58.00 | 275 | Bill Rooney | £50.00 |
| 225 | Adam Clayton | £58.00 | 276 | Thomas Trickett | £50.00 |
| 226 | Duke of Roxburghe | £58.00 | 277 | Cyril Stein | £49.50 |
| 227 | Peter Wood | £58.00 | 278 | Nicholas van Hoogstraten | £49.00 |
| 228 | Earl of Pembroke | £58.00 | 279 | John Coldman | £49.00 |
| 229 | Leonard Steinberg | £58.00 | 280 | Michael Gooley | £49.00 |
| 230 | Robert Sangster | £58.00 | 281 | Sir Anthony Jacobs | £49.00 |
| 231 | Celia Lipton | £58.00 | 282 | Earl of Mansfield | £49.00 |
| 232 | Colin Sanders | £57.50 | 283 | Stanley Cohen | £49.00 |
| 233 | Rory Guinness | £57.00 | 284 | Derek Crowson | £49.00 |
| 234 | Lady Louisa Guinness | £57.00 | 285 | Clive Smith | £48.00 |
| 235 | Lady Emma Guinness | £57.00 | 286 | Richard Biffa | £48.00 |
| 236 | David McMurtry | £56.00 | 287 | Gerald Weisfeld | £48.00 |
| 237 | John Haynes | £56.00 | 288 | James Gulliver | £48.00 |
| 238 | Michael Stone | £56.00 | 289 | Judah Binstock | £48.00 |
| 239 | Tom Wheatcroft | £56.00 | 290 | Arnold Clark | £48.00 |
| 240 | Sean Lennon | £55.50 | 291 | John Chedzoy | £48.00 |
| 241 | Simon Draper | £55.50 | 292 | Lady Paula Brown | £48.00 |
| 242 | Jonathan Harmsworth | £55.00 | 293 | Noel McMullen | £48.00 |
| 243 | John Beckwith | £55.00 | 294 | John Ray | £47.50 |
| 244 | Greg Stanley | £55.00 | 295 | Jim Raper | £47.50 |
| 245 | Clarice Pears | £55.00 | 296 | Peter Vardy | £47.00 |

# The Richest 500 People in Great Britain

| Rank | Name | Wealth(£m) | Rank | Name | Wealth(£m) |
|------|------|-----------|------|------|-----------|
| 297 | Peter Beckwith | £47.00 | 348 | Benzion Freshwater | £39.00 |
| 298 | Peter Thomas | £47.00 | 349 | Rod Stewart | £39.00 |
| 299 | Harry Solomon | £47.00 | 350 | Charles Dobson | £39.00 |
| 300 | Lord Margadale | £47.00 | 351 | Barbara Taylor Bradford | £39.00 |
| 301 | John Newsome | £46.50 | 352 | Martin Copley | £39.00 |
| 302 | Tim Mahony | £46.50 | 353 | John Zochonis | £39.00 |
| 303 | Nigel Mansell | £46.00 | 354 | Robin Phillips | £38.50 |
| 304 | Nigel Alliance | £46.00 | 355 | Lord Weinstock | £38.50 |
| 305 | Robert Gavron | £46.00 | 356 | Derek Thomson | £38.50 |
| 306 | Lord White | £46.00 | 357 | Paul Slater | £38.00 |
| 307 | Bernie Taupin | £45.50 | 358 | Ray O'Rourke | £38.00 |
| 308 | Nigel Wray | £45.00 | 359 | Everard Goodman | £38.00 |
| 309 | Tommy Sopwith | £45.00 | 360 | Duke of Richmond | £38.00 |
| 310 | Derrick Frost | £45.00 | 361 | Sir Adrian Cadbury | £38.00 |
| 311 | Earl of Lonsdale | £45.00 | 362 | Gordon Baxter | £38.00 |
| 312 | Mickey Duff | £44.50 | 363 | Ronald Diggens | £38.00 |
| 313 | Leonard Lewis | £44.00 | 364 | Tom Walduck | £38.00 |
| 314 | Dr Philip Brown | £44.00 | 365 | Richard Desmond | £37.50 |
| 315 | Peter Jones | £44.00 | 366 | Sir John Hall | £37.50 |
| 316 | Lord Tanlaw | £44.00 | 367 | Dick Francis | £37.50 |
| 317 | Nat Somers | £44.00 | 368 | Sir Nicholas Bacon | £37.00 |
| 318 | Clive Lewis | £44.00 | 369 | Countess of Lichfield | £37.00 |
| 319 | Sheena Easton | £43.50 | 370 | Mary Foulston | £37.00 |
| 320 | Rocco Forte | £43.50 | 371 | Lady Sheila Butlin | £37.00 |
| 321 | Nigel Raine | £43.00 | 372 | Lady Juliet de Chair | £37.00 |
| 322 | Mickie Most | £43.00 | 373 | Duke of Wellington | £37.00 |
| 323 | David Samworth | £43.00 | 374 | David Hood | £36.50 |
| 324 | Leon Litchfield | £43.00 | 375 | Earl of Halifax | £36.50 |
| 325 | Dame Barbara Cartland | £43.00 | 376 | Edwin Boorman | £36.50 |
| 326 | Paul McGuinness | £42.50 | 377 | Viscount Hambleden | £36.50 |
| 327 | Lady Anya Sainsbury | £42.00 | 378 | Bevitt Mabey | £36.50 |
| 328 | Michael Noble | £42.00 | 379 | Andrew Cohen | £36.00 |
| 329 | Philip Noble | £42.00 | 380 | Maria Phillips | £36.00 |
| 330 | George Harrison | £41.50 | 381 | Keith Chapman | £36.00 |
| 331 | Sir Sydney Lipworth | £41.50 | 382 | Michael Luckwell | £36.00 |
| 332 | Bruce Robertson | £41.00 | 383 | Adrian Berry | £36.00 |
| 333 | Stanley Thomas | £41.00 | 384 | Peter Moores | £36.00 |
| 334 | John Aspinall | £41.00 | 385 | Bill Ruffler | £36.00 |
| 335 | Greta Fenston | £41.00 | 386 | Robert Hanson | £35.00 |
| 336 | Lord Hanson | £41.00 | 387 | Sarah Bathurst | £35.00 |
| 337 | Ron Dennis | £41.00 | 388 | Chris Evans | £35.00 |
| 338 | Michael Peagram | £40.00 | 389 | Marquess of Normanby | £35.00 |
| 339 | Keith Richards | £40.00 | 390 | David McErlain | £35.00 |
| 340 | Robin Lodge | £40.00 | 391 | Peter Kane | £35.00 |
| 341 | Viscount Coke | £40.00 | 392 | Marquess of Douro | £35.00 |
| 342 | Ron Hickman | £40.00 | 393 | Vivien Duffield | £35.00 |
| 343 | Portia Kennaway | £39.50 | 394 | Margaret Barbour | £35.00 |
| 344 | Lawrie Lewis | £39.50 | 395 | David Kirch | £35.00 |
| 345 | Chris Wright | £39.50 | 396 | William Benyon | £35.00 |
| 346 | Louise White | £39.00 | 397 | Mark Birley | £35.00 |
| 347 | Duchess of Roxburghe | £39.00 | 398 | George Williams | £35.00 |

| Rank | Name | Wealth(£m) | Rank | Name | Wealth(£m) |
|---|---|---|---|---|---|
| 399 | Sir Leslie Porter | £35.00 | 450 | Eric Clapton | £31.50 |
| 400 | Viscount Leverhulme | £35.00 | 451 | Sarah Davidson | £31.50 |
| 401 | Lord Home | £35.00 | 452 | Peter Goldstein | £31.50 |
| 402 | Joe Bollom | £35.00 | 453 | Andrew Knight | £31.50 |
| 403 | John Delaney | £35.00 | 454 | Freddie Laker | £31.50 |
| 404 | John Draper | £35.00 | 455 | Doris Thompson | £31.50 |
| 405 | Tim Rice | £34.50 | 456 | Eric Norman | £31.00 |
| 406 | Sir Julian Hodge | £34.50 | 457 | John Cleese | £31.00 |
| 407 | David Gold | £34.50 | 458 | Dame Shirley Porter | £31.00 |
| 408 | Tom Walkinshaw | £34.50 | 459 | Harry Patterson | £31.00 |
| 409 | Jackie Stewart | £34.00 | 460 | Angela Yeoman | £31.00 |
| 410 | Ralph Gold | £34.00 | 461 | Roger Baker | £31.00 |
| 411 | Bill Wyman | £34.00 | 462 | Robert Rayne | £31.00 |
| 412 | Ian Hutcheson | £34.00 | 463 | John Reid | £30.50 |
| 413 | Lady Edna Samuel | £34.00 | 464 | Cliff Richard | £30.50 |
| 414 | Harry Shipley | £34.00 | 465 | Leigh Webb | £30.50 |
| 415 | John Shipley | £34.00 | 466 | George Michael | £30.00 |
| 416 | Richard Gabriel | £33.50 | 467 | Audrey Baxter | £30.00 |
| 417 | John Thornton | £33.50 | 468 | Ross Warburton | £30.00 |
| 418 | Vicountess Linley | £33.00 | 469 | Duchess of Westminster | £30.00 |
| 419 | David Padley | £33.00 | 470 | Allen Lloyd | £30.00 |
| 420 | Olga Polizzi | £33.00 | 471 | Robert Murray | £30.00 |
| 421 | Frank Williams | £33.00 | 472 | Richard Palmer | £30.00 |
| 422 | Deverok Pritchard | £33.00 | 473 | Malcolm Walker | £30.00 |
| 423 | Lindsay Bury | £33.00 | 474 | Peter Waterman | £30.00 |
| 424 | David Blackburn | £33.00 | 475 | Keith Bradshaw | £30.00 |
| 425 | Alan Clark | £33.00 | 476 | Trevor Burke | £30.00 |
| 426 | Earl Harrington | £33.00 | 477 | Bryan Morrison | £30.00 |
| 427 | Rodney Webb | £33.00 | 478 | Michael Pemberton | £30.00 |
| 428 | Baron Inverforth | £32.50 | 479 | Robert Johnson | £30.00 |
| 429 | Ken Follet | £32.50 | 480 | Douglas Gregory | £30.00 |
| 430 | Jeffery Archer | £32.50 | 481 | Dr David Horrobin | £30.00 |
| 431 | Sean Connery | £32.50 | 482 | Marquess of Zetland | £30.00 |
| 432 | Joseph McWilliams | £32.50 | 483 | Princess Alexandra | £30.00 |
| 433 | Nick Faldo | £32.00 | 484 | Michael Caine | £30.00 |
| 434 | Dave Stewart | £32.00 | 485 | Alf Gooding | £30.00 |
| 435 | The Princess Royal | £32.00 | 486 | Viscount Weir | £30.00 |
| 436 | Marquess of Hartington | £32.00 | 487 | Mary Mackinnon | £30.00 |
| 437 | Duncan Davidson | £32.00 | 488 | Miriam Louisa Rothschild | £30.00 |
| 438 | Jackie Collins | £32.00 | 489 | Michael Brinton | £30.00 |
| 439 | Samuel Whitbread | £32.00 | 490 | David Doyle | £30.00 |
| 440 | Julie Andrews | £32.00 | 491 | Richard George | £30.00 |
| 441 | Henry Hoare | £32.00 | 492 | Chris Lazari | £29.50 |
| 442 | Princess Margaret | £32.00 | 493 | Lawrie Barratt | £29.50 |
| 443 | Roger Moore | £32.00 | 494 | Alan Elliot | £29.00 |
| 444 | Prince Philip | £32.00 | 495 | Sir Ernest Harrison | £29.00 |
| 445 | Catherine Cookson | £32.00 | 496 | Earl of Cawdor | £29.00 |
| 446 | Gemma Maughan | £32.00 | 497 | Stanley Kalms | £28.00 |
| 447 | Jimmy Thomas | £32.00 | 498 | Joel Joffe | £28.00 |
| 448 | Kaveh Alamouti | £31.50 | 499 | Christopher Marshall | £27.50 |
| 449 | Ringo Starr | £31.50 | 500 | Bryce Alexander | £27.50 |

# Part Five
## *Rankings by Category*

## Richest insurers

| Rank | | Name | Wealth |
|---|---|---|---|
| 1 | (52) | William Brown | £187m |
| 2 | (78) | Matthew Harding | £145m |
| 3 | (88) | Ken Scowcroft | £132m |
| 4 | (160) | Sir Mark Weinburg | £75.5m |
| 5 | (222) | Grahame Chilton | £59m |
| 6 | (227) | Peter Wood | £58m |
| 7 | (279) | John Coldman | £49m |
| 8 | (331) | Sir Sydney Lipworth | £41.5m |
| 9 | (352) | Martin Copley | £39m |
| 10 | (498) | Joel Joffe | £28m |

## Richest pop stars

| Rank | | Name | Wealth |
|---|---|---|---|
| 1 | (13) | Paul McCartney | £482m |
| 2 | (30) | Tom Jones | £265m |
| 3 | (86) | Phil Collins | £135m |
| 4 | (123) | Engelbert Humperdinck | £102m |
| 5 | (143) | Elton John | £87m |
| 6 | (159) | Mick Jagger | £79m |
| 7 | (161) | Paul Hewson (Bono) | £75m |
| 8 | (187) | Mark Knopfler | £65m |
| 9 | (199) | David Evans (The Edge) | £63m |
| 10 | (200) | Larry Mullen | £63m |

## Richest aristocrats

| Rank | | Name | Wealth |
|---|---|---|---|
| 1 | (8) | Viscount Cowdray | £700m |
| 2 | (29) | Duke of Devonshire | £268m |
| 3 | (60) | Duke of Buccleuch | £175m |
| 4 | (75) | Duke of Atholl | £150m |
| 5 | (77) | Duke of Northumberland | £146m |
| 6 | (85) | Marquess of Northampton | £136m |
| 7 | (87) | Viscount Portman | £135m |
| 8 | (90) | Viscount Petersham | £130m |
| 9 | (92) | Marquess of Tavistock | £128m |
| 10 | (118) | Marquess of Chomondeley | £105m |

## Richest oldies

| Rank | | Name | Age | Wealth |
|---|---|---|---|---|
| 1 | (325) | Barbara Cartland | 93 | £43m |
| 2 | (455) | Doris Thompson | 91 | £31.5m |
| 3 | (401) | Lord Home | 91 | £35m |
| 4 | (406) | Sir Julian Hodge | 89 | £34.5m |
| 5 | (445) | Catherine Cookson | 87 | £32m |
| 6 | (300) | Lord Margadale | 87 | £32m |
| 7 | (413) | Lady Edna Samuel | 86 | £34m |
| 8 | (488) | Miriam Rothschild | 86 | £30m |
| 9 | (317) | Nat Somers | 86 | £44m |
| 10 | (213) | Lord Forte | 85 | £61.5m |
| 11 | (14) | Lord Cayzer | 84 | £400m |
| 12 | (8) | Viscount Cowdray | 84 | £700m |
| 13 | (154) | Christina Foyle | 83 | £82m |
| 14 | (35) | Patrick Murphy | 83 | £221m |
| 15 | (367) | Ronald Diggens | 82 | £38m |
| 16 | (195) | Earl of Inchape | 81 | £64.5m |
| 17 | (141) | Lord Laing | 81 | £90m |
| 18 | (21) | Sir John Templeton | 81 | £315m |
| 19 | (256) | Lord Rotherwick | 81 | £53m |
| 20 | (149) | Earl of Cadogan | 80 | £85m |

## Richest entertainers

| Rank | | Name | Wealth |
|---|---|---|---|
| 1 | (25) | Andrew Lloyd Webber | £290m |
| 2 | (26) | Cameron Mackintosh | £286m |
| 3 | (103) | Chris Blackwell | £116m |
| 4 | (241) | Simon Draper | £55.5m |
| 5 | (259) | Robert Earl | £52.5m |
| 6 | (269) | Michael Winner | £51.5m |
| 7 | (312) | Mickey Duff | £44.5m |
| 8 | (322) | Mickie Most | £43m |
| 9 | (326) | Paul McGuinness | £42.5m |
| 10 | (405) | Tim Rice | £34.5m |
| 11 | (431) | Sean Connery | £32.5m |
| 12 | (440) | Julie Andrews | £32m |
| 13 | (443) | Roger Moore | £32m |
| 14 | (457) | John Cleese | £31m |
| 15 | (477) | Bryan Morrison | £30m |

## Richest women

| Rank | | Name | Wealth |
|---|---|---|---|
| 1 | (23) | Chryss Goulandris | £300m |
| 2 | (31) | Lady Brigid Ness | £265m |
| 3 | (32) | Viscountess Boyd | £235m |
| 4 | (36) | Donatella Moores | £218m |
| 5 | (55) | Lady Grantchester | £185m |
| 6 | (59) | Patricia Martin | £179m |
| 7 | (72) | HM The Queen | £158m |
| 8 | (76) | Lady Elizabeth Nugent | £148m |
| 9 | (112) | Lady Virginia Stanhope | £108m |
| 10 | (116) | Lady Willoughby de Eresby | £106m |
| 11 | (117) | Lady Anne Bentinck | £105.5m |
| 12 | (128) | Pamela Harriman | £95m |
| 13 | (131) | Laxmi Shivdasani | £94m |
| 14 | (133) | Countess of Sutherland | £92m |
| 15 | (136) | Marchioness of Douro | £90m |
| 16 | (138) | Princess Victoria v Preussen | £90m |
| 17 | (154) | Christina Foyle | £82m |
| 18 | (164) | Baroness Thatcher | £75m |
| 19 | (165) | Patricia Kluge | £74m |
| 20 | (181) | Blanche Buchan | £67m |
| 21 | (197) | Mary Czernin | £63.5m |
| 22 | (206) | Ann Gloag | £62.5m |
| 23 | (208) | Lady Theresa Rothschild | £62.5m |
| 24 | (209) | Camilla Acloque | £62m |
| 25 | (215) | Anita Roddick | £61m |
| 26 | (216) | Jessica White | £60m |
| 27 | (234) | Lady Louisa Guinness | £57m |
| 28 | (235) | Lady Emma Guinness | £57m |
| 29 | (261) | Charlotte Morrison | £52m |
| 30 | (262) | Isabel Goldsmith | £52m |

## Richest car dealers

| Rank | | Name | Wealth |
|---|---|---|---|
| 1 | (34) | Robert Edmiston | £225m |
| 2 | (158) | Sir Tom Cowie | £76m |
| 3 | (170) | David Wickens | £71m |
| 4 | (237) | John Haynes | £56m |
| 5 | (260) | Tony Bramall | £52m |
| 6 | (290) | Arnold Clark | £48m |
| 7 | (296) | Peter Vardy | £47m |
| 8 | (390) | David McErlain | £35m |
| 9 | (424) | David Blackburn | £33m |

## Richest politicians

| Rank | | Name | Wealth |
|---|---|---|---|
| 1 | (49) | Paul Channon | £190m |
| 2 | (79) | Mark Lennox-Boyd | £145m |
| 3 | (104) | Tim Sainsbury | £115m |
| 4 | (133) | Michael Heseltine | £108m |
| 5 | (164) | Baroness Thatcher | £75m |
| 6 | (425) | Alan Clark | £33m |
| 7 | (430) | Lord Archer | £32.5m |
| 8 | (458) | Dame Shirley Porter | £31m |

## Richest motor racers

| Rank | | Name | Wealth |
|---|---|---|---|
| 1 | (63) | Bernie Ecclestone | £167m |
| 2 | (239) | Tom Wheatcroft | £56m |
| 3 | (303) | Nigel Mansell | £46m |
| 4 | (337) | Ron Dennis | £41m |
| 7 | (408) | Tom Walkinshaw | £34.5m |
| 5 | (409) | Jackie Stewart | £34m |
| 6 | (421) | Frank Williams | £33m |

## Richest youngsters

| Rank | | Age | Name | Wealth |
|---|---|---|---|---|
| 1 | (240) | 19 | Sean Lennon | 55.5m |
| 2 | (233) | 20 | Rory Guinness | £57m |
| 3 | (234) | 23 | Lady Louisa Guinness | £57m |
| 4 | (22) | 24 | Earl of Iveagh | £310m |
| 5 | (418) | 24 | Viscountess Linley | £33m |
| 6 | (198) | 25 | Viscount Wimbourne | £63m |
| 7 | (242) | 26 | Jonathan Harmsworth | £55m |
| 8 | (224) | 28 | Sir Euan Calthorpe | £58m |
| 9 | (343) | 28 | Portia Kennaway | 39.5m |
| 10 | (428) | 28 | Baron Inverforth | 32.5m |

## Richest royals

| Rank | | Name | Wealth |
|---|---|---|---|
| 1 | (72) | The Queen | £158m |
| 2 | (82) | Prince Charles | £142m |
| 3 | (435) | The Princess Royal | £32m |
| 4 | (442) | Princess Margaret | £32m |
| 5 | (444) | Prince Philip | £32m |
| 6 | (483) | Princess Alexandra | £30m |

# Part Six
## *Index*

# INDEX